'A promising young historian with a taste for the exotic.'

Stephen Fry

'There is so much to see at the Freak Show which Woolf provides his readers; and he makes it clear that it does the memory of these amazing artists a disservice to avert your eyes.'

Therese Oneill, author of *Unmentionable*

'Explores with subtlety and consideration the many facets of humanity's strangeness. A really excellent book and an important study of the physically marginalized and neglected.'

Clive Bloom, author of *Victoria's Madmen*

'Exceptional. *The Wonders* shines a bright light on the real human experiences behind Victorian freak spectacles. With carefully researched historical detail and a knack for storytelling, Woolf's style is impressive.'

Lillian Craton, author of *The Victorian Freak Show*

'An intriguing and fascinating look into the world of "freaks". Beautifully researched and well written.'

**Richard Butchins,
award-winning artist and disabled filmmaker**

'Fascinating and thought-provoking. A marvellously researched account of the freak industry – an extraordinary side of Victorian life which has been ignored for too long.'

Jane Ridley, author of *Bertie*

'John Woolf's book will dazzle you with details of extraordinary lives, long underestimated by history.'

Matthew Sweet, author of *Inventing the Victorians*

THE WONDERS

The Extraordinary Performers Who Transformed the Victorian Age

JOHN WOOLF

PEGASUS BOOKS
NEW YORK LONDON

THE WONDERS

Pegasus Books, Ltd.
148 West 37th Street, 13th Floor
New York, NY 10018

First Pegasus Books hardcover edition November 2019

ISBN: 978-1-64313-220-4

10 9 8 7 6 5 4 3 2 1

Printed in the United States of America
Distributed by W. W. Norton & Company

Dedicated to my granny, Anne Dickey, a true wonder

Contents

———

ACT FOUR: The Climax

Curtain Up

Buckingham Palace, 23 March 1844

O N A MILD spring evening in 1844, two Americans arrived at
Buckingham Palace: a 6ft 2in showman and his dwarf, General
Tom Thumb (real name Charles Stratton). Only six years old
and 25in tall, Tom was dressed in a powdered wig and a cocked hat that
framed his blond hair and rosy cheeks. A red velvet coat and breeches
hugged his small and well-proportioned body. He wore white stockings
and tiny black shoes, and he carried a miniature cane and ceremonial
sword. The showman, P.T. Barnum, wore a plain black court suit. Both
were dressed for an audience with the twenty-four-year-old queen.

On arriving at the palace, the Lord-in-Waiting gave Barnum and
Tom a crash course in court etiquette. They were forbidden to address
the queen directly and could not, under any circumstances, turn
their back to Her Majesty. They were then promptly led down a long
corridor and up a broad flight of marble stairs, arriving at the doors of
the Picture Gallery, renowned for the masterpieces hung on its 155ft
long walls. This was the palace's official space for entertaining guests.
Symmetrically arranged along the sides of the room were four marble
fireplaces, framed on each side by a pair of scantily clad female statues
holding palettes and brushes. These statues stared directly onto the
room, ready to witness the scene that was about to unfold.

The doors were thrown open and Tom Thumb entered with a firm step followed by a graceful bow. He exclaimed in his high-pitched voice: 'Good evening, Ladies and Gentlemen!'[1]

The royal entourage burst into laughter as Tom glanced up from his bowed position. About thirty dignitaries stood on the other side of the room, their eyes fixed on his body. Among the guests, sparkling with jewels and dressed in the latest fashions, was Queen Victoria, who by contrast looked inconspicuous in a plain black dress. She sat on a large chair next to her mother, the Duchess of Kent, and her first cousin cum husband, Prince Albert, who had just returned from Coburg following the death of his father, Ernst I.

For over an hour Tom entertained the dignitaries with songs, dances and imitations, including his comical impersonation of Emperor Napoleon. The queen was mesmerized. She took Tom by the hand and led him around the gallery, which he described as 'first rate'.[2] He asked to meet Victoria's son, the two-year-old Prince of Wales, but the queen explained that he was resting, and promised another meeting soon. Then Albert conversed with Tom, who answered in a dignified way, while Victoria interviewed Barnum. Who was this boy? Where did he come from? Who were his parents? And how did Barnum find him?

As instructed, Barnum began by answering the queen's questions via the stern Lord-in-Waiting. But never one for formalities Barnum soon dispensed with the advice not to address the queen directly and, with characteristic Yankee boldness, turned and spoke directly to Her Majesty. It was a huge breach of royal protocol, but the queen was unperturbed as she and the showman began discussing Tom Thumb's history, much to the smouldering consternation of the Lord-in-Waiting.

Just before they were about to go, Barnum and Tom remembered the second piece of advice: never turn your back to the queen. So instead of turning to leave, they began backing out of the gallery, keeping their gaze fixed on the queen's blue eyes. The Lord-in-Waiting was satisfied: order and protocol were restored.

But Tom's little legs could not keep pace with Barnum's long strides. He kept turning around and running a few steps to catch up, then swinging round to resume the formal backing-out position. Victoria's alarmed spaniel began barking and chased after the swivelling Tom, who promptly drew the small ceremonial sword from his belt and started battling with the dog. The Lord-in-Waiting was incandescent, but the royal crowd broke out in hysterics.

Charles Stratton, Tom Thumb, battling with Queen Victoria's spaniel at Buckingham Palace in 1844.

When the pair finally reached the anteroom, an attendant rushed in to check they were all right. Barnum and his prodigy simply laughed. The attendant implored them to return soon, while the Lord-in-Waiting huffed, according to Barnum, that if Tom Thumb was such a renowned figure, 'he should fear a declaration of war by the United States!'[3]

That night, before bedtime, Victoria wrote in her journal: 'After dinner we saw the greatest curiosity, I, or indeed anybody ever saw, viz: a little dwarf, only 25 inches high & 15 lb in weight. No description can give an idea of this little creature, whose real name was Charles Stratton ... He made the funniest little bow, putting out his hand & saying: "much obliged Mama".[4]

The queen had given the freak show her royal seal of approval. This was mercilessly exploited by Barnum, who, with the help of the queen and his star, Tom Thumb, unleashed 'Deformito-Mania' in Britain: a pervasive and popular fascination with the exceptional body.[5] General Tom Thumb was already an American celebrity, but now he would become an international one. And while the display of dwarfs, giants, wild men, bearded ladies and all manner of exceptional bodies had been around for centuries, this meeting with the queen was pivotal. It changed the story. A freak industry was born.

For the rest of her reign, Queen Victoria endorsed, patronized and met the great freak performers (and circus celebrities) of the century, as did numerous American presidents. Victoria's passionate interest became fodder for showmen, and the freak show became part of Victorian culture on both sides of the Atlantic. Through every conceivable expression of popular culture, the freak performer was there bringing awe, joy and disruption to the Victorian world.

This is a story that brings those performers centre stage, exploring their lives, triumphs and tragedies, and giving a voice to those frequently silent performers, who created the wondrous age of the freak.

Introduction

I N THESE PAGES, the Victorian Age of prudes and prigs, scientists and industrialists is reconfigured into the Age of the Freak: an era where wonders reigned supreme, where kings, queens, presidents and commoners came to gaze at nature's great diversity. This is an age that marvelled at the marvellous and wondered at the wondrous; an age when the freak show was never a marginal affair, but instead central to Victorian society. The image of the Widow of Windsor, Queen Victoria herself, is transformed into Her Majesty the fun-filled queen, a freak fancier and lover of the circus. Our modern age of celebrity, alternative facts and obsession with the body – seen everywhere from gossip magazines to our TV screens – is rooted in the nineteenth-century freak show.

The Age of the Freak opens at the beginning of the nineteenth century, but can also be seen as flowing back to the seventeenth and forwards into the twentieth. In this great expanse of time, the word 'revolution' repeats: in the scientific revolution of the Enlightenment, with its concerns for the rational and material, and the Romantic revolution, with its culture of feeling, imagination and introspection. The American and French revolutions were politically tumultuous, but the industrial revolution, commercial revolution, communications revolution and consumer revolution were equally monumental in disrupting the order of things.[6] Into this cauldron of change came the freak, reflecting and enhancing the fractious forces of history, while turning those deemed different into the celebrities of their age.

As we chart the international history of the freak and their shows, tackling sites of entertainment from dime museums to circus extravaganzas, the lives of these marginalized performers make their way back to centre stage. Often, their voices have been muffled by the passage of time, the legacy of others or the very nature of the sources. But we must confront these challenges head on: give attention to forgotten lives for which we have little direct or reliable evidence; negotiate and discuss the complexities of nuanced relationships between performers and showmen and audiences; and unpack sources that often dabbled in fiction, falsity and fantasy. Frequently, the moment you think you have found the performer behind the performance, they disappear. But in this search for the performer, the culture of the period stands out and new insights appear.

It is no coincidence that the heyday of the freak show occurred in the nineteenth century when an obsession with bodily matters was there for all to see. From fears of body snatching to the terror of dissection after death; from anxieties about premature burial to the struggles in burying the escalating dead; from inventions to dispose of faeces to public health reforms; this was a time when new norms were created around the body. Here was a century when 'science', 'scientist', 'normal' and 'disability' entered the lexicon; when bodies were starved, leading to riots and famines, and maimed by the new machinery that epitomized the age; when bodies were paraded and beautified by cosmetics, and a sex industry was born. Such exposure to the body was the *raison d'être* of the freak show: a commercial form of entertainment where biology was made into a commodity for the whole family to enjoy. Furthermore, the freak show emerged as industrialization, urbanization and modernity took hold. The rise of the middle classes, the introduction of the Saturday half holiday, the shift from agriculture to manufacturing, the spread of commercial leisure – each spurred the development of popular culture, the birth of the entertainment industry and the proliferation of stages where freaks could perform, all within the context of an internationalized freak industry that straddled the Atlantic.

S O, LET US cast our eyes back to the end of an epoch, when the freak show reigned supreme, and at the end of the lives of three individuals who changed the face of Victorian entertainment. Mountain Grove Cemetery is a rural burial ground which sits peacefully to the west of Bridgeport, Connecticut. Today, across 125 acres, the flat mowed lawns and winding footpaths are punctuated by thousands of gravestones and the occasional hill. A fountain splashes in one of the ponds as you walk around, observing the tombstones, crematory, chapel and mausoleums, located both above and below ground.

If you take the path to area nine, you arrive at one of the largest memorials, set off from the other graves by a low stone wall. Here is a fitting monument to P.T. Barnum, the man who helped found the cemetery back in 1849, the former mayor of Bridgeport and a giant of Victorian entertainment; 'A Cesar [sic] Among Showmen' ran one headline following his death on 7 April 1891, aged eighty.[7] And justifiably. Barnum popularized the freak show, the circus, ethnological shows (displays of foreign people), opera and blackface minstrelsy; he revolutionized museums, devised the first matinee shows and developed the display of exotic fish and marine mammals. He introduced the rhinoceros and herds of elephants to America and initiated the freak show, sideshow, modern-day advertising, fake news and alternative facts.

But Barnum was a myth as much as a man, and remains so today. He created his own image through autobiographies and professional humbugs. In life, as in death, he had numerous epithets that reflected his evolving mythical status: the Prince of Humbugs, the Genial Showman, the Greatest Showman, the Children's Friend and the Sun of the Amusement World.[8] Yet Barnum's legacy has often overshadowed those he managed: performers who achieved a similar level of celebrity and who, crucially, helped make the fame of the great showman.

Charles Stratton's grave at Mountain Grove Cemetery, Bridgeport, Connecticut. A life-sized statue of Stratton stands at the top.

It is fitting, therefore, that almost behind Barnum's monument, in area eight of the cemetery, is another monument to a star who in life, as in death, remained in close proximity to the showman. Raised high on a 40ft obelisk is a life-sized marble statue to Charles Stratton, better known as General Tom Thumb, who died on 15 July 1883, aged forty-five. He was discovered by Barnum, who thrust him onstage when he was only four years old and about 25in tall. But while Stratton was tiny, his stardom was huge: he was one of the world's first international celebrities; and he entertained such dignitaries as President Abraham Lincoln and Tsar Nicholas I of Russia. Ten thousand people came to pay their respects when he was buried with Masonic honours in a small walnut coffin.

He was joined at Mountain Grove Cemetery by his wife, Mercy Lavinia Warren, who passed away on 25 November 1919. Her small gravestone rests next to her husband's, dwarfed by his monument, although she had an incredibly successful career too: she found stardom in 1862 after signing a contract with Barnum. When twenty years old, and 32in tall, she was praised for her singing, dancing and physical beauty. In 1863 she married Stratton at Grace Church in New York. Despite the American Civil War raging, the nation was diverted by the so-called Fairy Wedding.[9] Even President Lincoln took a break to meet the newlyweds. A few years later they presented the world with their own child. Together they formed The General Tom Thumb Company, which travelled on a honeymoon tour and later, between 1869 and 1872, on a world tour.

Lavinia outlived Charles by thirty-six years. Later she married another performer of short stature, the Italian Count Primo Magri, and formed the Lilliputian Opera Company, which travelled across America. As late as 1915 Lavinia would write that 'the old name still draws the crowd (Mrs General Tom Thumb)'.[10] When she passed away at the age of seventy-seven, she was buried, on her instructions, next to her first husband, Charles Stratton.

In life the fortunes of all three – the Strattons and Barnum – were entwined. Their relationship did much to change Victorian culture. They left the world when the freak show was one of the archetypal expressions of popular culture, at the apex of a history that had roots going right back to the ancient world.[11]

Ancient Egyptians turned dwarfs into both gods and jesters. Aristotle, Cicero, Pliny and Augustine all pondered bodily difference.[12] In Ancient Greece and Rome monstrous babies were killed at birth, considered signs of cosmic chaos.[13] Yet the Romans also used monsters as the inspiration for gods (Janus, the god of time, is usually depicted with two heads), and monsters and angels could even operate in the same religious cosmology, monsters teaching what to fear, angels teaching what to love, and both igniting awe and devotion.[14] More than a thousand years later, representations of the anomalous body proliferated in early modern print culture, and monsters were often used in Protestant fables auguring divine punishment.[15]

But while the monster signified malevolence, a warning of impending danger, those with exceptional bodies were also paraded for public enjoyment. By the seventeenth century, 'monster shows' were frequent attractions in fairs, marketplaces, coffeehouses and taverns across Europe, while dwarfs were also being kept as pets inside royal courts and aristocratic households. The decadence of Charles II's reign (1660–85) led the writer Henry Morley to note that 'the taste for monsters became a disease'.[16] In the seventeenth and eighteenth centuries monster shows were a site for the mingling of all social classes.[17] Similarly, in colonial America, monsters or living curiosities travelled across the countryside, performing in towns and public gatherings. By the early nineteenth century monsters could be seen in rented rooms, museums and fairs in both America and Europe.

In the mid-nineteenth century, spurred by new railways, steamships and a developing popular culture, the display of exceptional bodies moved from being a predominantly local and informal affair to a professional and international business. Acts from around the world, and increasingly from colonized areas, crossed the Atlantic, with some continuing into Russia and to Constantinople, following what became an established freak show circuit.[18] A growing middle class, with more money to spend and time to enjoy, poured into the freak show which, by the end of the century, was firmly connected to all manner of popular entertainment, out of which grew the freak industry.

By the late nineteenth century, freak performers were regularly featured in circuses, music halls, theatres and seaside resorts; zoos, aquariums, pleasure gardens and dime museums; world's fairs, amusement parks, minstrel shows and carnivals. The freak performer was on the street; making arduous journeys with travelling fairs; and appearing in 'show shops', i.e. vacant commercial premises. They could even be seen in your home, a private performance for an extra fee, or staring at you from photographs, newspapers and journals.

The freak show eventually became a victim of its own staggering success, and forces were at work that would ultimately bring it down. The forces included a saturated entertainment industry, the rising power of medicine, changing tastes and the outbreak of the First World War. As such, historians have commonly defined the freak show's period as running from 1840–1940, although the peak of popularity was around 1840–1914. But, as we will see, we should be wary of neat parameters: freak shows never really died, but instead metamorphosed into different forms of entertainment that are still with us today.

BEFORE GOING FURTHER, there are certain matters that need addressing: concerns regarding language, voyeurism, prurience, exploitation and ridicule always linger under the surface of this subject. Engagement precipitates moral and political questions: 'how do we talk about freaks without re-inscribing the oppressive attitudes we attempt to critique?' as Rosemarie Garland-Thomson, professor of

English and bioethics, pondered.[19] How do we discuss a subject matter that titillates and excites curiosity while, at the same time, trying to transcend voyeurism?

The answer lies in the performers themselves and in the pursuit of focusing on their lives, because it is these lives that deserve recognition. I have decided to publish images because to withhold them would be just as tantalizing, and because images were part of the performance and constitute important historical evidence, also, not to shy away from the drama and the lights, for this would deny the reality and experiences of people who performed in freak shows. Which brings us to the ever-present question, was the freak show historically exploitative? As we will see, in some cases it was, at other times it was empowering. In this sense, it was much like the contemporary entertainment industry.[20]

Attention should also be directed towards the terms 'freak' and 'freak show'. The word 'freak' continues to hold negative connotations. The disability activist Eli Clare disliked it. Writing in 1999 he felt the word was even more harmful, hurtful and unsettling than terms such as 'queer' and 'cripple'.[21] Indeed, the advent of the Disability Rights movement sought social and political change to see the community accommodated rather than excluded, and the word 'freak' seemed a troubling throwback to a bygone age.[22] But some in the Disability Rights movement used the term 'freak' as a badge of pride. Katherine Dunn's novel *Geek Love* (1989) took its title from an infamous sideshow act, the geek, who was renowned for biting the heads off living rodents, chickens and snakes. Dunn explores the world of a travelling carnival, celebrating human difference and rejecting the vulgarity of normality, with Olympia – the albino, hunchback dwarf – proudly declaring: '... I win out by nature, because a true freak cannot be made. A true freak must be born.'[23]

But here in this book the term 'freak' is not used for political reasons, but rather because it was the terminology of the time and because the word 'freak' encircles individuals whose diverse experiences were joined.[24] According to the *Oxford English Dictionary* (*OED*), the 'freak', short for 'freak of nature', means 'an abnormally developed individual of any species; in recent use (*esp.* U.S.), a living curiosity exhibited in a show'. Thus the freak of nature is closely associated with the freak show, although the first usage of 'freak of nature' was as late as 1847 (the term 'freak' was around for even longer, however, indicating a sudden change of mind, a capricious humour, a prank or trick and, writes the *OED*, 'a product of irregular or sportive fancy': a 'mighty freak').[25] In addition to 'freak of nature', there was a litany of other terms used in the eighteenth and nineteenth centuries: 'monstrosities', '*lusus naturae*', 'oddities', 'prodigies', 'novelties', 'marvels' and 'wonders'; also novel or unknown 'races'. It was only from the 1840s that the term 'freak' was used consistently in the world of entertainment.[26]

In the freak show there were so-called 'born freaks', such as dwarfs and giants; what we might call 'exotic freaks', such as cannibals and savages; and 'self-made freaks', like the tattooed and those performing novelty acts, such as sword-swallowing, fire-eating and snake-charming.[27] The sociologist Robert Bogdan defined the word perfectly when he wrote: '"Freak" is not a quality that belongs to the person on display. It is something we created: a perspective, a set of practices – a social construction.'[28] The freak of nature was as much a 'freak of culture', crafted by the context in which it was created and the show in which it was displayed.[29] The freak, in short, was a creation and a presentation; it designated a persona, an identity, which existed onstage. It also functions as a useful analytical category, which has been deployed in numerous pieces of scholarship within the tradition of Freak Studies.[30] To be explicit: General Tom Thumb was a freak; Charles Stratton was a freak performer.

Bogdan goes on to describe the freak show as a 'formally organized exhibition of people with alleged and real physical, mental, or behavioural anomalies for amusement and profit'. It was distinguished, he added, 'from early exhibitions of single attractions that were not attached to organisations such as circuses and carnivals'.[31] The freak show, in other words, was an organized, commercialized and professionalized display of human difference, often with more than one freak performer being displayed within a permanent venue.[32] The show was often respectable – being described as educational – thoroughly theatrical and emphatically popular, open to all ages, genders and professions. It was also rather nebulous, occurring in a popular museum or circus sideshow. Incidentally, the term 'freak show' was not used until the mid- to late nineteenth century, coming among a plethora of others, from 'sideshow' to 'Odditorium'.[33]

Not all freaks were deformed, and they certainly were not defined as 'disabled' (a term which emerged later in the nineteenth century). In fact, the freak was neither infirm nor disabled nor a 'cripple' but, in nineteenth-century terminology, an able-bodied performer.[34] To quote from a freak celebrity, Carl Herrmann Unthan, known as the Armless Fiddler: 'I saw the first transport of wounded soldiers and heard their moans. The terrible visions arose before me. How would these many thousands endure the crippledom which had befallen them?'[35] When Unthan saw the reality of the First World War in the 'crippledom' of servicemen he decided: 'I'm going to teach the cripples in the hospitals how to do useful work and be happy in doing it.'[36] This he dutifully did, while continuing to give performances that demonstrated his skills with his toes, which ranged from rolling a cigarette to playing cards. He even impressed Kaiser Wilhelm, the grandson of Queen Victoria, with a shooting demonstration in Dresden. Wilhelm (who had a secret disability, a withered arm), was so impressed with Unthan's marksmanship that he took two bullets as souvenirs.[37] Although a freak performer, Unthan never saw himself as a cripple. Moreover, despite his armlessness, it did not follow that deformity was enough to make him into a freak, a constructed persona made for the stage.

As we start our story in earnest, we commence much earlier than Unthan: in the seventeenth century and in the presence of royalty, no less; for as we chart the history of the freak show, we must investigate its roots. And, strange to say, they were located in two paradoxical places: the highest echelons of Europe, and the lowest; the royal courts, and the stigmatized travelling fairs. And here, there and in between we meet a court dwarf who becomes a warrior, another who falls in love, a fat man who shapes national identity and a showman labelled a scoundrel.

And so, to begin …

ACT ONE

——◦◦——

DRESS REHEARSALS

CHAPTER ONE

JEFFREY HUDSON

LONDON, NOVEMBER 1626: the strong-willed King Charles I is on the throne. A year earlier the Great Plague had struck down upwards of 35,000 people, a terrible prelude to a tempestuous reign that would see new tensions with Parliament, war in France, war in Scotland and anger at the king's High Anglicanism, and end with the English Civil War and Charles's execution. But in November 1626 this was all to come, and the king and queen enjoyed a lavish banquet held in their honour by the ambitious and ingratiating George Villiers, Duke of Buckingham.

The banquet's likely location was York House, London, an impressive building with an Italianate water gate that connected the house to the Thames. There was music, sumptuous food, gifts galore and theatricals. At one end of the feast was a pair of curtains. When pulled apart they revealed a magnificent backdrop painted with a blue sky. Moments later fluffy clouds descended from the sky and, as if by magic, servants carrying plates of rich meat, vegetables and fish emerged from behind the clouds to serve the guests. The spectacle continued into the evening, with each new dish filling the hall with aromas of exquisite cooking.

After the feast, the bloated, jolly and perhaps tipsy party – but not too tipsy because Charles disliked drunkenness – moved into the banqueting hall. Here the culinary theatricals continued apace: march pane, the forerunner to our marzipan, was presented in beautiful shapes, a visual delight rather than a treat to be eaten, and at the climax of the banquet trumpets blared as two footmen entered carrying a glorious pie, gilded in gold leaf, 2ft high and wide. The pie commonly contained an amusing surprise: the long-standing tradition was live blackbirds, though this was a bit of a cliché by the early seventeenth century.

Still, anticipation mounting, the pie was placed before the fifteen-year-old queen, Henrietta Maria. Suddenly, a child's hand popped through the crust and a fresh-faced dwarf emerged (thankfully, the pie was cold, not hot). He had dark brown eyes and light brown hair. The dwarf, ever so slightly chubby but with a perfectly proportioned body, wore a miniature suit of armour and marched up and down the banqueting table waving a flag. He then returned to the queen and gave a low, theatrical bow. Henrietta Maria was mesmerized. Here was Jeffrey Hudson, seven years old and 18in tall. And he was the queen's to keep.[38]

HENRIETTA MARIA WAS a French Catholic in Protestant England. She felt entrapped in a loveless marriage and had recently been isolated further as her French entourage was expelled from court. But Hudson's performance – and now his presence – had temporarily broken her malaise.

After the celebrations, Hudson went to the queen's private residence at Denmark House (now Somerset House) in London, a white stone, Italianate building – the first Renaissance palace in England. There he joined Henrietta Maria's assortment of ladies-in-waiting, dogs, monkeys, birds, priests, servants and numerous rarities of nature.

There was the Welshman William Evans, a porter of the backstairs, who was reportedly 7ft 6in tall. Thomas Parr, or 'Old Parr', arrived in 1635 and was allegedly 151 years old, although he was probably only seventy. The dwarf Sara Holton arrived shortly after Hudson and remained with the queen until at least 1640. She was joined by the 'Queen's dwarf', Anne Shepherd, and Richard Gibson, the 'King's dwarf', who was renowned for his miniature portraits. When the two married, Charles I gave the bride away. The couple had nine children, two of whom became successful painters.

Ensconced inside Henrietta Maria's luxurious and orderly court, Hudson was provided a privileged life. Born in 1619, the son of a poor butcher from Oakham in the East Midlands, his father, John Hudson, and his mother, Lucy née Royce, were poor country folk. They agreed to release their seven-year-old son into the care of the wealthy Duchess and Duke of Buckingham. Then he became a gift served in a pie; then he became the queen's pet. Reportedly, Hudson declined to see his father once ensconced inside the royal court. Perhaps this was a rejection of his lowly origins or perhaps it would have been too painful an encounter for a boy ripped from his family. Nonetheless, according to Thomas Fuller's *History of the Worthies of England* (1662), the earliest contemporary account of Hudson's life, he lived at the court 'in great plenty therein, wanting nothing but humility, (high mind in a low body) which made him that he did not know himself, and would not know his father, and which by the King's command caused justly his sound correction'.[39] Sadly, we do not really know how Hudson felt because, like so many dwarfs and freak performers of the past, they are largely silent in the archives, their stories steeped in myth.

Indeed, the very terms 'dwarf' and 'little people' come from folklore. Dwarfs lurked in pre-Christian Norse mythology, and they were praised as gods in Ancient Egypt; Western folklore had them living in underground kingdoms with trolls, kobolds (German sprites) and gnomes. They were commonly described as tricksters, being lustful, avaricious and jealous, while also playful and childish.[40] These fables cascaded down the ages: it was noted, for example, that 'the ladies were very fond' of Hudson and 'he could make married men cuckolds without making them jealous.'[41]

Yes, he was a handsome child, but a cuckold of the court? More likely these rumours repeated the myths and long-held associations between dwarfs and wayward sexuality. Ancient Greek sculptures, for example, depicted Dionysian dwarfs in erotic postures; Julia the Elder (39 BC – 14 AD), daughter of Augustus, reportedly satisfied her sexual fantasies with her collection of dwarfs; and Emperor Xuanzong (685–762) allegedly had a harem containing dwarfs in his Resting Place for Desirable Monsters.[42] So how we read Hudson and what we know of him is filtered through these ancient legends and myths. The problem is exacerbated because there were only two contemporary accounts of Hudson published during his life, and collectively they amounted to just a few hundred words. Modern biographer, Nick Page, had to trawl through letters, reports, poems, plays, newspapers and a fair amount of fictional texts to reconstruct Hudson's life.[43]

Certainly, though, in the court of Henrietta Maria, Hudson and his queen were bound by dislocation, and together they forged an intimate, familial bond. During the years that Hudson was with the queen, she would emerge as a precocious force of nature who was fiercely loyal to her husband, the Catholic Church and the finer things in life, including jewels, Persian carpets and fresh flowers scattered across the palace floors. While occasionally self-indulgent and self-righteous, she knew how to enjoy herself, starring in the famed masques of the courts, designing gardens, commissioning artworks and architectural renovations, and epitomizing fashion. She was no sideshow to history either: she was on a mission to advance the cause of Catholicism, exercising power over her husband and taking part in international diplomacy.

Like Henrietta Maria, Hudson developed into a witty, lively and intelligent gentleman with an education befitting his station as the queen's trusted companion. Like her, he felt the forces of history and played a role in their unravelling. He was probably given basic schooling, learned to speak French, and was even provided with a personal servant and a supervisor who was also the queen's nurse. Aged fourteen, he was hunting and shooting in specially made clothes; every winter he would partake in the masques, balls and entertainments in the palace; and in summer he would join the queen on her royal progresses across the country. When twenty-one, he was given a salary of £50 per annum. Moreover, as the queen gave birth to seven children, most within the 1630s, he found himself part of a loving family. He was an integral part of the culture of the court and his relationship to Henrietta Maria was maternal and intimate. The servants were kept close, Charles taking a keen interest in their welfare.

Hudson was also a central feature of the court's flourishing arts programme. Everyone enjoyed the famed masques, a synthesis of operetta and theatre, and he often featured in them. He played the fairy-tale Tom Thumb in *The Fortunate Isles and Their Union* (1625) and featured in *Chloridia* (1631), where he emerged as 'a Prince of Hell, attended by six infernall Spirits; He first danceth alone, and then the Spirits: all expressing their joy, for Cupids comming [sic] among them'.[44] One of his earliest performances, on 23 November 1626, was held in celebration of the queen's seventeenth birthday. One scene involved William Evans, the giant porter, removing from his coat pocket a loaf of bread and, from the other, 'he drew little Jeffrey the Dwarf ... first to the wonder, then to the laughter, of the beholders,' wrote Fuller.[45] A week later Hudson was in another masque alongside the king and queen.

JEFFREY HUDSON'S PRESENCE in the English court was not a freak show as such (freak shows being best defined as a formally organized exhibition of human anomalies for the purpose of amusement and profit), but his life at the court was certainly a forerunner. He was kept for the purpose of entertainment. He was valued because of his body. He was exhibited in plays and paraded to royal guests, and he joined an assortment of other curiosities who later entered the Victorian freak show.

Before the United States of America was even an idea, dwarfs had been sold, swapped and even bred for European royal families. They were prevalent in the courts of Ancient Egypt, China and West Africa. Alexander the Great (356–323 BC) gathered a whole retinue of dwarfs. The Romans collected dwarfs as pets, placing some in gladiatorial rings to fight with 'Amazons', and tossing others across the amphitheatre for entertainment. By the Middle Ages dwarfs were kept side by side with monkeys, sometimes transported between royal households in birdcages. Hudson was not even the first dwarf to be served in a pie.[46]

Dwarfs belonged to the broad category that embraced 'monsters', 'marvels', 'wonders' and 'prodigies', terms that denoted something or someone out of the ordinary but within God's great scheme. They were grouped with phoenixes, werewolves, portents and miraculous natural occurrences. They were part of God's creation, merely miniature, the laws of nature contracted into diminutive proportions.[47] And they were united by the experience they engendered: the shock and awe at the unexpected and the pleasure at nature's eccentricities; the allure of the strange, the exotic and the novel.[48]

Dwarfs were brought into court because they were a valued rarity, because they enhanced the status of their owners and because they entertained. In an age where power rested heavily on the person of the ruler, proximity to power was everything. Companions to royals often came from the noblest of families; they were close to power but also potential threats. Hudson and other court dwarfs were never perceived as threats. Their value was more akin to that of jesters, slaves, eunuchs and pets. They were an extension of the royals' *Wunderkammer*, or Cabinet of Curiosities which, from the sixteenth century, contracted the world's wonders into a collection that enhanced the status of the owner. Moreover, court dwarfs fulfilled a function similar to ladies-in-waiting. Dwarfs were essentially owned by their masters, and entirely dependent on their will. As such, they offered the royals many things, and were ultimately moulded by the particular desire of their master.

Court dwarfs were also loved and, in some cases, treated as one of the family. Some were given special tasks, responsibilities and privileges. The dwarf Don Diego de Acedo, known as El Primo, was secretary and keeper of the king's seal in Philip IV of Spain's court. He was even painted by Diego Velázquez, who executed at least ten portraits of dwarfs in Philip's household. Velázquez presented them with an element of independence, dignity and humanity that reflected their valued position in the king's court. Velázquez also broke from the tradition of depicting dwarfs as creatures from mythology, steeped in symbolism – as Anthony van Dyck painted Hudson in 1633 – and instead depicted them with realism and sensitivity.

While van Dyck depicted Hudson with a monkey on his arm, living in royal luxury and with a maternal bond between him and Henrietta Maria, he was still the queen's pet. In some respects, he was not much different to that monkey, 'with whom, as a source of amusement, he was an equal', wrote one nineteenth-century commentator.[49] Hudson was part son to Henrietta Maria, but also part pet and part jester. While he was well treated, he was also frequently mocked and bullied at court: the friends of the queen's eldest son, Prince Charles (the future Charles II), used to throw him around in a blanket. Hudson's position at court was ambivalent and precarious: one moment he was mocked, the next praised; he was one of the family yet set apart. Ultimately, this ambiguity would be Hudson's downfall.

As Hudson's life illuminates, individuals who were defined by their different bodies were never, necessarily, marginalized: they could find themselves at the heart of culture, in the centre of the royal household no less, long before General Tom Thumb visited Buckingham Palace in 1844, and long before freak performers became the grand celebrities of the Victorian Age. By that time, however, dwarfs were more likely to be seen as nature's mistakes rather than its wonders, and dwarfs would no longer be living in royal courts but instead be parading their bodies for profit. While those developments came later, as Hudson's biographer stressed: 'Jeffrey was eventually to become a "wonder" at Court, but had he not ended up on display in London, he would have just become a curiosity among the fairgoers in the provinces', joining a 'child with 3 legs', 'the Indian King' or an 8ft 'giant' in the likes of Bartholomew Fair.[50] In other words, if not in the royal court, Hudson would probably have been displayed in the stigmatized fairs, dangerous marketplaces or rowdy wakes, festivities originally designed to commemorate a patron of the local church. One of the oldest and most notorious, Bartholomew Fair was described by William Wordsworth as a 'Parliament of Monsters' where performers, such as rope-dancers, puppeteers, fire-eaters and animal trainers frolicked as part of a Dionysian festival alongside kettle drums, trumpets, bagpipes and people with natural anomalies. The assortment of monsters on display included 'hermaphrodites, dwarfs, giants, giantesses' and 'a woman with three breasts, a boneless child, and a monster with one body, two heads, four arms and four legs, with teeth in each mouth'.[51]

Hudson might have joined this dangerous and transitory world of the fairs, populated by the 'itinerant professors of the art of amusing', wrote the nineteenth-century chronicler of London fairs Thomas Frost.

These itinerants 'were in the habit of tramping from town to town, and village to village, for at least two centuries before the Norman Conquest' in 1066, travelling between the fairs that had developed in medieval Britain 'under the protection of the baronial castles'.[52]

The travelling entertainers were known as glee-men, although there were an equal number of female glee-men too, a term that included 'dancers, posturers, jugglers, tumblers, and exhibitors of trained performing monkeys and quadrupeds'.[53] According to Frost, during Elizabeth I's reign (1558–1603), 'lusus naturae, and other natural curiosities had begun to be exhibited by showmen', thus joining the itinerant entertainers who, without roots, were seen as outsiders and viewed with suspicion. The Vagabonds Act of 1572 lumped wandering performers with thieves, fortune tellers and itinerant beggars. The Puritans 'regarded all amusements as worldly vanities and snares of the Evil One', claimed Frost, and this contributed to the itinerant's marginalization and bedevilment.[54] Such censure, however, did not put a stop to the travelling fairs, and they continued into the seventeenth century and beyond.

Hudson was fortunate: life in the royal court was a far better option than the fairs, but we should not create a false dichotomy between royal patronage and fairground displays. Some dwarfs did find more regular employment as artisans and tailors, while others worked on farms. And in ancient times some dwarfs had distinguished careers as poets and philosophers: Philitas of Cos (c. 340–285 BC) helped found the Hellenistic school of poetry, while the relatively unknown Alypius of Alexandria was a philosopher in the third century. There were even dwarfs in the clergy, such as John Baconthorpe (1290–c. 1346), a scholastic philosopher who allegedly taught at Cambridge and Oxford, and the Frenchman Antoine Godeau (1605–72), a contemporary of Jeffrey Hudson who was a renowned writer of romantic poetry and who entered the clergy in 1636.[55]

These individuals, though, were the exceptions not the rule. In the coldness of economic reality, dwarfs struggled to make a living; for the most part their lives were dependent on their families, defined by financial struggle and, if not patronized by royals or nobles, they often found their livelihood within public display.

⚯

J EFFREY HUDSON, PRESENTED as a gift as a young child, was arguably one of the lucky ones: freed from economic hardship, elevated far higher than the dwarfs displayed in the fairs, he was clothed, fed, educated and even paid by the English royals. Nonetheless, dependent and subservient to Queen Henrietta Maria, his life was entangled with the history of her court. For Hudson stability at court meant stability in life, so while Charles I ruled directly, and Parliament was shut down for eleven years, Hudson was relatively secure. However, his situation changed when the Parliamentarian cause was kindled and plots, counter-plots and revolution began to spread.

Hudson was living through an incredibly dangerous period of English history. The Civil War was part political, part religious and part personal, and led to a loss of life, as a proportion of the national population, greater than in the First World War. Indeed, the war brought devastation and disruption on an unprecedented scale and drove the royals from power. In 1642, to the shouts and screams of an angry mob, Henrietta Maria was forced from London with Hudson in tow. She travelled to Holland to raise funds and amass ammunition, and returned the next year accompanied by Hudson aboard a Dutch warship. (It was commanded by Van Tromp, whose name, incidentally, was later appropriated by a Victorian performing dwarf, Jan Hannema, who met Queen Victoria in 1849 and billed himself 'Admiral Van Tromp'.)[56]

They landed at the small fishing village of Bridlington on the north-east coast on 22 February 1643. At around 5 o'clock the following morning, Henrietta Maria and Hudson were awoken by the sounds of war: the Parliamentarians were firing cannons at Bridlington from six large ships. In the turmoil that ensued, the queen escaped but Hudson, aged twenty-two and fiercely loyal, stayed to fight. Apparently he rushed to the quayside with a sword and pistol but the Parliamentarians never left the ships and kept firing.

The cannon balls smashed into cottages and streets, killing one of the queen's servants. People ran for cover until the tide changed, and the ships left the bay. The queen's entourage emerged from the rubble. It was clear the Parliamentarians were after blood. They had targeted their queen, who was declared a traitor a few months later. Hudson, however, had shown extraordinary bravery.[57]

The queen and her entourage next went to York, a Royalist stronghold, before heading south to Stratford-upon-Avon and then Oxford. One night the cavalry commander, Prince Rupert, led Royalist forces in raids against the Parliamentarians and, according to Page: 'it is certainly possible that Jeffrey fought alongside the King and Prince Rupert at the battle of Newbury – a terrible slaughter which both sides claimed as a victory.'[58] But it is hard to know for sure. Walter Scott, in his historical novel *Peveril of the Peak* (1823), claimed that Hudson did fight in this battle and was even knighted 'Sir Geoffrey Hudson [*sic*]'.[59] The latter was definitely false, and Hudson's boast in the book – that he 'charged with my troop abreast with Prince Rupert' wielding a sword atop 'a tall, long-legged brute of a horse' – smacks of fiction.[60] There are no records of his fighting alongside Prince Rupert or the king or, indeed, having ever been commissioned in the army. Moreover – and this could read as either proof or disproof – there was a long tradition of court dwarfs being said to display courage and loyalty, and joining in fighting: in his invasion of northern China in the early thirteenth century, for example, Genghis Khan was apparently joined by his dwarf, Casan.[61]

However, if Hudson was not commissioned into the king's army, the queen had her own, and she could appoint whomever she wished. Hudson, it would appear, went directly to his queen to seek a title and a post that reflected his bravery and commitment. He was duly made Captain of the Horse and, some forty years later, towards the end of his life, he was still recorded as Captain Jeffrey Hudson in a list of people receiving donations from the king.[62] The title was a source of great pride to Hudson.

That new title created problems, though. In the summer of 1644, amid the bloody Civil War, the queen's court escaped to France. By October they were in Nevers, roughly 150 miles from Paris, where Hudson was mercilessly mocked by Charles Crofts, brother of the queen's Master of Horse. The joshing got too much for Hudson. His pride wounded, he challenged Crofts to a duel. Crofts reportedly thought the whole thing a joke. It wasn't.

Next to the castle of Nevers, the men mounted their horses and charged. Raising his weapon, Hudson fired first. The bullet penetrated Crofts' skull. It was a piece of extraordinary marksmanship that Hudson would come to regret. He had ignored the numerous decrees against duelling and killed an influential man in the royal court. Henrietta Maria had little choice: with tears and sobs she banished Hudson from her court.[63]

For Hudson this moment was a brutal reminder that his fortunes had always depended on the queen. He was never an independent, self-contained person. His ambiguous position was made absolute. Expelled from court, he set out on his return journey to Britain in the winter of 1644, but, incredibly (you can't make this up), his ship was captured by North African Barbary pirates and he was enslaved for twenty-five years. According to James Wright's *The History and Antiquities of the County of Rutland* (1684), the only other contemporary account of Hudson's life: 'It was a Turkish Pirate that took and carried him to Barbary, where he was sold, and remained a slave for many years.' We know practically nothing of his time in captivity, although Wright claimed it was one of 'hardship, much labour, and beating, which he endured when a Slave to the Turks'.[64] Wright, who wrote approximately two years after Hudson's death, recalled: 'I have heard himself several times affirm, that between the 7th year of his Age and the 30th he never grew any thing considerable, but after thirty he shot up in a little time to that highth [*sic*] of stature which he remain'd at in his old age, viz. about three foot and nine Inches.'[65]

Wright wasn't sure if this was true, but we do know that in May 1669 Hudson was back in England with a pension provided in part by the Duke of Buckingham, the son of his original patron. He was then about fifty years old, living in his home county of Rutland, probably with his brother, Samuel. Later that year he heard that Henrietta Maria was dead. King Charles had been beheaded in 1649 after the Civil War; then came the Commonwealth (1649–60) and the Restoration and the reign of Charles II, who was king when in 1678 Hudson returned to London … and more tragedy.

The capital, recently ravaged by plague and fire, was awash with anti-Catholic sentiment and Hudson was recognized as the dwarf of the Catholic queen. He was thrown into gaol, spending his sixtieth birthday in Westminster's Gatehouse Prison. Eventually released, he died an outcast around 1682 and was buried in an unmarked and unknown location.[66]

JEFFREY HUDSON BEGAN life as the son of a poor butcher. He had risen to court pet, then Captain of the Horse. He had been banished, enslaved, possibly tortured, imprisoned and rejected by society. How he felt about his life is conjecture. Mistreated? Betrayed? Abused? Angry? The latter part of his life would certainly suggest so. But the earlier part? He had lived in royal luxury; was loved, educated and clothed; was entertained and entertaining. Though he was mocked and bullied, he had escaped poverty and social marginalization, and was never displayed in the rowdy, licentious fairs. Perhaps he regarded his early life with pride and nostalgia.

With no record left by Hudson it is hard to go any further. But there is another way of approaching his experience: through the life of another court dwarf, a Polish gentleman, Józef Boruwłaski (1739–1837), who grew to a total height of 3ft 3in. Like Hudson, Boruwłaski was deemed attractive and was 'not one of those misshapen beings whom nature seems to have barely conceived'. He was 'favoured by nature, possesses every qualification which constitutes a man; distinctly organized, healthful, well-made, only differing in size'.[67] This was all written in the preface to a memoir authored by Boruwłaski: a rare source that gives our protagonist a voice, avoiding the muteness of dwarfs from the past and offering some realities against the prevalent mythologies and fictions.

CHAPTER TWO

JÓZEF BORUWŁASKI

JÓZEF BORUWŁASKI'S STORY reflects the life of a dwarf in the royal courts: the world of Jeffrey Hudson. But it also introduces us to a new trend of dwarfs being increasingly paraded in public for money: the world of Charles Stratton, aka General Tom Thumb. Unlike Hudson and Stratton, Boruwłaski left a memoir that was published in 1788 and ran into four editions, the last appearing in 1820. These memoirs provide a unique insight into how Boruwłaski viewed his experiences. They are the personal account of a man who was defined by his body yet who sought recognition beyond his unusual size. The memoirs, as we will see, should be taken with a pinch of salt; nonetheless they signalled an important moment, when the ancient mythologies concerning dwarfs were countered by a gentleman writing from his own perspective, in his own voice.

Boruwłaski was born in November 1739, measuring a mere 8in, in the town of Halych on the Dniester River, in today's Ukraine.[68] He came from an impoverished, noble family of six children, three of whom – Boruwłaski, his sister and his elder brother – were dwarfs and destined to be dependent on the sponsorship of richer families.[69]

'I had scarcely entered my ninth year when my father died,' he recalled, 'and left my mother with six children, and a very small share in the favours of fortune.' With little choice, his mother put Boruwłaski into the care of a family friend, the widowed Helena Stadnicka, later the Countess of Tarnowska, 'but not without tears'.[70] Unlike his average-sized siblings, who could enter the clergy or military, or marry into a wealthy family, this was probably the best and most realistic option for Józef. He lived with Helena for four years as her *Joujou*, meaning 'little joy', and was probably given basic schooling, learning arithmetic, the tenets of Catholicism, German and French.[71]

Boruwłaski's life was disrupted when the countess remarried and, as he wrote, she 'seemed no longer amused with my little prattling'.[72] He knew what he had to do: 'I considered it as my duty to double my efforts, that I might render myself agreeable to the husband of my benefactress.'[73] But he did not succeed and, aged around fifteen, was transferred to the ownership of Countess Anna Humiecka, then one of the wealthiest ladies in the country.

Boruwłaski spent the first six months at Humiecka's estate in Rychty (now Richta in Ukraine), a small town in the Polish-Lithuanian Republic, before travelling with her across Europe in late 1758 or early 1759. It was the start of his life as a travelling companion to the countess, being 'introduced' to the nobility and royalty of the European salons and palaces. 'Introduced' is not quite the right word, because essentially Boruwłaski was being displayed – paraded in lavish, often military, costumes, creating excitement contradictory to the Enlightenment, which embraced the rational and rejected the Baroque's obsession with the strange and freakish.[74] Jeffrey Hudson had been interpreted in one way, part of a world of wonders, marvels and monsters, and now Boruwłaski in quite another.

The seeds of modern science were planted in the eighteenth century when natural philosophers turned their attentions to the observable external world. The Enlightenment's concern was the rational – what could be seen and understood – not the irrational and imaginative.

Thus, increasingly, the supernatural was expunged from academic deliberations, but this was not a neat, chronological shift: according to the sixteenth-century French surgeon Ambroise Paré, the causes of monstrosity ranged from 'the glory of God' (i.e. supernatural wonders) to 'hereditary or accidental illnesses' (more in tune with the thinking of the Enlightenment).[75] But even in the sixteenth century Paré was moving towards a more materialist reading of monstrosities, emphasizing early development from fertilization to birth. Some forty years after Paré's publication, supernatural marvels were no longer part of rational explanations, and monsters were seen to be caused 'by virtue of a secondary plan of nature', according to the Italian scholar Fortunio Liceti.[76] Monsters became mistakes. In the eighteenth century the discussion moved on again: the French naturalist Étienne Geoffroy Saint-Hilaire began to classify monstrosities, believing they followed the same rules of nature that determined non-monstrous beings. Paré's distinction between the natural, the unnatural and the supernatural was no more: monsters were now forged by scientific forces and subject to the same rules. Monsters, as we will see, were actually rendered normal.[77] Certainly, they could be rationally explained and classified.

While new scholarly attitudes were evolving when Boruwłaski was being paraded by his countess, everyday reactions had not kept pace. He was a source of fascination and joy to all who saw him, including Maria Theresa, the Archduchess of Austria and Queen of Bohemia and Hungary, 'who was graciously pleased to say, that I exceed by far all that she had heard of me, and that I was one of the most astonishing beings she had ever seen'.[78] She even gave him a ring, previously worn by her daughter, who Boruwłaski believed was Marie Antoinette, who later became the Queen of France in 1774 (and was executed during the French Revolution).

After six months in Vienna, Boruwłaski and the countess went to Munich, where they met Elector Maximilian III Joseph and his wife, Maria Anna Sophia, before heading to Lunéville, then Paris, the Netherlands and back through Germany, impressing everyone from the Hapsburg statesman Wenzel Anton to the French writer Count Tressan, who helped ensure Boruwłaski's entry into the famous Enlightenment *Encyclopédie*. Boruwłaski was taught the guitar by Pierre Gaviniès, one of the most famous composers and violinists of his day, and was instructed by the ballet master, Gasparo Angiolini. When he returned to Warsaw, in the autumn of 1761, it dawned on Boruwłaski that 'first I was looked upon only as an object of mere curiosity' but now the nobility 'sought my society, because they took pleasure in my conversation'.[79] This was, after all, 'the age of conversation' and his witty, intelligent repertoire stood him in good stead.[80] But while the trip across Europe had refined his manners and character, he was also painfully aware of his predicament:

> *Those, however, would be much mistaken, who should imagine that, seduced by the repeated kindnesses bestowed on me, or wholly devoted to the pleasures afforded me, I did not sometimes labour under painful feelings, or that I could always be unconscious of being, upon the whole, only looked upon by others as a doll, a little more perfect, it is true, and better organized than they commonly are, but, however, only as an animated toy.*[81]

It is not hard to imagine such reflections being echoed by Hudson or Stratton. In one notable scene Boruwłaski recalled overhearing Humiecka say 'how pleasant it would be' to see if Boruwłaski could procreate with his sister, another dwarf. In ancient Rome dwarfs were kept in wealthy households to fulfil the erotic fantasies of their owners; as author Betty Adelson wrote: 'dwarfs, wandering naked except for jewels, were not an uncommon sight in the homes of the wealthy'.[82] And despite the Age of the Enlightenment, some things had not changed. On hearing Humiecka's cruel salaciousness, Boruwłaski wept bitterly: 'so strongly was I affected at the sort of contempt apparently implied in this project of uniting me with my sister; from which I thought I had to conclude, not only that they believed themselves entitled to dispose of me without my advice, but even looked upon me as a being merely physical, without morality, on whom they might try experiments of every kind.'[83]

The experiment never happened, but Boruwłaski was left in no doubt how he was perceived. And this was by no means the only indignity: the legend of Jeffrey Hudson was repeated when Boruwłaski was served in an urn during a banquet. On another occasion the court dwarf Nicolas Ferry, known as Bébé, grew jealous and tried to push Boruwłaski into a fire. Ferry was in the care of Stanisław I Leszczyński, twice elected King of Poland, who inflicted severe corporal punishment on his dwarf after the attempted murder.

Ferry was around eighteen years old at the time, but the early onset of ageing made him appear about thirty. Moreover, he had 'both in his mind and way of thinking, all the defects commonly attributed to us'. He was mentally slow, wrote Boruwłaski, who pleaded that Ferry be shown clemency: 'I sincerely pitied him, and would not have related this circumstance, but to remark, that the smallness of our stature does not prevent us from experiencing the power of the passions.'[84] Ferry died a few years later, in 1764, after suffering an infection, although it was rumoured he died of jealousy.

―⁃◌◌⁃―

FOR NEARLY TWENTY years, between 1761, when Boruwłaski was twenty-one years old, and 1780, when he was forty-one, Boruwłaski lived with Humiecka in her estates at Podole and Warsaw. He was given a doll-sized room with 'a small sofa, little tables, a small billiard set, and other games and toys'.[85] He may have been treated like a plaything, yet Boruwłaski was a man and, 'women, in my eyes, had taken quite a new form,' he wrote. 'I loved them all.'[86] Yet he viewed his situation with frustration: 'How much was my mind mortified on reflecting upon my stature, which I considered as an insurmountable obstacle to the happiness I longed for with so much ardour!'[87]

Boruwłaski overcame his fears. He would sneak out with so-called friends, visiting the theatres to find women, and eventually fell in love with a French actress, only to discover that his friends and the actress were laughing behind his back. The countess was also furious with him for stepping outside his assigned role as child-pet. Over the years love and lust were not easy to contain. Finally, when Boruwłaski was approaching his fortieth year in the late 1770s, the household was joined by Isalina Barboutan. She was a dark-haired, attractive, humorous French girl, twenty-three years younger than Boruwłaski. He was 'in love', besotted.[88] But he was also plagued with anguish: 'It was then I bitterly felt all the disadvantages of my size ... to be upon a level with other men, I would have sacrificed both the fondness of my benefactress, and the bounty.'[89]

Boruwłaski soon confessed his feelings to Isalina but she only burst out laughing, and Boruwłaski was confined to his bed for two months, possibly suffering depression. When he recovered he began writing love letters: 'Oh! that Nature had doomed me, by my stature, never to pass the narrow circle of childhood! Why then have given me a feeling heart, allotted me a soul capable of appreciating the qualities of your own, implanted in my bosom the seeds of a violent passion?'[90]

Isalina's letters were filled with rebuttals and rebukes, especially when the countess got wind of Boruwłaski's love and furiously expelled Isalina from her household: 'she makes me answerable for your madness', Isalina wrote on 4 November 1779, adding a week later that 'the whole town talk of this circumstance, and I cannot go anywhere, without being exposed to unpleasant and troublesome jokes'.[91] Boruwłaski was also expelled from the countess's home, having upended her desire for a childish plaything: 'My captivity, my charming friend, is now at an end', he wrote to Isalina on 20 November.[92]

In her letters Isalina reveals how she was then, in effect, forced into marrying Boruwłaski by her mother because he was promised a royal salary. In her letter of 26 November she wrote that 'somewhere else you might be punished for thus forcing my inclination; here you must be loved, since one cannot hate you.'[93] It is worth reflecting that, as a young woman in the eighteenth century, Isalina's choices were as limited as Boruwłaski's, perhaps more so. In 1779 they married; Isalina was seventeen, Józef forty.

J ÓZEF BORUWŁASKI WAS now independent and married, but his life was far from stable. He was outside the protection of a benefactor for the first time in his adult life. And his allowance of 120 ducats was not enough to sustain a comfortable lifestyle, especially after Isalina had three children in the early 1780s.

Over the next twenty-five years Boruwłaski walked a tightrope. On the one hand he was loath to publicly display himself for money: 'The education I had received, the manner in which I had lived till now, contributed to make me look upon this resource as beneath me.'[94] On the one hand the bibulous fairs carried a stigma that he wanted to avoid. On the other hand his options were limited. He had to earn money and his body was a prime source of revenue. He overcame this tension by giving 'concerts' across Europe, performing with his violin and guitar at expensive events for a select audience. He even dubbed himself Count Boruwłaski, a title that was pure fiction, but it elevated his status and emphasized his noble heritage.

He began his second tour of Europe in 1781, arriving in Vienna on 11 February. But the ruler, Maria Theresa, had recently died, and all public entertainments, including concerts, were suspended. A French diplomat reportedly told him: 'Do not believe ... my little friend, that concerts will always be sufficient to answer your expenses, and to procure you a support; you must needs give up pride, or choose misery; and if you do not intend to lead the most unhappy life; if you wish to enjoy, in future, a state of tranquillity, it is indispensable you should resolve to make exhibition of yourself.'[95]

Boruwłaski was shocked by this, and ignored the suggestion for a further year, holding more concerts and visiting the courts of Germany, where 'several charming ladies were eager to take me on their lap and clasp me in their arms'; 'the most cruel torment', he wrote in the first edition of his memoirs, especially because he was now a married man.[96] In Triesdorf, Boruwłaski and Isalina were forced to part with their youngest daughter, who was taken into the care of a wealthy family, as they continued across Germany to Strasburg, Brussels and Ostend, eventually arriving in England in March 1782.

Here they received the patronage of the fashionable Duke and Duchess of Devonshire. The duchess, Georgiana, was a compassionate woman who provided Boruwłaski with an apartment and introduced him to anybody who was anybody, including the Prince of Wales, heir to the throne (the future King George IV). On 23 May 1782 Boruwłaski met King George III, who treated him as a gentleman rather than an object of curiosity, much to his appreciation.

In the eighteenth century Boruwłaski's experiences were not necessarily unique: Matthias Buchinger (1674–1740), born without hands or feet and about 29in tall, travelled across northern Europe entertaining kings and nobles, and reportedly met King George I, although the sources differ on this point. Like Boruwłaski, Buchinger was a skilled musician, mastering the trumpet and flute among half a dozen other instruments, and he added magician, dancer and calligrapher to his portfolio of talents (his work was exhibited at the Metropolitan Museum of Art in New York in 2016). Moreover, like Boruwłaski, he was a married man and father. In fact, Buchinger reportedly married four times, fathering some fourteen children. There were even rumours of multiple mistresses.[97]

Like Buchinger, Boruwłaski found himself at the heart of fashionable society. But in a paradox that defined Boruwłaski's life, he struggled financially despite moving in the highest social circles. What's more, although he had successfully avoided public exhibitions, pressure was mounting: in May 1782 he was introduced to Charles Byrne, the Irish Giant, who was displaying himself for money. The meeting was arranged by aristocratic friends who were keen to see their contrast in size (the top of Boruwłaski's head reached Byrne's knee). Boruwłaski soon held his first London concert at Carlisle House, investing the huge sum of eighty guineas in the affair. He also hosted 'balls' in London, holding one on 30 May 1788 at the Crown and Anchor Inn on the Strand. As was advertised in the press, it was open to anyone who could afford the 5 shillings entrance fee, the high price sifting the rough from the refined – meaning Boruwłaski could tell himself that this was no monstrous performance for the great unwashed. Indeed, this was a fashionable social gathering where, between 8 p.m. and 1 a.m., Boruwłaski played host and entertained guests with his guitar and jigged a Cossack dance with his wife. Afterwards, he danced with the ladies.[98]

In her 2012 biography of Boruwłaski, Anna Grześkowiak-Krwawicz drew attention to a mysterious figure who appears to have helped Boruwłaski organize these concerts. This figure was sometimes referred to as the 'uncle' of Isalina, and was noted by Boruwłaski as a friend and generous man who travelled with him and his family across England and Ireland until at least 1787.[99] His help would have been invaluable: when Boruwłaski first arrived in England, he could not speak the language, instead conversing in French; he never fully mastered English, speaking with a pronounced accent and poor grammar. Moreover, it appears that Boruwłaski travelled with Isalina and the children (about whom, unfortunately, little is known; they are rarely mentioned in the sources), so perhaps the 'uncle' helped take care of the family. Also, being no taller than 39in and travelling around the country displaying his body was hardly safe, and Boruwłaski probably benefited from having protection.

⸺∘☙∘⸺

For a grand total of twenty years, Boruwłaski played host across Britain, holding promoted 'concerts', 'balls', 'breakfasts' and conducting special visits to people's homes for half a guinea per guest (again, not a public exhibition, although the claim was increasingly tenuous). He also greeted people in his own apartments, usually for 5 shillings, but the cost was gradually reduced: 'the pressures of want, and the call of nature, had stifled in my heart all that seemed shocking to me.'[100] Whether he liked it or not, Boruwłaski was moving ever closer to public displays.

In Birmingham, in 1785, he was visited by the young Catherine Hutton. She later wrote 'A Memoir of the Celebrated Dwarf, Joseph Boruwłaski' (1845), which noted: 'I never saw a more graceful man or a more perfect gentleman.'[101] He became a regular at the Hutton household, where Catherine was struck by the difference between his onstage and offstage persona: 'He spoke but little English. He uttered the few phrases he had learned with assumed veracity, when in public; but, at our fireside, where he was no longer obliged to exert himself, he was frequently silent, and sometimes sad.'[102]

A few years later Boruwłaski wrote his own memoirs. He had not been receiving the royal allowance of 120 ducats and his concerts and balls were failing to attract the crowds. He was in debt and faced the prospect of imprisonment. His memoirs therefore had a monetary motive; they were a new, textual form of display. He went from concerts, balls and apartments to performing on the page, outlining his trials and tribulations, but also his dignity, respectability and humanity as a dwarf who moved in the upper echelons of society. As we will see, by writing for a profit, Boruwłaski carefully constructed his memoirs to appeal to a broad audience.

And they were a success. The first edition secured four hundred subscribers and there was another edition, four years later. Copies were printed in English, German and French, and many were sold to visitors at his apartment, a forerunner to the exhibition pamphlets of the Victorian freak show, which outlined an often fanciful biography of the freak onstage. To conclude the second edition, Boruwłaski reflected:

Behold the cruel pangs of a husband and father; were I upon a footing with mortals, I might, like them, have supported myself and my family, by honest industry: but my size excludes me irrevocably from the common circle of society.—There are many persons who seem to pay no regard, nor even to consider me as a man, and an honest man, endued [sic] *with the most tender sensibility,— how painful a reflection!*[103]

In the following years, Boruwłaski continued displaying his body in concerts and 'social calls'. He placed announcements in the press and printed pamphlets to advertise his 'appearances' (but never public 'exhibitions' to the masses, he told himself). In 1788 he moved north with his family, performing in Cambridge, Norwich and Bury St Edmunds before travelling to Scotland. In 1790 he went to France, arriving in the middle of the French Revolution and almost exactly when the National Constituent Assembly declared the abolition of the nobility – Boruwłaski's prime audience. Worse, he was now in poor health and a conman stole his money. By 1791 he was in Guernsey on the start of a new journey, which took him through Warwick, Coventry, Birmingham and Liverpool, and on to Ireland in 1792, where it appears his wife left him.

Rumours abounded that there was trouble in the marriage. It was claimed, and is still repeated, that Isalina would lift Boruwłaski onto a mantlepiece and leave him there after serious quarrels.[104] Possibly, having been pressured into marrying Boruwłaski, Isalina found the whole affair humiliating and struggled with the transitory life of her family and a husband who essentially worked as a performing dwarf. It was probably during the trip to Ireland in 1792 that the couple separated, and Boruwłaski, who referred to his wife as an 'adored companion' and 'sincere friend' in his memoirs, later expunged these loving references in future editions.[105] What happened to Isalina is unclear, but in 1842 she was living with her second daughter on St Thomas in the Virgin Islands, where she died at the age of ninety in 1852. To the end, she used her married name.[106]

Boruwłaski stayed in Ireland for about six years, travelling across a troubled country that was threatened by French invasions led by General Humbert. He returned to England around 1799. By now he was in his sixties, tired of travelling, weary from displaying his body and anxious about the future. Luckily he would, eventually, find rest. In about 1805 friends and benefactors had raised enough money to invest in a lifetime annuity, which gave him an annual income of approximately £150. This provided Boruwłaski with the stability he so craved, but it was not enough to live in London, so he headed to Durham, a town he knew from earlier travels, and where his good friend and organist at the cathedral, Thomas Ebdon, lived.

Surrounded by luscious green countryside, Durham stood in the shadows of a magnificent castle and cathedral, with the River Wear running through the quiet city. According to one nineteenth-century traveller, the inhabitants lived 'a cheerful and happy life'.[107] Here was a place to find rest. Boruwłaski probably moved to Durham in 1806, initially living with the Ebdon family until Thomas died in 1811. Boruwłaski subsequently moved to 12 Old Bailey, close to Prebends' Bridge in the old part of Durham, which acquired the name 'Count's Corner'.[108] He remained close to the Ebdon family until his dying days.[109]

He lived in humble circumstances, surrounded by a varied and plentiful library of books on philosophy, history, theology and natural history, and with furniture scaled to his size.[110] He became a member of the Masons and could be seen walking around town with celebrated actors, local gentry and clergy. He was good friends with the actor Stephen Kemble and the comedian Charles Mathews, who 'regarded him as a gentleman' rather than a curiosity, according to Mathews' wife.[111]

Boruwłaski was, by most accounts, humorous, cheerful and amiable. He was acquainted with the Bishop of Durham, William Van Mildert, a key figure in the founding of Durham University who, in a book of verses, described Boruwłaski as 'one of nature's wonders'.[112] Boruwłaski spent the remainder of his days tending his garden, walking around the picturesque town where, it is said today, he was sometimes teased by the locals and enjoyed experimenting in alchemy. Around 1816 he sat down to write yet another version of his memoirs, which was published in 1820 and dedicated to King George IV. In letters held at Durham University Library, Boruwłaski shows a keen interest in ensuring the memoirs were properly advertised.[113] The following year, aged eighty-four, he visited George IV with Charles Mathews in attendance. It was one of the proudest moments of Boruwłaski's life.

THE 1820 MEMOIRS, however, were filled with falsity. Boruwłaski claimed that in the early 1780s he travelled through Hungary, Turkey, Russia, Finland, Lapland and through to the Arctic Ocean. He journeyed, so he wrote, across Scandinavia and Siberia, reportedly meeting the great traveller and Hungarian explorer Maurice Benyovszky, and together journeying into Tunisia in search of the 'philosopher's stone'. None of this was true but Boruwłaski was capitalizing on the fashion for travel stories; his memoirs were part of a literary genre.

This is equally true of the first three editions, which were published in the 'confessions' genre popularized by Jean-Jacques Rousseau in the eighteenth century. This genre of writing explains why Boruwłaski so openly confessed his feelings while largely ignoring the broader historical context, including the French Revolution, the partitions of Poland and the madness of George III. In this genre Boruwłaski had been dealing in introspection, reflection and emotions. However, the genre had become unfashionable by the time he was writing the fourth edition, so he replaced sentimentality with adventure.[114]

His memoirs, then, do not present an unmediated insight into his life, nor a reliable repository of historical fact. Indeed, all the memoirs and autobiographies explored in this book are better regarded in this way: not as private diaries but rather public presentations, moulded by specific agendas.[115] 'I belong to the public,' Lavinia Warren wrote in her memoir, and so too do these autobiographies.[116] Nonetheless, these first-person sources, and Boruwłaski's memoirs in particular, provide protagonists with a voice and some determination over their legacy. Their resurrection has its own value.

Boruwłaski passed away aged ninety-seven (remarkable at the time as dwarfs were not known for longevity). His belongings were valued and sold at auction. The Ebdons helped settle the outstanding affairs 'of our dear friend Count Boruwłaski', and he was buried in Durham Cathedral, near the west end of the north aisle, with a stone marked by the letters 'J.B.'[117] In the university's museum, a life-sized statue, two suits, his hat, hatbox, slippers, gloves, violin and walking stick were preserved (some are now in Durham's Town Hall alongside an oil painting).[118] In 1933 his wedding ring was added to the collection.[119]

In the west wall of the church of St Mary-the-Less, Durham, there is a black marble tablet that was meant to be placed in the cathedral but was allegedly refused as Boruwłaski was a Roman Catholic. It bears the inscription: 'Near this spot repose the remains of Count Joseph Boruwłaski, a native of Pokucia, in the late kingdom of Poland … he possessed a more than common share of understanding and knowledge. After various changes of fortune, borne with cheerful resignation to the will of God, he closed his life.'[120]

Throughout his life Boruwłaski demonstrated a strong sense of pride and propriety. Raised in aristocratic and royal circles, he was loath to display his body to the masses and he deliberately avoided becoming one of the 'monsters' of the marketplaces and the travelling fairs, which continued to attract social disapproval.

But he was not the only person with an exceptional body who sought to eschew such lowly displays. Daniel Lambert, a contemporary of Boruwłaski, also found himself destined for public exhibitions, though on account of his extreme corpulence. Like Boruwłaski, the sources detailing Lambert's life were constructed to fulfil a specific function that tarred facts with fiction. Like Boruwłaski, Lambert sought to elevate his displays. But, unlike the Polish dwarf, Lambert would in death, even more so than in life, be elevated by others: he would become a national legend and shape a national identity.

CHAPTER THREE

DANIEL LAMBERT

D ANIEL LAMBERT WAS born on 13 March 1770 in the parish of St Margaret, Leicester. He was raised in a rural setting surrounded by 'horses, dogs and cocks, and all the other appendages of sporting', according to a posthumous 1809 pamphlet.[121] His family were gamekeepers, huntsmen and keen sportsmen and, as a boy, Lambert shared these passions.[122] There was no indication that he would become morbidly obese and forced to display his body.

Aged fourteen, Lambert went to Birmingham as an apprentice to a die-casting and engraving business, serving four out of the standard seven years before returning to Leicester where he succeeded his father as keeper of the Leicester gaol, a small institution for men and women. Lambert's character shone: he was renowned for his compassion, and instigated a series of prison reforms that were praised. One prison inspection specifically referred to Lambert as 'a humane, benevolent man'.[123] He was a true gentleman, with a 'generous heart', claimed one biography; he was quiet, shy and unassuming.[124] When the prison closed in 1805, Lambert was granted an annuity of £50 for life, further proof of how highly he was held.

But while running the gaol his weight had increased. This was attributed to his confined and sedentary life, although contemporary sources claimed Lambert never ate or drank more than the next man. An 1806 newspaper stated: 'his diet is plain and the quantity very moderate, for he does not eat more than the generality of men. He drinks neither wines, spirits, or malt liquor, having for the last twelve years drank only water. He sleeps well, but scarcely as much as other people; and his respiration is as free as that of any moderate sized person.'[125]

Being fat was already then seen as a moral and mental failure. The Enlightenment taught that man was master over his body and so, as the eighteenth turned into the nineteenth century, corpulence was increasingly seen as one's 'own fault'.[126] But since Lambert's weight apparently was not due to gluttony, he was not morally culpable. He remained a dignified gentleman with an upright moral character.

His main passion was country pursuits, a proper gentlemanly interest, and he was a keen breeder of cocks, hens and dogs. A rare letter, written in his hand and dated 12 May 1805, acknowledged the receipt of two cocks and four hens, one of which he returned with the letter for 'she goes upon the nest every day, and comes from thence cackling but never lays—consequently she is of no service to me'.[127] He would have liked nothing more than to live a quiet rural life, but his weight kept burgeoning. Aged thirty-two he weighed 32st; at thirty-six he had ballooned to 52st 11lb.

The weight brought unwanted attention. When someone called at Lambert's home, his servant informed the caller that his wary master never received strangers: 'Let him know,' replied the curious visitor, 'that I called about some cocks.' Lambert overheard and reportedly called out: 'Tell the gentlemen [sic] that I am a *Shy-cock*.'[128] But however shy, Lambert was unable to keep the curiosity-seekers at bay. Eventually, despite his better judgement and natural reticence, he submitted to the prospect of being exhibited: 'he must either submit to be a closed prisoner in his own house or endure all the inconveniences without receiving the profits of an exhibition', wrote one nineteenth-century biography.[129]

This was not dissimilar to the experience of Celesta Geyer over a hundred years later who, in the 1920s, was told by a circus fat lady: 'You know, honey, everyone laughs at you now. Don't you think it would be a good idea to make them pay for their fun?'[130] So Geyer, who had a successful career outside showbiz, became Dolly Dimples. She joined the tradition of circus fat ladies who wore girlish attire, titillated inquisitive audiences and were reportedly jolly and happy, although many suffered from depression. Geyer, as testified in her own writing, appeared to have a binge-eating disorder: 'I was caught in the clutches of my own jaws,' she wrote.[131]

As to Daniel Lambert, he 'abhorred the very idea of exhibiting himself', claimed *The New Wonderful Museum and Extraordinary Magazine* (1808), and 'he is too noble a spirit to submit to be the hired puppet of any Show-man'.[132] But, we are told, he eventually, if reluctantly, conceded to a public exhibition and headed to London in April 1806. He rented an apartment at 53 Piccadilly, a respectable and increasingly expensive part of town on a busy road filled with expansive houses, inns, taverns and booksellers. His exhibitions were different to the fairs of the early nineteenth century and the commercial freak shows of the 1840s: he presented himself in apartments that 'had more the air of a place of fashionable resort than of an exhibition', said a posthumous pamphlet. It cost 1 shilling to enter, a price which ensured the riffraff stayed away.[133] It was a type of performance befitting Józef Boruwłaski's refined engagements, though Lambert never played music or danced as Boruwłaski did.

An advertisement in *The Times* read: 'Exhibition – Mr Daniel Lambert, of Leicester, the greatest curiosity in the world, who, at the age of 36 years, weighs upwards of 50 stone ... will receive company at his house.'[134] It was important that the apartment had the air of a home as this suggested respectability, and Lambert was at pains to stress that he was not a spectacle. Rather, his exhibition was designed as a social occasion, and 'there was not a gentleman in town from his own county but went to see him, not merely gazing at him as a spectacle, but treating him in the most friendly and soothing manner', claimed his posthumous pamphlet. When a group of Quakers visited, they felt compelled to remove their hats in deference; foreigners paid their respects; a party of fourteen travelled from Guernsey; and even Boruwłaski came to visit in an 'unexpected meeting of the largest and smallest man', which seemed, noted the same pamphlet, 'to realize the fabled history of the inhabitants of Lilliput and Brobdingnag', a reference to Jonathan Swift's *Gulliver's Travels* (1726).[135]

At these events Lambert was praised for being gentlemanly and manly. The latter was earned by mastering the external world through grit and discipline. It was a category linked to rugged individualism. Gentlemanliness, however, was more socially exclusive, and associated with affluence and politeness.[136] Lambert had all the markers of both. According to numerous nineteenth-century biographies, he was a true gentleman: 'he is an intelligent man, reads much, and possesses great vivacity'; his 'qualities and endowments of mind ... raise him above the level of the generality of men'.[137] He was also commended for his manners: 'very pleasing; well-informed, affable, and polite'.[138] Indeed, visitors were 'extremely pleased with the urbanity of his manners'.[139] One newspaper explicitly stated the effect: 'what adds to the pleasure of his company, he is in every respect a gentleman in his conversation and manners'.[140]

Lambert's manliness was expressed through 'frank straight-forwardness' in both action and speech.[141] It was claimed that one visitor crudely asked the cost of Lambert's coat and met the retort, 'if I knew what part of my next coat your shilling would pay for, I can assure you I would cut out the piece'.[142] On another occasion Lambert allegedly lost his temper and threatened to throw a rude visitor out of the window.[143] His manliness was further bolstered by his 'fondness for hunting, coursing, racing, fishing, and cocking'.[144] Lambert could converse with his upper-class visitors because his 'knowledge of what appertains to the Turf and the Sports of the Field, we believe is not excelled by that of any man in the kingdom', claimed the *York Herald*.[145]

But while Lambert's exhibition was largely met with respect – and, according to some accounts, he even met King George III – there were less favourable encounters. Anne Jackson Mathews, writing about her husband, the comedian Charles Mathews and friend to Boruwłaski, recalled his visit to Lambert's exhibition *c.* 1806: 'The half-courteous, half-sullen manner in which this "gross fat man" received the majority of his visitors met the humour of my husband, and he liked as well as pitied him; for it was distressing sometimes to hear the coarse observations made by unfeeling people, and the silly unthinking questions asked by many of them about his appetite, &c.'[146]

For a shy gentleman, with a keen sense of social propriety, the experience of publicly exhibiting his body must have been humiliating.

IN THE SUMMER of 1809 Lambert travelled to Stamford, Lincolnshire, for the horse racing. He rented a ground floor room at the Waggon and Horses Inn on 20 June, but the next morning was found dead, at just thirty-nine, a young age even then. He was older than Edward Bright, twenty-nine, a grocer from Essex, who weighed over 40st at the time he perished in 1750. Bright was renowned as one of the fattest men of his day and was frequently compared to Lambert, though Bright never displayed himself for money. When Lambert died his body surpassed Bright's, weighing a total of 52st 10½lb; he was 5ft 11in tall with a waist girth of 102in.

Such an extraordinary size required a purpose-built coffin, built on two axles and four wheels. His body was pushed down a gradual decline from the inn to the burial ground at St Martin's Church, Stamford. Elizabeth Gilbert, a local, wrote to her son describing the 'great crowd' at the funeral on 23 June 1809: 'such a sight was never seen at Stamford'.[147] It was said at the time: 'youth and hoar age were assembled, numbers of whom had been in expectation of seeing him alive, in propria persona, but were now obliged to content themselves with the mere sight of his coffin, which, to a contemplative mind, would create reflections on the mutability of all sublunary things'.[148]

The people of Stamford laid to rest a country gentleman who, through no fault of his own, through no overindulgence in food, was forced to display his body. After his death his numerous attributes were praised:

> *the moralist will delight to investigate the qualities of that mind which animated such a prodigious body. Shrewd and intelligent, Mr Lambert had improved his natural talents by reading and observation. In company he was lively and agreeable; the general information he possessed, and the numerous anecdotes treasured up in a memory uncommonly retentive, rendered his society extremely pleasant and instructive. ... With respect to humanity, temperance, and liberality of sentiment, Mr. Lambert may be held up as a model worthy of general imitation.*[149]

—◦◦◦◦—

ALL CLEAR? THE truth is that Lambert was (and is) a myth constructed through numerous biographies written during and after his life, each one fulfilling a specific function. Yet many historians have taken claims about him – that he was shy, reluctant to exhibit his body, ate very little – at face value. The picture is more complex. He may have been these things but the archives give another, equally probable, picture: Lambert was a keen self-promoter and businessman who relished the prospect of exhibitionism.

It seems that Lambert pursued all avenues to make his exhibitions successful. He advertised his shows in papers, printed handbills that were distributed to locals and even had a small publicity campaign 'for publishing by subscription a full-length portrait' of himself.[150] He also commissioned the construction of a large carriage to take him to London in 1806, very possibly a necessity on account of his size – or a clever publicity stunt, similarly adopted by the actor Stephen Kemble (another friend of Boruwłaski's) a few months later. Kemble rode into London in a specially crafted carriage to accommodate his 'monstrous size', a stunt that led one reviewer to write 'no wonder that the public curiosity was raised to a considerable pitch'.[151]

Moreover, Lambert did not confine his exhibitions to London. He exhibited in Birmingham, Coventry, Manchester, York, Cambridge and Huntingdon before travelling to Stamford, where he died. And he did not just exhibit in genteel apartments: in Leicester, he displayed himself during the local fair 'At Mr. Scott's Grocer, Market-Place'.[152] Lambert coupled these exhibitions with his business selling dogs. He posted adverts 'to the sporting world' and advertised the sale of his setters and pointers, earning 215 guineas, a huge sum that reflected the pedigree of his dogs and, possibly, the novelty of buying from the notorious Fat Man.[153]

It was commonly maintained that Lambert was too upright to associate with showmen who were seen as morally dubious, being associated with the stigmatized fairs. But if Lambert did conduct his own exhibitions, we can legitimately ask: who collected the fees, who placed the adverts, who decided on the touring route and who knew about the 'respectable' tradition of exhibiting human curiosities? Even

Boruwłaski had a mysterious figure who helped with his tours. As a supposedly reluctant exhibitor, Lambert seemed well attuned to the conventions of marketing his extraordinary body. Like Boruwłaski, with his concerts and balls, so Lambert sought to price himself into propriety. The shilling to visit him differentiated his exhibition from the penny shows, frequented by a rowdier audience. Lambert also exhibited in respectable apartments. As early as 1752 the dwarf John Coan had charged 2s 6d for his exhibition to price out the more 'disreputable' spectators.[154] And in 1782 Charles Byrne, the Irish Giant, stressed the propriety of his exhibition, which occurred within a 'large elegant room', much like Lambert's 'home'.[155]

These strategies attempted to project a respectable exhibition to counter the long-standing belief that spectacular exhibitions and popular fairs encouraged anarchy, licentiousness and violence, which ultimately culminated in censorship and suppression. Indeed in 1804, a couple of years before Boruwłaski moved to Durham, a petition was levelled against the fair at Elvet with the statement that 'it is high time that some method should be taken to prevent it in the future'.[156] All things considered, then, while many sources present a shy Lambert reluctant to exhibit his body, he could equally have been a shrewd businessman and a good showman who knew how to pitch his body.

THE SOURCES DETAILING Lambert's life also require some interrogation. His biographies, published in the nineteenth century, came in two forms. The first were 'life pamphlets', approximately twenty-eight pages long, by anonymous authors. A mere two days after Lambert's death in 1809, a local advert was placed calling for 'any particulars relative to the said Mr. D. Lambert', information that was used in the first edition of his life pamphlet published five days later and sold for 6d.[157] There were also 'eccentric biographies', a literary genre spanning the 1790s to 1900s. They came in numerous forms, from expensively bound books to cheaper pamphlets, enjoyed by a diverse readership.[158] They were essentially freak shows (or popular Victorian museums) in textual form, including anything they deemed 'eccentric' and 'wonderful', with misers, religious fanatics, 'curious products of art', but also, as in the freak show, corporeal 'deviations of nature, such as giants, dwarfs, strong men, personal deformity'.[159]

Crucially, the eccentric biographies had a pedagogic function, claiming to educate their readers in a moralistic tone. Many were even designed for instructing boys at home and in schools, but the didactic nature of these biographies was not just aimed at the young: eccentric biographies were designed for the whole family and they existed within a broader category of behavioural literature, which included courtesy books, conduct books and etiquette books.[160] All of Lambert's biographies entered a highly competitive commercial market, which was expanding due to technological advances that reduced the price of the written word, and made it increasingly accessible to the urban and literate population. Lambert existed within this broader print culture, which developed from the sixteenth century.[161]

Lambert's biographies catered to the demands and expectations of a growing readership, much like Boruwłaski's memoirs, which were constructed in the confessional and then the adventure genre. But while the former helped reveal Boruwłaski's personal experiences, Lambert's eccentric biographies (and indeed the life pamphlets) had a different function. Take, for example, the claim that Lambert was a 'model worthy of imitation', quoted in his life pamphlet: 'With respect to humanity, temperance, and liberality of sentiment'.[162] The phrase 'model worthy of imitation' suggested that Lambert could be studied as an exemplar, which was precisely the aim of nineteenth-century biographies: to be tools for edification filled with useful knowledge.

As early as 1750 Samuel Johnson had noted that 'no species of writing seems more worthy of cultivation than biography, since none can be more delightful or more useful ... or more widely diffuse instruction to every diversity of condition'.[163] Eccentric biographies were explicit: 'biography contributes perhaps more than any other species of writing to a knowledge of the nature of the human mind', and it 'teaches us that there is scarcely an affliction incident to our nature, however severe, which we are not capable of enduring', wrote *The Eccentric Mirror* (1806).[164] Biographies ensured that 'readers in general will be improved, as well as surprised', according to *The New Wonderful Museum* (1804).

Lambert's worthy character attributes were meant to appeal to the readership and conform to their expectations. The sources, then, were presentations of, not revelations about, him. As such, claims about Lambert's character become harder to verify. Take another example: the statement that Lambert never ate or drank more than others, despite weighing over 52st. This was an important assertion because, as explained, by the early nineteenth century being fat was predominantly seen as a personal moral failing (from the 1860s, in medical circles, fatness was largely seen as a pathological disease).[165] If Lambert did not eat more than the next man, his morals were not questionable and he remained a worthy exemplar. His displays were also justified, because while it was deemed indecent to stare at the sick, an educative curiosity towards the healthy body *was* acceptable.[166] And Lambert, we are told, had an 'uncommonly healthy constitution'.[167]

When the current *Oxford Dictionary of National Biography* reconstructs Lambert's life, claiming he was fond of walking, swimming, hunting, 'drank only water, and slept less than eight hours a day', it projects statements of questionable veracity.[168] The real

Lambert is harder to access. It is better to see Lambert as a construction in the archives, while never forgetting that underneath was a real man who lived, breathed and displayed his body.

⚬֊◦◦֊⚬

A S A RESULT of these numerous biographies, which reached a broad audience and were even published in America, Lambert attained a celebrity status that specifically rested on his national identity. By virtue of being placed within eccentric biographies, he was framed as a humorous character and an eccentric, two attributes connected to the UK and especially Englishness. *The Eccentric Mirror* (1806) explains:

> *It is universally admitted that no country in the world produced so many humourists and eccentric characters as the British Islands. This acknowledgement is an indirect eulogy on the political constitution and the laws under which the English enjoy the happiness of living, and by which each individual is suffered to gratify every whim, fancy, and caprice, provided it be not prejudicial to his fellow-creatures.*[169]

In other words, eccentricity and humour expressed political liberty. The character of the English was linked directly to the unwritten constitution which, since the Levellers and Glorious Revolution of 1688, was wedded to the idea of the freeborn Englishman.[170] And as an eccentric character, deemed an honourable English trait, Lambert was elevated to a national icon: a 'true son of John Bull', said his 1809 life pamphlet and, according to *The Magazine of Curiosity and Wonder* (1835), 'a true Englishman'.[171]

Lambert's connection to Englishness assumed a visual form through graphic satires (printed pictures with a political content), with Lambert depicted as John Bull – the personification of the UK (especially

England), and a symbol of English liberty and wit.[172] In widely circulated political caricatures, Lambert was presented as the defender of the nation, warding off the dastardly French. Indeed, the French Revolution and the resulting Reign of Terror, epitomized by the guillotine, had bolstered the importance of English liberty within a framework of constitutional monarchy. In December 1804 Napoleon was crowned Emperor of the French and Britain feared an attack. Under this threat of invasion a popular volunteer movement emerged, which was mainly made up of the propertied but also included the working classes.[173] Representations of John Bull were legion during this time because they offered what another national icon, the female Britannia, could not: assertiveness, aggression and, as a man, participation in the public sphere.[174]

In a caricature entitled 'Two Wonders of the World, or a Specimen of a New Troop of Leicestershire Light Horse' (1806), Lambert is dressed in a militia uniform, seated on a massive Leicestershire horse and brandishing a sword. He attacks the tiny Napoleon, who drops his hat and sword, and holds his hand in horror: 'Parbleu! If dis be de specimen of de English Light Horse vatvil de Heavy Horse be? Oh, by Gar, I vil put off de Invasion for an oder time!' With his sword and military uniform, Lambert was aggressively male and patriotic: a defender of English liberty, just like John Bull; and both men were decidedly fat.

Lambert was part of this national discourse, contributing to the idea of England as a land of liberty threatened by the French. Moreover, as an emblem of Englishness, he embodied the heart of English identity.[175] His fatness was a positive reflection of English values, and his name entered the national lexicon to signify largeness and greatness.[176] His portrait appeared on public houses and inns, while lithographs began to circulate after his death: commercial mementos in remembrance of a national hero. Furthermore, there followed a tradition of displaying fat men, fat ladies and fat babies well into the twentieth, and twenty-first, century. A fat child, the Miniature Lambert, was displayed as early as 1806 and P.T. Barnum showed fat people in his dime museums, while a 'Second Daniel Lambert' hit the freak shows in the 1870s.[177]

But Lambert should be not confused with these later freak performers. He was not performing in the Victorian freak show; rather, he was presenting his body at the beginning of the century in a social engagement rather than a commercial spectacle. Moreover, like Hudson and Boruwłaski, Lambert overwhelmingly refused to engage with the country fair scene or mass public exhibitions. Also, all three were elevated or sought to elevate themselves: Hudson in the royal courts; Boruwłaski in aristocratic circles and by his refined presentations; and Lambert in genteel exhibitions within his 'home'.

Yet they also demonstrate, on a sliding and chronological scale, the move away from royal courts towards public exhibitions: Hudson was firmly connected to the former, Boruwłaski straddled the two and Lambert did not have royal patronage. This shift reflects the gradual decline of ostentatious courts and the move to public displays. Furthermore, the three signal another trend that would help give birth to the freak show: embracing respectability. But we are not there yet and, in the early nineteenth century, the lowly fairs remained a prime location for freak performers. So what was it about itinerant entertainment that Hudson, Boruwłaski and Lambert sought to avoid? Why such fear of the fairs? Luckily, thanks to a first-hand account, we have a pretty good idea.

CHAPTER FOUR

GEORGE SANGER

THE YEAR IS 1795. Europe is capitulating to the French. The British prime minister, William Pitt the Younger, is war weary and national debt is mounting. On the brighter side, European and UK culture is thriving: Ludwig van Beethoven gives his debut performance as a pianist in Vienna and William Blake completes his first colour print of *Newton*.

That autumn two teenage boys walk along a muddy road from Salisbury to London. They carry a knotted handkerchief containing a few possessions. The brothers are escaping their family farm to seek their fortune. As they cross London Bridge there's a scream – 'Look out! Press gang!' – from a panicking, escaping crowd. The boys run. The younger, say eighteen years old, darts inside an apothecary shop, but the elder, James Sanger, is caught and, despite an exchange of fists, carried away.[178]

This was the start of his ten years' forced service with the Royal Navy, ending at the Battle of Trafalgar in October 1805 and the British victory over the Franco-Spanish fleet in the Napoleonic Wars. Sanger was on HMS *Victory* and allegedly one of twenty-six men who boarded a French frigate in the battle, losing three fingers and suffering a slash to his head. Soon afterwards he was discharged and granted a pension of £10 a year. He was also given a royal prescription that stipulated he could undertake whatever living he chose, so long as he conducted his business honestly and lawfully.

During his time with the navy, Sanger had befriended two Jewish men who, like him, had been press-ganged. The Harts, as they were known, had been strolling conjurors who wandered across Britain performing at fairs and wakes. They had taught Sanger some of their tricks, presumably to pass the time, and Sanger had lapped up the 'hanky-panky' (which then meant trickery) of these conjuring Jews. On his release, stirred by their stories, Sanger began a new life as a showman. He invested in a penny peepshow that he carried on his back, and in this primitive device displayed pictures of the Battle of Trafalgar, brought to life by his patter. And he had the scars to back it up. His first pitch was at Bristol Fair, where he met the woman who would bear him ten children, chief among them George Sanger.[179]

—•◦◦•—

GEORGE SANGER WAS born on 23 December 1825 at Newbury, Berkshire. He entered a world illuminated by dim tallow flames, at a time when the freak show was in the ascent, and he left the world, with its electric bulbs, in 1911, when the freak show was in the descent. Fortunately he left us with an autobiography, *Seventy Years a Showman*, published in 1910, which reveals why the likes of Hudson, Boruwłaski and Lambert desperately tried to avoid and distance themselves from the fairs.

Although George has been dwarfed by the legacy of P.T. Barnum, he was a monumental figure in Victorian England, and his life and career presents a broader story of the rise of popular culture. Moreover, his autobiography illuminates the world of the travelling fairs, complete with a rag-tag community of itinerant performers, 'living curiosities', peddlers and tradesmen who were united by the pressures from the outside world.

He started life in the travelling fairs, which formed part of England's pre-industrial landscape where traditional recreations thrived, including cockfighting, bull-baiting, dogfighting and communal celebrations. The agricultural festival of Plough Monday, for example, was a carnivalesque celebration where farmers trailed their ploughs to collect money, singing and dancing in the merriment of the gathering which, by the middle of the century, was denounced by the urban middle classes as 'rude' and 'vulgar', totally unbecoming for modern, civilized Britain.[180] But this was Sanger's world.

In his autobiography George explains that his father, James, was a kind, resourceful and self-sufficient man who in winter earned a living dealing in fish, fruit and toffee apples sold on a stall in Newbury. Over summer he and his wife travelled the countryside in a caravan made of thin sheets of iron, and ran a peepshow at fairs – that melting pot of classes, commerce and juggling, acrobatics, mimicry, foolery, music, etc. dating right back to the twelfth century. James supplemented his peepshow with living curiosities: the foreign-sounding Madame Gomez, billed as 'the tallest woman in the world', and the Savage Cannibal Pygmies of the Dark Continent, performers known as Tamee Ahmee and Orio Rio, aged ten and nine, who wore feathers, beads and facial paint to give them their 'savage' appearance.[181] Unfortunately George does not give us their biography, so we do not know much about them, and indeed tracing the lives of 'human oddities' who performed solely in the early fairs is nigh on impossible because, unlike the commercial Victorian freak shows, there are hardly any textual accounts to reconstruct their lives. Still, we do know that Madame Gomez and the 'cannibal pygmies' were fake.

Madame Gomez was neither foreign nor tall but surreptitiously raised on a platform. And Tamee and Orio were not cannibals, pygmies or African: they were born to a black mother and a white Irish father. But James was a natural showman. He was flexible with the truth and a gifted talker who could pull a crowd. When introducing the savage cannibal pygmies he would begin: 'Ladies and Gentlemen: These wonderful people are fully grown, being, in fact, each over thirty years of age. They were captured by Portuguese traders in the African wilds, and are incapable of ordinary speech. Their food consists of raw meat, and if they can capture a small animal they tear it to pieces alive with their teeth, eagerly devouring its flesh and drinking its blood.'[182]

The Victorian showman Tom Norman wrote in his autobiography: 'But you could indeed exhibit anything in those days, yes, anything from a needle to an anchor, a flea to an elephant, a bloater, you could exhibit as a whale. It was not the show, it was the tale you told.'[183] It was about the 'gift of the gab', as the sharpshooter Florence Shufflebottom wrote in her family history notes.[184]

Shufflebottom recalled the travelling fairs of her great-grandfather's days where an act, the Fall of China, was announced by a showman. His spiel would spike the interest of a curious crowd, who'd part with a penny to see the magnificent representation of China's fall. Led away into the tent, they were shown broken glass on a table ... China's fall ... and the showman, with a smile, would say: 'if you want to have a laugh at your friends – Don't tell them what you have seen, tell them to come and see this show, and have a good laugh at them as they leave'.[185] The appeal was all in the story. 'The Man with Two—No Ladies Admitted, Gentlemen Only', barked one showman but inside his tent was a man with two thumbs on one hand.[186] The disappointed spectators were hoping for something more salacious.

JAMES SANGER WAS forced to abandon his display of Madame Gomez and the savage pygmies when the authorities got wind of his deceptions and tried to have him arrested. 'At that period', his son wrote, the law 'sternly dealt with the show-folk as "rogues and vagabonds"'.[187] The fairs, once patronized by the aristocracy, were also increasingly abandoned by the well-to-do from the middle of the eighteenth century, while the authorities were trying to shut them down: Southwark Fair was abolished in 1762, May Fair in 1764, Peckham in 1827 and Bartholomew in 1855. This was quickly followed by the demise of Camberwell in 1855, Greenwich in 1857 and Stepney in 1860. It was part of a trend in censorship and suppression, culminating in government legislation such as the Vagrancy Act (1824), the Regulation of Markets and Fairs Act (1847) and the Theatres Act (1843). In 1823 the Bow Fair Field was closed on the grounds of its supposed immorality, with an 'Elegy' penned in the press:

> *Take warning then, ye fair! from this fair's fall! ...*
> *Listen, oh listen, to Law's serious call,*
> *For fun and pleasure lead but to undoing!* [188]

The assault on the fairs, which was underscored by religious disapproval and political fears concerning congregating working classes, was why the showmen and freak performers had to find new, different sites, particularly from the 1830s. This was part of a new approach that hinged on the nature of respectability, a nebulous term incorporating everything from avoiding the workhouse to wearing appropriate clothes and adopting appropriate manners.[189] In the world of entertainment, respectability meant a move towards propriety, order and appealing to the right classes. When Boruwłaski and Lambert were on display, they predominantly targeted the upper classes, but deeper into the nineteenth century showmen began to court the middle classes too. They also adopted the rhetoric of 'rational recreation', which reached a heyday in the 1830s and 1840s, and was embraced by middle-class reformers with the belief that 'leisure activities should be controlled, ordered, and improving'.[190] By billing their freak shows as edifying, educative, domesticated, morally permissible and even uplifting, showmen were helping to tame 'rough' amusements.[191]

When George was a boy, the fairs were rough amusements showing the likes of dwarfs, giants, limbless wonders and other human curiosities. In the British Library there are amazing relics from these early nineteenth-century fairs, including coloured cards cut in intricate patterns and adorned with beautiful writing explaining, 'cut by Miss Museell at Camberwell Fair with her toes' (1832), and from another 'armless wonder' is an 'autograph of John Murray written with his toes' (1842).[192] Thomas Frost's *The Old Showmen, and the Old London Fairs* (1874) documented a plethora of other fairground acts including 'Maria Teresia, the Amazing Corsican Fairy, who has had the Honour of being shown three Times before their Majesties'.[193]

Yet despite the rhetoric, these fairground performances were generally perceived as degrading and humiliating. In his *Sketches by Boz* (1836), Charles Dickens describes Greenwich Fair, noting that 'the best thing about a dwarf is, that he has always a little box, about two feet six inches high, into which, by long practice, he can just manage to get'. The box was painted like a six-roomed house, from which the dwarf rings a bell or fires a pistol from the first-floor window to get the attention of the boisterous crowd. 'Shut up in this case', Dickens continued, 'the unfortunate little object is brought out to delight the throng by holding a facetious dialogue with the proprietor: in the course of which, the dwarf (who is always particularly drunk) pledges himself to sing a comic song inside, and pays various compliments to the ladies, which induce them to "come for'ed" with great alacrity.[194]

—◦☜☞◦—

B Y THE TIME George Sanger was born in 1825, his father had developed his peepshow and added a makeshift roundabout too. In 1833 the peepshow included twenty-six peep glasses, enabling twenty-six people to see the pictures pulled up and down by strings. At night tallow candles were placed behind the pictures for illumination. George, when only six years old, thought this 'the greatest show on earth'. He became determined to follow in his father's footsteps, soon learning the patter and enticing audiences to 'Walk up!'[195]

The peepshow could also be a form of sensational news, a counterpart to the highly illustrated penny dreadfuls, and James cleverly capitalized on notorious murders to attract paying customers. In October 1833, for example, he travelled to Berkshire to catch the last fair of the year, the Statute of Wantage, where, according to George's autobiography, James witnessed the decapitation of the landlady in a local inn. She'd got into a fight with several labourers, one of whom used a 'fagging-hook', or sickle, to slash off her head. The murderer was promptly jailed, and James returned to the fair and altered some pictures to depict the decapitation. The next day he was advertising 'the authentic representation of the terrible murder at the Red Lion, as described by an eye-witness of the dreadful deed'.[196] With the murder the talk of the town, the peepshow made a nice profit.

As James bellowed to fairgoers, George by his side, his shouting formed part of a cacophony of sounds and a sensory assault. Other vendors proclaimed their gingerbread stalls, pickled salmon, oysters, snails and cheese; there were clouds of cheap cigar smoke; feet were caked in mud; and the crowds were overwhelming. Dickens wrote of Greenwich Fair (1839):

Imagine yourself in an extremely dense crowd, which swings you to and fro, and in and out, and every way but the right one; add to this the screams of women, the shouts of boys, the clanging of gongs, the firing of pistols, the ringing of bells, the bellowings [sic] of speaking-trumpets, the squeaking of penny dittos, the noise of a dozen bands, with three drums in each, all playing different tunes at the same time, the hallooing showmen, and an occasional roar from the wild-beast shows; and you are in the very centre and heart of the fair.[197]

This was the world in which George and his family lived and travelled, in a community where differences that divided people outside the fairs were largely immaterial inside: 'the show business was mainly in the hands of the Jews, who in my day outnumbered the Gentile entertainers by two to one, and were always good friends and comrades to us,' he recalled years later.[198] The Romani community were a different matter, however: 'The gipsies, it is true, went from fair to fair, but it was as horse-dealers, hawkers of baskets and tinware, workers of the lucky-bag swindle, fortune tellers, and owners of knife and snuff-box shies.' The 'proper' showmen, George emphasized, always kept their distance from the Romani and, while the showmen marvelled at their ability to make money, they mocked the gratuitous display of wealth, in the form of finery and trinkets, designed to outshine the rival Romani tribes.[199]

Despite some differences, the showfolk were united by the dangers, pressures and hostility from the outside world. Travelling on primitive roads was an arduous task, even harder in wet weather and when diseases like smallpox and cholera struck. When his daughter contracted smallpox, in the absence of any treatment, James devised his own form of inoculation. He applied her contaminated pustules to his healthy children with the assistance of a long needle. The latter developed the disease, but only in a mild form, and they were effectively inoculated. Poverty was another issue: 'Many found only a bare hand-to-mouth living in the summer months,' George recalled, 'and in winter had to exist as best they could.'[200] The community relied on one another for help, with disastrous consequences if pride barred appeals for assistance. This was the sad fate of a Mr Thompson, the Scottish Giant, who, falling on difficult times, refused to ask for help and starved to death in his caravan.

Rivalries among showmen could be fierce, and one of George's earliest recollections was 'The Battle of Oxford Road' in May 1833, when he was eight. He and his brother William nearly died in the fight. After the May Day gathering, the showmen quickly packed up their caravans in Reading and headed to Henley. Wombell's and Hilton's menageries raced each other, each determined to arrive first and secure the best location. When Wombell's menagerie tried to stall Hilton's, one of the latter 'knocked one of Wombell's drivers off his seat with a tent-pole', creating pandemonium: 'In a minute all was confusion; grooms, drivers, and carriage attendants of the two menageries left their posts and, catching up any weapons they could lay their hands on – crowbars, tent-poles, whips, etc. – attacked each other with desperate ferocity.'[201] Everyone got involved, 'even the freaks', Sanger said; 'the fat man made for the living skeleton with a door-hook; the living skeleton battered at the fat man with a peg mallet'.[202] The elephants went ballistic, Sanger's horse did a runner and many were injured.

It was a tough, violent world – the authorities did not care for showmen, seeing them as criminals, rogues and vagabonds and their fairs as licentious, anarchic and vice-ridden – and Sanger learned to use his fists from an early age. You could not rely on the authorities; the police force was meagre and not officially formed until 1829.

Furthermore, showmen were frequently at the mercy of the mob and had to administer their own form of justice: 'the showman's law'.[203] Once, at Lansdown Fair, the Sangers were attacked by 'roughs' from Bath, 'led by a red-headed virago, a dreadful giantess of a woman, known as "Carroty Kate"', Sanger said.[204] In the evening, Kate and her crew wrecked the fair, nearly beating to death the owners of the drinking booths and helping themselves to the barrels and bottles of liquor. In retaliation the showmen banded together and located Kate and her gang. They chucked the men in the pond and then hauled them out for a whipping of thirty-six lashes. Next, they turned to Kate: 'two strong women administered a sound thrashing' as 'she screamed and swore horribly, and writhed about, so that the half-dozen stout show-women who were holding her had a difficult task'.[205]

When the fairs packed up for winter, life remained equally perilous for the Sangers. Travelling from London to Newbury, having purchased some fish, fruit and vegetables, George and his father gave two strangers and their conspicuous parcel a lift in their wagon. George, on his horse behind the wagon, glimpsed the parcel illuminated by the bright moon: 'It was a bulky, long, shapeless sort of bundle contained in a big sack, and it wobbled in a fashion that made it seem, to my boyish eyes, as though it had something alive in it.'[206] Eventually his curiosity got the better of him and he peeped inside. 'Oh! My God, the horror of that moment!' he recalled, 'the face of the dead woman before my eyes seeming to bob at me with every movement of the animals'.[207] They were Resurrectionists or grave robbers, who lurked in graveyards, digging up the dead and selling the corpses to anatomy schools. They were detested by the public and James handed them over to the authorities, lest they were all lynched by an angry mob.

IT IS HARD to imagine that out of this alloy of violence, danger and perceived immorality arose the institutions of Victorian popular culture: the magic shows rooted in the fairground conjurers, the zoos emerging from the travelling menageries, the ethnic shows from displays of exotic foreigners, and the Victorian freak shows from conglomerate circuses.

Indeed, the modern circus was invented in the late eighteenth century when the fairground entertainers joined the equestrian performers in the so-called riding schools, where equestrian masters gave horse-riding lessons to the upper classes and demonstrated their own feats of horsemanship in public performances to bolster their income. It was when these equestrians introduced acrobats, jugglers, dancers and rope-dancers between their horsemanship shows that the modern circus was born (defined by the combination of equestrianism, acrobatics, visual comedy, theatre and dance).[208] Freak performers were not then included. The modern circus was a permanent, respectable site that later in the nineteenth century would provide freak performers with one of their most lucrative venues.

It is commonly held that the inventor of the modern circus is Philip Astley (1742–1814), son to an English cabinetmaker. Astley fought in the Seven Years' War, a war almost on the scale of a world war, before forming Astley's Riding School on Westminster Bridge Road in 1769 (this was not his first school, or his last). The entertainment featured Astley's horsemanship skills, developed from his time in the cavalry. The open-air, circular ring (known as the circle or circus) was enclosed by a fence, behind which stood the spectators, who were protected from the weather by a roof, while others sat in a small wooden building.

On the street side were colourful banners (akin to posters), while Astley barked 'step right up, step right up' at the steps leading to the front gate. According to Thomas Frost, Astley had an 'imposing appearance, being over six feet in height, with the proportions of a

Hercules, and the voice of a Stentor, [which] attracted attention to him'.[209] His golden-haired wife, Patty, collected the admissions fee: 1 shilling for standing or 2 for a seat in a box. As the spectators entered, they were hit by the smell of moist soil and sawdust. One account of a performance, dated 1770, outlines some of the feats performed by Astley, billed as the 'original English Hussar':

He makes his horse lie down, imitating death
He rides at full speed standing with one foot on the saddle
He balances himself without holding at full speed, standing on
   the saddle
He picks up a sixpence from the ground at full speed
He sweeps his hand along the ground
At full speed he springs from the saddle to the ground and from
   the ground to the saddle
He then rides two and three horses.[210]

None of these performances were new, but Astley injected the flare of the showman. He addressed the audience directly and concluded his show with the words, 'When you have seen, all my bills expressed/ My wife, to conclude, performs the rest', to which Patty emerged standing on her head on the back of a horse, or firing a pistol while balancing on two horses or even sometimes on a horse covered in a swarm of bees.[211]

When Astley realized that something more was needed to maintain the audience's interest, he recruited entertainers from the fairs to perform between the equestrian acts. They included a clown (borrowed from the Elizabethan theatre) performing on a slack rope, an Italian strongman balancing his children on his feet, and jugglers, acrobats, rope-dancers and a musical band. The modern circus was born, soon leading to imitations that spread across the UK, Europe and America.[212]

Considering this close association between the fairs and the circus, it is not surprising that George Sanger formed his first circus on 14 February 1854 at the King's Lynn Charter Fair. Four years earlier he had married Ellen Chapman, a lion-tamer from the travelling fairs. The Sanger circus was an appendage of the travelling fairs and followed their routes through Lincoln, Cambridge, Norfolk and Suffolk. By the 1860s, with his wife and brother John, George owned ten permanent circuses in the UK which were largely divorced from the fairs and stood in their own right. In 1871 the Sangers bought the lease of Astley's Amphitheatre. Running the amphitheatre for twenty-eight years, George dominated the English circus scene and the circus became firmly established in Victorian culture: a popular, respectable, commercial and international form of entertainment.

This development closely mirrored the history of the freak show, which was initially rooted in the English travelling fairs before emerging as a commercial institution. The historian Dominique Jando recognized in relation to the circus: 'Since the decline of the fairs ... acrobats, jugglers, rope-dancers and all kinds of itinerant entertainers were looking for new venues to exhibit their talents.'[213] The riding schools were the perfect venues: they received noble patronage and were permanent, respectable sites, unlike the temporary, disreputable fairs. A similar transition occurred in the freak shows as human oddities were 'upgraded' from the travelling fairs into permanent venues from the 1830s onwards.

The fairs did not completely disappear. As late as 1890 Accrington's August Fair was denounced as a 'carnival of vice' and 'a horrid nuisance', and despite evangelicals condemning fairs more generally as 'popish festivals', freak performers could still be seen at these sites: the travelling Hull Fair in the 1890s, for example, had five fat women shows alone.[214] The fairs actually helped ensure the ubiquity of freak shows, as they guaranteed that performers could be seen in urban centres and rural communities. Indeed, the elements of spectacle, sensory experience, showmanship, illusion and freakery continued to thrive in the fairs well into the twentieth century.[215]

But as we enter the 1830s, there's a change. With Hudson, Boruwłaski, Lambert and Sanger we have charted a move from the highest echelons of the royal courts to the lowest form of public exhibitionism in the fairs. Next comes a transition, back and forth between the world of itinerant displays in pre-industrial environments and the world of permanent, commercial and respectable freak shows in a modern urban setting. Time to meet, among others, a Hottentot Venus and the 161-year-old Nurse of George Washington. We open with a pair of Siamese twins performing in a public museum. The age of the Victorian freak beckons.

ACT TWO

SHOW TIME

CHAPTER FIVE

CHANG AND ENG

I N NOVEMBER 1829 Chang and Eng were ready for their London public. The twins had already been paraded in Boston, New York and Philadelphia, and poked and prodded by London's medical fraternity. Now the doors to the Egyptian Hall, 'The Home of Mystery', were about to be thrown open.

Originally designed to hold 'upwards of Fifteen Thousand Natural and Foreign Curiosities, Antiques, and Productions of the Fine Arts', the Egyptian Hall in Piccadilly was open daily from noon until dusk.[216] It was created in the ancient Egyptian style of architecture and ornament, which reflected Britain's fascination with pharaohs and sphinxes, sparked by Napoleon's Egyptian Campaign of 1798–1801. The facade copied the ancient Temple of Tentyra, with inclined pilasters and sides covered in hieroglyphics. At the front of the building, two giant statues of Isis and Osiris stared down at the visitors as they proceeded into the Great Room, lined with ancient-looking columns and topped with an impressive dome that beamed light into the expansive space.

Hundreds queued along Piccadilly, holding the half-crown entrance fee for what the press proclaimed would be a spectacle that could not 'offend the delicacies of the most fastidious female'.[217] When the doors to the Egyptian Hall opened at midday, the eighteen-year-old Chang and Eng greeted their excited audience. The twins were respectfully dressed in foreign clothes. Their hair, about 30in long, was 'braided and arranged upon their heads in the Chinese style', according to an exhibition pamphlet.[218] The only flesh on view was the band, around 2in thick and 4in long, that connected the boys below the breastbone. What couldn't be seen was their connected livers.

A freak show exhibition pamphlet, for sale at 1 shilling, provided fascinating descriptions of the twins, detailed information about their lives and country and an array of medical testimonials. But that was nothing compared to their live performance. Captain Coffin, their 'protector', or James Hale, their manager, began by introducing the twins to the seated audience. The brothers then conversed with the crowd in clear, albeit limited, English, answering their questions. If the questions were anything like those asked in Boston, a few months earlier, they included:

Q: *Are you the same size?*

A: *We weigh 180lb.*

Q: *Do you enjoy being joined together?*

A: *There is no choice, according to the doctors. We try to make the most of our situation.*

Q: *Do you mind people staring at you and asking you questions?*

A: *We know we are different and people are curious. It is a way of earning a living, and we are grateful.*[219]

Chang, who stood to the left as the audience looked at them, was the more vivacious twin and probably did most of the talking. By some accounts he was also more intelligent, quick-witted and dominant, the natural leader, while Eng was more ponderous and generally happy to follow his brother's lead. The pamphlet added: 'their feelings are warm and affectionate, their manners docile, and their conduct amiable and well regulated'. Yes, they were grateful for any 'act of kindness, or affectionate treatment of any description', but it was also made clear that an 'injury offered to the one, is equally resented by his brother'.[220]

After the questions, the act really took off. It required an equality of action and a unison of movement that left the audience spellbound. The brothers performed acrobatics with somersaults, backflips and leaps of surprising agility. In Boston they'd lift audience members into the air and carry them around the room and now, in England, they added the game of battledore and shuttlecock (a popular English sport and forerunner to badminton). Each brother held a miniature racket (the battledore), before hitting the shuttlecock to and fro. On account of their connecting ligament the twins stood a mere 4–5in apart, so this fast-paced hitting of the shuttlecock was a spectacle of agility, harmony and speed. The press reported: 'In their ordinary movements they resemble two persons waltzing ... without being in the least disgusting or unpleasant, like almost all monstrosities, these youths are certainly one of the most extraordinary freaks of nature that has ever been witnessed.'[221]

After the cheering and clapping, the twins – who renamed themselves the Siamese Twins in the early 1830s – could be manhandled by the curious. Their ligament was the subject of the fondling and, in one report, one of the boys (probably Chang) even scolded someone for touching them with cold hands.[222]

Chang and Eng's 1829 performance was one of the first freak shows staged in Britain: an organized, theatrical and popular performance in a permanent venue connected to commercial entertainment. The Egyptian Hall was a respectable venue run on commercial lines; it catered to middle-class men, women and children and housed three or four exhibitions at any one time. It was initially run by the naturalist William Bullock, whose collection of natural history specimens was designed to educate the public, but, by the time Chang and Eng were displayed, ownership of the hall had transferred to Bullock's nephew George Lackington, who sought to increase profits with more popular displays that included the exhibition of freaks.

Incidentally, the Egyptian Hall was opposite the apartment where Daniel Lambert had exhibited some twenty-three years previously. Back then, however, Lambert presented himself in a privately rented apartment where he met visitors who came to converse. He never performed an act, there were no mementos to purchase, he seemingly operated without a manager and there was no showman introducing his performance, which was merely a conversation with visitors. Lambert's display was no freak show, but Chang and Eng's was. They had a manager who introduced the twins through an oral spiel or lecture, there were visual and textual accounts of the twins, most notably their exhibition pamphlet sold at their show, and there was a performance of acrobatics. These were the crucial elements that comprised the freak show, although the term was not yet used.

Chang and Eng's early career marked a transitional phase in the history of freakery between, on the one hand, traditional displays in carnivalesque fairs and, on the other, modern displays in commercial and respectable venues. Indeed, in the early nineteenth century most performers were still shown at fairs, at wakes and within rented apartments. At Bartholomew Fair in 1827–28 there were giants, dwarfs, albinos, fat people, 'New Zealand Cannibals', and a 'nondescript' with the head of a pig, the ears of a wolf and the body of a human claimed the publicity.[223] Sometimes these shows were priced according to social status: 'Ladies and Gentleman, 1s; Trades People, 6d; Servants and Children, 3d'.[224]

The twins' freak show was joining a fast-evolving, commercial entertainment scene, which included minstrel shows and menageries. In the 1820s and 1830s freak performers could also be seen in assembly rooms, 'large and commodious rooms' and exhibition halls throughout the capital, including the Argyll Rooms on Regent Street, which hosted Ivan Ivanitz Chabert, 'the only Really Incombustible Man', who played with fire (a forerunner to the 'self-made freak' common in later circus sideshows).[225] Developments in transport and the expansion of the empire ensured an increasingly steady supply of freak performers who filled the growing number of venues while the fairs were being reformed or shut down.

Chang and Eng's performance constituted a freak show, but their display also moved into the realms of what historians have variously dubbed 'ethnic shows', 'ethnic displays' and 'human zoos'.[226] The Egyptian Hall hosted an array of these exhibitions, such as Laplanders in the 1820s and Native Americans and 'African Bushmen' (San people) in the 1840s. To the Victorians, ethnic shows were entertaining and edifying, thus attracting both the working and middle classes. Usually what the audiences learned about the 'Fiji Cannibals', for example, did not reflect the realities of the Fijian people, yet in an age when travel was limited for most, the ethnic shows were often the only means of seeing and learning about foreign people.

Ethnic difference and freakishness were not necessarily the same thing so, arguably, ethnic shows and freak shows should be treated as separate phenomena.[227] But the Siamese Twins constituted a prime example of the crossovers between the two forms of entertainment at a time when they were still developing. The twins were freakish on account of their connecting ligament and ethnically different on account of their heritage, and both these categories of 'abnormality' were simultaneously presented in their show.

CALLED CHUN AND IN (later Chang and Eng), the brothers were born in May 1811 in the Kingdom of Siam (today's Thailand) under the reign of Rama II, who was known as the 'Poet King' on account of his love for the arts. They were raised in Meklong, a fishing village outside the capital of Bangkok, surrounded by 'floating bazaars, fine pagodas and gardens', wrote an early nineteenth-century missionary.[228] Yet no birth records exist, and no documentation of their young lives have been discovered. Instead we have stories passed down by word of mouth and contained in dubious materials.

It was claimed that their father, Ti-eye, was a fisherman from southern China; their mother, Nok, was half Chinese, half Siamese and a resourceful woman who bore a total of nine children. The family lived on a small houseboat, with a thatched roof made of leaves, that floated on the Meklong River. In this floating home, moored to the riverbed by large bamboo sticks, the twins were brought up speaking Chinese (possibly Cantonese) and probably gained a basic level of literacy and arithmetic.[229]

At the front of their home their father would sell fish he'd caught, but this was a poor family and life was tough, especially when, in the spring of 1819, cholera killed Ti-eye and five of the children. Nok was left widowed in her thirties and with four young children to support. She tried her hand at numerous ventures, assisted by Chang and Eng, who, according to their freak show pamphlet, contributed to the family budget 'by fishing, manufacturing cocoa-nut oil [sic], and other arts, at which they were remarkably expert'.[230] One of those 'other arts' was raising ducks and selling their eggs, a Chinese skill developed over centuries.

Then in August 1824, while the boys were fishing, perhaps for the highly nutritious shellfish that were good for the ducks, they were spotted by Robert Hunter, a British merchant living in Siam, who, the story goes, 'mistook them for some strange animal'.[231] On realizing that they were remarkable humans, Hunter determined to have Chang and Eng exhibited in the West. Hunter's business partner was Captain Abel Coffin, an American trader of tea, sugar and guns.

The presence of Hunter and Coffin in Siam was testimony to the gradual prising open of a kingdom which, for over a century, had remained isolated from the West. In 1785 the British occupied the island of Penang, so gradually expanding its possessions; in 1818 commercial contracts were forged between Portugal and Siam; from 1824 the Anglo-Burmese War raged next to Siam and proved the naval and technological prowess of the British; and in 1826 the Burney Treaty was signed between the new Siam king, Rama III, and Henry Burney, an agent of the British East India Company. Creeping colonialism and commercialization were accompanied by the saving of souls as missionaries poured into Siam.

Determined to bring the twins to the West, Hunter and Coffin first secured the consent of King Rama III, who owned everything in the dominion and who reportedly had summoned the twins to his palace, where they crawled before the corpulent king as he sat cross-legged on his throne. Eventually Rama III agreed to let the boys leave the country, so Coffin and Hunter began working on their mother. She was allegedly paid $3,000 (the twins later claimed it was just $500) in a transaction akin to purchasing slaves. A contract was signed by Chang and Eng on 1 April 1829, which stipulated that they'd go to America and Europe with Coffin under their own 'free will and consent'. All their expenses would be paid, and they would return to Siam after five years.[232]

In March 1829 the twins joined the cargo on the ship *Sachem* and began their 138-day journey from Siam to America. Their first stop was Boston where, in a tent, they were displayed at 50 cents a ticket.

They excited 'the greatest interest among scientific and professional men', reported one British scientist, and after eight weeks in Boston were shipped off to New York City and Philadelphia.[233] Chang and Eng's stage performance developed from answering audiences' questions to performing somersaults, backflips and feats of strength to challenging spectators to a game of checkers. In October 1829 they travelled to England where, the next month, they were examined by the medical fraternity and then paraded in the freak show at the Egyptian Hall.

Chang and Eng were an exceptionally rare sight in London. Conjoined twins were usually stillborn or died very shortly after birth. Indeed, before 1829 the last living display of conjoined twins in London appears to have been the Hungarian Sisters, Helena and Judith, in 1708: 'One of the greatest Wonders in Nature that ever was seen,' declared the publicity.[234] Remoter precedents were the Biddenden Maids, Mary and Eliza Chulkhurst, allegedly born in Kent in 1100, and the Scottish Brothers of the mid-fifteenth century, who lived at the royal courts for most of their lives, although both these sets of conjoined twins are mired in mystery and little is known about them. In the seventeenth century King Charles I hosted Lazarus and Joannes Baptista Colloredo, Italian conjoined twins who toured Europe, but Joannes was a parasitic twin who did not speak and kept his eyes closed.

Chang and Eng's contemporaries were the fascinating Millie and Christine – the Two-Headed Nightingale – conjoined twins born in 1851 who became exceptionally popular later in the century. And in the twentieth century Daisy and Violet Hilton became celebrity personalities, featuring in the films *Freaks* (1932) and *Chained for Life* (1952). But in London in 1829–30, Chang and Eng were the ones causing the excitement. They were 'racial freaks', notes a historian, and another that, for Chang and Eng, it was the 'combination of racially and biologically framed qualities that made them such highly bankable performers'.[235]

—•ⓠⓠ•—

THE TWINS WERE billed as 'Siamese', but the London papers noted that their colour and features 'point them out at once as belonging to the Chinese race'.[236] This was a few decades before Chinese immigrants supposedly transformed the East End with opium dens and parlours for prostitutes and gambling, and the Chinese and Siamese were still a rare sight in London. The twins were exotic spectacles and curiosities to the English, who, in the early nineteenth century, enjoyed exhibitions of Asian artefacts and people including, in April and May 1827, two 'Chinese ladies' shown at a 'Chinese exhibition' where 'genuine Chinese goods' were sold.[237]

But were the twins Chinese or Siamese? It wasn't clear. Their publicity stressed their Chinese heritage, and the press duly reported the brothers' Chinese features. Being Chinese certainly had an advantage, as the Siamese were generally considered to be inferior to the Chinese. Yet being Chinese also meant different things to different people. China could be seen as mystical, luxurious and influential (its aesthetics copied in Victorian chinoiserie), but China could also be despotic, mendacious and even violent (with malign stereotypes evolving into twentieth-century characters like the fictional villain Dr Fu Manchu).[238]

Furthermore, in Britain race was not just about skin colour: the Irish, Jews, Italians, French and even the white working class were often seen as racially different. Race was frequently less significant as a marker of difference than class, and interracial marriage was common, although this would change as attitudes to race hardened.[239] Underpinning Western perceptions of race was a Christian orthodoxy that saw humans as a single species, the product of a single act of Divine creation, a view known as monogenesis. Differences between people were explained using a variety of factors, from complexion to religion to socio-economic organization. These differences between people, it was usually argued, were the result of environmental influences and not inherent physical differences. So, while we tend to think of nineteenth-century views of race as biologically deterministic, in the early part of the century the dominant view was more nurture than nature.

In 1796, for example, Henry Moss, a second-generation African American who had previously fought in the Continental Army during the War of Independence, was displaying himself in a Philadelphian tavern. He was billed as 'A Great Curiosity' and it cost a quarter of a dollar to see his body; half price for children.[240] Moss had undergone a metamorphosis in 1792 when, aged thirty-eight, he started to turn white with patches emerging across his body and face, most likely a sign of what today we would call vitiligo or leucoderma. But, at the time, neither the presumably terrified Moss nor the learned community knew the reason for his physical change. Members of the American Philosophical Society, one of the first and most renowned scientific institutions in America, flocked to his exhibition, furiously debating the potential causes of his transformation from black to white. One interpretation, based on monogenesis, maintained that Moss, having come from a hot climate and living outdoors, had slowly turned white because of the cooler American climate.[241]

Polygenism, which asserted that human races were of different origins, offered another possible reason. This theory became increasingly popular during the Age of Discovery from the late seventeenth century, as the West was exposed to people whose culture and bodies were seen as wildly different to their own. The comparative anatomist Georges Cuvier, while not a polygenist, nonetheless laid the groundwork for this theory by arguing that three distinct racial types existed: Caucasians, Mongolians and Ethiopians.[242] According to the polygenists, there were biological and material distinctions that separated the races. Benjamin Rush, the politician, social reformer and physician who is sometimes mistakenly dubbed a proponent of polygenism, nonetheless offered a more materialistic reading of Henry Moss's body. In 1792 Rush argued that blackness was a symptom of leprosy and so, as Moss turned white, he was experiencing a 'cure' of his condition; he was being healed.[243]

Into these ongoing debates stepped Chang and Eng, whose differences were never clear-cut; they were neither clearly Siamese nor Chinese and how they were viewed depended on whom you asked. In their exhibition pamphlet, they were said to be merely distinct on account of a 'wonderful caprice of nature'.[244] The 'appellation of monsters ... is a harsh word and should not be used', someone wrote to *The Times*, while an unknown Sophia thought they were quite beautiful and apparently fell in love with both.[245] She wanted to marry them but, being two men, the marriage would have been bigamous.

Sophia's story – eagerly reported in the press – was probably bogus, an invention of Chang and Eng's manager, but it expressed a conundrum felt by the many who came to stare: 'Two Bodies: are they two men?' asked a later exhibition pamphlet.[246] People also asked, did they have one soul or two? At a time when both salvation and individualism were important, the twins complicated the boundaries of the soul and the self.

Here, then, we are edging ever closer to the ambiguity of the Victorian freak. The philosopher Elizabeth Grosz has argued that freaks disrupted categories and dichotomies common in Western thought (male–female, animal–human); an 'intolerable ambiguity' that turned freaks into beings who were 'considered simultaneously and compulsively fascinating and repulsive, enticing and sickening'.[247] But the response to the twins was less revulsion and more positive inquisitiveness: they were complex, contradictory, confusing and, as such, a sensation.

Reportedly, more than 100,000 people saw the Siamese Twins during their seven months in London, with another 200,000 paying to see them touring the provinces; 2,000 copies of their exhibition pamphlet were sold in 1830 alone. Their popularity spanned the classes, right up to the likes of Queen Adelaide (wife of King William IV), Prince Esterházy (Austrian ambassador to England), dukes, duchesses and the much-loved Duke of Wellington, who had defeated Napoleon at the Battle of Waterloo fourteen years earlier. Even King Charles X of France, later exiled in the UK after the July Revolution in Paris, escaped his woes to see the twins in Liverpool.

Thomas Carlyle, the Scottish philosopher, lamented this freak frenzy: 'May we not well cry shame on an ungrateful world … which will waste its optic faculty on dried Crocodiles, and Siamese Twins?'[248] This was an early utterance of condemnation against the popular appeal of the freak show; an indirect rebuke to the Egyptian Hall for diluting their cultural exhibitions for the display of freaks. Many, however, did not agree with Carlyle.

CHAPTER SIX

SCIENCE AND SIAM

A S THE FREAK show was emerging, medical men were inspecting, probing and gawping at the monstrosities on display. Before their public display at the Egyptian Hall in November 1829, Chang and Eng had been inspected in Boston by the renowned doctor John Collins Warren, professor of anatomy and surgery at the Harvard Medical School, who wrote a widely circulated report that focused on the twins' connecting ligament. Then, in Philadelphia, the twins were inspected by the so-called 'father of American surgery', Philip Syng Physick, president of the Philadelphia Medical Society and inventor of the stomach pump and, brace yourself, the artificial anus. Everywhere they went, Chang and Eng confronted medical science, always encouraged by James Hale, their manager.

On 24 November 1829, shortly before the twins' public exhibition at the Egyptian Hall, Hale invited London's medical establishment to a private inspection of the living Siamese Twins. Learned gentlemen descended on the hall, including some of the greatest luminaries of the day. There was Honoratus Leigh Thomas, president of the Royal College of Surgeons, and previous presidents such as Astley Cooper, Anthony Carlisle and William Blizard. There was also a cohort from the Royal College of Physicians, which included Francis Hawkins,

Charles Locock and Henry Halford, who was president of the college when he gawped at Chang and Eng.

After fondling the twins, the satisfied gentlemen (around thirty in total) signed a statement that praised the 'remarkable and interesting youths', stressed the reliability of the performance ('in no respect deceptive') and emphasized the respectability of the show ('nothing whatever, offensive to delicacy').[249] The statement was printed in the twins' exhibition pamphlet and was included in a book open for inspection at their public performance. A personal statement by Joshua Brookes, a leading London anatomist, also appeared in the pamphlet: 'Having seen and examined the two Siamese Youths, Chang and Eng, I have great pleasure in affirming they constitute a most extraordinary *Lusus Naturae*; the first instance I have ever seen of a living double child.'[250]

In the eighteenth and early nineteenth centuries there was a professional pride in the sciences not sensationalizing, but rather observing, monstrosities with a detached gaze.[251] Here, however, Brookes and the other medical signatories were promoting the freak show. Many of these medical reports, gamely reprinted in the pamphlet, focused on the twins' connecting band. According to the doctors this piece of flesh was the key to unlocking the mystery of their physiology:

The ensiform cartilage at the end of each sternum, is united to its fellow, and has been in part ossified, forming a hard, elastic upper edge to the band which connects these boys. This is convex upward, and concave below, becoming the upper boundary of a canal which is in the band … the canal is necessarily lined by a continuation of the natural peritoneal membrane of the cavities, and the whole of this is covered by common integuments. Thus the connecting link is constituted.[252]

Most would have been befuddled by this scientific jargon, but that was not the point. Hale included this report to demonstrate the educative element of the freak show, while aiding the upgrade from monstrous displays at low-class itinerant fairs to respectable spectacles in commercial venues. Furthermore, medicine was slowly modernizing and becoming more professional, gaining social respectability and cultural authority, and so these attributes were transferred to the freak show. What's more, the medical seal of approval confirmed the authenticity of Chang and Eng, a bonus when many showmen were displaying deceptions (such as Madame Gomez and the Savage Cannibal Pygmies of the Dark Continent, as paraded by James Sanger).

For Hale, the support of the medical fraternity was a coup. But it went both ways. Associating with Chang and Eng was also an opportunity for the medical men to understand the brothers' exceptional bodies. In popular parlance the twins were described by an assortment of terms such as 'freaks of nature', which was used interchangeably with 'human oddities', 'prodigies', 'novelties' and 'monstrosities'. The medical fraternity offered their own terms as they battled to categorize the twins: 'United Twins', 'lusus natuare', 'double living child', 'Siamese Twins' and 'double monstrosities' (only from 1861 was the term 'conjoined twins' used).[253] Until the twins' death, and even after, the medical fraternity debated the nature and meaning of Chang and Eng's monstrosity.[254]

In fairness, medical men were moving ever closer to a more definite understanding. As we saw in Act One, Jeffrey Hudson had belonged to that amorphous category which embraced monsters, marvels, wonders and prodigies, denoting something or someone out of the ordinary, but within God's great scheme. In the eighteenth century Józef Boruwłaski toured the royal courts of the Enlightenment, when natural philosophers turned from marvelling at the supernatural to observing the natural world, and the science of monstrosities (called teratology) had been spearheaded by the French anatomist and natural historian Étienne Geoffroy Saint-Hilaire. By the time Chang and Eng were displayed, an even more secular and scientific understanding of the monstrous body was being established. Monstrosities and marvels were liberated from the mythology of centaurs, sphinxes, mermaids and Cyclopses, leaving behind the narrative of wonder and God's design, and entering the light of teratology, physiology and pathology. Increasingly under the clinical gaze, monstrosities that were once 'wonders' were now 'errors'; what was once 'marvellous' was now 'deviant' (although, as we will see later, the narrative of wonder never fully died).[255]

Moreover Saint-Hilaire's son Isidore emphasized the proximity of the normal and monstrous in his publication on the history, organization and classification of anomalies (1832–36): 'monsters are also normal beings; or rather, there are no monsters, and nature is one whole'.[256] The anatomist Richard Owen similarly declared in an 1837 lecture that 'monsters are, like the Beings called Normal, subject to constant rules'.[257] Monsters were normal because they were subject to natural rules rather than supernatural interventions. Monsters had been naturalized.

Still, things were in flux. The twins were not necessarily perceived within a simple binary of normal and abnormal. The former only emerged as a recognizable concept between the 1840s and 1860s, and 'abnormality' only entered the Oxford English Dictionary in 1847 to denote 'an unusual form' in a medical and biological sense.[258] Even the term 'scientist' was not coined until 1833, when William Whewell used it to distinguish those studying the material world.[259] This remained a period of transition, with natural philosophy moving towards science, and this instability spurred the medical fraternity to investigate Chang and Eng and seek to work out what the twins meant and how they fitted into the scheme of life; and while their bodies invited comprehension, the conclusions were still unclear. This, in turn, made Chang and Eng an exciting prospect for experimentation.

⚬⟨∞⟩⚬

THE LONDON PHYSICIAN Dr George Buckley Bolton was lucky enough to enjoy prolonged proximity to the twins. He had been designated their personal doctor shortly after their arrival in London, and he maintained this role during the twins' seven-month stay in the capital in 1829 and 1830. In his desire to unearth the mysteries of Chang and Eng's physiology, Bolton conducted intrusive experiments and even allowed some of his colleagues to inspect and test the twins' connecting ligament. In his report to his colleagues, at the Royal College of Surgeons on 1 April 1830, he was keen to assert, not entirely correctly, that: 'I have neither instituted, nor permitted to be made, any unjustifiable experiments upon these youths; considering myself bound, by professional responsibility, as well as by a sense of national justice, to resist all such improper proposals.'[260]

In his widely circulated report, Bolton outlined his experiments to the gathered surgeons. He had tested the sensitivity of the twins' connecting band by poking it with a pin. Both boys shrieked, so Bolton concluded that the ligament carried nerves, arteries and veins that connected the pair. However, 'when slight punctures be made at the distance of half an inch from the centre of the band, then the sensation is only felt by the individual to the side punctured'. Bolton concluded 'that the united twins would be subject to certain distempers in common, although each possesses a distinct existence, and even different constitutional peculiarities'.[261]

Bolton fed Chang an asparagus to decipher the 'sanguineous communication' between the twins. Chang's urine had 'the peculiar asparagus smell' but not Eng's, which, Bolton said, 'tends to corroborate the opinion I entertain of the possibility of effecting a separation of the twins by a surgical operation'.[262] This would be a source of contention, with others who claimed separation was impossible; such debates, exaggerated by showmen, helped create a 'psychodrama starring the doctors who make normal humans out of monsters', noted the critic Leslie Fiedler.[263]

Nonetheless, Bolton decided the twins comprised 'two distinct persons' who were remarkably similar: 'They are exceedingly affectionate and docile, and grateful for every kindness shown them. It is not often that they converse with each other, although their dispositions and tempers agree, and their tastes and opinions are similar.'[264] He added that they both liked music and drama but had different dreams; they were 'quick in intelligence' and shared a 'moral and physical intimacy': 'these extraordinary individuals are the most remarkable instances on record of perfect and distinctly formed human beings united together'.[265]

Bolton concluded his report with an important thanks to Chang and Eng's protectors. He was grateful for the 'liberal manner in which they have uniformly afforded the means of investigating so curious an object of philosophical inquiry'.[266] Beneficence was, of course, key in justifying the treatment of Chang and Eng. Moreover, the repeated assurances that the twins were 'docile' was part of a strategy to infantilize the twins, emphasize their willingness to be inspected and displayed and comfort audiences that the twins, though exotic, were not dangerous.

As we shall see when examining the archives, Chang and Eng were not wholly pleased with Bolton, their protectors or the swarms of medical men who buzzed around their bodies. But, for now, they had to put up with it.

THIS 1831 AMERICAN satire clearly understood why medical men were so keen to associate with the conjoined twins:

> *Sir Astley bid high to secure them,*
> *To cut up when the spring was o'er;*
> *He had, he begged leave to assure them,*
> *Cut up 'The Skeleton,' before.*
> *T'was much, they'd see if they reflected,*
> *To be with care and skill dissected;*
> *And if next year they would prefer—he*
> *Was not at present in a hurry.*[267]

The interest in the living Chang and Eng was compelled in part by a desire for the dead Chang and Eng. The market in cadavers did not escape the notice of the twins' protectors: Coffin carried embalming fluid in case of the twins' sudden death. Indeed, one notable inspector and signatory to the twins' exhibition was William Clift, curator of the Hunterian Museum at the Royal College of Surgeons, which had a collection of approximately 18,700 anatomical preparations created in the second half of the eighteenth century by John Hunter, the anatomist-surgeon.

From at least the eighteenth century, exceptional bodies were prime specimens for the medical establishment. In the 1780s the body of Charles Byrne, the Irish Giant who met Boruwłaski, was secured by Hunter. Although Byrne's dying wish was to ensure his body went nowhere near the anatomist's table, Hunter reportedly bribed the undertaker and claimed the corpse. The giant was then dissected and displayed in Hunter's collection.

Similarly, five years before Chang and Eng's exhibition in London, Caroline Crachami, described as the nine-year-old Sicilian Dwarf (also dubbed the Sicilian Fairy, who in truth was probably only three years old), was acquired by Clift for the Royal College of Surgeons after being sold by Dr Gilligan, a quack cum showman. Gilligan had promised Caroline's father that he would cure her cough by taking her to England to enjoy the congenial air. Instead, Gilligan displayed her from his apartment in Bond Street. For a shilling she could be viewed; for an extra shilling, handled. No wonder *The Times* wrote: 'her great antipathy is to Doctors; these have offended her by examining her too minutely, and whenever they are mentioned she doubles her filbert of a fist, and manifests her decided displeasure'.[268] She died, possibly of tuberculosis, in 1824. Her father tried to obtain her body and eventually found it lying on the anatomy table at the Royal College of Surgeons surrounded by Clift and his assistants, eagerly dissecting her corpse. Apparently, the distraught father grasped her dismembered body and screamed in anguish. (This account was reported in the press, suggesting public disapproval of such treatment.) Gilligan escaped to France and Caroline's skeleton was displayed next to Byrne's. Well into the twenty-first century they were still on show together at the Hunterian.

On 23 November 1829, a day before Chang and Eng's private medical show at the Egyptian Hall, another pair of conjoined twins were under the knife in Paris. The Sardinian Ritta and Christina Parodi, born into a poor family in March 1829, had died suckling their mother, who had only just taken them to France in the hope of earning some money by presenting her babies to the public and learned societies. They certainly got a close look when the conjoined twins died and were subsequently dissected in the amphitheatre of the Muséum National d'Histoire Naturelle at the Jardin des Plantes. At this examination was Georges Cuvier, the comparative anatomist, who had previously dissected Sara Baartman in 1815.

A Khoekhoe woman from South Africa, Baartman was dubbed the Hottentot Venus, a stage name which suggested savagery and sexuality, ('hottentot' being a pejorative term invented by the Dutch to describe pastoral communities, Venus being the Roman goddess of love). She was renowned for her steatopygia (fat around the hips and buttocks) and macronympha (large labia). Her exhibition, as noted by historians Gilles Boëtsch and Pascal Blanchard, marked the 'birth of the practice of human zoos' in Europe, a tradition in which Chang and Eng were partly displayed.[269] Moreover, they continued, 'this young woman … had the dubious honour of being an original, having served, in turn, as an object of entertainment, an object of media attention, a "sexualized" object, a monstrous object, and a scientific object'.[270] She was displayed for amusement, profit and learning, and, in her death, she was ultimately raped by science; strong but appropriate language.[271]

UNTIL RELATIVELY RECENTLY very little was known about Baartman's early years, but archival discoveries reveal that she was born in today's Eastern Cape in the 1770s (not the Gamtoos River Valley as often reported). She was raised on a colonist's farm amid settler violence and was given the name Sara Baartman, which essentially meant 'savage servant' (Sara, in Dutch, was spelt 'Saartjie'). She was sold to one Pieter Cesars, an itinerant trader and employee of a Cape merchant, who moved Baartman to Cape Town in the mid-1790s. By this point both her parents were dead (her father had been killed by a pack of bandits). She spent more than a decade in urban Cape Town working as a domestic servant, although she was kept like a slave. She was under the charge of Cesars' employer, the German-born Jan Michiel Elzer and, following his death in 1799, she moved into Cesars' small house. Ultimately it would be Pieter Cesars' brother, Hendrik, who brought Baartman to London. He was joined by Alexander

Dunlop, a Scottish surgeon to the Royal Navy and exporter of museum specimens. Dunlop possibly met Baartman at a slave lodge in the city, where she may have been forced into prostitution, as he was working as the doctor of the lodge around this time. In 1810, when Dunlop and Cesars decided to ship Baartman to England, she was in her thirties and had mothered three children; all had died in infancy, their names unrecorded.[272]

She ended up at 225 Piccadilly, where it cost 2 shillings to see her display and both male and female spectators rubbed shoulders as they observed and prodded her. She wore a tight-fitting costume to highlight her large buttocks and to give the impression that she was naked. She sang onstage and one reporter, for the *London Times*, noted how she was 'produced like a wild beast', placed in a 'cage' on a raised platform and 'ordered to move backwards and forwards' by her manager.[273] Her exhibition was akin to that of a performing animal, although some historians have also noted that she was treated like a celebrity: carried on a chair and presented to a duke, riding in a carriage on Sundays and visited by many of London's fashionable, with songs and poems composed in her 'honour'.[274]

Baartman could not speak English but, as the *London Times* noted, her manager 'was seen to hold up his hand to her in a menacing posture' until she obeyed his command.[275] The English actor and comedian Charles Mathews, who was friends with Boruwłaski and a visitor to Lambert's 1806 exhibition, also attended Baartman's display. He recalled his experience to his wife, who later wrote:

He found her surrounded by many persons, some females! One pinched her; one gentleman poked her with his cane; one lady employed her parasol to ascertain that all was, as she called it, 'nattral'. This inhuman baiting the poor creature bore with sullen indifference, except upon some provocation, when she seemed

inclined to resent brutality ... On these occasions it took all the
authority of the keeper to subdue her resentment.[276]

Baartman's exhibition was challenged in October 1810 when abolitionists objected to it. The case eventually went to court and hinged on the question of whether she was a free agent at liberty to make her own decisions. A dubious contract between Dunlop and Baartman was produced, suggesting that, yes, she was a willing participant. Baartman also gave her own testimony, under the watchful eye of Dunlop, claiming she 'came by her own consent'.[277] The judge ruled in Dunlop's favour, and the show continued.

It appears Baartman was baptized in Manchester in December 1811, with permission granted by the Bishop of Chester, and she even got married, although nothing is known of the groom. She was displayed in Manchester, Bath and Limerick before being paraded in Paris, where, in the spring of 1815, she spent three days at the Jardin des Plantes under the observation of professors at the Muséum National d'Histoire Naturelle. Here she posed naked for images that appear in the first volume of Étienne Geoffroy Saint-Hilaire and Frédéric Cuvier's *Histoire Naturelle des Mammifères* (1824). She was pictured in a book featuring apes and monkeys.

In December 1815, Baartman was dead; no one was interested in the cause of death, but she most probably died of pneumonia.[278] Now science could claim the ultimate prize: Georges Cuvier (the brother of Frédéric) dissected her body, decanted her brain and genitalia, and made a cast of her body. In the name of science Cuvier immortalized Baartman as a biological and racial specimen. He took his time dissecting her, particularly focusing upon her buttocks and genitals, which Baartman had refused to show him when she was alive: 'science as rape, institutionalized', wrote her biographers, saying Cuvier molested the cadaver.[279] Baartman's genitals were preserved in a jar, and her skeleton joined Cuvier's collection, before he reached his 'scientific' conclusion: the Hottentot was closer in lineage to apes than humans.

For nearly two hundred years, in Case Number 33, Baartman's brain and skeleton were displayed at the Jardin des Plantes, the world's foremost museum of natural history. Campaigns were launched to 'Bring back the Hottentot Venus' and, following interventions from presidents Nelson Mandela and Thabo Mbeki, her body was finally repatriated in April 2002. She was buried in her home country later that year.

⁓≪≫⁓

B AARTMAN'S HUMANITY WAS stripped. The practice of dissecting exceptional bodies showed that the humanity of the individual was immaterial compared to the scientific importance of the material body. It is worth noting that before the Anatomy Act of 1832, which enabled surgeons and anatomists to access the unclaimed corpses of the poor, dissection was legal only if the cadaver was an executed criminal. But with such corpses in short supply and demand insatiable, surgeons and anatomists relied on the dreaded Resurrectionists and body snatchers.

In America and England dissection was seen as worse than death – there was no 'rest in peace' if you were dissected, no guarantee you would ascend to heaven, and certain humiliation and degradation as your corpse was prised apart by surgeons and anatomists in training. But Sara Baartman, like Chang and Eng, had a higher rating: they were ethnically different *and* physiologically exceptional. This not only made them more valuable as subjects for science and entertainment, but also aided the separation of their humanity, which was necessary if in death they were to be treated like criminals.

Being ethnically different also played into the much broader story of the period. Between 1790 and 1830 the Royal Navy assigned the naturalists on their trading expeditions to promote scientific exploration. Curiosities, including humans, were brought back to the UK for classification and display. William Clift was curator at the Hunterian, a dissector of the Sicilian Dwarf and endorser of Chang and Eng's performance. He also dealt in a range of these transported natural history specimens, from lumpfish to Chinese skulls, many of which were displayed in public exhibitions.[280] Just a year after Chang and Eng's London display, the twenty-two-year-old Charles Darwin sailed on the *Beagle* as the ship's naturalist, observing and classifying plants, animals, rocks and fossils and returning almost five years later with over 1,500 zoological and geological specimens. That voyage also included three Fuegians who had failed to be properly 'civilized' in England, and who were now being returned with a missionary preacher in tow.[281] Sara Baartman, and Chang and Eng, were shipped to the West as part of a broader movement of goods and people.

Agents of empire – whether missionaries, merchants or naturalists – were all involved in the display of foreign artefacts and people. In 1803, when the Dutch took control of the Cape of Good Hope, a Dutch missionary preacher displayed a male and two female Hottentots, declaring that they 'have become civilised and espoused Christianity under his Ministry and by his exertions'.[282] Remarkably, in 1844, George Henry, an Anishinaabe tribe member from North America, who had converted to Christianity around 1825 became a 'missionary manager'. He exhibited unconverted members of his own tribe in London and Paris through the 1840s.[283]

Like Baartman, Chang and Eng were displayed within the context of colonialism. Coffin and Hunter seized their opportunity as foreign merchants (they also assisted missionaries in the region), placing Chang and Eng onstage because, as Hunter wrote, he knew they would 'prove profitable as a curiosity'.[284] And exoticism was a defining feature of the twins' shows. They were presented through the prism of Orientalism which, simplistically stated, was a way of seeing, imagining and creating Middle Eastern, Asian and North African people as exotic, backward and uncivilized.[285] The Orient, then, was as much a construct as the freak identities onstage, and this Orientalism informed how the twins were viewed. Indeed, when Bolton examined the twins, he read their bodies against the Western standard: 'They are much shorter, and appear less advanced in puberty, than youths of this country at the age of eighteen years; but the average stature of their countrymen is less than that of Europeans.'[286]

Chang and Eng, the Siamese Twins, in an Oriental setting, c. 1830.

By comparing the twins against Western bodies, Bolton highlighted the belief that the Caucasian body was the normative standard at the summit of a racially graded scale.[287] The historian Douglas Baynton has showed how the emergent concept of normality in the nineteenth century depended on perceived social and biological hierarchies which merged race and disability into a single category of difference and inferiority. Down's syndrome, for example, was labelled 'Mongolism' in 1866, while Chang and Eng's billing as the Siamese Twins also established a supposed link between race and disability.[288]

Hale, the show manager, capitalized on the public's fascination with Orientalism with the lithograph opposite. He depicted Chang and Eng with dark skin, bulbous foreheads and slanted eyes. Dressed in pantaloons and brocaded tunics, they stand barefoot in an opening between palm trees and other vegetation. In the background are wooden huts and domed architecture, which evoke both North Africa and west Asia, thus subsuming distinct geographies into a singular 'Orient'.[289] The image was recycled on handbills and tickets in America and England, part of a broader production of Orientalist landscapes that featured in optical entertainments such as panoramas, dioramas and cosmoramas and promised an engagement with the exotic.[290]

Chang and Eng's exhibition pamphlet also peddled these Orientalist stereotypes. The text claimed that, during Coffin's time in the Orient, he witnessed the incarceration of the Prince of Laos and his family, who were 'confined in an iron cage, loaded with heavy chains', after which the prince 'was to be taken to the place of execution and there hung by a hook to be inserted under his chin; he was afterwards to be seated on sharp pikes five inches in length; then to be placed in boiling oil, and finally pounded to pumice in an immense mortar'.[291] This is Coffin, Western observer of 'degraded' Siamese practices, a character which anticipated later freak show pamphlets that themselves copied imperial adventure novels.

Notions of violent and despotic Orientalism were well established by the time Chang and Eng were displayed. Since the failed British embassy to China in 1816, when Lord William Amherst refused to partake in the kowtowing ceremony, the 'cruel Orient' had become increasingly prevalent in nineteenth-century art and literature, and even appeared in the theories of Karl Marx, who attributed Asiatic despotism to acrid climates.[292] Crucially, and mendaciously, the twins' supposedly cruel homeland turned their presence in England into a form of liberation. No wonder they loved their protectors, claimed the pamphlet; no wonder they never wished to return home: 'The youths have never expressed any anxiety to return; on the contrary, they say they are so much better pleased with their present manner of life, that if their mother were with them, they should not have the least desire to revisit Siam. They often say she would be astonished to see how much like little kings they now live.'[293]

Offstage, however, the realities were very different.

CHAPTER SEVEN

THEIR OWN MEN

C HANG AND ENG were resentful. They had begrudged their twenty-seven-day journey from New York to England in October 1829. They'd been placed in steerage while the rest of the group, including Captain Abel Coffin, his wife Susan, Robert Hunter and James Hale, had first-class cabins. While Coffin and co. enjoyed the culinary perks associated with this status, Chang and Eng, along with their companion Tieu, a Chinese neighbour and servant from Siam, were on daily salt beef and potatoes.

On arrival the twins had the indignity of an intimate medical examination by George Bolton, who wrote: 'their genital organs are like all their other external parts, regularly formed; but the youths are naturally modest, and evidence a strong repugnance to any close investigation on this subject'.[294] They then had a gruelling performance schedule in London, followed by a tour of the wider British Isles. They covered around 2,500 miles, with exhibitions in the likes of Bath, Windsor, Reading, Oxford, Birmingham and Liverpool.

Granted, their display at the Egyptian Hall was in a respectable venue and they never perceived themselves as deformed or disabled. They even apparently offered a one-eyed spectator half price admission and gave a cripple with no arms or feet a crown and some cigars.[295] But in many ways they were continuously being cut down.

The 1830 exhibition pamphlet infantalized the eighteen-year-old twins, claiming 'for Captain Coffin and his Lady, they have a paternal regard, calling them very frequently father and mother'.[296] Similarly, Coffin wrote to his wife that 'I feel that I shall always do by them as by my own children may God bless you all and may you be as happy as I could wish.'[297] In 1830 Coffin's wife wrote to her children that the twins were 'very good boys indeed': 'they say that they love your mother much I tell them some times I am going home to America thay say No No I shall cry mamah if you go home and leave me [sic]'.[298] This infantilizing reflected a paternalism common in colonialism: the colonized were frequently collapsed into the figure of the child requiring nurture and parental care.[299] And as often the case in the colonial subjugation of people, Coffin was also hard on the twins, instructing his wife that 'you must not let them have too much' and noting that if he was harsh it was for their own good.[300] Chang and Eng found their treatment hard to bear; ultimately, they would revolt quite sensationally. For now, however, their resentments simply simmered.

The group dynamics became unstable when, in January 1831, Abel Coffin left to pursue business in the East Indies while Hunter left for Singapore, taking the twins' friend Tieu home to Siam, which greatly upset the increasingly homesick brothers. The management of the twins was then left to Hale under the authority of the overbearing Susan Coffin. The group left London in January 1831 and travelled across the Atlantic for a tour of North America.

This was the start of an arduous eight-year journey, going backwards and forwards from the East, Midwest and South of the States, travelling north to Canada and south to Cuba. Chang and Eng were beginning a new life as itinerant performers in cities, towns, hamlets and villages, visiting fourteen of the then twenty US states. In many ways they were cast back to an older, pre-industrial age which echoed the life of George Sanger in the travelling English fairs. At the Egyptian Hall, in respectable Piccadilly, they were freak performers in an urban environment, praised by dukes, duchesses, the middle classes and the medical men. But now the twins were being recast as travelling entertainers, and they'd face abuse, censure and condemnation as they roamed the landscape. Moreover, under rapacious and repressive protectors, their resentments were compounded.

BETWEEN 1831 AND 1839 Chang and Eng crossed a bloody landscape during a turbulent time in history, with slave rebellions, abolitionist agitation and the first attempted assassination of an American president. There were wars with Native Americans and the forcible removal of thousands from their ancestral homelands. Threats of succession exposed the cracks in the Union, ultimately erupting two decades later in the Civil War. The 1836 patent for the revolving gun symbolized the often-explosive violence that plagued the fledgling, ideologically divided nation.

James Hale and the twins travelled by stagecoach, boat and train. An enclosed wagon was obtained so they could be hidden from view. There was an extra wagon for the baggage, three horses and a man named Tom Dwyer who travelled with the twins as hired help. Susan stayed in Boston, instructing Hale to keep her updated on the exhibitions through letters. He would go ahead of Dwyer and the twins to secure the venues. In large cities, Chang and Eng performed in hotels for a few days or even weeks; in smaller towns and villages they performed in lodging houses or inns for one or two nights. The admission was 25 cents, sometimes raised to 50.

Their routes – what one historian has called the 'channels of itinerancy'– were well trodden before, and especially after, the American Revolution.[301] During the sixteenth and seventeenth centuries, and gathering pace in the 1750s and 1760s, a stream of itinerant entertainers had piled into British North America from Europe, bringing their wares and entertainments.[302] They wandered the landscape to sell manufactured goods; there were tinsmiths, artisans, furniture makers, portrait painters, 'peddler poets', book traders, lecturers and medicine men.

During the early to mid-eighteenth century they were joined by religious zealots, fired up by an evangelical revival called the Great Awakening, who rode on horseback giving sermons to troubled souls. Galloping beside them were judges following the circuit courts to dispense justice and uphold the rule of law. Then came the entertainers: puppeteers, fire-eaters, magicians and phrenologists, who'd read your skull and facial features to reveal your 'true' character. These entertainers performed in railway houses, taverns, inns and fairs, often stopping in larger urban centres with better spaces for entertaining. Other showmen on the circuit had to schlep dioramas, kaleidoscopes, automata, waxworks and hot-air balloons; some had menageries that included lions and tigers, monkeys and giraffes; circus troupes had to shift canvas tents, sometimes requiring thirty employees and ten wagons. And, of course, there were the human oddities: girls with no limbs, black men with white spots, bearded ladies and the Siamese Twins.

The itinerant experience in America was harsh, dangerous, transitory and lonely. Itinerants travelled vast distances with a horse and cart along near impossible roads. Although America had concentrated cities like New York, this was a country with vast terrain: in 1800 less than 4 per cent of America's population lived in areas with a population greater than 10,000. By 1850 the figure had only increased to 12 per cent.[303] In an unidentified diary, written by an Irish peddler from 1807–08, the author records travelling up to 32 miles a day across Virginia: 'Rain increased, Mountains Bad, the Land being very Rich made the Hills so slippery tha[t] our Horses had enough to do to get along'.[304] Travellers confronted difficult tavern-keepers; they kept pistols by their side; and they might have come across the thousands of displaced Native Americans fleeing white settlers.

By October 1831 Hale had left the group after constant fighting with Susan. He was replaced by an Irish friend, Charles Harris, who wrote frequent letters on behalf of the twenty-year-old twins. These letters highlight the range of problems confronting the group – not just the troublesome journeys but how, in the winter of 1830–31, the freezing weather severely reduced audiences, and was matched in ferocity by a scorching summer sun.[305] The twins were worked like dogs. They were homesick. They got ill, and there were accidents on the road.

In Virginia, March 1832, the group were subject to an entertainment tax that threatened to kill their profits. The tax was aimed at 'Exhibitions of Jugglers, Sleight-of-hand men & others who might corrupt the public morals of the Community'. This was extended to exhibitions 'of the same class' where 'large masses of People in the open Air … endanger the public peace'.[306] Just like the clampdown on the English fairs, denunciation and censorship trailed the American itinerants. And puritanical condemnation rained down on the types of entertainment connected to Chang and Eng's itinerancy. In 1773, for example, Connecticut passed an Act for Suppressing of Mountebanks, censoring 'any games, tricks, plays, juggling or feats of uncommon dexterity and agility of body' which, it was maintained, corrupted manners, promoted idleness and threatened 'good order and religion'. In 1819 New York State prohibited the exhibition or performance 'for gain and profit any puppet show, wire dance, or any other idle shows, acts or feats'.[307]

Within this context, then, the legislature in Virginia would be damned if they'd allow two monsters like Chang and Eng to perform a potentially disruptive show without at least paying for the privilege. But the twins believed their exhibition was educational and virtuous, not bawdy and immoral, informing people about the wonders of the human body. Had not men of medicine endorsed their performance at the Egyptian Hall in London? But away from their permanent venue, which wrapped respectability around their show, they were mere monsters on the move, part of a ragtag rabble who threatened public morality. The twins and their protectors appealed directly to Virginia's General Assembly, asking for an exemption from the tax that threatened to ruin their business. The assembly rejected their appeal.

Yet what really offended the twins was the claim, made in the assembly, that they were slaves who had been bought from their mother. Chang and Eng were mortified, incensed, incandescent: 'they feel themselves aggrieved in being made ... liable to be spoke of as "slaves" bought and sold', Harris wrote.[308] But seven months prior to their arrival, Nat Turner had instigated a slave rebellion, leading to its brutal suppression and the execution of some eighteen slaves, plus the eventual conviction and execution of Turner; and just two months before the twins arrived the assembly had been debating slavery and emancipation; so, being ethnically 'Other' and travelling with protectors, Chang and Eng were perceived through these debates.

That the twins should take this personally is important. Clearly they did not consider themselves to be slaves. When they first arrived back in America in 1831, they even scolded a reporter for calling them 'boys' which, they told the reporter, in England meant a 'servant boy – cook boy – school boy'.[309] They were none of these things, and they did not like being considered subservient to the will of others.

Further, as they toured America the twins frequently asserted their own will. In December 1831, for example, they asked for an increased allowance of $3 a week to cover the costs of repairs for their chaise and wagon in addition to their monthly expenses.[310] Susan ignored then rejected their demands. Chang and Eng felt it was 'an intended act of unkindness'.[311] She maintained, however, that the twins could do with the carriage as they wished, but they would not receive any increase in their allowance. Charles Harris wrote on behalf of the twins (who seemingly struggled to write in English): 'it was like taking a bird, clipping off its wings, and then holding it up in one's hand and saying "now you may fly if you wish".' He also added and underlined: '(*This latter sentence is in their own words.*)' – stressing that Chang and Eng were taking sole responsibility for the complaint. Indeed, they signed the letter themselves.[312]

The twins felt exploited and ignored. They resented lining the pockets of others and they resented the tiring performances and constant travel, so in the summer of 1831 they took a little holiday. They spent a few days resting in Lynnfield, Massachusetts, enjoying fishing in the ponds and shooting in the woods. But despite their desire for privacy and respite, they were followed by about twenty to thirty intrigued locals: 'the nineteenth-century equivalent of paparazzi'.[313] According to the press, the 'mob ... were as zealous as if in pursuit of a wild beast'.[314] Chang and Eng were effectively hunted like animals, with stones and insults thrown. They retaliated, hitting one of the mob, a colonel no less, with the butt of their gun and even firing a bullet at him. They were subsequently hauled before the courts and fined $200.

By 11 May 1832, their twenty-first birthday, they had had enough. They had been insulted in Virginia, attacked in Massachusetts and dubbed 'slaves' and harbingers of carnivalesque immorality. Ever since they had come to the West, they had been shipped around like colonial possessions; their bodies had been invaded by medical men; their labours exploited by so-called protectors who were greedy, harsh and infantilizing. So they did something drastic: they cancelled their contract with the Coffins and declared themselves 'Their Own Men'.[315]

---◦◈◦---

THIS WAS A rupture that cannot be underestimated. Chang and Eng were twenty-one. They had reached the age of maturity and wanted to no longer be subservient to their protectors; they wanted to be in charge and of their own shows and their own lives. The Siamese Twins broke away to become independent, self-employed performers. They went from being exhibits to exhibitors, from performers to showmen.

Susan was furious but there was little she could do. It wasn't until October 1832 that her husband, after a lengthy 'wildgoose chase', eventually tracked the twins down and admitted reluctantly that 'they seem to feel themselves quite free from me'.[316] Chang and Eng were now in charge. They were businessmen, bosses and beneficiaries of their labour. They hired Harris at the same rate he'd received from the Coffins, keeping a detailed record of his expenses.[317] They hired servants, often 'negro' boys, to help with their performances.[318] They treated themselves to little luxuries like ice cream and seeing other entertainments, and they began a series of tours, earning considerable sums of money.[319] Crucially, they kept all the profits.

In May 1833, in correspondence with their old manager Hale, they requested a new exhibition pamphlet. It was published three years later as *A Few Particulars Concerning Chang-Eng, The United Siamese Brothers, Published Under Their Own Direction*. It explained: 'The pamphlets concerning Chang-Eng, which have been published previous to this time, were written before the period at which they became of age, and also before they understood the English language. Under these circumstances, the present statement has been written with their knowledge, and under their supervision.'[320]

The new emphasis was on Chang and Eng's 'own direction', and in some respects it flatly contradicted the old text. The 1830 pamphlet declared that the twins were from a 'poorer class' in Siam while the 1836 edition said they had been self-sufficient businessmen, 'pretty keen at striking a bargain' and bequeathing 'a very flourishing business to their brother' as they left home for America.[321] The old text said the King of Siam wanted them executed, the new text that the king had honoured them with gifts. The old version highlighted a violent Orientalist landscape, the new one provided a six-page treatment of the European landscape that Chang and Eng had enjoyed on their tours, presenting the twins as seasoned travellers. Finally, the new pamphlet reversed the gaze of curiosity, as Chang and Eng now became observers of *American* exoticism. Admitting the 'superstitious adherence to particular days and hours' in China, the pamphlet commented that this 'is no worse than the twins themselves have met with in this country'.[322]

Notably, the new pamphlet did not mention that Chang and Eng were sold by their mother, the rumour which had deeply offended them in March 1832: 'the idea of persons looking on them as children who had so hard-hearted a mother has sunk but too deeply in their minds', Harris wrote.[323] Moreover, the new pamphlet asserted that neither Chang and Eng nor their mother thought they'd be gone for so long; and 'since they left home, they have had several opportunities' to hear from her, a claim verified in private correspondence.[324]

In the new 1836 pamphlet the twins were no longer just objects of curiosity, but active participants in the construction of their onstage identities. The twins became the creators of their identities, rather than playing the freak personas moulded by others, and like Boruwłaski and Lambert they sought to elevate themselves. While the veracity of the information contained in both pamphlets is perhaps doubtful, and the versions of events questionable, this was not the point. What counts was that this was now their show, their choice, and their priorities were different to those of their old protectors.

It is common, in current academic literature, to separate the 'freak' and the 'freak performer'. The freak is the constructed, performing persona brought to life onstage by the freak performer, the private individual who lives a life offstage.[325] But there was a very close relationship between the two; onstage and off, public and private, were not separate realms. The personal life of the twins closely mirrored their presentations onstage: when Chang and Eng had protectors, they were presented as boys, ethnically and medically different; when Chang and Eng became 'Their Own Men' offstage, they changed how they were seen onstage.

Now Chang and Eng wanted to give the impression that they were gentlemen from Siam, respected in their country of origin. They were in the West of their own free will, not slaves but independent performers. And to show how far they had come, in 1839 they commissioned a lithograph depicting themselves within a lavish interior fitted with Chippendale furniture, corded drapes, carpet and a checkerboard; this interior suggested domesticity and affluence. They had lighter skin tones, short-cropped hair and were dressed in Western attire, wearing polished leather shoes. The image stands in marked contrast to the 1830 lithograph, which firmly placed Chang and Eng in an Oriental landscape, wearing native garb and sporting highly racialized features. Now, in 1839, they were respectable gentlemen.

After declaring themselves 'Their Own Men' in 1832, Chang and Eng continued to travel along the channels of itinerancy, but they promoted themselves and their exhibitions as respectable. And they were good at what they did: in 1833 they amassed a small fortune in the Deep South, grossing more than $500, for nine days, in Nashville; in November they boasted profits of $985.75; in December, $1,447.[326] They performed in Cuba and Canada, and they kept all the profits for themselves. By 1839 they had managed to save $10,000, which made them among the richest men in Wilkes County, North Carolina, where they chose to settle, leaving behind their lives as travelling freak performers (only temporarily, as it would turn out).[327]

Chang and Eng's commissioned lithograph, 1839. Eng is holding the book.

They opened a retail store in Traphill, an isolated community nestled near Stone Mountain in the Blue Ridge Mountains. Here they bought their first piece of land in October 1839, and built a two-storey house with a veranda, wide staircase and large windows to take in the views. That same month they successfully petitioned for American citizenship, formally renouncing their allegiance to the King of Siam and changing their names to Chang and Eng Bunker (purportedly chosen as a result of an intimate friendship with the Bunker family whom they met in New York around 1832).

Their lives changed even further when, on 13 April 1843, they married two local white sisters, Adelaide and Sarah Yates, aged nineteen and twenty respectively. They were the daughters of Nancy and David Yates, a wealthy planter with acres of land, who was one of the largest slaveholders in the census district of Mulberry Creek, situated roughly 12 miles from Traphill. Chang's marriage to Adelaide and Eng's to Sarah was another crucial juncture in the twins' lives, marking their transition from performers and businessmen to members of the Southern elite.

While some historians and biographers have declared that the marriages caused uproar in the community, there's no compelling primary evidence to back up that claim; at the same time there was certainly condemnation, prurience and derision in the national press. Moreover, the fact that the twins did marry raises interesting questions as to how they circumvented both the 1790 Naturalization Act, which limited obtaining citizenship to 'free white persons', and anti-miscegenation laws which outlawed interracial marriage. Yet, as the academic Joseph Orser has showed, while the twins were regarded as 'monsters' in popular culture, legally they were 'white' as the categories of 'Asiatic', 'Mongolian', 'Oriental' and 'Chinese' were not officially sanctioned at the time they married in 1843.[328]

So, as white married men, Chang and Eng settled down in rural

Traphill where they and their wives shared a house. Soon they had children: on 10 February 1844 Sarah gave birth to Katherine Marcellus; six days later Adelaide had Josephine Virginia; just over a year later, on 31 March 1845, Sarah had Julia Ann; and eight days later Adelaide had Christopher. Between them, they brought twenty-one children into the world (two died before the age of three; two were born deaf and mute). In the spring of 1845 the two couples and their burgeoning families bought a small dwelling and a 650-acre farm in Surry County, near Mount Airy village, gradually increasing their property portfolio over the next two years. Between 1845 and 1853 they moved between properties in Traphill and Surry County, where they farmed wheat, Indian corn, oats and potatoes, and lived a typical Southern life.

It was typical only to a point, however. Offstage Chang and Eng were the Bunkers, farmers, fathers and husbands, but they did return to the stage as the Siamese Twins, rejoining the freak show circuit in 1849 to earn more money to support their growing families, which, at this point, included a total of seven children. Perhaps they toured reluctantly (they deliberated for some time before returning to the stage), yet still they took the plunge, billing themselves as 'The Living Siamese Twins Chang-Eng and Their Children'. The five-year-olds Katherine and Josephine performed with their father and uncle onstage. The children were regarded as just as exotic as their fathers, with the press commenting on their 'Siamese cast of countenance', 'coarse black hair' and 'swarthy' complexion.[329] The children, in short, became freak performers and, for the remainder of their lives, Chang and Eng would appear in freak shows alongside their offspring, switching between their domestic lives in North Carolina and the world of the freak show.

At home the Bunkers continued to develop their farms from the mid-1840s. They invested in agricultural technology to maximize profits from their land, and they chewed tobacco, raised livestock and enjoyed hunting, fishing and music. Their homes were fitted with the best furniture and cutlery imported from the North; they hosted friends and lived as part of the Southern gentry. Their farm reportedly had a blacksmith and shoemaker's shop, testifying to the twins' entrepreneurial spirit.[330] They also kept slaves.

In 1843 their father-in-law's wedding gift was a slave, called 'Aunt' Grace Gates, who served as nursemaid to the Bunker children. In September 1845 Chang and Eng bought two more girls (aged seven and five) for $450, plus a three-year-old boy for $175. In February 1846 they bought another girl for $325. By 1848 they claimed to have thirteen slaves between them and by 1860 twenty-eight. Furthermore, their home in Traphill had two smaller buildings adjacent to the main home: one for the kitchen and one for the slaves and horses. At their Surry County farm they had 'house slaves' like Grace Gates and 'field slaves' who worked the land. Reportedly, they lived in poor conditions.[331]

Chang and Eng deliberately purchased young slaves, under the age of eight, who were put to work until their early twenties when they were sold at a profit or traded for younger individuals who were also less likely to revolt. It was asserted in the press that the twins were cruel masters, using the 'lash without mercy'.[332] They vehemently denied this 'fabrication and infamous falsehood', saying that they treated their slaves with love, care and kindness, perhaps echoing the claims of their own earlier freak show protectors.[333] Whatever the truth (and let's hope it was compassion rather than cruelty) perhaps owning slaves was their ultimate claim to independence, self-sufficiency and power. Or, more likely, this was the reality of life in the South.

Other freak performers were not so well-off. In 1835, as Chang and Eng were lumbering along the channels of itinerancy, doing the circuits with preachers, peddlers and showmen, a woman was being displayed, and unlike Chang and Eng, she was a slave. Today her owner, for that's what he was in all but name, is remembered as the 'greatest showman on earth'. He is a man who did much to create the age of the freak. He did much to revolutionize entertainment and advertising. But he was building on the success of performers like Chang and Eng, and it should never be forgotten that he started showbiz with a slave.

CHAPTER EIGHT

JOICE HETH

W HEN PHINEAS TAYLOR Barnum first observed Joice Heth at the Masonic Hall in Philadelphia, in July 1835, she was infirm and possibly suffering from dementia. Her eyes sank into her skull, almost hiding her eyeballs in their dark cavities. Her skin was so wrinkled it appeared to be falling off her skeletal frame. A grey mass of hair curled around the top of her head. She had no teeth. She was almost completely paralysed. The nails on her hands were around 4in long. But to Barnum her decrepit figure spoke of opportunity.

Barnum's journey to Philadelphia began some months earlier. In his autobiography he alleges that he had been living hand to mouth, flitting between dead-end jobs ever since he moved to New York in the winter of 1834–35. Before then, in his hometown state of Connecticut, he had worked as a clerk, proprietor of a village store, newspaper editor and involved himself in lottery schemes. In New York, with his wife and child, he became a drummer coaxing customers into stores and earning a small commission on sales. He flicked through newspapers looking for work. He found numerous dodgy enterprises usually requiring a capital investment for some questionable speculation. Eventually Barnum was able to open a small private boarding house and purchased an interest in a grocery store in New York. He felt like Wilkins Micawber, a clerk from Charles Dickens' *David Copperfield* (1849–50), who ever optimistically believed that something would 'turn up'.[334] Luckily for Barnum, in July 1835, it did.

An old friend, Coley Bartram, came to see the twenty-five-year-old Barnum at his store, and brought exciting news. Bartram had recently been in possession of 'an extraordinary negro woman', Barnum later wrote, but had sold his interest to his partner, R.W. Lindsay, who was now exhibiting this woman in Philadelphia.[335] Lindsay was struggling as a showman and was anxious to sell. Bartram handed Barnum a copy of the *Pennsylvania Inquirer* and, as Barnum began to read, his eyes lit up:

CURIOSITY— The citizens of Philadelphia and its vicinity have an opportunity of witnessing at the Masonic Hall, one of the greatest natural curiosities ever witnessed, viz., JOICE HETH, a negress aged 161 years, who formerly belonged to the father of Gen. Washington. She has been a member of the Baptist Church one hundred and sixteen years, and can rehearse many hymns, and sing them according to former custom. She was born near the old Potomac River in Virginia, and has for ninety or one hundred years lived in Paris, Kentucky, with the Bowling family.[336]

Barnum was intrigued: here was a woman, allegedly 161 years old, associated with George Washington, the 'Father of the Nation', the first president of the US, whose life story was read by millions of American schoolchildren and adults. Barnum's entrepreneurial spirit was sparked: he sensed a new opportunity and the chance of earning some dollars. He travelled at once to Philadelphia (which, in a sad irony, had been home to the first American Anti-Slavery

Society Convention in 1833) where he was 'favourably struck', as he wrote. He gazed at Heth as she lay 'upon a high lounge in the middle of the room; her lower extremities were drawn up, with her knees elevated some two feet above the top of the lounge.' Despite her paralysed state, she was, claimed Barnum, sociable, lively and talkative, sharing with Barnum stories of 'her dear little George', at whose birth she was present; 'in fact,' she said, 'I raised him.'[337] She talked about God and her membership of the Baptist Church, and even regaled him with ancient hymns.

For the young, ambitious Barnum, Heth was too good to be true. Never one to be deceived (he preferred deceiving others), Barnum asked Lindsay, the owner of her exhibition, for proof of Heth's age. Barnum was presented with a bill of sale, dated 5 February 1727, which confirmed that Heth was the slave of Augustine Washington, the father of George Washington. Still sceptical, Barnum enquired further, asking why Heth was only recently discovered as the 161-year-old slave of the Washington family. Lindsay said that for many years she had been living in an outhouse belonging to her later slave owner, John S. Bowling of Kentucky, and no one had bothered to enquire about her age. The story only came to light when Bowling's son discovered Heth's bill of sale in the records office in Virginia. It was good enough for Barnum, who figured that any public scepticism could be used to good effect: if people weren't convinced, they might be encouraged to attend the show and discern the truth themselves. As for Barnum, he later claimed he was satisfied that Heth was really 161 years old and connected to Washington. Her stories about Washington seemed so unscripted and truthful and, as he later stressed, 'I taught her none of these things.'[338]

Yet Barnum would also claim otherwise. In fact, at one point he admitted coercion and cruelty; he even said he had crushed Heth's will with drink and starvation. But these assertions came later, and they came in a jocular tone. For now, in 1835, Barnum was earnest. He paid Lindsay $1,000 for the right to exhibit Heth, $2,000 less than the asking price, essentially leasing this elderly woman. She became his property – and his means to a new profession in freakery.

UNFORTUNATELY, WE KNOW very little about Heth, which is not uncommon considering the lack of records kept on the lives of slaves. But thanks to the painstaking research of Benjamin Reiss, professor of English and cultural historian, we have some clues.[339] Reiss concludes that she was possibly a trusted slave to William Heth through at least the 1790s, and she may have been present at his wife Eliza's miscarriage in 1793. Joice then travelled to Louisville with William's brother Andrew, and at some point after Andrew died in 1803 she was transferred to John S. Bowling, who had connections with the Heths. At this point Joice was about fifty. R.W. Lindsay then acquired from Bowling the right to exhibit her, displaying her in Ohio and the South but with limited success. Lindsay then sold on the right to exhibit her to Barnum in 1835.

It was with William and Andrew that Joice may have acquired her fascinating yarn, for the Heth family were proudly connected to George Washington, a relationship that constituted the single most important fact of their lives. Reiss wonders whether Joice may have heard the stories of the family 'fighting with, strategizing with, dining with, riding with, walking with the man whom whites already referred to as their mythical "father".'[340] Perhaps she privately mocked or publicly cajoled William, who reportedly had a good sense of humour and may have encouraged, or at least forgiven, the occasional teasing by a trusted slave. Perhaps this developed into a fully developed satire. If so, Reiss asks, 'could the career of the greatest entertainer of the nineteenth century have originated with a slave's subtle mockery of her master?'[341]

It certainly wasn't rare for slaves to mock their masters. Moreover, it is all too easy to fall into the trap of assuming that freak performers, especially black performers, were mere victims at the mercy of white tyrants. Chang and Eng proved the opposite and the picture is often, although not always, more complex. For example, Hendrik Cesars, who brought Sara Baartman to London in 1810, was actually a free black man who owned slaves. Moreover, once Baartman was onstage, there is reason to assert that she was not a passive pawn: she performed as the Hottentot Venus, thus contributing to the formation of that role. She was also possibly the publisher of certain Hottentot Venus images.

With this in mind, it is also possible to imagine that when Joice later suffered with dementia, she came to believe her make-believe routine was actually true. Indeed, she never dropped out of character and was reportedly sincere when retelling her tales. Apparently she did not even realize how famous George Washington had become. But maybe she was a good actor. Or perhaps retreating into this fantasy was better than facing her reality. Without this story her future would have been even more uncertain; perhaps she saw its value and clung to it.

AFTER ACQUIRING HETH in the summer of 1835, the same year that Chang and Eng embarked on their tour of Cuba, Barnum ambitiously proceeded with his exhibition. He hired the young lawyer Levi Lyman, a 'shrewd, sociable, and somewhat indolent Yankee' according to Barnum's autobiography, who was engaged to work as an assistant. Lyman 'possessed a good knowledge of human nature; was polite, agreeable, could converse on most subjects, and was admirably calculated to fill the position for which I engaged him', Barnum wrote.[342]

Next, Barnum struck a deal with William Niblo, an Irish immigrant who in 1828 had purchased a large plot of land on the north-east corner of Broadway and Prince Street, where he opened Niblo's Garden. This fashionable pleasure garden had an air of respectability not dissimilar to the Egyptian Hall's. Niblo's was a refuge for the 'better sort', who wandered around its grounds lined with trees and exotic flowers. Guests could rest in the large, wooden enclosures or loll under the parasols. In their signature white aprons and blue belts, African Americans served the white clientele lemonade and ice cream; no other African Americans were allowed in the garden unless they were performing. Visitors could stroll into the Hermit's Cave or Marine Cavern, or gaze at dioramas of London's Great Fire and the Israelites leaving Egypt. Come the evening, the place was ablaze with coloured-glass lanterns. The expensive entrance fee barred the lower sorts, and women could only enter if chaperoned by a man, which kept the prostitutes at bay and ensured respectability.[343] This was the right site for Heth's exhibition.

The real brains behind Niblo's Garden was Mrs Niblo: 'a shrewd business woman' who 'always attended to the details of the establishment in person, examining and auditing all the bills of the concern, and keeping a sharp eye to receipts and expenditures', according to one contemporary account.[344] It was Mrs Niblo who ran the enterprise and 'had the tact and good sense to keep her little fussy husband in the background'.[345] Nonetheless, according to Barnum, it was with William Niblo that a deal was struck: Barnum would provide an exhibition space for Heth's display, would pay for printing and advertising and even pay for a ticket-seller. In return Niblo, or more accurately his wife, would receive half the profits.

Heth was then bundled into a railway carriage and sent from Philadelphia to New York. The senile slave was about to encounter the largest city in America.

NEW YORK CHIMED with Barnum's personality: big, bustling and full of energy. The port was thriving, the recently completed Erie Canal linked the metropolis to vast agricultural regions and, by the 1830s, the city was home to around 250,000 people. New York was not yet the sprawling metropolis of today. It was certainly big, the biggest in America, filled with houses, offices, theatres, industrial buildings and warehouses, but it was more akin to an overgrown village.[346] But like modern New York, it was aggressive, pushy and fast.

There were traders, bankers, speculators, shipbuilders, craftsmen, canal diggers, cart-pullers and construction workers. A downtrodden Irish immigrant community, centred around the Five Points neighbourhood, had brought Catholicism to mostly Protestant shores. A free African-American population moved around Manhattan and Brooklyn, and a rising tide of abolitionism offered some hope to the African-American middle class, who called for equal rights.

Artisans and craftsmen lived above small businesses in places like Corlears Hook on the Lower East Side, one of the first tenement buildings in the city. New Yorkers with money could be found in the less cramped areas above Houston Street, living in marked contrast to the overcrowded quarters of New York's poorest, who were squeezed between churches, breweries and single-family homes.

Sanitation was bad. People used outhouses in the street, behind or between buildings, mixing the stench of human and animal faeces with the cloud of toxins from the tanneries, slaughterhouses and distilleries. Cholera hit in 1832, taking approximately 3,500 lives. Prostitution, public drunkenness, begging and crime were facts of life, a ripe background to the penny press' sensational stories of murder, sexual immorality and you name it. Before the formation of a professional police force in 1845, the city was patrolled by night watchmen and marshals, who struggled to contain the rising tide of crime.

New York was also one big playground. Theatres were open to all social classes, although sitting was segregated along class lines. People went not just for the plays but the acrobats, jugglers and trained animals between the acts. New York also had circus amphitheatres, such as the New Circus on Broadway and the Zoological Institute's menagerie, where for 25 cents (half price for children) New Yorkers could gaze at amazing animals, including an ostrich, a zebra, a rhino and elephants. The American Museum displayed paintings, waxworks, taxidermy and live animals. Things were slightly rougher around the Bowery, a neighbourhood in the south of the city, an 'urban underworld' thriving on cheap dance halls and popular blood sports like cockfighting.[347] Taverns and hotels held itinerant entertainments. And when you had had enough of that, the Vauxhall Gardens was one of several pleasure gardens that, from the mid-eighteenth century, began offering New Yorkers an escape from the city.

Barnum threw Heth into this world, whipping up publicity as best he could: 'I was aware of the great power of the public press,' he wrote on reflection, 'and I used it to the extent of my ability.'[348] The first thing he did was invite members of the penny and traditional press to a private viewing. Heth was laid out in Niblo's Saloon, an old converted stable in Niblo's Garden, and allegedly the editors believed her story, no doubt convinced by Barnum's and Levi Lyman's bribes. They were ready to fill their pages: 'The greatest curiosity in the world, and the most interesting, particularly to Americans, is now exhibiting at the Saloon fronting Broadway.'[349]

Heth's exhibition was worked up in an aggressive advertising campaign as Barnum commissioned posters and 'transparencies, two feet by three feet in size', which were mounted on a 'hollow frame and lighted from the inside'. They were, he wrote, 'painted in colors with white letters' reading: 'JOICE HETH 161 YEARS OLD'.[350] A short memoir of her life was also published, claiming she was born in Madagascar in 1674 and, aged fifteen, 'cruelly torn from the bosom of her parents' and imported to America as a slave.[351]

On 12 August 1835 the doors to her exhibition opened, initially from 8 a.m. to 10 p.m., but the hours were soon reduced as Heth found the displays too draining. The public entered a private chamber to confront 'this marvellous relic of antiquity', claimed one newspaper.[352] Heth was forced to shake their hands. She felt, although she couldn't see, people touching her hair and skin, some even taking her pulse. She experienced the indignity of children screaming and laughing in her face, poking and prodding her ailing body. She tried to swat them away like flies.

Once the audience had settled, the showman turned to his script. According to Barnum, 'our exhibition usually opened with a statement of the manner in which the age of Joice Heth was discovered, as well as the account of her antecedents in Virginia'.[353] Then her bill of sale, the document that denied her humanity, was read aloud. And finally Heth performed, which, because of her decrepitude, only involved answering questions that invariably explored her relationship with the Washington family. Apparently a punter asked, 'Joice, do you remember about the peach tree?' – a reference to a popular tale in which Augustine Washington finds his favourite tree chopped down and his son, George, confesses to the act. 'Yes, dat I do, very well,' Heth allegedly responded in a parody of African-American dialect. 'Well, tell it,' shouted the patron. And Heth obliged:

> 'Wy, de boys be playing in de garden—de garden be away up by
>   Missy Atwood's—de boys play, and George be dere'.
> 'Well, what did they do?', interjected the patron.
> 'Dey damage de peach tree very much—break de branches'.
> 'Well, what said master to that?', enquired the patron.

'Old Massa Wassington be very angry—de boys deny dey did'em—
young Massa George stood up like a man—"Fadda, I do
'um"—old Massa den not whup'em.'
'Why did he not whip him?', asked the patron.
'Why?—'cause he tell de truth, dear boy—'cause he tell de truth.'[354]

It's said that Heth, ever the religious woman, would frequently break out singing church hymns, waving her long-withered arm to keep the beat of the music.

This performance in a respectable and permanent venue, coupled with Barnum's advertising campaign and the presence of a lecturing showman, turned Heth's display into a freak show in all but name. For two and a half weeks the crowds poured in. Editorials proclaimed that she 'has created quite a sensation among the lovers of the curious and the marvellous; and a greater object of marvel and curiosity has never presented itself for their gratification'.[355] The Jacksonian penny press was particularly enthralled, and Barnum and Niblo were making an average of $1,500 a week. Heth received nothing, and no one seemed to question the display of a slave in a state that had outlawed slavery in 1827.

⁘⊙⊙⊙⁘

SARA BAARTMAN'S DISPLAY, back in 1810, had instigated the tradition of ethnic shows or human zoos in Europe. Chang and Eng, as racial freaks, were displayed within this tradition. So was Heth, whose exhibition, according to Reiss, marked the conception of ethnic shows in America, developed by Barnum and others later in the century.[356]

Her exhibition echoed the mocking of African Americans seen in blackface minstrels, in which African Americans were depicted as comical, lazy, backward, loud and grotesque. By the mid-nineteenth century, this racial derision extended to the Irish, Native Americans and Asians, with Chang and Eng parodied by the minstrel performers Charles Fox and Frank B. Converse.[357] Heth's disability was another crucial component of the 'show', placing her in the tradition of freak shows: 'Her appearance is very much like an Egyptian mummy,' wrote the *New York Evening Star*; 'her weight is said to be less than fifty pounds; her feet have shrunk to mere skin and bone,' noted the *New York Sun*.[358] Much like Chang and Eng (and indeed Baartman), the lines between ethnic shows and freak shows were blurred: racial and physical difference could meet together onstage.

As with the ambiguity of the freak, there was a tension in Heth's display. While she was positioned as racially and physiologically inferior, she was also associated with the Father of the Nation, which made her special and part of America's story. This led one irate reader of the *New York Sun* to write to the editor denouncing the exploitation of one so closely connected with the nation's hero: 'She is the common property of our country – she is identified with the foundation, rise, and progress of our government – she is the sole remaining tie of mortality which connects us to him who was "first in war, first in peace, and first in the hearts of his countrymen" – and as such, we should protect and honor her, and not suffer her to be kept for a show, like a wild beast, to fill the coffers of mercenary men.'[359]

Despite this, Heth remained 'property'. And this property was about to be transported across the eastern frontier following the same channels of itinerancy that Chang and Eng were taking at exactly the same time.

CHAPTER NINE

STARDOM OF SORTS

A CCORDING TO THE *New York Herald*, Joice Heth was 'bundled up for a tour through the country to make the people stare – the curious wonder – and all contribute their half dollar to see the sight'.[360] For five further months she was hauled across the north-east, displayed in taverns, inns, museums, railway houses and concert halls. During this tour, on the 27 August 1835, she was placed on a steamboat destined for Providence, Rhode Island, a conservative, religious, abolitionist capital. Shortly after arrival, Barnum audaciously claimed that Heth's exhibition favoured the abolitionist cause, promising that the proceeds of the performance would go to freeing her enslaved grandchildren. 'Viva la humbug!' Barnum later added.[361]

Abolitionists in Providence, unaware of Barnum's humbug, were supportive of the good cause the exhibition was allegedly advocating. The *Providence Republican Herald* reported that 'we look on this extraordinary specimen of humanity, with something bordering on awe and veneration'.[362] After her success she was shipped off to Boston where, according to Barnum, 'the fame of Joice had preceded her, the city was well posted with large bills announcing her coming, and the newspapers had heralded her anticipated arrival in such a multiplicity of styles, that the public curiosity was on tip-toe'.[363] But the *Boston*

Courier was not so positive about her display: 'We had not anticipated a sight so melancholy and so disgusting.'[364]

These mixed responses revealed a cultural discomfort which, at the root, arose from the question of whether culture should be a populist free-for-all (a view subscribed to by the newspaper editors in New York) or controlled, managed and refined (agreed the Boston media who aligned more with the genteel classes).[365] The same disagreements applied when Chang and Eng were the subjects of censure at the General Assembly in Virginia, and even earlier when they performed at the Egyptian Hall in London and some lamented the commercial, popular and 'frivolous' displays of freaks.[366] Chang and Eng, and indeed Heth, were not just crossing large territories but two different epochs: an earlier era that condemned itinerant shows and a new age that thrived off the commercialization of fun.

Barnum was immune to these concerns; he was seeking to make Heth's exhibition popular and more lucrative, and when audience numbers began to decrease in Boston he unleashed more humbug by peddling the story that Heth was not, in fact, a human being: 'What purports to be a remarkably old woman,' ran the press, 'is simply a curiously constructed automaton, made up of whalebone, india-rubber, and numberless springs.'[367] Suddenly, people flocked to Heth's exhibition to decipher, by look and touch, whether this old woman was really living or simply a machine. In the process Barnum was refining his particular mode of popular culture: an 'artful deception' that provoked questions of authenticity and reliability while weaving illusionism and realism into the exhibition.[368]

After Boston, Heth was brought back for performances in New York, then New Haven, back to New York, Newark, New York again, and then to Albany and on and on. As she was transported, she suffered. She grew increasingly tired, weary and ill. Her gruelling schedule, performances six days a week for up to eight hours a day, were draining. By January 1836 Barnum had no choice: the exhibitions were cancelled. Heth was exhausted and sent to Bethel to recoup in the house of Barnum's half-brother Philo. A month later a horse-drawn sleigh arrived at Barnum's boarding house in New York. The driver handed Barnum a letter: Joice Heth had died; the corpse was in the sleigh. The display of Joice Heth was about to take an even darker turn.

ON 25 FEBRUARY 1836, at the City Saloon exhibition hall, a diorama display was opened to the public. However, the throng that filled the saloon, which stood next to the American Museum on Broadway, were not going to see a three-dimensional model. They were attending an 'anatomical examination'.[369] The 1,500 spectators paid 50 cents' admission to Barnum, the smiling showman; physicians, students, clergymen and the press crowded in, ostensibly in the name of science.

Around 12 o'clock Heth's body was brought into the amphitheatre and placed on an operating table made especially for the occasion. Encircling the table were four men: Dr David L. Rogers, professor of surgery at the New York College of Physicians and Surgeons, Barnum, his sidekick Lyman and a reporter.

Rogers placed his instruments on the table. He rolled up his sleeves and, as Barnum later wrote, 'with an air of triumph upon the assemblage ... looked, and doubtless felt, as if this was the proudest moment of his life'.[370] Overcome with anticipation and emotion, Rogers began the circus with an announcement that amounted to a showman's spiel: 'Gentlemen, you see before you the most important subject that ever graced a dissecting table. Never since the flood, have we heard of a person reaching the astonishing age which this woman undoubtably has. We shall, unquestionably, in the course of this examination, make many important discoveries not laid down in our medical books.'[371]

Rogers informed the audience that he expected hardened arteries and organs as proof of Heth's extreme age. He had been present at a previous postmortem in Italy, on a woman allegedly 116 years old, so he knew what to look for. He probably injected the cadaver with a concoction of mercury, varnish, spirits and vermilion to suppress the odours and preserve the tissue.[372]

He cut into Heth's chest, which appeared natural and healthy. He sliced open the heart. With some difficulty and force he proceeded to prise open her skull. This was not so much a medical investigation as a ghastly spectacle of dissected flesh, a 'bloodily invasive circus' in front of a live audience.[373] Echoing the fate of Sara Baartman, and many others too, this was science as rape, and the 'entertainers' Barnum and Lyman made around $700 off it.

The climax of the event occurred when Rogers, after dissecting his cadaver, was forced to conclude to an astonished audience: 'Joice Heth could not have been more than seventy-five, or, at the utmost eighty years of age!'[374] Everybody had been duped.

ON 26 FEBRUARY 1836 the *New York Sun* ran the story: 'DISSECTION OF JOICE HETH.—PRECIOUS HUMBUG EXPOSED'.[375] A day later the *New York Evening Star* refuted the revelation: Heth *was* around 161 years old.[376] The *New York Sun* declared that 'the exhibitor of this old negress, admitted … that she was not "the oldest woman in the world"'.[377] Astonishingly, the editor of the *New York Herald*, James Gordon Bennett, declared in his paper: 'Joice Heth is not dead. On Wednesday last, as we learn from the best authority, she was living at Hebron, in Connecticut.'[378]

Just a few days later, on 1 March 1836, the *New York Sun* enjoyed a good dig at Bennett, claiming that the exhibitors of Heth 'have been amusing themselves with hoaxing some stupid editors'.[379] The gibe was justified: Bennett had been humbugged, although he defended the story and even published fictitious certificates to corroborate his piece. Yet behind his peddling of fake news and alternative facts, Bennett was livid because he knew he'd been fooled.

This 'best authority' was Levi Lyman, Barnum's sidekick. In September 1836 Lyman offered to make good by offering Bennett the real story of Joice Heth. The first instalment was published on the *Herald*'s front page on 8 September 1836. The paper had only recently started to use their front page for news rather than adverts, so this article, entitled 'The Joice Heth Hoax', was one of the first front-page news stories in American history. Bennett also published an illustration of Heth in the third installment, one of the first times an illustration had accompanied a news story in American history.[380] Bennett was making media history, but he was making it with fake, freak news.

The first installment claimed that 'a gentleman from New England' (read Barnum), discovered 'an old negro woman who had been blind and in her bed for 30 years, and otherwise was a great natural curiosity'. The New Englander decided to display her and began spinning the yarn that she was born and raised 'in the family of the sainted Washington'. The paper went on: 'Joice herself, after a good deal of trouble was taught her lesson – how to respond to questions respecting Washington. In completing this part of the business they had some difficulty. She would occasionally get cross and angry. On such occasions she burst forth "God damn you".'[381]

To calm her down, it was claimed Heth was given whiskey, muttering in thanks, 'well massa, dat be good'. The story added that Heth, who previously had a 'wild, huge, and unregulated appetite', was denied proper food and instead fed eggs and whiskey, 'till she was brought down to mere muscle and bone'. This supposedly improved her mental powers and also left her with an emaciated figure that made her appear older, which was an effect helped when her teeth were forcibly removed.[382]

Bennett continued publishing these tall tales until he finally realized he was being humbugged yet again and the installments of the Joice Heth hoax abruptly ceased. According to Barnum, Bennett had peddled a 'ridiculous story, being a ten times greater humbug than the one before'.[383] But despite the lies, something novel was happening: Joice Heth had become a cultural phenomenon, and the history of freakery had entered new terrain.

By the mid-1830s newspapers were undergoing a revolution. Previously they were largely the preserve of the elite: supported by political parties, government contracts and individual subscriptions from wealthy readers. Between 1790 and 1835, however, newspapers rose in numbers from 106 to 1,258, spurred by the federal government's postal system and the Postal Service Act of 1792, which subsidized papers. And the content changed. In came sensational stories that included news about common people, for common people. The fairground barkers morphed into newsboys in the streets who'd shout out the latest headlines.[384] The pages had adverts for the likes of Joice Heth and 'living curiosities' on display. The new penny press was cheap, prolific and contributing to the emergence of a mass urban culture, built in part on increased urbanization, better communication and travel, and a population hungry for entertainment.[385] And now Heth's story was at the centre of the penny press, and thus popular culture too.

This, in turn, marks a crucial shift in the history of freakery. Thanks to an emerging popular culture, the once transitory and localized displays of living curiosities were no longer marginal. Another audience was also being created, a secondary public that did not necessarily attend the shows but knew about them through the press. A new public curiosity developed: intrigued about the performers in the papers but unclear as to whether they were genuine or fake, which was a great boost to the shows themselves.[386]

The 1830s, then, was a decade of freak show evolution. Heth and Chang and Eng had roamed the landscape, exhibiting in traditional inns and taverns, but were also attached to more formal, respectable and commercial organizations. At the same time, thanks to the press, freak performers were finding a new stage at the centre, rather than at the margins, of popular culture. Collectively these developments foreshadowed the coming of the Victorian 'freak industry'.

———•⊚⊚•———

BARNUM HADN'T QUITE finished with Heth. In 1841 he wrote another version of events that closely mirrored Lyman's account to Bennett. *The Adventures of an Adventurer: Being Some Passages in the Life of Barnaby Diddleum* was a satirical, semi-autobiographical novella published in the *New York Atlas* over twelve weeks. The readers of this periodical were, like those of the New York penny press, white-collar workers and Jacksonian Democrats. The *Atlas* dealt in lowbrow entertainment and serialized fiction, and had a massive circulation, being sold at some 150 locations in Lower Manhattan alone, which was on a par with the more respectable 'Sunday Sheets'.[387]

In this satire, which had an air of authenticity, Barnum claimed he discovered 'the negro wench' who, 'having been bed ridden for twelve years was so wrinkled and shrivelled and drawn up by disease, that her appearance indicated great longevity'. Barnum decided to make Heth look even older by extracting her teeth, 'which caused her cheeks to sink in, and then I stated that she was the nurse of the immortal George Washington'. His novella reeks of coercion: 'My black beauty', wrote Barnum, was 'commanded at my sovereign will and pleasure'. He continued: 'I soon got Joyce [*sic*] into training, and ... as willing to do my bidding as the slave of the lamp was to obey Aladdin. I discovered her weak point. It was discovered in seven letters—W-H-I-S-K-E-Y.'[388]

Barnum revealed how he taught Heth the Washington stories and doctored documents to attest to her extreme longevity. On one level this satire, like the *Herald*'s Joice Heth hoax, was fiction. We know, for instance, that Heth was displayed as the nurse of George Washington before coming under Barnum's management. Yet the stories were 'by no means *all* a fantasy', as Reiss noted.[389] They were repeated years later in another satirical text, *The Autobiography of Petite Bunkum* (1855), most likely written by Barnum.

But then in Barnum's autobiographies, published in 1854 and 1869 (bestsellers running into multiple editions), he distanced himself from the Heth hoax. He abandoned his earlier claims of control. Yet these later accounts were written when Barnum was remoulding his public identity towards social respectability. By 1865, after thirty years shaping popular culture, he was also entering politics as an abolitionist Unionist Republican. No wonder he wanted to sanitize the Heth stories and minimize his involvement.

In his earlier years, however, he was desperate to make a name for himself and we should not discount his propensity for cruelty while, of course, recognizing that he was a man of his times. He may have starved and brutalized Heth's body (not least in her public dissection), and his own claims of coercion, and tone of contempt, cannot be discounted as pure fiction.

Indeed, this was not the last time he brutalized a slave. Between 1837 and 1838 Barnum bought another slave and, when he suspected him of stealing, whipped him fifty times and sold him at auction in New Orleans.[390] Furthermore, throughout his career he faced allegations of animal and child cruelty. Barnum, then, was not as lovable as Hugh Jackman's portrayal in the 2017 Hollywood blockbuster, *The Greatest Showman*.

CHAPTER TEN

THE AMERICAN MUSEUM

I N 1836, WITH Joice Heth dead and dissected, Barnum joined a circus. He accompanied the scores of itinerant performers travelling across America, working with the Old Columbian Circus run by Aaron Turner, an old showman and 'original genius', wrote Barnum, who was 'a good judge of human nature', a 'practical joker' and a man from whom Barnum could learn.[391] Barnum worked as the secretary, treasurer and ticket-seller, journeying with wagons, horses, tents and carriages in an outfit of thirty-five people, including equestrian performers, a magician (who doubled as a clown), a band and Signor Vivalla, who executed 'remarkable feats of balancing, plate spinning, stilt walking'.[392]

The circus moved from Connecticut, where it was outlawed, into Massachusetts and then down into South Carolina, joining the dozen or so small-scale circuses travelling around the East Coast. During his six months with Turner, Barnum learned the tricks of the trade and, by October 1836, having made around $600 profit, he ventured out alone with, as he recalled, 'Vivalla and a negro singer and dancer' and 'several musicians, horses, wagons, and a small canvass tent'; a motley crew more variety show than circus, which travelled south to Alabama, then into the Carolinas.[393]

Aged twenty-six, Barnum was learning on the job, but this was a life he didn't like. He lacked a base and life as an itinerant entertainer was marked by near-death moments, accidents on the road, longing for family, trouble from the law, unreliable crew members and dodgy business partners. Circuses were seen as morally dubious and disreputable, so the ever ambitious Barnum was lumping himself with social pariahs. He wrote: 'I was thoroughly disgusted with the life of an itinerant showman; and though I felt that I could succeed in that line, I always regarded it, not as an end, but as a means to something better in life.'[394] That 'something better' was, as he wrote, 'a respectable, permanent business'.[395]

In autumn 1841 an opportunity presented itself: Scudder's American Museum in New York was for sale. Situated on the corner of Broadway and Ann Street, the museum contained around 150,000 natural curiosities, including natural history specimens such as minerals, fossils and stuffed animals. To attract a broader range of customers, John Scudder Jr. introduced variety performances, minstrel shows and living freak performers. His showmanship helped turn a healthy profit for the museum despite the financial crash of 1837, and the museum was earning an average of $7,000 annually.

Scudder had started the process of transforming these once civic institutions into centres of entertainment, appealing to a mass audience with variety entertainment (much like William Bullock's nephew, George Lackington, did at the Egyptian Hall in London). But Scudder's had also seen better days: once valued at $25,000, the museum was now going for $15,000, although even that reduced rate was way beyond Barnum's price range. Yet in a series of Barnumesque moves and manoeuvres, proudly retold in his numerous autobiographies, the Great Showman struck a deal with the museum's owner, Francis Olmsted. Barnum outwitted a company of speculators and managed to purchase the museum on credit. Within a year he'd paid back every cent, and in the process he'd established the freak show at the centre of the amusement industry.

THE AMERICAN MUSEUM, a white stoned building five storeys high, became Barnum's world. With his wife, Charity, and daughter Caroline, he moved into the museum's billiard hall, which was converted into a ground-floor apartment. All necessities were nearby: his hairdresser was a block to the east at 2 Beekman Street; lunch and dinner could be had at Sweeney's Restaurant, Ann Street; and, for business, the newspaper district, including the *New York Herald*, *New York Sun* and *New-York Tribune*, was just behind the museum to the east. Nearby Chatham Street was lined with laundries and shops, while the Bowery had working-class entertainments and saloons. From these quarters, future customers would descend.[396]

A hand-coloured lithograph looks south from City Hall Park, a popular meeting place among the wealthy, and shows Barnum's American Museum to the left and the recently built white-granite Astor House hotel to the right. Directly opposite the museum, slightly covered by a tree, is St Paul's Chapel, which was completed in 1766 in the late Georgian style. In the distance is the steeple of Trinity Church.

Broadway, that 'Great Avenue', ran for more than three miles from the Battery in the north, heading south into country lanes. The main stretch was one of the busiest in the world, with more carriages, horses, wagons and people than any street in London or Paris. It was fashionable yet dirty, with pedestrians spitting, pigs roaming and horse manure festering as well as badly managed sewers. Yet it was a 'moving panorama of human life', as one observer noted, where 'you may see the lean lanky Puritan from the east, with keen eye and demure aspect, rubbing shoulders with a coloured dandy, whose ebony figures are hooped in gold'.[397] At the intersection of upper- and lower-class neighbourhoods, the full pantheon of New York life paraded. And right in this mix stood Barnum's American Museum.

Broadway, New York, c. 1846. You can see Barnum's American Museum on the left.

There was, however, steep competition, with New Yorkers being distracted by a plethora of theatres, museums and pleasure gardens, not to mention the concert halls, lecture halls, saloons, restaurants, hotels and even churches, all of which provided some form of entertainment. By 1850 Barnum would be competing against six theatres, four summer pleasure gardens and over sixty other amusements halls.[398] He needed to grab his audience's attention and so he embarked on an impressive transformation of the building. As he wrote: 'It was my monomania to make the Museum the town wonder and town talk.'[399]

He flew large, colourful national flags along the museum's rooftops and, on the second floor, built a balcony for guests. On the roof he installed a massive lighthouse lamp, the city's first spotlight, which beamed up and down Broadway at night. He also astonished New Yorkers when, one morning, they saw large, garish posters between the hundred windows of the museum. They advertised all forms of exotic animals, from polar bears to lions, transforming the drab building into an exciting centre of wonders which, for a mere 25 cents, could be viewed by all, with half price for children and even African Americans allowed on certain days.

By June 1842 Barnum had established a roof garden where customers could take in the magnificent views while listening to a brass band that apparently played so terribly that passers-by beneath escaped into the museum to avoid the racket. If you survived the band there were comfortable chairs beneath the awnings, ice creams, other refreshments and, at night, illuminated balloons. A one-hundred-jet fountain was later installed on the top floor.

And the excitement did not stop there. Barnum bolstered the collection of curiosities which, by 1849, included around 600,000 artefacts (by 1864 the collection had ballooned to over 850,000 items). The museum's Lecture Room (really a large theatre) hosted afternoon and evening performances featuring even more curiosities. Visitors were struck by the array of acts: a Chinese juggler, a serpent charmer, magicians, ventriloquists, gypsy fortune tellers, trained fleas, Indian chiefs from the Rocky Mountains and performing animals including chickens, dogs and a python. There were also dioramas, panoramas, animated tableaux, musical instruments, a model city of Paris, the skin of a bald eagle, dwarfs, albinos, giants, fat people and 'armless wonders'.

It would be no good, Barnum reasoned, if people went inside only to be disappointed with what they found. But 'To send away my visitors more than doubly satisfied, was to induce them to come again and to bring their friends.'[400] This was as true for genuine exhibits as it was for the fake ones, and these were a veritable draw, contributing to his reputation as the self-proclaimed Prince of Humbugs which, according to the nineteenth-century edition of

Merriam-Webster's dictionary, as a noun meant 'imposition under fair pretences' and, as a verb, 'to deceive; to impose'.[401] In Barnum's book *The Humbugs of the World* (1866), he was keen to stress that a humbug did not include criminals and swindlers, and that a humbug might be 'putting on glittering appearances' to 'suddenly arrest public attention, and attract the public eye'; he is an 'honest man' who gives the public their money's worth.[402] So, as Barnum wrote in his autobiography:

> *If I have exhibited a questionable dead mermaid in my Museum, it should not be overlooked that I have also exhibited cameleopards, a rhinoceros, grisly bears, orang-outangs [sic], great serpents, etc., … and I should hope that a little 'clap-trap' occasionally, in the way of transparencies, flags, exaggerated pictures, and puffing advertisements, might find offset in a wilderness of wonderful, instructive, and amusing realities.*[403]

Under this philosophy of humbug, Barnum had no qualms advertising the American Museum's 'Great Model of Niagara Falls With Real Water' (in reality an 18in miniature model), the 'Captain Cook Club' used to kill the British explorer (in reality one of many Indian war clubs owned by Barnum), or the 'Wonder of Creation – the Fejee Mermaid', depicted as a beautiful, naked mermaid (in reality a fish's tail sown onto a monkey's head).[404]

Barnum got his hands on the mermaid in 1842 thanks to his friend Moses Kimball, proprietor of the Boston Museum. Barnum knew mermaids didn't exist, so he sourced Dr Griffin, a supposed agent of the Lyceum of Natural History in London, who confirmed the veracity of this 'mermaid taken among the Fejee Islands'.[405] At the same time Barnum sent excited letters about the mermaid to New York editors. The city started to get curious.

Luckily for Barnum, Griffin was also a seemingly respectable and educated gentleman who happily showed his mermaid to the proprietor of a hotel in which he stayed in Philadelphia. Mesmerized, the proprietor invited his friends – including newspaper editors – to take a peek, and they spread the news through their pages. The story reached New York again, and the city's curiosity was piqued yet further.

Griffin's next stop was New York, and reporters rushed to his hotel when he arrived. He kindly let them see the mermaid. Naturally, the editors wrote this up and Barnum provided them with woodcuts that depicted three beautiful siren mermaids. They did not encapsulate the reality, a dried-up-looking piece of taxidermy, but no matter: they were printed and curiosity reached fever pitch. This was fuelled as Barnum printed ten thousand pamphlets confirming the authenticity of mermaids in natural history; they were distributed by boys in the street and sold for a penny.

Some were credulous, others incredulous, but when the mermaid was finally shown at the Concert Hall, 404 Broadway, people wanted to see for themselves. The crowds poured in, greeted by Griffin, who told the story of the mermaid, provided a scientific explanation and willingly answered questions. No one seemed to realize that Griffin was actually Levi Lyman, Barnum's accomplice, who some years earlier had helped arrange the exhibition of Joice Heth. No one seemed to realize, either, that the Lyceum of Natural History never existed. The whole thing was a hoax. Yet people were aware that 'the large transparency in front of the hall, representing a beautiful creature half woman and half fish, about eight feet in length', Barnum gleefully reported, was in reality 'a black-looking specimen of dried monkey and fish that a boy a few years old could easily run away with under his arms.'[406]

Still, they had already parted with their money and Griffin, the press and the pamphlets reported the possibility of mermaids, so, they reasoned, perhaps this really was a true wonder of nature. When the display transferred to Barnum's American Museum after only a week at the Concert Hall, the showman cashed in, making thousands and putting his museum on the map.

———◦◦◦———

OVER THE YEARS, the American Museum would host a dizzying array of exhibits both fake and real, from the Lancashire Bell Ringers who used their bells to create melodious sounds to the Orpheon Family of incredible gymnasts. The American Museum would even become a theatre, featuring plays such as *Beauty and the Beast*, *Uncle Tom's Cabin* and *The Drunkard*, an affair about temperance (Barnum's religious calling), which was the first New York premiere to run to over a hundred successive performances, delivered by a newly formed acting company connected to the museum. But the greatest events were the freak performers, who were promoted as a central part of Barnum's museum.

There was Vantile Mack who, aged seven and displayed by his mother, weighed 18st with a 21in chest; Mme Josephine Fortune Clofullia, a Swiss Bearded Lady; the Infant Esau, her body covered in hair; the Wonder of the World, the armless 4½ft high Mr Nellis; and an assortment of other 'born freaks', 'exotic freaks' and 'self-made freaks'. Their presence at the American Museum marked the culmination of shifts and developments that were detectable in the 1830s with the likes of Chang and Eng and Heth.

Barnum's American Museum did one better than the Egyptian Hall, Niblo's Garden and the American Museum under Scudder's management: he turned his museum into an unashamedly popular, commercial and respectable venue that was a central part of an emerging entertainment industry. This, in turn, marked a turning point in the history of freakery. Before the 1840s, generally speaking, living curiosities, be they dwarfs, giants, Siamese twins, bearded ladies, savages, fire-eaters or exotic animals, were displayed in transitory and informal sites, often as single attractions connected to carnivalesque fairs and other channels of itinerancy. Occasionally, these curiosities were managed by an itinerant showman. Sometimes, a human curiosity could be seen in a museum, but they were not a central part of the collection; they were merely a living addition to the inanimate marvels inside. This was broadly the experience of all the performers we have met thus far. But Barnum's American Museum ensured that human curiosities were a big part of the attraction. Freak performers streamed into his museum and, as a result, found themselves attached to a formal, urban and modern organization which, thanks to Barnum, was becoming a central pillar of popular culture.

Barnum also effected a great personal transformation. Before 1841 he was merely one of many showmen who travelled the itinerant circuits, displaying an array of exhibits. He was a pre-industrial showman, living hand to mouth 'at the bottom round of fortune's ladder', he claimed, a wanderer barking and hawking dubious goods but harking after a more respectable, permanent enterprise.[407] He found this at the American Museum.

Barnum's museum brought elite and popular culture under one roof. The working, middle and upper classes, natives and immigrants, children and adults, men and women would all rub shoulders in a dizzying and dazzling display of wonders packaged within an intensely democratic experience. For the same small fee, just 25 cents, nearly everyone and anyone could enjoy the miscellaneous collection of curiosities and freak performers, ensuring an element of egalitarianism that dismantled class divisions (although once again it is worth noting that African Americans were only allowed in on certain days). In many ways his museum was popular culture's answer to the ideals of Jacksonian democracy which, during the 1830s, was asserting the rights of the 'common man'. These same people, who were now enjoying the penny press, were warmly invited inside the American Museum.

What's more, Barnum designed a space that was safe and respectable for middle-class women and families. The American Museum prided itself on being devoid of lewd behaviour; shows were morally uplifting and thoroughly (well, ostensibly) educational: 'We Study to Please' was the slogan of Barnum's theatre.[408] The museum was more entertainment than edification, but by promoting the latter, with a rhetoric of 'moral elevation, scientific instruction, and cultural refinement', Barnum catered to the widespread (often middle-class) belief that leisure should be constructive and didactic, not wasteful and idle.[409] In short, he appropriated high culture and brought it down to the level of commercial entertainment, accessible to all classes of people.

This mirrored a general trend between the 1840s and 1860s when all manner of popular amusements drifted towards what the historian LeRoy Ashby described as a 'middle-class consumerism' that bolstered profits and cemented a new mass culture open to every social class.[410] A similar move was detectable in Britain too, where violent pre-industrial entertainments often associated with the working classes were slowly reformed to pacify the middle classes; although, as we will see in the Final Act, this narrative was by no means simple or absolute.[411] The courting of the middle classes, who cherished the values of domesticity and respectability, was part of a broader 'taming of rough amusements', seen in the legislative assaults on the fairs in England and the ingenuity of Barnum's American Museum.[412]

Barnum also transformed the very nature of museums from early nineteenth-century proprietary museums (similar to Europe's Cabinets of Curiosities), where patrons could pay to see instructive artefacts in centres of science, into the popular dime museum, a place of respectable amusement for a mass audience. As Andrea Stulman Dennett noted, Barnum 'made the dime museum a fixture of the American cultural landscape'; 'his museum was the prototype – all later museums followed his pattern'.[413]

This is crucial for understanding the age of the freak, as the dime museum became a prime spot for freak performers, especially from the 1870s, when the museums spread across America and featured in almost every city (often with three or four in any one location).[414] The dime museum, an American journalist wrote in 1896, 'is simply an exhibition of monstrosities, genuine and artificial, and the public is admitted to view them on payment of a dime', which ensured a broader audience could attend. 'These monstrosities, known in the "profession" as "freaks",' the piece continued, 'seem to be produced in quantities to supply the demand', a reminder that some patrons recognized the fabrication of freak identities on stage.[415] There was plenty of false advertising and freak identities that were pure fiction: the Wild Men of Borneo were Irishmen, for example, and the Chinese Sword Swallower a Frenchman. But, as was Barnum's earliest intention, these humbugs occurred in a space akin to a respectable family resort, thus permissible to the middle classes, with any deceptions 'done for the amusement and instruction of the public', claimed one dime museum proprietor.[416]

B ARNUM HAD THE skill, business acumen and showman's hullabaloo to make his enterprise a success. By late 1842, a year after Barnum purchased the museum, he had earned $28,000, which was $17,000 more than the previous year. He sold more than 30 million tickets in the years he ran the establishment, until 1865, when the museum burnt to the ground.[417] During this period, he was tireless in developing his palace of wonders.

In the 1850s Barnum invested $50,000 in the museum. The Lecture Room (renamed the Moral Lecture Room, in a nod to the middle classes) was transformed into a three-storey auditorium with a balcony, box seating and 3,000 seats. A new grand staircase was constructed, leading patrons to the Cosmorama Department, the Second Saloon (with natural history specimens) and the Third Saloon of miscellany. There was also the Aquaria Department, the Fifth Saloon (with paintings and taxidermy), the Sixth Saloon of yet more curiosities and the Seventh Saloon that included the Happy Family – over sixty animals of different species allegedly living happily together in one cage.

During the Civil War the museum became a shrine to the Unionist cause. The giants, dwarfs and automatons were dressed in Yankee uniforms, patriotic dramas were held twice daily and war-related exhibits were brought to the museum. In June 1864 Miss Major Pauline Cushman, the famous Unionist spy, described her exploits and adventures. The Civil War photographer Mathew Brady, who had a studio directly opposite the museum, took a *carte-de-visite* portrait of Cushman, plus numerous freak performers, which were sold at the museum.

Due to his success, Barnum could add to his entertainment portfolio. Two years after he purchased the American Museum, he bought Peale's New York Museum; in 1845 he bought the Baltimore Museum and in 1849 the Philadelphia Museum. His wealth was epitomized in Iranistan, an oriental mansion loosely modelled on the Royal Pavilion of King George IV, which synthesized Moorish, Byzantine and Turkish architecture with arches, columns, domes and towers that created a dreamlike fairy world of exotic grandeur.

Between 1850 and 1852 he managed a highly lucrative tour with the operatic singer Jenny Lind, the Swedish Nightingale, once again courting a respectable form of entertainment, and in 1851 he established Barnum's Great Asiatic Caravan, Museum and Menagerie – a forerunner to the conglomerate circuses that would secure his legacy as a giant of the amusement world (and which we'll return to later). The Asiatic Caravan was essentially a circus but, by refusing to use that term, Barnum was once again presenting his entertainment as respectable (the circus was still seen as disreputable), just as he had done with the freak show.[418] Already by 1854 he was being praised as 'the most celebrated man for enterprise, and second in wealth'.[419]

Nonetheless, for all the success, Barnum still needed good performers. He had the ingenuity, the perfect stage and the changing economic and cultural conditions on his side, but he also needed the stars. And there was one in particular who, a year after Barnum purchased the American Museum, helped cement and build his celebrity and legacy. This performer, Charles Sherwood Stratton, made his debut at the American Museum in 1842, quickly becoming one of the greatest performers of the century, the first freak performer to meet Her Majesty Queen Victoria, and the first to meet with numerous American presidents. Stratton was one of the world's first international celebrities; he popularized the freak show in America, Britain and Europe; and he was the man who married Lavinia Warren in a ceremony that distracted the nation during the height of the Civil War. Alongside Barnum, Stratton helped turn the freak show as a newly formed Victorian institution into an international entertainment industry. And when Barnum first met Stratton in the winter of 1842, displaying him at the American Museum before the year was out, Charles Stratton was only four years old.

ACT THREE

❧

DOUBLE ACT

CHAPTER ELEVEN

BRIDGEPORT BABY

A T FIVE MONTHS old, Charley, as his mother called him, stopped growing. He measured around 25in, his feet were 3in long and he weighed approximately 15lb. On his first birthday, on 4 January 1839, he remained exactly the same height and weight.

This was peculiar because, in every other respect, Charley was normal; in fact, he was born a large baby, weighing 9lb 2oz. He was 'perfectly' proportioned with his arms, legs, back and head all symmetrical. He was not sickly. He was not malnourished. Charley's parents had no idea why their baby had stopped growing. Their doctor, a graduate of New Haven Medical College, was equally perplexed.

One answer, which worried Charley's parents, suggested that it might have something to do with the theory of maternal impressions. This ancient idea maintained that if a pregnant woman was exposed to an external shock that induced stress, the child in her uterus could be 'marked' in some way.[420] And, indeed, just before Charley was born, his mother, Cynthia Stratton, had seen the family puppy drown in the Pequonnock River, so she worried that she was to blame for her son's stunted growth. The doctor assured Cynthia that this was not the case, but he could offer no explanation why their son was so small.

It was certainly not hereditary as there was nothing in the family line to account for Charley's size.[421]

Today we know that his pituitary gland was not producing enough growth hormone, but at the time people could only wonder why he was so small. It remained a source of anxiety to the family and a cause of curiosity for the residents of Bridgeport, Connecticut, where Charley was born and raised.

⁘

W HEN CHARLES STRATTON was born, Bridgeport was still a fledgling community in the state of Connecticut. It was nestled in the south of Fairfield County, along the coast of Long Island Sound, and was originally home to Pequonnock Native Americans of the Paugussett tribe. From the seventeenth century Bridgeport emerged as a small Puritan community with around two hundred settlers who worshipped at the small Congregational church. This was in a rural setting with flat meadows, rolling hills, muddy streets, gravel sidewalks and roaming cows. The geography ensured that early colonists fished and whaled in the Atlantic Ocean and farmed the broad meadows. At the falls of the Pequonnock River, the first mill to produce white notepaper had been running since 1826. That same decade free African Americans started settling in a neighbourhood that became known as Little Liberia, in today's South End of Bridgeport.

In 1836, two years before Charles Stratton was born, the Housatonic Railroad was chartered, paving the way for a new railway and the growth spurt of the town. By 1840 Bridgeport was connected to New Milford, with trains travelling back and forth from New York City. As a result East Bridgeport was transformed from farmland into an industrial landscape: bridges were constructed over the Pequonnock River; the population of the town increased; a business district was established;

local hotels and convenience stores popped up; and Bridgeport's economy shifted from agriculture into a mercantile and manufacturing hub. The city was fast becoming an economic powerhouse producing everything from sewing machines to ammunition.

Charles could be spotted sitting on the wagon of the local Dutch baker, Henry Seltsem, who travelled across town selling buns, or with his mother as she cleaned the Daniel Sterling House, a hotel situated at Main and Wall Streets. He may also have been seen on Sundays at St John's Episcopal church, where he was baptized. His mother, Cynthia, was a disgruntled, illiterate woman, prone to swearing and criticizing her first cousin cum husband, Seth Sherwood, a local carpenter who had served as a private in the Light Artillery of Bridgeport but was poorer and seemingly less able than the rest of his family. Sporting a black beard, Sherwood could frequently be seen at the local watering hole, drinking heavily with friends, and was later chastised by his wife for never amounting to anything. The family were relatively poor, living in a traditional New England saltbox house with their son and two daughters, Frances Jane and Mary Elizabeth. But things soon changed when Barnum came to town.[422]

⟋ ∞⟍

THE WINTER OF 1842 was exceptionally cold on the East Coast of America. The Hudson River was frozen, and no boats were sailing. Barnum, who was in Albany on business but needing to get back to Manhattan, boarded the Housatonic Railroad. He stopped for one night in Bridgeport, where he met his half-brother Philo Fairchild Barnum, who managed a local hotel, the Franklin House, and who'd previously put up Joice Heth following her illness from the tours with Barnum. The showman was still revelling in his purchase of the American Museum which, a year into his ownership, had become the talk of New York City, and he was always on the lookout for novelties to add to his ever growing collection. So when Philo told Barnum about the young Charles Stratton – four years old and still the same height as when he was five months old – Barnum immediately invited the Strattons to his brother's hotel. Barnum recalled:

He was the smallest child I ever saw that could walk alone. He was not two feet in height, and weighed less than sixteen pounds. He was a bright-eyed little fellow, with light hair and ruddy cheeks, was perfectly healthy, and as symmetrical as an Apollo. He was exceedingly bashful, but after some coaxing he was induced to converse with me, and informed me that his name was CHARLES S. STRATTON, son of Sherwood E. Stratton.[423]

There are numerous stories about this meeting. Barnum claimed Philo effected the introduction, but others in Bridgeport wanted the credit. Theodosia Fairchild, who was married to the tavern keeper at the Daniel Sterling hotel where Stratton's mother worked, claimed she instigated the introductions, even making Charles a blue velvet suit for the occasion and encouraging Cynthia to meet the showman. Henry Folsom, one of Sherwood's drinking companions, later claimed he was the broker in the meeting, fully aware that the boy would be a perfect addition to Barnum's American Museum. Whatever their veracity, these tall tales reflect the magnitude of the occasion, which only dawned on the townsfolk a little later.[424]

Barnum certainly saw something special in Charles. Physically, he was a handsome, miniature child with blond hair, rosy cheeks, blue eyes and a high-pitched voice. He was also sharp, lively and seemingly intelligent but initially timid as he stared at the tall stranger. Barnum decided to experiment. He wanted to hire Charles on a four-week contract at $3 a week – 'all charges, including travelling and boarding of himself and mother, being at my expense'.[425] The plan was to exhibit Stratton at the American Museum.

Perhaps Stratton's parents were initially reluctant. We don't know what they thought, but they could well have had their doubts about this showman from the big city. Yet they may have reasoned that a month's experiment was acceptable, and they were not signing their son's life away. Perhaps they thought this was an opportunity for their son (and themselves) to earn some additional income. Charles's life opportunities would certainly be restricted, arguably even more so than in the days of Józef Boruwłaski, because by now court dwarfs and sponsorship by noble families were rare. Dwarfs were usually dependent on their own families, their community or, increasingly, showmen who paraded them in exhibitions. Indeed, with the decline of ostentatious royal courts, public exhibitionism became the reality for many dwarfs in the nineteenth century, although some did work in professions outside the world of entertainment; and some, like American-born Mary Rutherford Garrettson (1794–1879), made an impact independent from their bodies: she was a Christian educator, strongly opposed to slavery, and author of two children's books.[426]

Whatever their thoughts and feelings, the Strattons agreed to Barnum's proposal. As for Charles, he was four years old and ignorant of the transaction. As for Barnum, we can only take him at his word: he was unsure whether Charles would be a success, but a short four-week experiment was a small gamble, so he got to work elevating Charles Stratton into General Tom Thumb.

———•◦◦•———

B ARNUM SPENT MANY hours, days and even nights training Stratton in the ways of the stage. The showman taught the child how to play different characters, carry himself onstage, project his voice, sing and dance, and adopt the airs and graces of a refined adult. According to Barnum, Stratton had 'native talent and an intense love of the ludicrous', and he proved himself adept at mastering a routine.[427] It is worth repeating that Stratton was just four years old. These skills were being mastered by a child barely more than a toddler.

Next, Barnum altered Stratton's identity, which forever blurred the lines between his private character and his public persona. Barnum dubbed him Tom Thumb, a name that evoked Richard Johnson's *The History of Tom Thumb* (1621), where the hero, no bigger than his father's thumb, embarks on various adventures. Tom is swallowed by a cow, becomes the favourite of the legendary King Arthur, is blessed with magical powers from his godmother, 'Queene of Fayres', and is even knighted as Sir Thomas after fighting for 'God, King and Country', and duelling with a giant and becoming victorious through brains not brawn. Calling Stratton 'Tom Thumb' instantly connected him to the Victorian craze for fairies – expressed in everything from paintings to opera – and further linked him to a folklore legend that would define his own life.

From the outset, then, Stratton's public persona straddled myth and reality. But the new name itself wasn't enough to make the act a success, so Barnum made other changes. Stratton's age was inflated from four to eleven because Barnum wanted people to regard Stratton as a dwarf, rather than a small child who had yet to develop: 'The thing I aimed at was, to assure them that he was *really a dwarf* – and in *this*, at least, they were not deceived.'[428] Next, a change of national identity: Stratton went from being American to English as Barnum was fully aware of 'the American fancy for European exotics'.[429] An English dwarf would fit the bill, being more foreign and otherworldly than a bog-standard American dwarf. Finally, Barnum made Tom Thumb a 'general'. In part this reflected the heroism of the fairy-tale Tom Thumb who bravely fought against giants but being a general was also part of a strategy to 'aggrandize' certain freak performers, imbuing them with elevated status and rank.[430]

Collectively, through a combination of these fictions, deceptions and the skill of the performer, Stratton was transformed into General Tom Thumb, a Victorian freak.

ONCE THE ICE had defrosted on the Hudson River in early December 1842, Barnum, Stratton and his mother left Bridgeport aboard the *Nimrod* steamship. Together they were embarking on a new adventure and forging a long-lasting relationship. According to Barnum, by this time Stratton had grown 'very fond of me' and he, in turn, was 'sincerely attached to him'.[431] It was the blossoming of a strange father–son relationship in which the father cum showman cared for his son, almost loved him, but, arguably, primarily for financial reasons.

They were perfect companions: Stratton, with his love for the ludicrous, and Barnum, who loved to laugh. Barnum was, according to Lavinia Warren, the 'life of every gathering': a true force of nature, brimming with energy, ambition and optimism.[432] Although he had numerous blotches on his moral record, he was a complex man of his time with a public persona moulded through his numerous writings and a private life that was seemingly at odds with his public character, the Prince of Humbugs. He was charitable and a committed Christian. It is little wonder that, later in life, Stratton would speak fondly of Barnum and help him in the showman's greatest hour of need. But now, in early December 1842, the trio arrived in New York. The announcements proclaimed: 'TOM THUMB, ELEVEN YEARS OLD AND ONLY TWENTY-FIVE INCHES HIGH, JUST ARRIVED FROM ENGLAND!!!'[433]

CHAPTER TWELVE

CONQUERING AMERICA

O N THANKSGIVING DAY, 8 December 1842, General Tom Thumb made his debut at the American Museum. Beginning in the Hall of Living Curiosities, the General, with his tiny outstretched palms and a chirpy 'How d'ye do?' greeted the spectators, their eyes staring down at him, marvelling at this miniature being so 'lively, agreeable, sprightly, and talkative, with no deficiency of intellect', wrote Philip Hone, the former mayor of New York, in his diary.[434] Up close and personal, people knew this was no Barnum humbug, no Joice Heth hoax or Fejee Mermaid. Tom Thumb was the real thing.

Tom Thumb naturally and easily conversed with the audience. One of Barnum's favourite tricks, which he adopted frequently in the early years of Tom Thumb's performances, was to enter the room in one of his large overcoats and, amid the chatter and commotion, shout 'General Tom Thumb! General, General! Where are you?' before Tom Thumb emerged from his coat pocket with a 'Here I am, sir', to the delight of the audience.[435] It was a performance straight from the days when Jeffrey Hudson, at the court of Henrietta Maria, was plucked from the pocket of the court giant.

The museum's Lecture Room was where the theatricals took place, and it was packed for the occasion. In the early years of the museum, this room was 'narrow, ill-contrived and uncomfortable', recalled Barnum, but it had a stage and today it contained an eager crowd.[436] Barnum began by introducing Tom Thumb, 'the rarest, the tiniest, the most diminutive dwarf imaginable', who followed onstage to deliver a series of scripted puns that played on his size and alleged nationality. In a mock Cockney accent he proclaimed, 'I am only a Thumb, but a good hand in a general way at amusing you for though a mite I am mighty.'[437] Laughter. Applause.

From the audience Barnum picked a young boy to come onstage, but Tom Thumb quipped, 'I'd rather have a little miss', earning himself a reputation as a lady's man, and confirming to all that Tom Thumb was quick-witted, although this was probably also scripted.[438] When the young boy stood next to Tom Thumb, the verdict was confirmed: this really was the smallest dwarf anyone had seen, even tinier than the boy onstage, and the audience muttered in amazement. All agreed that this was no monster as they marvelled at his handsome features, proportional body and beautiful, bright blue eyes.[439]

The performance continued with Tom Thumb astounding the crowd with a mixture of skits, tricks and impersonations. He appeared as an American Revolutionary soldier dressed in a white wig, black cocked hat, blue coat, white waistcoat and breeches with a 10in sword in his hand. He went through the practice of a military drill while singing 'Yankee Doodle' in his high treble voice:

> *Yankee Doodle came to town*
> *Riding on a pony*
> *Yankee Doodle keep it up*
> *Yankee Doodle Dandy*
> *Mind the music and the step*
> *And with the girls be handy.*[440]

The audience were captivated; this was a sound they had never heard before. It was high pitched but melodious, more akin to the sound of a bird than a human. The tone and the lyrics were clear, gentle and sweet.[441] When the evening came to a close, Barnum returned home to the converted billiard hall next to the museum, while Cynthia slept on the fifth floor of the museum with her son. When the reviews came out, no one was in doubt that Tom Thumb was a hit. The *New-York Daily Tribune*, which reviewed the debut performance, declared: 'General Tom Thumb, Junior, the Dwarf, exhibiting at the American Museum, is by far the most wonderful specimen of a man that ever astonished the world.'[442]

And let us be very clear: this debut performance was yet another decisive moment in the history of displaying exceptional bodies. The venue itself had been one turning point, providing a permanent, respectable and commercial venue for freak performers. Additionally, as Michael M. Chemers, the theatre historian, perfectly summarized: 'His debut on the New York stage was to mark a turning point in the history of the exhibition of "human curiosities," which almost overnight developed from a marginalized, disreputable carnival diversion into one of the most popular forms of mainstream theatrical entertainment in the United States, and would remain so for a century.'[443] Chang and Eng and Heth had pre-empted this move to the respectable; they had performed in public museums like the Egyptian Hall in London and Niblo's respectable pleasure garden in New York. But as they toured across America, they were still perceived as harbingers of carnivalesque corruption.

Tom Thumb, though, was no threat to the moral fabric of the nation. His freak show was a form of theatre contained within the respectable American Museum which, thanks to Barnum, welcomed the middle, upper and working classes. And Stratton's performance was unique: he was not simply paraded in front of the curious; neither did he perform acrobatic tricks associated with itinerant entertainers and the morally dubious circuses. No, Charles Stratton had mastered a performance piece, aged only four years old, and he displayed comic ability, musical ingenuity and skilled mimicry. This was theatre, pure and simple.

CHARLES STRATTON WAS seemingly made for the stage. He performed two shows a day in the Lecture Room and, between performances, rehearsed new songs and routines. He developed a range of impersonations and, performing beside a straight man (either Barnum or one of his employees), played different characters in specially made costumes: the student from Oxford University, the Scottish Highlander, the American sailor and Emperor Napoleon.

Standing on the stage of the Lecture Room, Tom Thumb and his straight man (in this early script, the 'Doctor') would deliver their routines to a rapturous audience:

Doctor: *What dress is this, General?*
Tom: *It's my Highland costume.*
Doctor: *What is that in your hand, General?*
Tom: *My claymore. [A double-edged sword.]*
Doctor: *To what use do you put it to?*
Tom: *I fight with it.*
Doctor: *Fight! I'd like to know if you've ever been in battle.*
Tom: *How could I be a general if I have never been in battle?*
Doctor: *Why, sir, I know several generals who have never smelt gunpowder ... Will you favour the audience with a Scotch song?*
Tom: *Yes, sir.* [444]

At this moment, Tom Thumb would sing the Scottish ballad, 'Come Sit Thee Down'. His high-pitched voice, strangely beautiful and certainly original, had audiences spellbound. Next ...

> Doctor: *Now, General, will you be kind enough to astonish the audience by dancing the Highland fling?*
> Tom: *Yes, sir.*[445]

There followed a comic dance. Then, finally, the sale's pitch:

> Doctor: *I will here state the General has an interesting book containing an account of his life and travels and also a lithographic portrait which the audience can procure in the room below at the conclusion of the performance. What do you charge for them, General?*
> Tom: *A stamped receipt.*
> Doctor: *And what is a 'stamped receipt'?*
> Tom: *A kiss.*[446]

The pamphlets and lithographs were sold for money; the kisses were an additional offering, taking the interactions between audience and freak performer to a sensual level. With the showman's introduction, the theatrical performance and the textual and visual accounts of Tom Thumb, the hallmarks of the Victorian freak show were firmly established.

In these early years, and in a manner echoing Daniel Lambert, Tom Thumb was constructed as both manly and gentlemanly. In exhibition pamphlets he was described as 'a sort of mental and physical concentration, a chemical synthesis, in which manhood has been boiled down'.[447] The early to mid-nineteenth-century associations between gentlemanliness, affluence and politeness were emphasized:

he had 'all the grace and dignity of the finished gentleman'.[448] And while Lambert's manliness was articulated through his direct speech and love of hunting, Tom Thumb's manliness was sexual, expressed through those kisses: his 'strange beauty, has made many persons, and especially ladies, so strongly attached to him as to become his almost daily visitors', claimed a later exhibition pamphlet, which continued by asserting that Tom Thumb 'boasts, among his other adventures, of having kissed six thousand ladies'.[449] At four years old, he was roguish and gentlemanly.

The ever-present reference to Stratton's 'proportional' figure reflected what the Victorians perceived to be the ideal classical body: symmetrical, neat and constrained.[450] Stratton's physique was thus deemed perfect, albeit contained within a miniature form. His intelligence refuted the popular 'science' of craniometry, which stipulated that the size of the brain related to the size of the skull.[451] Stratton was diminutive, but he was not dim. He was not considered monstrous or grotesque, which was a common response to those with achondroplasia dwarfism (a bone growth disorder leading to disproportionate limbs and an enlarged head): 'Little people are most generally deformed in some respect or other,' claimed a freak show pamphlet in the 1840s, 'and for which reason very little interest is excited by their appearance.'[452] But not so with Stratton. According to his exhibition pamphlet, he was 'altogether free from the deformities which generally disfigure such manikins'; characters like the dwarf Quilp, from Charles Dickens' *The Old Curiosity Shop* (1840–41), who haunted angelic Nell 'by a vision of his ugly face and stunted figure'.[453] Instead, Tom Thumb's proportionate body connected him to the world of fairies, while achondroplasia dwarfs occupied the domain of the monstrous.[454] Being merely a child but trained to act like a gentleman, Tom Thumb occupied a liminal space between child and man: he was gentlemanly and manly *and* tiny; he was a beautiful Victorian freak; an ambiguous being and a delight.

Towards the end of December 1842 the positive reviews continued, with Tom Thumb packing out the American Museum: 'I went last evening with my daughter Margaret,' Philip Hone wrote in his diary, 'to see the greatest little mortal who has ever been exhibited.' Usually, Hone noted, 'I have a repugnance to see human monsters, abortions, and distortions … but in this instance I experienced none of this feeling. General Tom Thumb (as they call him) is a handsome, well-formed, and well-proportioned little gentleman.'[455] A correspondent for the *Baltimore Sun*, attempting to come to terms with the boy he had seen onstage, wrote: 'I cannot describe the sensations with which one looks upon the diminutive specimen of humanity. Were he deformed, or sickly, or melancholy, we might pity him; but he is so manly, so handsome, so hearty, and so happy, that we look upon him as a being from another sphere.'[456]

Such discombobulation perfectly reflects what the sociologist and philosopher Zygmunt Bauman has described as 'ambivalence': a 'language-specific disorder'.[457] When an object cannot be contained within a single category, it is hard to find the right language to define, contain and segregate that object. For Chang and Eng, the problem of language was apparent in medicine's inability to define their anomaly. For Tom Thumb, the problem was reflected in the reactions from the *Baltimore Sun*. And, as with Chang and Eng, this ambivalence generated success: 'General Tom Thumb, as you may well imagine, attracted crowds; indeed, not less than thirty thousand persons visited him at the American Museum', the *Baltimore Sun* announced.[458]

Many women were drawn to Tom Thumb because they found him cute, if not sexually appealing: people wanted to be near Tom Thumb, to pet him, handle him, grope him, kiss him.[459] It was an experience Hudson and Boruwłaski had known only too well. And

Barnum played on this strange sort of desire by initiating one of Tom Thumb's closing acts in which he would appear wearing only an elastic body stocking that clung tightly to his figure as he posed in a series of statues: Cain raising a club, about to kill Abel; brandishing a spear, ready to fly like Romulus; and posing as the biblical Samson. To add variety to his shows, Barnum staged mock battles between Tom Thumb and the museum's giants, the Frenchman M. Bihin and the Arabian Colonel Goshen; and new characters and skits were added, including the character Mary Ann (Tom Thumb's female impersonation).[160]

Tom Thumb was proving a triumph so, once the initial four-week contract ended, he was re-engaged by Barnum for a year at an increased salary of $7 a week, lodging and travel included, with the right to exhibit in any part of the US. This time Stratton was joined by both his parents, whose travel expenses were covered by the showman. Barnum also promised a 'gratuity of fifty dollars at the end of the agreement', as he wrote in his autobiography.[461] The contract was signed by Cynthia and Sherwood, with $3 going directly to Sherwood, who assisted Barnum on their travels.[462]

In 1843 the group visited the major towns and cities of America, often accompanied by Barnum's business manager and friend, Fordyce Hitchcock, a 'genteel, industrious' man whom, Barnum wrote, knew 'the ways of the boy well'.[463] Generally, things ran smoothly, as Stratton improved his performance routine and was well received wherever he went. But Sherwood was erratic. When Tom Thumb performed for six weeks in Boston, Sherwood refused to leave his hotel room. He sat there, brooding, perhaps feeling inadequate as his son become the breadwinner, or perhaps merely feeling redundant. Indeed, when Sherwood was finally given a proper role, to act as the ticket seller for the shows, his mood seemed to improve; yet his sulk was an early signal that Sherwood was battling with demons.[464]

There were, however, no such demons onstage. Tom Thumb was enthralling audiences. In letters to his friend and fellow museum proprietor Moses Kimball, Barnum boasted that Tom Thumb had earned $280 at a farewell benefit in Philadelphia; 'Did you ever hear the like?'[465] And while Barnum had promised Kimball that Tom Thumb would perform at the Boston Museum in March 1843, in a letter dated 8 March, Barnum admitted to being 'greedy and was keeping Tommy longer south than he promised', for Tom was proving such a hit.[466] Yet Tom Thumb did make it to Kimball's Boston Museum (an establishment that mirrored Barnum's American Museum), performing between May and June, and was a monumental success. By the end of the year Barnum increased Stratton's weekly salary to $25. He'd 'earned it', wrote the showman.[467]

—◦◦◦—

CHARLES STRATTON'S TOM Thumb was quickly becoming as popular as the fairy-tale Tom Thumb, who outwitted ogres and giants. His folklore freak persona also combined with the trope of the Yankee, a shrewd, hard-working character who outmanoeuvres those in power.[468] Both the folklore Tom Thumb and the Yankee challenged power, which played perfectly in America where, by 1842, the Yankee had become a popular figure in melodrama.

Further, just like Barnum's egalitarian American Museum, the Yankee reflected the ideals of Jacksonian democracy, which championed greater rights for the 'common man' against established aristocratic power. General Tom Thumb brought together the Yankee character and the fairy-tale Tom Thumb in a way that chimed with the times. Stratton should be regarded within the field of theatre history because, through vaudeville-style performances, he became a celebrated actor who could charm audiences across the social spectrum, developing a persona that reflected common characters in the American theatre.[469]

Amid the success of the star General Tom Thumb, Barnum renegotiated Stratton's contract for another year's service, doubling his salary to $50 a week, all expenses included. This time, however, there was a new condition: 'with the privilege of exhibition in Europe'.[470]

CHAPTER THIRTEEN

---•◦•---

MAN IN MINIATURE

A S THEY BOARDED the *Yorkshire* transatlantic steamer on 19 January 1844, the sound of 'Home Sweet Home' could be heard being played by a New York brass band. The musicians had come to pay homage to the heroes of American entertainment, a strange pair of national celebrities: the showman P.T. Barnum and his prodigy, the now six-year-old Charles Stratton. Thousands came to see Tom Thumb before he set sail for Europe. In the morning he gave them one last show, then the band escorted the pair as they made their way from New York City to Sandy Hook, New Jersey, a protruding barrier strip that separated the mainland from the Atlantic Ocean. It was on these perilous waters that Barnum and Stratton would set sail to find new riches in the Old World; for Barnum had conquered America, and now he wanted to conquer the globe. As the ship's bell rang at half past one, announcing the moment of departure, Barnum and Stratton waved goodbye to America. It would be three years before Stratton returned home.[471]

Amid the excitement and trepidation, Barnum wept. 'I was decidedly in the "melting mood",' as he later wrote in his autobiography.[472] He was naturally prone to fun; he instinctively saw the lighter side of life, taking personal struggles in his stride with a belief in God by his side. But as Barnum looked out at the open ocean, 'toward the wide sea with its deep mysteries', his heart clung to family and home.[473] He was entering the unknown, a path poorly travelled, operating on an instinct that his American dwarf would receive fame and fortune in Britain.

It was a massive gamble, and he knew it. The showman and his prodigy had transformed the state of freak shows in America, but Britain was another story. Since the Middle Ages, dwarfs had been seen in coffeehouses, inns and fairs; by the nineteenth century they were a staple of the licentious and riotous fairs that travelled around the country in summer and spring. But these fairs had been abandoned by the well-to-do. These days it was mainly the lowly and rowdy who attended, and they usually paid no more than a penny to see dwarfs perform alongside other 'monstrosities'.[474] London, for sure, had hosted successful freak performers like Chang and Eng, and dwarfs such as Józef Boruwłaski even earlier. But Boruwłaski represented a different age for dwarfs, when they were connected to royal courts and noble households, and Chang and Eng, back in 1829, were medical and ethnographic curiosities who brought scientists into the shows.

Tom Thumb had a different allure as a 'man in miniature', and it was by no means enough to ensure success. Indeed, by the early 1840s, as Barnum realized, 'dwarfs were at rather a low figure in the fancy-stocks of England'.[475] They had a reputation for drunkenness and mischievousness, they supposedly lurked in the shadows of the travelling fairs, and their friends, if they had any, were social pariahs: showmen and other ne'er-do-wells who stood outside the social structures of their time. On the *Yorkshire* steamer, Barnum had a sense of foreboding.

There was also significant competition. From 1837 to 1901, the years of Queen Victoria's reign, leisure pursuits and amusements proliferated, everything from recreations in the home, such as the piano, board games, gardening and needlework, to the likes of art galleries, museums and public lectures. Street performers were prolific, with bands, minstrels, dancing bears, acrobats and Punch and Judy shows a familiar sight. Public houses and beer shops were not just places for working men to drink but sites of entertainment that offered a range of activities. There were excursions to the countryside, flower shows, debates and meetings of friendly societies, not to mention dancing and music and, at the lower end of the scale, prostitution, gambling, cockfighting and ratting (when terriers would kill as many rats as possible against the clock). Diversions were dizzying; we could add music halls, theatres, the circus, sports, fancy-dress balls, even a good church sermon to the list, all of which threatened to drown out Tom Thumb.[476]

Barnum did make some adjustments. He now sold Tom Thumb as an American dwarf and he sent press releases in advance to whip up excitement. Before they even arrived, therefore, it was being claimed that Hudson and Boruwłaski 'would seem to have been perfect giants in stature' compared to Tom Thumb.[477] 'Sir Geoffrey Hudson [sic] and the Polish Count were each sufficiently wonderful,' declared another, 'but their dwarfish reputation must be eclipsed by the new marvel, "General Tom Thumb", if the particulars which appear in the American papers concerning him are correct.'[478]

Still, this was hardly enough to ensure success, and in a time before the 'special relationship', the British were decidedly ambivalent about the Americans, who had expelled their government during the War of Independence and then had the gall to continue, as republicans, with the abominable institution of slavery, which the British had abolished throughout the empire in 1833. Indeed, Barnum would find himself defending the institution of slavery against the 'rabid fanaticism of some abolitionists' which, he maintained, was 'more reprehensible than slavery itself'.[479] Furthermore, the English literary hero Charles Dickens had warned his countrymen about the Americans, who, aside from the atrocious system of slavery, prided themselves on 'Universal Distrust', '"smart" dealing' and profits above culture.[480]

These fears swirled around Barnum's head for nineteen days as he and Charles Stratton made their voyage across the Atlantic, arriving in Liverpool in early February 1844. They stayed and performed in the city of docks for a couple of weeks before heading to the imperial, commercial, industrial and entertainment capital of the world.

—◦◦◦—

IN 1844 THE six-year-old Charles Stratton found himself in London: 'a Human awful wonder of God', wrote the poet William Blake, an overpowering metropolis that increasingly sprawled into the countryside year by year, as urbanization engulfed village greens and the population grew from just under 1 million in 1801 to an astonishing 4.5 million by 1901.[481] The capital was described in the very language of monstrosity, the journalist Henry Mayhew deeming London a 'monster city' that bred its own deformed creature, the working class – a 'race of dwarfs', 'City Arabs' or, in the words of Charles Booth in the 1890s, 'wild' and 'dwarfish'.[482]

A large section of the population was packed into filthy, overcrowded living quarters where crime, disease and poverty were rife. The German philosopher Friedrich Engels, writing about the conditions of the working class, foresaw revolution in this smouldering atmosphere, where criminals lurked around every corner: 'A *Times* of September 12, 1844, falls into my hand, which gives a report of a single day, including a theft, an attack upon the police, a sentence upon a father requiring him to support his illegitimate son, the abandonment of a child by its parents, and the poisoning of a man by his wife.'[483]

In a city increasingly reshaped by road improvements, bridge construction and slum clearances, the agents of vice did not just roam above but underground. The sewers – rebuilt and improved from the 1860s – offered a labyrinth beneath the gaslights where gangs of sewage hunters, known as Toshers, sifted through London's filth to gather pieces of silver and other valuables.

London might have been a scary space for the young Stratton, the crowds being noisy, pushy and aggressive. Or perhaps he was excited: a new country, new adventure, new city. In some respects, London was not that different to New York, with its growing population, noisy crowds bartering along the Hudson River and impressive buildings lining the cityscape. We do not really know how Stratton felt: he did not leave a record of his feelings as a six-year-old. What we do know is that Stratton had been taught to conceal his fears and to behave like General Tom Thumb, Barnum's invented identity. The boy was to be as brave as the fairy-tale Sir Thomas who battled evil. Onstage and off, there was no place to show any fear or confusion; such emotions had to be buried deep inside. Besides, Stratton had his London debut to focus on.

BUILT OF PORTLAND stone, the Princess's Theatre stood proudly on Oxford Street, one of the longest and finest arteries of London, amid a plethora of architecturally eclectic buildings, from the Duke of Westminster's mansion to rickety one-storey houses and shops. The theatre was managed by the supposedly mean-spirited and tight-fisted John Medex Maddox. The journalist George Augustus Sala called him 'a Jew – an "Ebrew Jew" whose real name was Medex: the Maddox being an ornamental suffix, added for purposes best known to himself' (probably because of vitriolic anti-Semitism).[484] His brother, Sam, kept a cigar shop opposite the theatre which, on Tuesday 20 February 1844, was hosting a night of farce, vaudeville and Italian opera (Maddox's staple offering). He offered cheap entertainment for raucous aristocrats, hardened soldiers, blood-stained medical students and wannabe gentlemen.

It was quite a dissolute crowd for Tom Thumb's opening night, and a far cry from the more respectful audiences at the American Museum in New York. The riotous London audience cheered, jeered, fought and haggled with prostitutes as Stratton waited in the wings. Then, between the second and third act of Donizetti's comic opera *Don Pasquale* (1843), Barnum confidently strutted onstage to announce, 'General Tom Thumb!' Stratton took his cue and emerged from the wings; he toddled down to the footlights at the front of the stage where the reflectors from the pit hid a good portion of his body, and was greeted with shouts, jeers and the laughter of surprise.[485]

'The droll little dwarf', one reviewer wrote, 'informed the audience that he was the renowned American General Tom Thumb, that he was a Yankee by birth, and he hoped he should be as well received in this county as he had been in his own.'[486] In his high-pitched voice, Tom Thumb continued telling the rowdy crowd that he was twelve years old (in reality, he was only half that age), his height was 25in and his weight was 15lb. He then disappeared offstage to change costume and return as Napoleon. Tom Thumb walked across the boards mimicking the French despot with salutes, the clicking of his heels and the swirling of his cane. He concluded his act striking classical poses in the elastic body stocking. The crowd whistled, whooped and cheered. By the end of the night, despite battling a nasty cold, Stratton had impressed a tricky, lively audience.[487]

Unfortunately, however, the *Illustrated London News* hoped never to see Tom Thumb again: 'The production of this little monster affords another melancholy proof of the low state the legitimate drama has been reduced to,' it lamented.[488] The Princess's Theatre was among a range of minor theatres deemed incomparable to the great legitimate theatres of Drury Lane and Covent Garden. These minors catered to the rising number of pleasure-seekers who desired a night of fun rather than didactic theatre.[489] The Princess's Theatre vied for attention, competing with London's magic shows, menageries, variety museums, makeshift circuses, pantomimes, panoramas and automaton shows. And in the context of popular entertainment, Tom Thumb was deemed no more than a 'little monster', indistinguishable from the 'disfigured' dwarfs who prowled the fairs.

Barnum had perhaps made an error of judgement. He was, as he wrote, 'a stranger in a strange land', who did not fully understand the English, or their popular culture.[490] The reviews were not good enough. Tom Thumb needed to redefine the dwarf act as he'd already done in America. Barnum needed to think again.

LUCKILY, HIS INSTINCTS were good. Barnum had rented a house in Grafton Street, Mayfair, a stone's throw from respectable Piccadilly. The land around this L-shaped street was bought in 1723 by the 2nd Duke of Grafton with three of his neighbours, and its row of neat Georgian houses sat in the heart of the West End. It was the perfect location to solicit a respectable following and project an image of wealth.

The West End was home to court and government, where the wealthy, leisured classes promenaded down clean, wide-open streets and propriety was in abundance: it was an angelic side to monstrous London. Barnum's neighbours were Britain's finest pedigree of aristocrats – his rented house was once occupied by a lord – and Barnum dropped any hint of being a showman; rather, he presented himself as a dignified American citizen, the guardian of a special guest in the capital.[491]

Barnum sent letters of invitation to the press and nobility. He enclosed Tom Thumb's calling cards, placed inside tiny envelopes. When intrigued visitors arrived they were greeted by a servant, 'dressed in the tinselled and powdered style of England', who ushered them into the impressive Georgian house, which boasted Tuscan columns and pediments.[492]

After climbing a fine staircase, visitors were amazed at the sight of Tom Thumb: 'an adult in manners, with the babyhood size of six months'.[493] They knew he was young, although not how young, but what was truly amazing was his size and shape. He *was* different to the disfigured dwarfs who could often be seen for a penny at the fairs. He laughed, chatted and sang, and had warmth and charm. He was well-mannered, lively and intelligent, and was dressed in a splendid suit. He knew how to create a spectacle. One mesmerized journalist wrote: 'We yearned to bring him away with us in our pocket, and to make him eat, drink, and be merry with us. General Tom Thumb! It may indeed be said of thee: "We ne'er shall look upon thy like again".' [494]

Crested carriages soon lined Grafton Street as word spread. Then invitations arrived. He was called to the mansion of Baroness Charlotte von Rothschild, the wealthy, philanthropic daughter of Carl von Rothschild, who lived at 148 Piccadilly. After passing through the illuminated hall and climbing the broad flight of marble stairs, Stratton proceeded to entertain about twenty lords and ladies by singing, dancing and playing his hornpipe. With this performance, and the deposit of a hefty sum of money in Barnum's pocket, word spread even further. Soon Tom Thumb was meeting the Duke and Duchess of Buckingham, the Duke of Bedford and the Duke of Devonshire.[495]

This was key. It was the upper classes who set the fashions: the theatres, concert halls and pleasure gardens thrived when lofty society offered their endorsement. The glory years of the travelling fairs only began to wane when, according to Thomas Frost, 'the nobility and gentry withdrew their patronage'.[496] There was a dependency between successful commercial entertainment and upper-class support. And now, with the upper classes behind him, Barnum ramped up the publicity. Posters advertising Tom Thumb were plastered across London; newspapers were filled with announcements:

> *In answer to the many letters received from the nobility and others, it is respectfully announced that the PUBLIC EXHIBITION of this remarkable phenomenon will be OPENED … Charles S Stratton, known as General Tom Thumb, is the smallest person that ever walked. He is of fine symmetrical proportions, lively, sociable, intelligent, graceful, and perfectly free from all deformity. It is impossible to form a just conception of his wonderful diminutiveness without seeing him.*[497]

The public exhibition was scheduled for the Egyptian Hall, where Chang and Eng had ignited a 'freak frenzy' back in 1829–30. In early March 1844 Barnum passed under the Egyptian Hall's imposing statues of Isis and Osiris and entered the Great Room, where a giant wigwam, 25ft high, stood underneath the dome. Six hundred paintings of Native Americans lined the walls: pictures of Native American chiefs, warriors and hunters, including scenes of them dancing and fighting. Over 3,000 costumes, weapons and artefacts were piled high. They emitted a musty smell and could be touched and examined by the curious: the relics of a culture and people slowly being destroyed as the republic expanded.[498]

Fortunately for Barnum, the man who had assembled the exhibition, George Catlin, was down on his luck. To entice people in, he had brought nine living Ojibwe Indians to perform war dances among the paintings and artefacts. But they had defected to another manager and enthusiasm for Catlin's exhibition had receded. With the high rent for the venue and three months left on his contract, Catlin was happy to strike a deal with Barnum: he would sublet the space on the condition that his collection remained in place.[499]

When the doors to Tom Thumb's Egyptian Hall performance finally opened, in March 1844, the well-to-do flocked to see the dwarf. Thanks to Barnum's prolific publicity, the middle classes followed, and then the working classes tried to catch a peek. All paid a shilling for the privilege. Even the Duke of Wellington came to see Tom Thumb. In a widely publicized encounter, the duke saw Stratton's impersonation of Napoleon Bonaparte, whom Wellington had defeated at Waterloo in 1815. Tom Thumb, dressed in full military uniform, marched up and down the stage, taking snuff and looking meditative. The duke asked what he was thinking: 'I was thinking of the loss of the Battle of Waterloo,' quipped Tom Thumb. It was a fabulous display of wit 'worth thousands of pounds to the exhibition', wrote Barnum.[500]

But this paled into insignificance when, on 23 March 1844, and in echoes of the lives of Hudson and Boruwłaski, Barnum posted a large placard on the door of the Egyptian Hall: 'Closed this evening, General Tom Thumb being at Buckingham Palace by Command of Her Majesty.'[501]

CHAPTER FOURTEEN

QUEEN VICTORIA'S PET

S HE WAS DUBBED 'the little queen' and 'her little majesty', in part a reflection of Victoria's age, in part an attempt to neuter the threat of a female sovereign (the last one, Queen Anne, having been deemed fat, inept and rather unsuccessful).[502] But Victoria was also known as 'the little queen' because, like Charles Stratton, she was tiny, growing just 4ft 11in tall; 'everybody grows but me', she lamented in her journal.[503] In 1838 the eighteen-year-old queen shared her corporeal fears with her dashing prime minister, Lord Melbourne, with whom she had a close and flirtatious relationship: 'I lamented my being *so* short, which he smiled at and thought no misfortune.'[504]

It might be a stretch to conclude that Queen Victoria was drawn to meeting Tom Thumb because of an affinity with bodily matters but, certainly, there were connections that united Tom Thumb and the queen. On the one hand, of course, they were polar opposites: Victoria was the head of state, the richest and most powerful woman in the world; Charles was a dwarf from Connecticut; he the entertainer, she to be entertained. But Victoria and Charles also shared more in common than either perhaps realized: both were small, both outsiders, both far from the norm. In fact, from birth, each had been marked as different, and both queen and dwarf experienced abnormal childhoods – controlled, public and isolated from their peers.

---·◦◈◦·---

VICTORIA'S FATHER, THE Duke of Kent, had died before Victoria reached the age of one, leaving her mother, the Duchess of Kent, penniless and widowed. A German with a poor grasp of the English language, the duchess was trapped in a foreign land, parasitic on her brother and the British government, which reluctantly paid for widow and child to occupy rooms in the dilapidated Kensington Palace.

Victoria's childhood was miserable – 'a very unhappy life', she recalled.[505] She was incarcerated in the palace and lived amid an unspoken but evident sexual dynamic between her mother and her comptroller, John Conroy, 'the Monster and Demon Incarnate', as Victoria later condemned.[506] She was caught in the 'Kensington System', which stifled the passionate princess, who was constantly watched by her mother. She was not allowed to sleep or even walk down the stairs on her own.

Victoria developed coping strategies. She escaped into a fantasy world with her dolls, diaries, dog and the opera, and had a close relationship with her governess, the German Baroness Lehzen, a loving but strict disciplinarian who oversaw Victoria's education. Victoria also found escape in the circus. In 1833, at the age of fourteen, she saw the handsome and graceful equestrian Andrew Ducrow at Astley's Amphitheatre performing *St George and the Dragon*. She was so mesmerized that she returned home and sketched a picture of the scene, writing in her diary how Ducrow had 'acted *uncommonly well* and rode *beautifully*', underlining the words to stress her wonder.[507]

Her passion for the circus continued during her reign, which began a few weeks after her eighteenth birthday. On Thursday 10 January 1839, not long after her coronation, Victoria was enthralled by the handsome Isaac A. Van Amburgh, an American animal trainer who pioneered the combination of menagerie and circus. He was performing at Drury Lane during the Christmas season. Victoria was initially grumpy at having to sit through the 'noisy and nonsensical' pantomime, *Harlequin and Jack Frost*, but she was awestruck in the eleventh scene when a 'miracle of a performance took place', with Van Amburgh manhandling six large cats, including a lion, tiger and cheetah.[508]

To the young queen, this was all quite beautiful, and she stared enamoured at the scene, wishing she could do the same. She imagined herself in the lion's cages grappling with the beasts. There was something about the display of power, the exercise of authority, the taming of the wild animals, which appeared beautiful and miraculous. She couldn't get the lion tamer out of her mind, talking incessantly about Van Amburgh to Lord Melbourne, and excitedly returning to Drury Lane on 24 January 1839, deliberately arriving late to miss the pantomime but catch Van Amburgh and the wild beasts. Obsessed, she saw Van Amburgh at Drury Lane seven times over six weeks.[509]

Her love of the lions was noted disparagingly by the English actor William Charles Macready, who wrote in his diary, with a tone of depression, 'Heard that the Queen was going to pay a third visit to Drury Lane theatre to see the lions.'[510] She was gaining a reputation as a queen who preferred the spectacular to the graceful, the foreign to the British, the circus to the drama. Worryingly, her preferences appeared more popular than refined. Yet Victoria was unmoved by cultural snootiness. She remained a lifelong lover of the circus. Soon, she would be enamoured with the freak show too.

———⁌❀⁍———

Left: Queen Henrietta Maria with Jeffrey Hudson. Painted by Sir Anthony van Dyck, 1633.

Right: Jeffrey Hudson at thirty years old with King Charles I. The engraving, made in 1821, claims Hudson was 'eighteen inches high'.

Right: Józef Boruwłaski with
an unidentified woman, 1821.

Left: Daniel
Lambert, who
came to shape
British national
identity.

Political caricature of Daniel Lambert and Napoleon: 'Two wonders of the world, or a specimen of a new troop of Leicestershire light horse', 1806.

Left: 'Wonderful Characters'. The Living Skeleton (Claude-Ambroise Seurat), Daniel Lambert, Jeffrey Hudson and an unidentified giant, surrounded by eight vignettes of other characters.

Right: George Sanger, the famous circus proprietor, and his wife, Ellen Sanger.

Above: The Egyptian Hall (also known as Bullock's Museum or London Museum), Piccadilly, London, 1828.

Right: Chang and Eng, the Siamese Twins, aged eighteen. The twins played badminton in their exhibition at the Egyptian Hall, c. 1829.

THE GREATEST
Natural & National
CURIOSITY
IN THE WORLD.

JOICE HETH.

Nurse to Gen. GEORGE WASHINGTON, (the Father of our Country,)

May be seen in NEW MILFORD
On WEDNESDAY & THURSDAY, the 10th and 11th of Feb.

JOICE HETH is unquestionably the most astonishing and interesting curiosity in the World! She was the slave of Augustine Washington, (the father of Gen. Washington,) and was the first person who put clothes on the unconscious infant, who, in after days, led our heroic fathers on to glory, to victory, and freedom. To use her own language when speaking of the illustrious Father of his Country, "she raised him." JOICE HETH was born in the year 1674, and has, consequently, now arrived at the astonishing

AGE OF 161 YEARS.

She Weighs but FORTY-SIX POUNDS, and yet is very cheerful and interesting. She retains her faculties in an unparalleled degree, converses freely, sings numerous hymns, relates many interesting anecdotes of *the boy* Washington, and often laughs heartily at her own remarks, or those of the spectators. Her health is perfectly good, and her appearance very neat. She is a baptist and takes great pleasure in conversing with ministers and religious persons. The appearance of this marvellous relic of antiquity strikes the beholder with amazement, and convinces him that his eyes are resting on the oldest specimen of mortality they ever before beheld. Original, authentic, and indisputable documents accompanying her prove, however astonishing the fact may appear, that JOICE HETH is in every respect the person she is represented.

The most eminent physicians and intelligent men in Cincinnatti, Philadelphia, New York, Boston, and other places, have examined this *living skeleton* and the documents accompanying her, and all, *invariably*, pronounce her to be, as represented, 161 *years of age!*

A female is in continual attendance, and will give every attention to the ladies who visit this relic of by-gone ages.

She has been visited in Philadelphia, New-York, Boston, &c., by more than TWENTY THOUSAND Ladies and Gentlemen, within the last three months.

Hours of Exhibition, from 9 A. M. to 1 P. M. and from 3 to 5, and 6½ to 10 P. M.

ADMITTANCE 25 Cents, CHILDREN HALF-PRICE.

Printed by J. BOOTH & SON, 147, Fulton-st N. Y.

Left: Handbill for an appearance of Joice Heth, allegedly 161 years old, in New Milford, Connecticut, 1835.

Right: Barnum's American Museum, New York, 1853.

Above: P. T. Barnum and the young Charles Stratton, c. 1850.

Right: Charles Stratton, aged around four or five, and a man thought to be his father, Sherwood E. Stratton, c. 1843.

Left: P. T. Barnum with the 'Fairy Wedding Party'. Front row, from left to right: George Washington Morrison Nutt (Commodore Nutt), Charles Stratton (Tom Thumb), Lavinia Warren and Minnie Warren (Lavinia's sister), 1863.

GEN. TOM THUMB, WIFE AND CHILD.

Right: 'General Tom Thumb, Wife and Child', *cartes-de-visite*, *c.* 1860s. It was later revealed that the child was a hoax and that the couple never had children.

Advert for an exhibition of Maximo and Bartola, the Aztecs, *c.* 1867–1899.

Left: Handbill for P. T. Barnum's Greatest Show on Earth, 1881.

Above: Poster advertising the Barnum & Bailey circus, *c.* 1899.

Right: A poster likely seen by Buckland and Munby featuring Julia Pastrana, the 'Nondescript', advertised for exhibition at the Regent Gallery, London, *c.* 1857.

Above: Julia Pastrana,
photographed in the early
1860s. Allegedly, the dress was
her own creation.

Right: Francis Trevelyan
Buckland, lover of the freak
show, surrounded bu his natural
history specimens, 1879.

Left: Anna and Martin Bates, reportedly taken on their wedding day, 17 June 1871. Allegedly, Anna's wedding dress was a gift from Queen Victoria.

Right: Millie and Christine McKoy, conjoined twins known as the Two-Headed Nightingale, aged nineteen, 1871.

'The Barnum and Bailey Show, Department of Prodigies',
Olympia, London, 1898–1899.

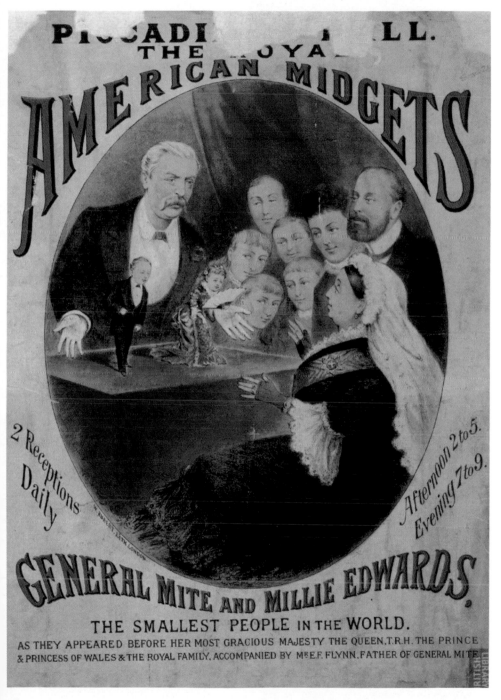

The so-called 'Royal American Midgets', advertised to preform at Piccadilly Hall, London, seen here being introduced to Queen Victoria, *c.* 1880.

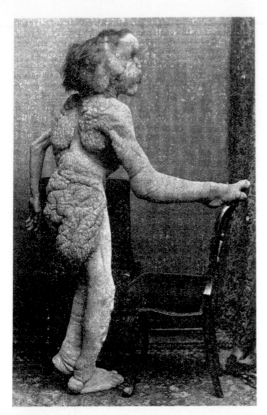

Left: Joseph Merrick, the Elephant Man, 1889.

Below: Dr. Eugéne-Louis Doyen separating the so-called 'Hindoo Twins' or ;Orissa Twins', Radica and Doodica, 1902.

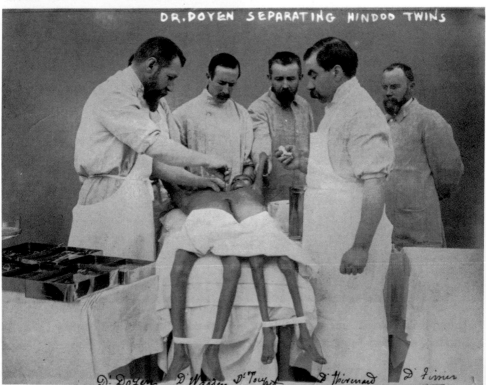

In THE YEAR when Victoria fell in love with Van Amburgh, an even greater love stole her heart. Victoria proposed to Albert on 15 October 1839. He was the nephew of Victoria's mother, and thus the queen's first cousin. Raised in an adulterous German household, Albert rebelled against his parents by becoming earnest, morally upright and serious. He was also very German. Victoria and Albert, who married on 10 February 1840, introduced the German tradition of a Christmas tree, a trend that soon caught on. And Albert's brother, Ernst of Coburg, was clear with his younger sibling, writing in 1844: 'Since the Family originates from a pure German House, it is essential to direct attention at all times to remaining a pure German.'[511]

Alongside a commitment to Germany, this was a royal household where the heads were bound together by a shared sense of duty, love and sexual attraction. Victoria was infatuated with Albert's blue eyes, perfectly shaped nose and pretty mouth, neatly framed by a delicate moustache and slight whiskers. Victoria enjoyed nothing more than to gaze at Albert during his morning shave. Together, they loved to listen to music, dance, dine and gaze at freak performers.

On 23 March 1844 Barnum and Tom Thumb stepped into the palace. This was a momentous occasion and the realization of Barnum's plan. When he first arrived in England, he had pursued his contacts with the American ambassador, Edward Everett, who had met Stratton and Barnum on 2 March 1844 and wrote of the former: 'A most curious little man. Should he live, and his mind become improved, he will be a very wonderful personage.'[512] Everett promised to exercise his influence to secure a royal engagement. On 8 March he invited the pair to meet the Master of the Queen's household, Charles Murray. When Barnum informed Murray that he planned to send Tom Thumb to meet the King of France, Murray – unable to countenance the King of France meeting Tom Thumb before the Queen of England – duly granted Charles Stratton an audience with Her Majesty.[513]

Thus, the first meeting occurred in the Picture Gallery on 23 March 1844. The last time Victoria had come face-to-face with a dwarf, he had tried to kill her. In 1842 a 'hunchback dwarf' had attempted to shoot the queen in a botched assassination attempt, which resulted in the police rounding up all the 'hunchbacks' they could find, and eventually arresting the mentally disturbed seventeen-year-old John William Bean, who, at 5ft 6in tall, was not actually a dwarf but was portrayed as such by some in the press.[514] With Tom Thumb, though, things were very different. He wowed the royal crowd, conversed with the queen and battled with her spaniel. He was issued another invitation on 1 April 1844, this time meeting Queen Victoria in the Yellow Drawing Room of Buckingham Palace, so named because of the yellow satin drapery that hung over the walls, couches and chairs. Tom Thumb proudly wore his court suit for the second time.

'I think this is a prettier room than the picture gallery; that chandelier is very fine,' Tom Thumb reportedly remarked as he surveyed the magnificent room lined with gold-painted panels and beautifully carved cornices.[515] Victoria smiled and introduced Tom Thumb to Bertie, the two-year-old Prince of Wales, thus marking his lifetime association with the freak show. 'How are you, Prince?' said the General, shaking Bertie by the hand and remarking: 'The Prince is taller than I am, but I feel as big as anybody', whereupon he 'strutted up and down the room as proud as a peacock amid shouts of laughter from all present', Barnum wrote in his autobiography.[516]

The queen also introduced Tom Thumb to her three-year-old daughter, Vicky, the Princess Royal, and together they made a touching picture frolicking on a miniature sofa Barnum had brought for the occasion. The royal party, which included Queen Victoria's mother, the Lady of the Bedchamber, and the Lady Superintendent of the Royal Children, cooed at the sight. Later that evening Queen

Victoria wrote in her diary: 'Saw the little dwarf, in the Yellow Drawing room, who was very nice, lively, & funny, dancing & singing wonderfully ... Little "Tom Thumb" does not reach up to Vicky's shoulder.'[517]

Victoria was so enthralled with Tom Thumb that he was invited to visit yet again, on 19 April 1844, when he sang 'Yankee Doodle', the American revolutionary song, to a royal crowd that included Leopold, King of Belgium, and his wife, Louise of Orléans, who 'were much surprised at' Tom Thumb, Victoria wrote.[518] Tom Thumb was truly in vogue. He was even visited by the Russian tsar Nicholas, and received an invitation to St Petersburg. But Tom Thumb's acceptance into the highest echelons of Victorian society was not quite enough to make Barnum rich. Now he needed to convert royal approval into an even greater public appetite.

BARNUM SKILFULLY CAPITALIZED on the commercial opportunities offered by the nineteenth century to effectively advertise Tom Thumb's new friend, Queen Victoria. He wrote all the reviews of the meetings between Tom Thumb and the queen, which were quoted verbatim by the *Court Circular* and splashed across the press. He printed promotional posters emblazoned in large letters: 'Under the distinguished patronage of Her Majesty'. Adverts were placed in the daily newspapers explicitly stating Tom Thumb's new association: 'under the especial patronage of Her Most Gracious Majesty the Queen'. Barnum even created souvenir medals with the inscription, 'Under the patronage of the Queen and Court of England'.[519]

Queen Victoria became part of the freak show. Her patronage was utilized by the master showman to package Tom Thumb as a dwarf with royal connections. He was not simply an amusing American dwarf; he was the queen's dwarf, 'The Pet of the Palace', wrote *Punch*, the satirical but shrewd social commentary magazine.[520] Queen Victoria was now directly associated with Tom Thumb and her patronage propelled Tom Thumb into the centre of British culture. Suddenly his shows were packed. On one occasion at the Egyptian Hall, one hundred students from a military school in Chelsea sang 'God Save the Queen', followed by Tom Thumb's own recitals.[521]

Barnum commissioned a miniature carriage in deep blue ultramarine with crimson and white trappings, and lined with expensive silk. Shetland ponies, measuring a mere 28in high, pulled the coach along the streets of London with Tom Thumb waving to astonished pedestrians, who read the motto 'Go Ahead' emblazoned on the side of the carriage.[522] The newspapers kept up the excitement: 'GENERAL TOM THUMB, the American Dwarf, under the especial patronage of Her Most Gracious Majesty the Queen, H.R.H. Prince Albert, the Queen Dowager, H.R.H. the Duchess of Kent, and the Queen of the Belgians, &c.'.[523]

Tom Thumb had come a long way since his lukewarm press reception at the Princess's Theatre. Now Charles Stratton the performer was fast becoming a 'celebrity', a term which assumed its modern meaning at precisely this time.[524] Barnum had effectively marketed Joice Heth in the 1830s, and thanks to the penny press she was propelled into popular culture, but by the 1840s commercialization was taking an even greater hold. The daguerreotype, for example, was providing the first commercially successful photographic process, which bolstered Tom Thumb's visibility on an unprecedented scale. Photographs of Tom Thumb appeared; his portraits ran in pictorial papers; polka music and quadrille dances were named after him; and songs were sung in his praise. He became quite the cultural phenomenon. According to *Punch*:

In the first place, the 12,000 people who visited Tom Thumb did not visit the mere dwarf. No. it was not unmixed curiosity for a joke of Nature, (and Nature, be it said with reverence, makes in the way of human creatures, very dull jokes at times)—no, it was to pay a reverence to one whom royalty delights to honour. Tom Thumb is not to be considered as a dwarf, but as an abstraction of highest taste.[525]

In addition to setting fashions and trends of the day Queen Victoria also exemplified the virtues of upright character, duty, modesty and domesticity, so her approval ensured both Tom Thumb's public renown and his respectability. A trickle-down effect occurred: the highest echelons endorsed Tom Thumb, which piqued the interests of the middle and working classes. This, in turn, kicked off a dwarf craze. As Barnum wrote to his friend Moses Kimball: 'There are at least 20 General Tom Thumbs now exhibiting in various parts of England, but that only paves the way for the approach of the "conquering hero".'[526] *Punch* cried out, in a sarcastic and mocking tone, that the 'successes' and 'victories' of Tom Thumb 'have called forth dwarfs from every nook and corner of the earth. England has taught human nature the exceeding advantage of being little. Hence, we have had German dwarfs – Spanish dwarfs – and, very recently, dwarfs from the Highlands.'[527]

Dwarf performers, including Richard Garnsey from Somerset, renowned as 'the most symmetrical dwarf in the world', flocked to London to ride the wave of Stratton's success.[528] Don Francisco Hidalgo, measuring 29in high, who had been attached to the court of King Ferdinand VII of Spain, left retirement aged forty-two also hoping to make his fortune in London (he didn't, and retired back to Spain).[529] Although Garnsey and Hidalgo failed to meet Queen Victoria, others did. Amid the vogue for dwarfs, Buckingham Palace and Windsor Castle became a revolving door for dwarf performers.

On Monday 16 December 1844 Victoria penned in her journal: 'After dinner we saw 3 German dwarves, aged 22, 18, & 13. The girl of 18 is a pretty, healthy looking little woman, but the boys are very frightful.'[530] The performers at the palace were Henrick Christian Brockstead, his sister Maria and brother Christian. The tallest among them was 36in. The dwarf siblings danced a dramatic ballet entitled 'Napoleon's Generosity', which echoed Stratton's successful imitation of the French despot. They repeated this performance to the public, who were charged 1 shilling for the privilege, and details of their lives were published in a memoir that could be purchased for an additional 6 pence. On the front page of the exhibition pamphlet, it was explicitly noted that the dwarfs were 'under Royal and Noble patronage'.[531]

Another trio of siblings who visited Queen Victoria were the Highland Dwarfs. Victoria wrote of them: '3 Highland Dwarves, who though certainly not pretty are very extraordinary. They are 2 brothers & a sister, aged 22, 19 & 18, – all of the same height, of a child of 6 & very strongly built. They danced & sang.'[532]

The Highland Dwarfs appealed to Victoria's love for all things Scottish, 'the brightest jewel in my crown', she wrote.[533] They hailed from the county of Ross, where they had been employed as shepherds before an Edinburgh showman persuaded the siblings to come to London, perhaps promising a reception that would match Tom Thumb's. They gained access to the queen, who 'was graciously pleased to express her approbation', and then they performed for the public too.[534]

Stratton and Barnum had established a new mode of presenting dwarfs (and freak performers more generally): secure royal approval and then go to the public. In the process, and thanks to Queen Victoria, they had ushered in a new 'age of the monsters', declared *Punch*; a period of 'Deformito-Mania', an obsession with deformity.[535]

I N LETTERS TO his friend the showman Moses Kimball, Barnum boasted about the riches flowing from Tom Thumb in London: 'Since New Year's (the new Tom Thumb administration) my profits have averaged $800 per week, & I think if the General lives I may safely count on clearing $25,000 per annum. You may well say it is a "fairy business". The Strattons are crazy – absolutely deranged with such golden success.'[536]

'Tom Thumb administration' reminds us that this was all business to Barnum. And 'if the General lives' was an ominous reminder that the life expectancy of dwarfs was low and that Barnum's previous hit, Joice Heth, had died on the job. The word 'crazy' seems to effectively capture how the Strattons, and indeed Barnum, felt: they were becoming ludicrously rich. The newfound wealth and fame went straight to the heads of Cynthia and Sherwood Stratton, 'vulgar, ignorant, common people', Barnum would surreptitiously write.[537]

But not everyone was happy with Queen Victoria's endorsement of dwarfs. The British writer and journalist Angus Bethune Reach lamented in the press: 'Let public opinion confess its error; and in future, when a dwarf is born, let its parents tend with the holiest love the unhappy being thus arriving, a monstrous creature, into the world. Let retirement be the lot of the being whom nature has prevented from mingling freely with its fellow-citizens. Let the brand be covered, the stigma hid. Let the secrecy of private dwelling or public asylum enwrap it.'[538]

This tension between displaying and concealing the anomalous body was a matter of political and moral dispute, which became more pronounced later in the century. But, for now, the public favoured the freak show. *Punch* was having none of it, however, denouncing with 'due gravity' Victoria's fascination, as did Prime Minister Robert Peel.[539] He felt that Victoria's obsession was an unhealthy distraction during a time of political and industrial unrest. The Chartists were on the march, and there were wage riots, high levels of unemployment, a looming potato famine and menacing Irish republicanism. Society was changing rapidly yet the queen seemed more interested in the wretched 'Deformito-Mania'.

CHAPTER FIFTEEN

TRIUMPH AND TRAGEDY

T HE GENERAL 'RAISED hell in England': he took London by storm, claimed victories across Britain and Ireland, before heading to France in March 1845, where he 'nearly killed the people' who were soon bowing down to the 'conquering hero' (to adopt Barnum's terminology).[540] Paris had emerged from a tumultuous past of revolutions and revolts, and was looking forward to the future (although 1848 would signal another rupture as revolution began). The restoration of churches destroyed by the French Revolution was underway; the first railway stations were being built; stone paths and trees were placed along the River Seine; and in 1853 Georges-Eugène Haussmann got to work building wide boulevards and parks, an opera house, a central market, aqueducts and sewers.

The Paris of the 1840s was one large pleasure land populated with artistic, literary and scientific exhibitions; museums, salons, gardens, theatres, balls and the Louvre. New classes of people were emerging from the shadows, disrupting the tripartite division of aristocracy, bourgeoisie and workers. These included the Bohemian students, artists and other creative types, unencumbered by cares about the future or the mores of the present, and the *flâneurs* who, donning long socks and dark-coloured gloves, were unburdened by the need to earn a living and, with a steady, fixed income, lived their days wandering along the boulevards, loitering in the gardens at the Palais Royal and drinking and eating at the numerous cafés and restaurants scattered around the city.[541]

Paris, of course, also had its share of dark, winding alleyways with dilapidated buildings, and there was the medieval Gothic Notre Dame, whose bells were rung by the disfigured hunchback Quasimodo in Victor Hugo's *Notre-Dame de Paris* (1831). But 'if a constant succession of gaieties and amusements be the attraction', declared a mid-nineteenth-century guidebook, the rue Vivienne 'containing almost all that Paris can boast' was the place to wander: 'on no part of the habitable globe are to be found so many attractions within so small a compass'.[542]

It was right here that Barnum intended to present Tom Thumb, 'in a central and fashionable quarter close by the boulevards', he wrote, finally settling on the 3,000-seater Salles de Concert.[543] According to Barnum, 'The élite of the city came to the exhibition; the first day's receipts were 5,500 francs, which would have been doubled if I could have made room for more patrons.'[544] Performances were packed out every afternoon and evening: 'The season was more than a success, it was a triumph,' recalled Barnum.[545]

But what ensured this level of success was the king. Indeed, Tom Thumb met King Louis Philippe, his wife, Queen Maria-Amalia, and other distinguished figures of the court shortly after arriving in Paris. Queen Victoria had made this possible: Louis Philippe was the father of Louise of Orléans, Queen of the Belgians, who was present at Tom Thumb's third introduction to Queen Victoria. Thanks to her patronage, Victoria had opened the doors to European royalty, and Barnum and Tom Thumb stepped right in. At the immense Tuileries Palace, situated on the banks of the Seine, the king was highly amused and gratified at the sight of Tom Thumb, who danced and performed for His Majesty. Philippe even presented Tom Thumb with a large emerald brooch set with diamonds and, on Barnum's request, granted permission for Tom Thumb to attend the forthcoming Longchamps celebration, a festive display of wealth. Deformito-mania was spreading to Paris.

In his elegant miniature carriage, pulled by Shetland ponies and led by children dressed as coachman and footman, Tom Thumb promenaded down the crowded, fashionable boulevard of the Champs-Élysées and the Park Bois de Boulogne. As Barnum recalled, 'thousands upon thousands cheered for "General Tom Pouce"' (his French moniker): 'There never was such an advertisement; the journals next day made elaborate notices of the "turnout," and thereafter whenever the General's carriage appeared on the boulevards, as it did daily, the people flocked to the doors of the cafés and shops to see it pass.'[546]

Tom Thumb had become 'the pet of Paris'.[547] The papers sang his praise, his statuette appeared in shop windows and even a fashionable café changed its name to Le Tom Pouce. Artists were desperate to paint him, actors wanted to associate with him and, 'meanwhile,' Barnum boasted, 'the daily receipts continued to swell, and I was compelled to take a cab to carry my bag of silver home at night'.[548] Charles Stratton was now an international celebrity. He stayed in Paris for nearly four months before beginning a tour of Belgium, rural France and Spain, spreading the Tom Thumb brand yet further.

There was one snag, however: the French levied a heavy tax on 'natural curiosities', a quarter of the gross receipts, which was far greater than the 11 per cent theatrical tax imposed on actors. Indeed, the French authorities could be difficult: back in the 1830s they denied Chang and Eng a travel permit for fear their 'monstrous' bodies would cause an outbreak of maternal impressions, the very same theory that had worried Stratton's parents when their son stopped growing. Although Continental Europe had a long tradition of displaying 'natural curiosities', the French tightly regulated what they dubbed *phénomènes*, and one way of policing these exhibitions was through taxation.[549] But Stratton was hardly ever described as a monster. Unlike Chang and Eng and other freak performers we'll encounter, Tom Thumb's exhibitions were not promoted in tandem with medical science.

Initially, Barnum had managed to avoid paying the full tax, but it was a struggle to keep the French authorities at bay. In a letter copybook, recently deposited at the Barnum Museum in Connecticut, are Barnum's letters from France, and one explains: 'The General is not exhibited simply as a natural curiosity, for as a natural curiosity he would not receive 100 francs per day. But the chief attractions of his exhibitions are his performances, which consist of the Poses Académiques, dancing-singing, imitations of celebrated characters such as Grand Frederick etc.'[550]

Barnum's claim was strengthened when, in the summer of 1845, Stratton performed in his own personalized play, *Le Petit Poucet* ('The Little Thumbling'), written by the acclaimed playwrights Louis Clairville and Philippe Dumanoir. It was based on the ancient fairy tale, popularized by the mythographer Charles Perrault, in which the clever Poucet, played by Stratton, goes from being an abandoned woodcutter's son left to die in a forest to a local prince who saves a kingdom during war, outwitting an ogre in between. The seven-year-old learned French for his star performance.

Stratton performed in the capital throughout the summer and was widely praised for his acting abilities; he could even boast membership of France's acting society, l'Association des artistes dramatiques.[551] Eventually, the authorities were forced to agree with Barnum: Stratton was certainly no monster likely to cause an outbreak of maternal impressions and he was much more than a natural curiosity. As such, Stratton would be subject to a lower theatrical tax in recognition of his status as an actor. Child performers were not rare onstage, in either America or Europe, but child dwarf actors certainly were. And none were as skilled as the seven-year-old Stratton. As Barnum wrote in his autobiography, 'he was more attractive as an actor than as a natural curiosity'.[552]

---❖---

B Y THIS TIME the group consisted of twelve people: Barnum, Stratton, his parents, Professor Pinte (interpreter and tutor) and an assortment of musicians and actors. Barnum needed to arrange the transport for the four Shetland ponies, the miniature carriage and the stage set for *Le Petit Poucet*, arranging for a post-chaise (drawn by six horses) carrying six people, plus a separate vehicle (pulled by four horses). There was a third vehicle (pulled by two horses) for the luggage and stage set. 'All this folly and expense,' Barnum wrote, 'in exhibiting a person weighing only fifteen pounds!'[553]

But it was a great way of advertising Tom Thumb, who travelled, among other places, to Rouen, Toulon, Orleans, Nantes, Brest, Bordeaux, Toulouse, Montpellier and Marseilles. Barnum would go ahead, arriving in each location a week before the entourage to secure 'the largest theatre or saloon to be found in the town', he wrote.[554] This was the travelling life once more, the life Barnum had hated, but this time he had a base back at his American Museum, and rather than having to drum up an audience, he was merely satisfying the huge appetite for Tom Thumb, which was caused, in large part, by the endorsements of the Queen of England and now the King of France.

Besides managing the crowds, Barnum had to manage the inter-personal dynamics of the travelling entourage. Stratton was the easiest. Despite his newfound celebrity status, he was, wrote Barnum, 'in no sense a "spoiled child," but retained throughout that natural simplicity of character and demeaner which added so much to the charm of his exhibitions'.[555] He still had a mischievous streak and liked nothing more than to play around, setting booby traps for Barnum and his parents. He'd place string between tables and chairs and watch in hysterics, rolling on the floor with laughter, as Barnum pretended to trip on the rather obvious trap.

It's said that Stratton loved to sit on Barnum's lap and listen to nursery rhymes and stories like 'Ali Baba and the Forty Thieves'. Barnum would sometimes pretend to be too sleepy to continue, just at the best bit, joshing Stratton that he'd need to pay to hear the rest. Stratton would begrudgingly part with his money: 'Please don't ever play such a trick as that on me again,' he allegedly moaned.[556]

Barnum took a keen interest in Stratton's education, paying for a private tutor who taught him French, reading and writing as well as the piano and violin. He constantly enquired after Stratton's well-being and forbade him from performing after 9 p.m. He seemed to genuinely care about Stratton, although he was also protecting a valuable asset, and the pair formed a loving bond. Stratton appeared content too: he loved the ponies and horses, although his pet monkey, which remained in London, was his favourite; he was well looked after; he was the centre of attention and was making everyone around him rich. He even grew to enjoy his lessons, and there was always some peace and quiet in the evenings when he retired to a room with his parents.[557]

Professor Pinte was a challenge, however. When the entourage reached the Belgium border, Barnum was infuriated to learn that Pinte had forgotten his passport, scolding him that he 'would never make a good showman, because a good showman never forgot anything'.[558] Barnum also struggled with Stratton's parents, claiming Cynthia was haughty, bad-tempered, hot-headed and interfering, which was particularly irritating because, from 1 January 1845, she and Sherwood were receiving half the profits. Sherwood, forever brooding and clueless, was paranoid and difficult, and he and Barnum conversed coldly on business.[559] Despite these tensions, Barnum's letters from France reveal that, with Stratton as the 'great little wonder of the age', the group had 'as much money as we want'.[560] This helped enable Barnum to occasionally return to New York to catch up with his museum business and his family.

In Brussels Tom Thumb performed for King Leopold and Queen Louise-Marie, who had previously seen him in London, then, in September 1845, Barnum and Tom Thumb were in Spain performing for the fifteen-year-old Queen Isabella II, and joining Her Majesty at a bullfight.[561] In the royal box, Barnum, Stratton and Isabella – a petulant and infantile queen – relished the bloodbath. In November 1845 Tom Thumb was again performing for King Louis Philippe. As one historian noted: 'The dwarf's trip to Europe had been not so much a tour as a royal progress.'[562]

———— ·◦◎◦· ————

IN DECEMBER 1845 great crowds warmly welcomed Tom Thumb back to England, where he soon performed at the Lyceum Theatre in London's fashionable West End. Boasting neoclassical columns and an internal balcony overhanging the dress circle, the Lyceum put on highbrow opera, adaptations of Charles Dickens's novels and, from March 1846, a play specially written for Stratton by the author, entertainer and mountaineer Albert Smith: *Hop o'My Thumb; or, the Ogre and His Seven League Boot,* an English adaptation of *Le Petit Poucet.*

Hop o'My Thumb transported the audience into a world of fairy tales and nursery rhymes, with the seven-year-old Stratton memorizing dialogue in rhyming couplets, learning several new songs and mastering stage directions that saw him outwit an ogre, ride a miniature horse and disappear offstage in a miniature chariot. The audience included the likes of Charles Dickens, the British actor William Charles Macready and Sir Edwin Henry Landseer, a renowned artist who specialized in painting animals. With his confidence, delivery and poise, Stratton was the star of the show.[563]

He was also booked at the Egyptian Hall for the Christmas season of 1845, where he continued to draw crowds until July 1846. Barnum had booked one of the two rooms upstairs. In the adjacent room, further down the corridor, Benjamin Robert Haydon had booked another. Haydon was a renowned English painter. He had studied at the Royal Academy of Arts under the 'terrible', magnificent Henry Fuseli, and, aged twenty-one, had even exhibited there. He toured the country giving well-attended and highly praised lectures, his success all the more remarkable because of his bad eyesight. Ever since an illness in childhood he had been troubled by the 'weakness of my eyes', he wrote in his diary.[564] On his sixtieth birthday, 25 January 1846, he pleaded: 'O God! continue my eyes and faculties to the last hour of my existence.'[565]

Despite his disability, he predominantly worked in the genre of history painting, which depicted great historical moments in a classical and idealized style known as 'high art'. He was also a man on a mission, to enlighten the tastes of the English, his motto: 'Grand Art sought for, wanted, & protected'.[566] This was not without resonance for a middle class who from the 1830s was particularly keen on 'rational recreation'.

Yet not everyone believed that art was important. The prevalence of evangelicalism from the 1780s, with its rejection of worldliness, instilled an upper-middle-class indifference towards art. When the British Institution for Promoting the Fine Arts was established in 1805, it fell short of a permanent national collection. When the National Gallery was established in 1824, it received limited funds. There was a sense that art was an aristocratic decadence, and that collections were for private rather than public consumption.[567] In September 1835 Haydon delivered a speech at the London Mechanics' Institution in Chancery Lane, railing at the 'degeneracy of taste' prevailing in England.[568] He was even more perturbed when, in 1843, he lost a national competition to paint a new fresco in the House of Lords.

Yet an inner voice propelled him forward ('Is it the whisper of an evil or a good spirit?' he wondered in his diary), and by January 1846 he had finished two grand paintings he intended to show to the public: *The Banishment of Aristides* and *Nero Harping while Rome Burned.*[569] Both paintings reflected the flaws of government and, perhaps, Haydon's own belief that the system was out to get him. Indeed, *The Banishment of Aristides* was very possibly a self-portrait.

Nonetheless, Haydon was ready to win over the public. He marched to the Egyptian Hall in January 1846 and defiantly rented an exhibition room. Together with his daughter, he prepared four hundred invitations for his private viewing on 4 April. On the first day only six people came. The rain poured outside as Haydon sat slumped in the empty room next to his daughter. One witness, who passed Haydon's exhibition, recalled the painter: 'stout, broad-shouldered ... rather shabbily dressed, with a general air of dilapidated power. There was something fierce and bitter in the expression of his face as he glanced across to the groups hurrying to see Tom Thumb.'[570]

Haydon believed his support lay with the people. Throughout his life he had coped with numerous failures and humiliations by comforting himself that his true genius was recognized by them. But in the storm of 'Deformito-Mania', amid the celebrity of Tom Thumb, things didn't look promising as the sixty-year-old painter opened his exhibition to the public on Monday 6 April 1846. It fared no better than his private viewing, and Haydon responded with the last gasp of a drowning man, paying for a desperate advert in the press: 'Exquisite Feeling of the

English People for high Art – General Tom Thumb last week received 12,000 people, who paid him £600, B.R. Haydon, who has devoted forty-two years to elevate their taste, was honoured by the visits of 133 ½, producing £5 13s. 6d.'[571]

The half visitor was a little girl. *Punch* wrote mockingly: 'That ½ is touching. What sort of ½ was it? Did it run alone, or being brought to drink in High Art, was it a baby or a breast?'[572] Haydon was no showman. His adverts merely broadcast his own failures, while elevating and advertising the success of Tom Thumb.

After a humiliating, financially crippling exhibition, Haydon was forced to concede in May 1846: 'the people have been corrupted ... Next to a victory is a skilful retreat; and I marched out before General Thumb, a beaten but not conquered exhibitor.'[573] One month later Haydon slit his throat, then snuffed out his life with the assistance of a pistol (the cuts to his throat failing to do the job). He left open his diary on a table in his painting room:

God forgive me. Amen.
Finis
of
B.R. Haydon.
'Stretch me no longer on this rough world' – Lear[574]

———•⌒◦⌒•———

AFTER HAYDON'S DEATH, as during his life, Stratton and Barnum said nothing about the artist. But the English felt guilty. 'Deformito-Mania' had come at a cost. Suddenly, people paid attention to the ruined artist; around £2,000 was publicly raised for his widow, who was also granted a pension of £50 per annum from the Civil List. The press thundered: 'The display of a disgusting dwarf attracted hordes of gaping idiots, who poured into the pockets of a Yankee showman a stream of wealth one tithe of which would have redeemed an honourable English artist from wretchedness and death.'[575]

At Haydon's inquest extracts from his diary were read aloud, reflecting where the culpability lay: 'April 13. Receipts £1 3s 6d. ... They rush by thousands to see Tom Thumb. They push, they fight, they scream, they faint, they cry help and murder! and oh! and ah! They see my bills, my boards ... and don't read them. Their eyes are open, but their sense is shut. It is an insanity, a *rabies*, a madness, a *furore*, a dream. I would not have believed it of the English people.'[576]

Haydon's death brought into relief the financial success of a dwarf and his showman, representatives of a nation criticized for 'their love of "smart" dealing' in Dickens's *American Notes* (1842).[577] Moreover, the suicide of Haydon was perceived as a battle between two modes of culture. It was, as *Punch* wrote, '"HIGH ART" *versus* "TOM THUMB"'.[578] The cultural clash was captured in George Cruikshank's 1847 etching, published in the popular *Comic Almanack*. It depicts the 'genius' painter sitting impoverished and broken in a dark studio as a dwarf reclines on an expensive chaise longue, eating grapes. Genius is rewarded with poverty; deformity is privileged with wealth.

The cultural concerns underpinning the freak show exploded onto the scene as *Punch* declared: 'Let "High Art" in England obtain the same patronage – let it receive as cordial a welcome at the Palace, as again and again has been vouchsafed to Tom Thumb and crowds of snobs, for such only reason, will rush to contemplate it – or to think they contemplate it.'[579]

Punch blamed the queen for Tom Thumb's popularity, but the underlying issue was a fear that culture was being diluted in favour of freak frivolity. Britain was the birthplace of Shakespeare, after all, but now it was enamoured with the commercial freak show. The rise of popular culture threatened to undermine elite culture, yet the laments largely fell on deaf ears as Barnum and Stratton embarked on a final tour of the provincial towns.

'Born a Genius and Born a Dwarf' by George Cruikshank, featuring Benjamin Robert Haydon and Tom Thumb, 1847.

———❦———

IN JANUARY 1847 Charles Stratton was giving his last performances at the Theatre Royal in Liverpool, where he acted scenes from *Hop o'My Thumb*. On 2 January as Stratton turned his attention home, *The Times* delivered a parting shot: 'we were indebted to Tom Thumb for all the physical deformities that contested for public favour … IT has not died a natural death … Thousands rush to look at it, as thousands rushed to kiss and touch the deformity aforesaid.'[580]

On 4 February 1847 the Tom Thumb entourage set sail on the *Cambria* steamer. Stratton had not seen home for three years but, since his departure, he had effected a monumental transformation, both personal and historical. Merely four years old when discovered by Barnum, Stratton had become a national celebrity and then an international star. He had been graced by kings and queens, adored by thousands and praised as an actor. The boy from Bridgeport, raised by a part-time cleaner and a struggling carpenter, had made fortunes for himself and his family. He made Barnum rich and famous too. In the process he had unleashed a cultural transformation in Europe. Prior to their transatlantic journey they had entrenched the shift from the carnivalesque to the commercial freak show as Tom Thumb performed theatricals at the American Museum, the new centre of popular culture. In Europe the pair had a similar effect. As the statistician Adolphe Quételet noted a few years later: 'Tom Thumb was the celebrated dwarf, whom the United States have offered to the admiration of Europe. I say "admiration", for I think the different classes of society have never shown a greater eagerness to see any other man.'[581]

The freak show had gone mainstream. For hundreds of years dwarfs and human curiosities had been performing, but Stratton and Barnum created a winning combination with a unique novelty performance, royal endorsements and a highly advertised show. In the process the Victorian freak show had become the freak industry: internationalized, professionalized and formalized within European popular culture.

From this moment, in Britain, Europe and America, the freak show would proliferate in a range of venues: amusement parks, travelling fairs and shopfront shows; in circuses, vaudevilles, music halls and seaside resorts; in museums, theatres, world's fairs and carnivals; in aquariums, zoos, pleasure gardens and even homes. The freak show was a central pillar of popular culture; in fact, it *was* popular culture, respectable, permanent and permeating; a transformation that occurred when General Tom Thumb, played by Charles Stratton and managed by P.T. Barnum came to town. *Punch* was perplexed by this phenomenon yet equally clear where the culpability lay:

We cannot understand the cause of the now prevailing taste for deformity, which seems to grow by what it feeds upon. The first dose administered to this morbid appetite was somewhat homeopathic, being comprised in the diminutive form of Tom Thumb; but the eagerness with which this little humbug was devoured – at least by female kisses – has caused the importation, on a much larger scale, of all sorts of lusus naturae *and specimens of animated ugliness, which form a source of attraction to the public ... There seems to be a sort of fascination in the horrible; and we can only hope, as the mania has now reached its extreme, a healthy admiration for the 'true and the beautiful', as the novelists call it, will immediately begin to show itself.*[582]

Fat chance. The age of the freak was only just building up steam.

CHAPTER SIXTEEN

FINDING CHARLES

C HARLES STRATTON'S LIFE was only just beginning too. When he returned to America in 1847, it was reported that he was now educated and accomplished, puffing on miniature cigars, sleeping in a rosewood bed imported from France (a gift from Barnum) and enjoying the mansion he shared with his parents – built from their new wealth – and their servants. He sent his two sisters to private school, while he continued touring and soaring to new heights. On 13 April 1847 he met the eleventh president of the United States, James K. Polk. He travelled across the US, Cuba and Canada, and went back to Europe too. By the 1860s, in his twenties, he owned his own property, pedigree horses and a yacht he sailed on Long Island Sound. He was a Knight Templar and a thirty-second-degree Mason. He was an independent man forging his own contracts and connections.[583]

In 1863, during the height of the Civil War, when the North had recently suffered a terrible defeat at Fredericksburg, Virginia, a 'furore of excitement' was described in the *New York Times* because 'The Loving Lilliputians', Charles Stratton and Lavinia Warren, were getting married at Grace Church in Manhattan.[584] Lavinia Warren Bump, shortened to Lavinia Warren, had been signed by Barnum a year earlier. When she first met Charles, aged twenty-one years old and 32in tall, she was bright-eyed, fresh-faced and intelligent, with an air of gentility that reflected the respectable New England family from which she came. She also had a mischievous glint: she had disobeyed her parents when, eager for adventure and travel, she abandoned her job as a schoolteacher to join her cousin's 'floating palace of curiosities' on the Ohio and Mississippi rivers, performing beautiful, sentimental songs, dancing gracefully and impressing with her natural beauty. No wonder Barnum signed her on a multi-year contract.

Of her eight siblings, only one was a dwarf: Huldah Pierce Warren, known as Minnie, who was signed by Barnum shortly after Lavinia. Aged sixteen years old, Minnie was maid of honour when Lavinia and Charles tied the knot.[585] The best man was George Washington Morrison Nutt, who went by the stage name Commodore Nutt. Barnum claims that Nutt visited the American Museum in December 1861 when he was struck by this 'most remarkable dwarf, who was a sharp, intelligent little fellow, with a deal of drollery and wit'.[586] At the time, Nutt, the son of a farmer from Manchester, New Hampshire, was 30in tall and thirteen years old. He was blue-eyed, fair-haired, humorous, witty and lively; a gifted singer, dancer, comic and actor who, the publicity claims, was signed by Barnum at the astonishing rate of $30,000 for three years, earning him the nickname the '$30,000 Nutt'.[587] (The actual contract amounted to $4,888 plus expenses for a five-year period.)[588]

Barnum had assembled a company of performing dwarfs and, before the big wedding day, he displayed the betrothed at the American Museum, 'crowding the Museum, and pouring money into the treasury', he wrote.[589] He even offered the couple $15,000 if they would postpone their wedding for a month, so he could keep their exhibition going as his profits were flowing. The couple flatly refused: 'Not for fifty thousand dollars,' exclaimed Stratton.[590] On the day itself, police erected barricades to contain the crowds, while inside the church was 'a gay assemblage of the youth, beauty, wealth, and worth of the metropolis': governors, members of Congress, generals and the richest and finest in New York.[591] Shortly afterward, the newlyweds went to meet President Abraham Lincoln.

The quartet formed the General Tom Thumb Company, which travelled on a honeymoon tour and later, between 1869 and 1872, on a world tour managed by Sylvester Bleeker, one of Barnum's friends and a former employee. The group travelled across America and Europe and then to Japan, China, Australia, India, Egypt and beyond.[592] By the late 1870s the company was disbanded, but the Strattons continued to tour intermittently, until Stratton passed away aged forty-five on the morning of 15 July 1883.

Despite his international profile, maintained throughout his career, we know little of Stratton from his own writings. It is remarkable considering his ubiquity. There was an industrial production of Tom Thumb memorabilia, which reflected his celebrity status and the commercial context: the numerous exhibition pamphlets, children's books, medallions, lithographs, daguerreotypes, engravings, prints and *cartes-de-visite*.[593] He was even depicted on trading cards, paper dolls, tiny 'Tom Thumb Segs' (heel plates) and 'Tom Thumb Jujubes' (candy pieces).[594] His clothes and carriages became commodities. Yet amid all this, Stratton the man remains largely elusive. Unlike his wife or Barnum, Stratton left no memoir or autobiography. His life, as we know it, was lived through his persona, General Tom Thumb.

His private life offstage was part of the public show, mirroring the experiences of Chang and Eng, whose wedding was treated for public consumption and whose children eventually hit the freak show stage. In Stratton's case, courtship and marriage were framed as fairy tales. In his autobiography Barnum gleefully reported how Nutt fell in love with Lavinia, as did Tom Thumb, whom she ultimately chose – Nutt and the General even getting into a fight over her. Nutt was allegedly heartbroken when he learned of the impending nuptials, but Barnum's retelling of the events closely echoed the stories of the literary Tom Thumb. In all probability, Barnum was writing fairy-tale fiction that obscured the realities.[595]

On the wedding day the whole affair was promoted as a fairy wedding, with tickets and souvenirs being sold. The couple's lives offstage were co-opted into the freak show world, framed as a freak fairy tale. Furthermore, Stratton's marriage propelled his freak persona into the realms of respectable domesticity and away from his earlier rakish persona. Just like Chang and Eng, whose onstage persona developed as their lives offstage transformed, so a similar interrelationship between the private and public occurred for Stratton and his persona Tom Thumb. The rogue who once boasted of having kissed thousands of ladies became a family man when he wed. This played to the cultural expectations of the mid-nineteenth-century 'cult of domesticity' that emphasized the importance of the family, and perceived marriage as the vehicle of respectability and stability.[596] By getting married, Tom Thumb was playing to his fan base and Barnum was upping the freak show ante. And yet, amid the publicity and showmanship, there was a personal relationship between Charles and Lavinia that was filled with affection and warmth.

Barnum went even further when he announced that the couple had become parents. Mathew Brady, the American Civil War photographer, took a portrait of the family that was reproduced throughout America and Europe. In truth, or so it seems, they had rented a baby from a foundling hospital. When they later toured Europe in the 1860s, Lavinia revealed: '... we exhibited English babies in England, French babies in France, and German babies in Germany. It was – they were – a great success.'[597] (The child may have even been presented to Queen Victoria in 1865.) But Barnum worried the public would suspect the baby hoax so, effectively, he killed the child by spreading the rumour that it had died of an inflammation in the brain. Years later, in a 1901 interview, Lavinia was emphatic: 'I never had a baby.'[598]

However, the historian and researcher John Gannon has unearthed information that complicates the picture. It is certain that a baby named Minnie Warren Stratton (sharing the first name of Lavinia's sister) died on 25 September 1866. Her death certificate notes that she was two years old, 'daughter of Charles Sherwood Stratton', whose occupation was penned as 'Exhibitor'. The cause of death was recorded as 'Congestion of Brain' and 'effusion into Ventricles and Convulsions'.[599] Furthermore, press reports indicate that Lavinia cancelled her performances to attend to the child at the Norfolk Hotel, Norwich, before she died. After the baby's death, both Lavinia and Charles attended the funeral at the Norwich Cemetery. Hundreds were in attendance and a gravestone, which still stands today, was erected.

It was strange that Lavinia never mentioned the child in her autobiography: perhaps a sense of shame, embarrassment or ... ? But it is highly probable that the child, although legally the Strattons', was not their biological daughter and, indeed, a delivery would have been dangerous (Lavinia's sister Minnie died in childbirth in 1878). Yet in this world of freak shows, with all the characteristic deception and humbug, one is rarely sure of anything.

—◦◦◦—

STRATTON DID LEAVE some words but they are few and far between and, as we will see, hard to divorce from his public persona. He was always General Tom Thumb when giving interviews or writing to acquaintances. We are in the territory of the modern celebrity, where never more so have people had to live their life in public: on social media, in gossip magazines, being photographed. Their lives *are* the entertainment, and we see the roots of this modern-day celebrity culture here.

But how, then, can we gauge Stratton's perspective on his life and experiences? It all began so young, when he was only four years old. How he felt about his early performing life is hard to discern. Did he relish the attention and the applause of his newfound fame? In an 1878 interview, when he reflected on his first travels around Europe, he admitted, 'I can't remember everything.'[600] In another interview that year, he mistakenly credited Queen Victoria with giving him the title 'General':

> *Previous to my presentations to the Queen, at Buckingham Palace, in 1844, I had been known simply as Tom Thumb; but the Queen, when I had been presented to her in that form, said, with a smile: 'You ought to have a title. I think I shall have to call you General Tom Thumb.' The Duke of Wellington and several others of the nobility were present at the time, and of course Her Majesty's words were instantly adopted, and I became a General from that time onward.*[601]

It is unsurprising that Stratton's recollections were hazy, being only a child when he went to Europe in 1844, although he did profess to have enjoyed certain parts of his tour. He recalled with fondness his encounter with the Duke of Wellington, where he had quipped that he was thinking about the loss of the Battle of Waterloo: 'when I look back at the scene, I can't help thinking that it was a pretty cute thing for me to have said to him'.[602] He was seemingly proud of his early achievements, commenting: 'I have been brought into contact with almost everybody of any note as I went along; all were very kind and I have the most pleasant recollection of the years I spent in Europe.'[603]

After his European tour, Philip Hone, the former mayor of New York, claimed Stratton 'does not appear to be fatigued or displeased by his incessant labours' and, since returning to America, could kiss 'the good-looking women, a favour which he does not grant indiscriminately'.[604] Caroline Barnum, the daughter of the showman, spent time touring with Tom Thumb in 1848 and noted that Stratton – whom she referred to as the 'General' – was 'full of fun' and 'full of sport', although 'I think he has a little pride'.[605] Reportedly, in his early performing life, Stratton would return a mocking stare to his audience.[606]

At times Stratton found the crowds tiresome and irritating, being mobbed wherever he went. He revealed in a later interview that they 'crowd up to my carriage and cry out, "Tom, don't you want a drink?" It's terribly insulting and disagreeable.'[607] The minstrel performer Charley Howard, who travelled with the ten-year-old Stratton in 1848, noted how 'he was always in a bad humour, and would get up every morning crying'.[608] Revealingly, Lavinia wrote in her autobiography: 'He had often remarked that he never remembered having been a child, being placed on exhibition when he was but four years of age, and was then educated to act the part of the man and put childish things away.'[609]

Stratton drank wine from the age of five, smoked cigars from the age of seven and chewed tobacco from the age of nine. The child was killed off when General Tom Thumb was created, and the balance of his life was a performance. There is no escaping this air of tragedy, underpinned by what, essentially, was financial exploitation.

But if Stratton did struggle with his predicament, he appears to have found solace in God, writing to a Reverend Sprague and noting that, 'in accordance with your request, I send you a *little* note'. That Stratton felt he should poke fun at his size in a letter to a minister perhaps exposes just how much he lived and breathed his performance:

I have travelled fifty thousand miles been before more crowned heads than any other Yankee living, except my friend Mr Barnum, and have kissed nearly two millions of [sic] *ladies, including the Queens of England, France, Belgium and Spain.*

I read the Bible everyday and am very fond of reading the New Testament. I love my Saviour and it makes me happy. I adore my Creator and know that He is good to us all. He has given me a small body, but I believe he has not contracted my heart, nor brain, nor soul. I shall praise His name evermore.

Time compels me to make this note short like myself.

Charles S. Stratton, known as General Tom Thumb.[610]

Perhaps Stratton's faith was a crucial part of his coping mechanism. His little boast of kissing numerous ladies and his commitment to God reflect both his pious and roguish nature, which were noted by contemporaries. That Stratton should refer to Barnum as 'my friend' is also revealing. There is no evidence to indicate that, in their personal relationship, Stratton and Barnum had anything other than admiration for each other. And while initially all the power was in Barnum's hands, over the years this would change as the pair went their separate ways. In 1856, when Barnum went bankrupt following some dodgy investments, Stratton came to the rescue, writing to his old friend:

My Dear Mr. Barnum,—

I understand your friends, and that means 'all creation,' intend to get up some benefits for your family. Now, my dear sir, just be good enough to remember that I belong to that mighty crowd, and I must have a finger (or at least a 'thumb') in that pie. ... I have just started out on my western tour, and have my carriage, ponies and assistants all here, but I am ready to go on to New York, bag and baggage, and remain at Mrs. Barnum's service as long as I, in my small way, can be useful. Put me into any 'heavy' work, if you like. Perhaps I cannot lift as much as some other

folks, but just take your pencil in hand and you will see I can
draw a tremendous load. I drew two hundred tons at a single
pull to-day, embracing two thousand persons, whom I hauled up
safely and satisfactorily to all parties, at one exhibition. Hoping
that you will be able to fix up a lot of magnets that will attract all
New York, and volunteering to sit on any part of the loadstone, I
am, as ever, your little but sympathizing friend,
  GEN. TOM THUMB [611]

Barnum claims he refused the offer of help, but in January 1857 the
pair were in Europe with Stratton playing Tom Thumb and helping
Barnum back on his feet. It says a lot about Stratton and his relationship
with Barnum.

⸺⟨⊙⟩⸺

WITH FEW WORDS from Stratton himself, and the boundaries
between the reality and the performance impossibly blurred,
how we read Stratton's life largely depends on how we view the type of
entertainment he popularized: the freak show. For some historians it
was a practice of exploitation: 'I want to establish from the start', David
Gerber wrote in his article on the 'careers' of those exhibited, 'that I do
not approve of freak shows and thus find condemnation of them, past
or present, a compelling purpose.'[612]

Understandably, he viewed Stratton's life as a tragic one, a life
which Stratton ultimately realized was tragic too. Gerber argued that,
as Stratton grew older: 'a note of gravity entered his personality, as if
he wished to be taken more seriously or at least to take himself more
seriously'. He stopped doing his comic routines and simply made personal
appearances. By the time of his death, aged forty-five in 1883, he had
grown fat, tired and weary, and had spent most of his wealth in a manner
that suggests 'compulsory striving'. Gerber was in no doubt: 'I have seen

Stratton as tragic, a prisoner of conditions over which he, as a dwarf, had little control and that both profited and humiliated him.'[613] Perhaps revealingly, his companion Nutt, who was displayed from the age of sixteen, succumbed to alcoholism and gambling.[614] Similarly, Stratton's father, Sherwood, who appeared to battle with demons throughout his life, ended his days a desperate alcoholic confined to a mental asylum, dying four days after Christmas in 1855, aged forty-four.[615]

In the view of other historians, however, the freak show fulfilled a necessary function: it was the vehicle through which those with exceptional bodies found employment, exercised agency over their lives and achieved material wealth and success. As Robert Bogdan wrote in reference to America: 'With an urbanizing country, no social security, discrimination in employment, architectural barriers, and strained personal relations, persons with anomalies found refuge in a world where there were others similarly situated.'[616] For him, Stratton's life could be read more positively, although Bogdan was also aware that 'he looked like a millionaire because he spent like one, not because he invested wisely', leaving his widow with an estate valued at a meagre $16,000, plus some small real estate, which was a pittance considering what he was once worth.[617]

Certainly, Stratton exists in the realm of the modern-day celebrity. He was hounded and celebrated across the globe; his image was everywhere. And he was rocketed to stardom in the American Museum, the institution that centralized the freak show in American popular culture. This was a form of entertainment that was sometimes exploitative, sometimes empowering. In fact, the freak show could be both at once.

Stratton was exploited as a child performer, clearly having no choice when he was thrust onstage aged four, but he was also empowered as a dwarf who operated in an able-bodied world organized against him. He achieved a level of security and public renown not available to most dwarfs in the nineteenth century. There were obviously trials and tribulations, but the source material is simply not there to assert, with confidence, how Stratton viewed his own life. What General Tom Thumb said and did is not necessarily proof of what Stratton experienced. In the end, however, his wife, Lavinia, left a fitting tribute that perhaps gets closest to the real Charles Stratton: 'His excellent qualities were numerous. I never knew a person so entirely devoid of malice, jealousy, or envy; he had the natural instincts of a gentleman. He was kind, affectionate and generous.'[618]

What we do know for sure is that through Stratton's relationship with Barnum, the golden age of freak shows dawned and the freak industry was born. It was a form of popular culture that peddled freak show entertainment which was more grand, commercial, international and integrated with the emerging entertainment industry than anything before the 1840s. Thereafter, thanks to this unique relationship, the freak show would grow in leaps and bounds, with whole troupes of freak performers acting together in a range of diverse venues, travelling around the globe under the auspices of showmen and managers with whom they were engaged in contractual arrangements (for the most part, at least). After Barnum and Stratton, freak shows were usually aggressively advertised; they comprised a unique novelty performance; they came with royal endorsements; they were highly mobile and international; and they were a central pillar of Victorian popular culture.

ACT FOUR

THE CLIMAX

CHAPTER SEVENTEEN

MAXIMO AND BARTOLA

MAXIMO AND BARTOLA were supposedly found in 1849 deep in the mountains of Central America, worshipped by pagans in a city named Iximaya. Two intrepid explorers had already lost their lives trying to locate the place: one was killed with a spear brandished by a wild Indian, the other was sacrificed on a high altar by bloodthirsty priests. But another adventurer, Señor Pedro Velasquez, had penetrated the fortified Iximaya and found the two children, Maximo and Bartola, squatting on an altar being revered as idols. They were, so the later publicity ran, relics of the ancient Aztecs, 'forbidden, by inviolably sacred laws, from intermarrying with any persons but of their own caste'. As such, they had 'dwindled down, in the course of many centuries, to a few significant individuals, diminutive in stature', 'imbecile in intellect' yet 'held in high veneration and affection by the whole Iximayan community, probably as living specimens of an antique race'. Velasquez escaped the citadel of sin with the children, fighting off the murderous Iximayans and managing, eventually, to launch Maximo and Bartola on the freak show stage. Well, that's the story.[619]

Unlike Charles Stratton, we know very little about the true background of Maximo and Bartola: both their origins and later lives are mired in mystery, communicated through freak show material that is sensationalist, dubious and at times downright fictitious. But although the details will likely never be known, the two did possibly hail from Central America – specifically, the province of San Miguel, El Salvador. It has been claimed that a Spanish trader, Ramon Selva, offered to take the siblings from their peasant parents, Innocente Burgos and Marina Espina, promising he would cure the youngsters of their 'imbecility'. Whatever their feelings, the parents agreed to part with their children, but Selva betrayed them and sold the siblings to an American showman, perhaps a Mr Knox, of whom little is known, who appears then to have sold the children to yet another showman, Mr Joseph Morris, about whom, again, we know little.[620]

A freak identity was constructed for Maximo and Bartola. They were dubbed 'The Last of the Ancient Aztecs of Mexico', given garish Aztec-themed costumes and saddled with the bogus Iximaya story, which was published in a freak show pamphlet that built on a successful travelogue by John Lloyd Stephens, *Incidents of Travel in Central America, Chiapas, and Yucatan* (1840s). In 1849 the siblings were thrust onstage in New York and Boston. Maximo, the boy, was around seven or eight years old and 33in tall; his sister was between four and six, and around 29½in tall. Their skin, it was noted, appeared similar in colour to that of Native Americans, and their hair was jet black. Their heads were described as elongated and small, and they did not speak English or any other recognizable language, although they were able to comprehend what was being said. They could, however, be heard among their 'unintelligible jargon of sounds' to utter the words 'Papa' and 'Mama'.[621] In their habits and actions, Maximo and Bartola appeared like children aged two or three.

Today we know the siblings had the condition microcephaly, but this term only emerged in the late 1850s and was only applied to the siblings in 1863. Instead, Maximo and Bartola were generally described as 'idiots'. In the Victorian period, now with a prominent freak industry, that often meant being put on show.[622]

———◦⦿◦———

MAXIMO AND BARTOLA were the talk of the scientific community in Boston. In 1849 they were displayed at the Society of Natural History; they were inspected by the renowned Boston physician Dr Jonathan Mason Warren, and they featured in his paper, published in the *American Journal of the Medical Sciences*, which called them 'Indian dwarfs' rather than ancient Aztecs. Warren claimed that although they had 'very low mental organization, they cannot be pronounced idiots of the lowest grade', because 'their senses of sight, hearing, smell, taste, and touch, as well as that of tact, seem complete'.[623] The editor of the *New-York Daily Tribune*, Horace Greeley, claimed: 'To the moralist, the student, the physiologist, they are subjects deserving of careful scrutiny and thoughtful observation.'[624]

Allegedly, Maximo and Bartola met the mayor of Boston, members of the Senate and House of Representatives and, at the White House, the thirteenth president, Millard Fillmore. Then, in a career resembling General Tom Thumb's, in June 1853 the two Aztecs were taken to England. According to the passenger list for the steamship *Europa*, which sailed from Boston and docked in Liverpool, the group comprised Joseph Morris, their manager-owner, a 'Professor Anderson', who acted as the showman, another 'lady, and boy ... and nurse', who probably cared for the siblings when they were not onstage.[625]

As they set sail, the *Era* reported the 'Arrival of More Wonders': 'Our eyes have scarcely recovered from the injurious effects of overstraining to get a glimpse at ... Thomas Thumb, when they are again summoned to gaze upon the two little Aztecs.'[626] Maximo and Bartola did not perform in Liverpool but they were introduced to local journalists, who whipped up interest. According to the *Liverpool Mercury*, 'the Aztec Lilliputians are not introduced to the public as dwarfs, or freaks of nature in human organisation – though in this light they may and will be regarded as the greatest natural and living curiosities extant – but they are exhibited as types and specimens of a race of people long since supposed to be extinct – living links between the most remote ages and the present'.[627]

Maximo and Bartola had entered a nation that perceived itself as the shining light of civilization: industrially strong, imperially powerful and politically secure (sheltered, as it was, from the 1848 European revolutions). Underpinning this optimism was a belief in the superior Caucasian race. While the Enlightenment taught that man would progress from a savage to a civilized state, through the 1840s and 1850s new theories were increasingly challenging this progressive narrative. Instead, it was largely maintained that there were some peoples who were not progressing and could not progress. The Aztec siblings exemplified the point: they were representatives of a race that had failed to civilize and had largely perished – except, of course, for Maximo and Bartola.[628]

With the Liverpudlian press promoting them, the Aztecs headed to London. Much like Chang and Eng in the 1830s, Maximo and Bartola were displayed before the medical fraternity. They did the rounds among the 'principle members of the Royal College of Surgeons, the Royal Institution and the Geographical and Ethnological Societies', the press claiming that the doctors 'pronounced them to be unparalleled by any specimens yet discovered alive'.[629] Apparently, at the Royal College of Surgeons, the children were mesmerized by the skeletons of the Irish Giant and Sicilian Dwarf that were displayed in the Hunterian Museum.[630]

Interest in the siblings was propelled by broader debates between proponents of monogenism, which argued for the common ancestry of humans, and polygenism, which stressed the different origins of human races. These were the same theories that had animated members of the American Philosophical Society when they went to see Henry Moss – the African American who developed white patches of skin – in 1796. But by the 1840s ethnology had emerged as a distinct discipline investigating the relationship between different people using physical, social and linguistic factors to account for human variations. The Ethnological Society of London, founded in 1843, gave institutional authority to the monogenesis theory as confidently asserted by the English physician James Prichard: 'all the tribes of men are of one family'.[631] Yet in America, through the 1840s and 1850s, polygenism trumped monogenism in scientific thought, largely to justify the continued subjugation of black slaves. And when James Hunt established the Anthropological Society of London, he delivered a paper in 1863 claiming there was 'good reason for classifying the Negro as a distinct species from Europeans'.[632] Thus, polygenism was institutionalized in Britain too.

Maximo and Bartola were examined while these issues were being debated. The siblings were intimately studied by the monogenist professor Richard Owen, a comparative anatomist who concluded they were 'instances of exceptional arrest of development, not representatives of any peculiar human race'.[633] Despite the showman's claims that the Aztecs represented a new race, Owen declared categorically that they were neither a new race nor even Aztecs. He was supported by the psychiatrist John Conolly, who delivered a paper to the Ethnological Society in 1855 stating that, despite 'numerous and diverse theories', Maximo and Bartola were 'merely examples of arrested development'.[634]

The comparative anatomist Robert Knox, who once gave a lecture during an 'ethnic show' of San people in 1847, begged to differ.[635] He linked Maximo and Bartola to the long-lost Aztecs, and wrapped his interpretation in the trendy polygenesis view. As he wrote in his article on the Aztecs: 'Mankind is composed of one great natural family, comprising many distinct species, unalterable and unaltered by time or circumstances.'[636] One family, for sure, but with biologically and hierarchically different species and, as he declared five years earlier, 'in human history race is everything'.[637] Maximo and Bartola might have been following the template established by Barnum and Stratton, but they were denigrated as racially inferior.

—◦◦◦◦—

HOT ON THE heels of the 'Deformito-Mania' of the 1840s, the Aztecs were summoned to Buckingham Palace on 4 July 1853, before they had even been subject to a public performance. It is not clear how this meeting was organized but, according to the press, it was Sir James Clark, the physician to Prince Albert, who helped secure the meeting.[638] Around a month earlier, Queen Victoria and Prince Albert had met the 'Zulu Kaffirs', a group of eleven men, one woman and one child who were performing in London, with Victoria describing them as 'most curious, wild, fine looking people.'[639] That same year the royals also met the so-called Earthmen, known only as Martinus and Flora, approximately sixteen and fourteen respectively, from South Africa, with Prince Albert collecting photographs of both the Earthmen and Zulus.[640] Clearly, 1853 was a year when Victoria and Albert were particularly interested in 'ethnographic curiosities'.

This interest was spurred by the Great Exhibition of the Works of Industry of All Nations (1851), housed in the magnificent Crystal Palace in London, which had been constructed with sheets of glass held by a central iron transept, 33m tall. Britain occupied half of the space, boasting exhibits from home and the colonies, and confirming what the early Victorians knew to be true: Britain was the greatest nation on earth. She was the supreme industrial, imperial and naval power; her sovereignty stretched across India, Africa and other colonies, and her tentacles of trade reached into Asia and Latin America.

The Great Exhibition had been the brainchild of Prince Albert, who hoped, as he had declared in an October 1850 speech, 'that the first impression ... upon the spectator will be that of deep thankfulness to the Almighty for the blessings which He has bestowed upon us'.[641] In March the following year, he declared at a formal banquet at Mansion House that 'the distances which separated the different nations and parts of the globe are rapidly vanishing before the achievements of modern invention'.[642] Prince Albert decided on almost everything associated with the Great Exhibition, including its motto: 'The Earth is the Lord's and all that therein is.'[643] And as a result he paid a heavy personal price; the period 1850–51 was one of the busiest in his life. His health was failing and he was frequently sick (he died aged just forty-two in 1861). However, his work left a lasting legacy, uniting the royal family with an event that epitomized Victorian optimism.

Crucially, the Great Exhibition fuelled interest in foreigners, who were usually seen as subservient to British civilization. The Indian section occupied several courts and was given the central location, a symbolic gesture to the importance of India to Britain's imperial crown. There were also smaller courts devoted to the Ottoman Empire, as well as Egyptian, Turkish and Tunisian areas. The last had an 'obliging native custodien [sic]' who guided visitors around the displays of 'North African tribes'.[644] Other London attractions at the time included the Vauxhall Gardens, which hosted an Algerian family in Arab costume, and the Egyptian Hall's presentation of a Syrian troupe in a 'Holy Land' panorama. Two years later, Earthmen, Zulus and Aztecs were being received by the nation and their queen.[645]

Now, on 4 July 1853, inside Buckingham Palace, Maximo and Bartola were introduced to Prince Albert, Queen Victoria and three of their children: their eldest daughter, Victoria, Princess Royal; their eldest son, Edward, Prince of Wales; and Princess Alice, their third-born. For over an hour the royal family gazed at the Aztecs; presumably Morris and Anderson were in attendance, answering any questions. The *Standard*, which ran the headline 'The Aztecs at the Palace', noted that 'these strange and wondrous arrivals from an unexpected part of the earth' were met with the 'most eulogistic terms'.[646] Like Barnum and Tom Thumb, Morris and Anderson made the most of this royal endorsement, printing in a freak show pamphlet that 'the excitement they occasioned at the Palace was far greater than that which their Guardians had expected'.[647] But Victoria was notably disappointed, even disgusted, with Maximo and Bartola. She wrote in her journal: 'we saw 2 horrid little monstrosities … They are a sad spectacle of humanity & are evidently idiots, who cannot speak. The like of them has never been seen before & their origin is a mystery. They … have the smallest most dreadful skulls imaginable. Altogether, they quite give one the creeps, but they are worth seeing.'[648]

After their introduction to 'scientific societies, and distinguished members of the medical profession', plus that visit to Buckingham Palace, the 'Aztec Lilliputians – Patronised by her Majesty', were finally ready for their London debut.[649] Clearly, Morris was following the route established by Barnum and Stratton: whip up public interest, aim for the palace and then go public.

There was, however, one big difference. Stratton reversed the assumptions of the pseudoscience phrenology, which linked the smallness of the skull to intelligence, whereas the Aztecs, according to one phrenologist, testified to the phrenological claims: Maximo and Bartola had 'an extremely defective condition of their mental constitution'.[650] And while Stratton was a skilled performer who could grab an adult audience, Maximo and Bartola could only play children's games while onstage. It's hard to escape the conclusion that, in this instance, the display of two children with cognitive disabilities was exploitation, pure and simple.

———◦◦◦———

IN JULY 1853, at the Hanover Square rooms, in a hot, stuffy and poorly ventilated space, Maximo and Bartola were displayed for up to seven hours a day, six days a week. Having been excited by the posters that littered the streets of London, and the loud announcements in the press, spectators piled in, with possibly 3,000 attending in the first two days.

The show began with the showman, perhaps Anderson, telling the fabulous story of the Aztecs being found in the city of Iximaya and worshipped as idols by pagan Indians. Then stepped forward their 'guardian-in-chief', perhaps Morris, who introduced Bartola and Maximo to the room. The audience were wonderstruck: 'The first glance at them utterly astounds the spectators. They are so small – their heads are so strangely formed – their little limbs are so meagre – their cries are so shrill – their pranks so strange, that in the first flush of astonishment one thinks rather of sprites and hobgoblins than of human beings.'[651]

According to a reporter from *Household Words*, 'They began their performance by running very obediently together, like horses in a circus, round the long platform in the middle of the room. Then they were put upon the platform and played monkey tricks for the amusement of the public.'[652]

The audience went wild. They clamoured around the platform, thrusting pieces of cake into the palms of Maximo and Bartola, who were also kissed and fondled. Their small heads were prodded and stroked by clammy hands. The showman declared that ladies were particularly fond of the Aztecs and that Her Majesty had had the pleasure of their company, his boasts drowned out by the incessant chatter of the crowd that mobbed the eleven- and eight-year-old siblings.[653]

One 'enthusiastic lady ... made the air alive with cries of "Kiss me, darling. Come, Maximo, dear kiss me ...".'[654] According to another reporter, one besotted woman from Belgravia begged: 'Oh! What a dear delightful little thing! Pray sir, will you permit me to take that love of an oddity home with me in the carriage?' Others pondered the reality of the Aztecs: some thought they were puppets, others that they belonged to a monkey tribe; one little girl thought they might be a mermaid and merman.[655] A hired hand – a young boy who also played with the Aztecs perched on their platform – sold the freak show pamphlet, *Illustrated History of the Aztec Lilliputians*. Price, 1 shilling; a daguerreotype sold for half a guinea too.

How Maximo and Bartola understood this experience is anyone's guess, but this was now their everyday reality. And they were only just beginning their lives as performers in the freak industry.

FOLLOWING IN GENERAL Tom Thumb's footsteps, Maximo and Bartola went on a Continental tour, appearing before stupefied audiences including, so the publicity stated, 'the Kings and Queens of Bavaria, Saxony, Hanover, Holland and Prussia ... the Emperors and Empresses of France, Russia, and Austria, and ... all the Nobility and Gentry'.[656] In 1860 they were back in America, this time performing at Barnum's American Museum which, following extensive renovations in the 1850s, was an even bigger attraction. The Aztec Children, as they were also known, were visited here by the eighteen-year-old Edward Prince of Wales, who had first seen them at Buckingham Palace in 1853. Bertie, as he was known, had grown up seeing the freak performers who visited his parents: he had been only two years old when he first met General Tom Thumb and, like his parents, maintained a lifelong acquaintance with freak celebrities.

Bertie's tour of Canada and the States in the summer and autumn of 1860 was the first overseas royal tour to North America. Thousands lined the streets to catch a glimpse of the prince. In Detroit 30,000 Americans awaited his arrival; in Chicago 50,000 people cheered. Bertie met President James Buchanan at the White House (shortly before the election of Abraham Lincoln); he attended a ball at the Academy of Music in New York (dancing being one of his favourite activities); and in October 1860, still in New York, he visited the Astor Library, the Deaf and Dumb Asylum and Barnum's American Museum.

Remarkably, however, the great proprietor was in Bridgeport when Bertie came to visit, so John Greenwood Jr, the manager of the museum, showed the prince around. Yet Barnum wrote about the visit as if he had been there:

Presently they arrived in front of the platform on which were exhibited the various living human curiosities and monstrosities. The tall giant woman made her best bow; the fat boy waddled out and kissed his hand; the 'negro turning white' showed his ivory and his spots; the dwarfs kicked their heels, and like the clown in the ring, cried 'here we are again'; the living skeleton stalked out … the Albino family went through their performances; the 'What is it?' grinned; the Infant Drummer-boy beat a tattoo; and the Aztec children were shown and described as specimens of a remarkable and ancient race in Mexico and Central America.[657]

The prince, according to Barnum, 'seemed pleased, and Greenwood was duly delighted', while Barnum waxed lyrical that his museum 'was the only place of amusement the Prince attended in this country'.[658] Although Barnum had instructed Greenwood to remove the wax model of Queen Victoria, which had been in the museum for nineteen years, Bertie did catch a glimpse of the wax figures of Chang and Eng Bunker, the Siamese Twins, displayed in the wax figure hall. He would have seen them in the flesh too: they were being displayed for a short period of time, performing with the Albino Family, and featuring two of Eng's children, twelve-year-old Montgomery and ten-year-old Patrick. Chang and Eng, who had briefly left their plantations in the American South, were paid $100 a week (apparently they did not like Barnum, finding him abrasive and stingy).[659]

According to the private secretary of the Duke of Newcastle, Gardner Engleheart, who assisted Bertie on his travels, the prince had actually made just a 'flying visit to Barnum's Museum'. But Engleheart visited the museum later in the day and wrote in his journal: 'The Albinoes [sic], the Siamese Twins, and the *What-is-it*, were considered the chief attractions ... the *What-is-it* appears like a horrible link between humanity and the brute; but it is pronounced by complete authority to be an idiotic and deformed negro.'[660]

So what was the 'What Is It?' He (not an 'It') wandered about the museum with his 'keeper', using a stick to support his awkward walk, and did little tricks, as 'lively and playful as a kitten', the press noted.[661] It is not certain who played the part of the What Is It? when Bertie visited, but it was possibly William Henry Johnson, born around 1840 in New Jersey.[662] Like Maximo and Bartola, Johnson was a person with intellectual disabilities and probably had microcephaly. But to the audience, including Prince Edward, what was particularly intriguing about the What Is It? was the claim that he was a 'nondescript' and a 'Man Monkey', captured by explorers near the River Gambia. The keeper informed the prince that he was discovered in 'his natural position ... on all fours; and it has required the exercise of the greatest care and patience to teach him to stand perfectly erect, as you behold him in the present moment'. The keeper promised that 'scientific men' have pronounced him 'to be a CONNECTING LINK BETWEEN THE WILD NATIVE AFRICAN AND THE BRUTE CREATION'. [663]

Back in 1815 Sara Baartman, the Hottentot Venus, had been declared closer to apes than to humans. Maximo and Bartola were also described in relation to monkeys. In Boston in 1849, for example, Dr Warren had drawn comparisons between the Aztecs and the 'Simian tribe'.[664] But by 1860 the correlation between ape and man would have new significance – and it would alter the way in which many freak performers, including the Aztecs, were seen.

CHAPTER EIGHTEEN

DARWIN ON DISPLAY

F OR A MAN who did much to reconfigure how the human body was seen, it is perhaps ironic that Charles Darwin suffered his fair share of bodily ailments. He was plagued by nausea, vomiting and flatulence; dizziness, abdominal pain and boils; and he experienced such terrible eczema that he decided, in 1862, to grow a beard to cover his blotchy face.[665] A few years earlier Darwin had shared his bodily predicaments with the world. *On the Origin of Species by Means of Natural Selection* (1859) had confused the separation between ape and man, injecting a level of ambiguity into man's position in nature that would have made any freak showman proud.

Darwin proposed that populations evolve through a means of natural selection, rooting mankind in one common descent. Although part of a much wider debate, Darwin implied, without directly stating, that a strict dichotomy between ape and human was misleading as both were connected on an evolutionary scale.[666] This was not a new idea: the Great Chain of Being – which vied with Darwin's theory of evolution – had been around for centuries, placing God, then white mankind, at the top of a hierarchy of nature which lumped Africans and apes into a similar category of inferiority. 'In whatever respect the African differs from the European, the particularity brings him nearer to the ape', the

English physician Charles White wrote in 1799.[667] Furthermore, the idea of 'missing links' between man and ape had been in circulation since at least the middle of the eighteenth century.[668] Even the theory of evolution had been around in numerous forms from the 1820s, and it was Robert Chambers' *Vestiges of the Natural History of Creation* (1844) that arguably made the theory of evolution less threatening, and more respectable, to a nation that still believed God was the mover and shaker of all creation.[669]

But with Darwin's text these issues became more salient. His ideas propelled the notion that a missing link could exist between ape and man, and this idea became increasingly prevalent in literary and scientific writings during the 1860s.[670] Caricatures of evolution proliferated in the press, fiction, satire, burlesque and, of course, the freak show.[671] In other words, Darwin's theory of evolution did not just impact the world of science, it impacted the world of entertainment.

———⁙———

SHOWMEN WERE QUICK to capitalize on Darwin's new theory. The display of the What Is It? – gazed at by Prince Edward at Barnum's Museum in 1860 – was a prime example. In March 1860 the *New York Herald* asked: 'Is it a lower order of man? or Is it a higher development of the monkey? Is it both in combination?'[672] The Aztecs were also brought into these debates; significantly, in 1870 they were displayed next to the monkeys at the Crystal Palace.[673] Moreover, in the 1880s the 'ape-girl', known as Krao, who was younger than ten when displayed in European freak shows, was exhibited as the Missing Link by a German showman, the so-called Great Farini. According to the publicity, he sent an agent to Laos to acquire one of the ape-people living in the forests, and this agent returned with Krao. She was, according to the press, 'A Living Proof of Darwin's Theory of the Descent of Man'.[674]

This clever publicity capitalized on another of Darwin's texts. In *The Descent of Man* (1871) Darwin uttered the word 'evolution' for the first time in any of his works and admitted that it is 'scarcely possible to exaggerate the close correspondence ... between man and the higher animals'.[675] While this suggested that all of mankind came from monkeys, a triumph for the monogenesis view, *The Descent of Man* also used the term 'the survival of the fittest', first coined by the social theorist Herbert Spencer in 1864. He applied Darwin's idea of natural selection to argue that humans existed in a perpetual, competitive struggle.[676] These ideas gave credence to imperialist endeavours, while also breathing new life into ethnic shows.[677]

These shows had come a long way since the early nineteenth century, when Sara Baartman and Joice Heth had instigated the tradition in Europe and America respectively. By the time Maximo and Bartola were displayed, contracts for the display of foreigners were relatively common and, by the later nineteenth century, they were standard practice. Moreover, unlike Chang and Eng, who in 1829–30 were displayed in a context of exploration and empire, now ethnographic curiosities were explicitly sought. Ethnologists and anthropologists eagerly attended the shows, keen to learn about different human races, just as the medical fraternity sought to fathom the mysteries of the anomalous bodies in the freak show.

As Maximo and Bartola were paraded in freak shows across Europe and America, ethnic shows were burgeoning. In London alone, between 1830 and 1860 there were displays of North Americans such as Ojibwes, Iowas and Hurons; groups of Khoe-San, tribes of Zulus and Australian Aborigines; Inuits, Fijis and others.[678] The Aztecs, presented as members of a race near extinction, were part of this growth in displaying 'exotics'. Much like Chang and Eng, the exhibition of Maximo and Bartola testified to the thin line between the ethnic and freak shows.

In 1853, the same year that the Aztecs arrived in England, the Earthmen – Martinus and Flora, who we've already briefly met – were also being displayed (and would similarly meet Victoria and Albert). It was claimed in the press that the teenagers 'burrow in the ground, and hence derive their name' the Earthmen, although members of the Ethnological Society labelled them 'Bushman-Troglodytes, or Troglodyte-Bushmen'.[679] Their parents were killed in South Africa following protracted violence in the Cape of Good Hope, and the siblings were subsequently taken into the custody of a merchant company, which allegedly hoped to educate the orphans so they might be civilized. This job was given to 'Mr George of Croydon', who took charge of Martinus and Flora when they first arrived in England in 1851. The siblings were filled with an equal measure of curiosity and fear as they found themselves in a foreign culture surrounded by strange people. Around 3½ft tall and wearing their native beads, feathers and 'strips of skin', they could only communicate in their own language, 'a few guttural and uncouth sounds'. Their keeper, George, managed to teach them English, musical instruments, dancing and singing and, by 1852, they were ready to go on public display. They were described as lively, witty and intelligent, regaling audiences with their songs 'Buffalo Girls', 'I'm Going to Alabama' and 'Britain Never Shall Be Slaves'. While the Earthmen were generally perceived as 'destitute of every vestige of civilization', they impressed audiences by displaying an air of European civilization, proving that 'savages' could be 'civilized'.

In 1853, the same year that the Earthmen and Aztecs were onstage, Londoners also saw the 'Zulu Kaffirs', that group of eleven men, one woman and a child who also met the queen and Prince Albert. The Zulus were brought to England by A.T. Caldecott, a South African merchant who persuaded them to travel 'by dint of continual perseverance; by telling the poor fellows the grand sights which awaited them; by engaging one this month and another the next; and by promising to each a good and just reward for their services', as he wrote in their exhibition pamphlet.[680] But Caldecott also required the permission of the colonial government, as trafficking in slaves had been abolished, and so agreed to various conditions including: 'a recognizance, binding himself in a sum of £500 and two sureties in £250 each'; that the Zulus be 'well treated on the voyage'; that it be proven their display was voluntary; and that they were returned to their home country. Caldecott was subsequently issued with a certificate from the government, and the Zulus were placed in the steerage compartment of the steamer *Sir Robert Peel* and brought from South Africa to England with Caldecott and his son, Charles H. Caldecott, who acted as the group's interpreter.

The Zulus were placed onstage at St George's Gallery (formerly the Chinese Museum) at Hyde Park Corner. Here was a quintessential ethnic show: Charles Caldecott opened with a lecture on the habits, manners and customs of the Zulus, using information largely mined from Nathaniel Isaacs' *Travels and Adventures in Eastern Africa* (1836). Borrowing from Isaacs, Caldecott presented the Zulus as bloodthirsty, irreligious and immoral: 'Behind his agreeable outward bearing, he conceals the most vindictive feelings, and a capacity for perpetrating the most atrocious cruelty. Impulsive, emotional, and excitable even to frenzy, he makes no effort to control his impulses, nor at any time reasons upon the abstract justice of his deeds.'[681]

After denigrating Zulu culture, Caldecott introduced the Zulus onstage.[682] They performed against a backdrop of beautifully painted scenes executed by Charles Marshall, a leading painter and set designer of his day. In the first scene they danced and sang around their huts; next they argued among themselves; then they performed a 'Meal Song' as they ate; and then came the 'Charm Song' to banish evil spirits. And so the show continued with scenes 'typical' of Zulu life.

What made the show such a success was the performance: the Zulus were compelling performers who offered a theatrical extravaganza. Thanks to the scenery and costume they were ostensibly placed in their native habitat, demonstrating 'the whole drama of Caffre life', wrote *The Times*.[683] The English had long been interested in the Zulus, having heard stories about their military expertise since the reign of Shaka Zulu (the monarch of the Zulu Kingdom, 1816–28). In the 1830s and 1840s the English read stories of massacres between the Zulus and Boers and, as Dutch-speaking settlers moved deeper into South Africa, tales of skirmishes spread further. Moreover, while black people were a common sight in London, most were ex-slaves from North America and the West Indies who were largely Westernized. Zulu tribes, on the other hand, were rare.

Charles Dickens visited the Zulus' exhibition and wrote, in an essay entitled 'The Noble Savage': 'My position is, that if we have anything to learn from the Noble Savage, it is what to avoid. His virtues are a fable; his happiness is a delusion; his nobility nonsense.'[684] In a sarcastic tone, he ripped into the romantic myth of the 'Noble Savage' and the dignity of primitive people. He borrowed from both the descriptions of Caldecott and Isaacs to portray the Zulus as backward and uncivilized, lambasting ethnographic shows and concluding, in reference to the Noble Savage, that 'the world will be all the better when his place knows him no more'.[685]

But there was no stopping the rise of ethnic shows. Some of the displayed savages and natives were fake, sourced from urban centres and costumed up, but many were genuine. The German-born Carl Hagenbeck and his heirs organized around seventy ethnic shows between 1874 and 1932, using recruitment agents to acquire such diverse people as Lapps (Sami), Nubians, Inuits, Indians, Sinhalese, Patagonians, Mongolians, Sioux, Samoans and Somalians, to list but a few. In 1907 he introduced 'native villages' into his permanent zoo, the Tierpark.[686] These constructs, commonly seen from the 1870s, enabled spectators to walk around a supposedly authentic village, observing the inhabitants in their everyday activities from cooking to dancing to smoking.

The villages were also installed in international expositions, or world's fairs, which combined trade and industrial fairs with freak shows, museums and art galleries. The Paris World's Fair of 1878 featured foreigners in custom-built pavilions and native villages, with around four hundred natives from the French colonies. The Greater Britain Exhibition of 1899 included 'A Vivid Representation of Life in the Wilds of the Dark Continent', with African animals and 174 natives from South Africa separated into four native villages.[687] This show occurred at the height of the so-called Scramble for Africa, when European powers carved up territories in the continent. This land grab was supported by Darwinian ideas that proclaimed the survival of the fittest by means of natural selection.

———— ·ⓞⓔ°· ————

D ARWIN'S IDEAS EMERGED when science reached a new level of professionalism. Back in 1829, when Chang and Eng were first displayed at the Egyptian Hall in London, medicine still had some way to go: Darwin was soon to set sail on the *Beagle* (a journey that led him to ponder transmutation, ultimately leading to his theory of evolution); the word 'scientist' had not yet been introduced; and teratology had not realized the aim of its founder, Étienne Geoffroy Saint-Hilaire, who hoped to integrate an understanding of monstrosity with all forms of evolution. Although Saint-Hilaire's work signalled a break with the mythology of supernatural wonders, which had informed how the likes of Jeffrey Hudson, the court dwarf, were seen, it would take the work of Darwin and his contemporaries to realize Saint-Hilaire's intentions.

On the Origin of Species had marginalized the importance of monstrosities in the process of evolution, but in *The Variation of Animals and Plants under Domestication* (1868) Darwin referenced the science of teratology as he discussed monsters as an extreme case of variations in nature.[688] In his private notebooks and letters, he also recognized the possibility of a link between origins and monstrosities, later praising the work of Camille Dareste, who, in the field of teratology, was seeking to understand the origin of species through a study of monstrosities.[689] Similarly, in the late nineteenth century, the biologist William Bateson considered monstrosities in relation to evolution.[690] At this point, thanks to Darwin and his contemporaries, monsters were within the realm of evolution. And while Darwin's theory that humans were similar to apes was threatening, and his side-lining of God borderline heretical, the freak show thrived off these ideas. Moreover, Maximo and Bartola were about to confirm a popular understanding of Darwin's theory: some races would eventually face extinction in the great struggle for existence.

IN JANUARY 1867 Maximo walked with a 'jerky gait' to the registrar's office in Hanover Square. His copper-skinned body was encased in evening dress with trousers too baggy for his short legs. A red camellia protruded from his buttonhole, the chain from his pocket watch rested against his white waistcoat and he donned a strip of crimson ribbon to denote some fabled foreign order to which he allegedly belonged. His sister, Bartola, wore a white satin dress, reportedly costing £2,000. It was cut low and ornamented with silver chains, showing off the sparkling diamonds that rested on her neck and bosom. She wore a wreath of orange blossoms in her hair. A lace veil, which she constantly played with and which caused her some annoyance, covered her face.[691]

At the registrar's office a genuine marriage certificate was signed: Maximo Velasquez Nunez, twenty-six years old, a bachelor gentleman, married Bartola Velasquez, a twenty-one-year-old spinster. The duplication of the name Velasquez indicated their possible familial connection. It was also the name of Señor Pedro Velasquez, who allegedly found the Aztecs in the city of Iximaya. Joseph Morris, the owner-manager, signed as the witness.[692] A large wedding party celebrated the occasion and a lavish breakfast was provided at Willis's Rooms, a fashionable venue in St James's, with *cartes-de-visite* for sale.

Once again, Morris followed the template established by Barnum and by Stratton, who had married Lavinia Warren four years before. But unlike Tom Thumb's fairy wedding, the Aztec wedding was seen as a specifically racial one. Claims that they were brother and sister were largely ignored in the press. That the Aztecs would eventually marry had been insinuated from the beginning of their freak show careers: the Aztecs were, after all, 'forbidden, by inviolably sacred laws, from intermarrying with any persons but of their own caste', claimed their early promotional material.[693] And in marrying each other, Maximo and Bartola, the Last of the Mysterious Aztecs, were propelling themselves towards further denigration and extinction.[694] They were destined to lose the battle in the struggle for existence.

The marriage was clearly a publicity stunt. It was also a union between an alleged brother and sister who had little or no comprehension of what they were doing. The marriage, however, was legally binding, another example of freak performers living their performance, and surely, particularly if they were brother and sister, another case of exploitation. The union had echoes of Countess Humiecka's desired experiment back in the eighteenth century, when she thought 'how pleasant it would be' to see her dwarf, Józef Boruwłaski, procreate with his sister. In Boruwłaski's memoirs he concluded that Humiecka and those closest to him must have regarded him 'as a being merely physical, without morality, on whom they might try experiments of every kind'.[695] This was also a fitting conclusion for Maximo and Bartola's marriage. And much like Tom Thumb's alleged child, the marriage raises questions. Were Maximo and Bartola really brother and sister? If so, why were they allowed to marry? (The Victorians could countenance cousins getting married but not siblings.) Why did their manager, Morris, decide on a legally binding marriage if this was a publicity stunt? And how did Maximo and Bartola view their marriage? As is often the case, there are more questions than answers.

AFTER THEIR WEDDING the movements of Maximo and Bartola become harder to trace, but the Aztecs continued to be displayed in England and Europe, often in their wedding clothes, and they appeared in the literature for the Barnum and Bailey Circus in the years 1888, 1889 and 1890. At this time Maximo and Bartola were under a new owner (allegedly their sixth), being displayed in mammoth circuses. In 1889 they were probably with Barnum's Greatest Show on Earth when it sailed from America to England on three massive ships. There were around 1,240 performers, a fully stocked menagerie, Roman chariots, miles of circus equipment, a herd of 380 horses and 8 tonnes of posters that were hung by 38 employees around London. Twice daily, 12,000 people flocked to see the Greatest Show. Barnum was hailed as an international celebrity, honoured by the likes of Randolph Churchill and Oscar Wilde.[696]

Eventually Maximo and Bartola disappeared into obscurity, vanishing from the archives by 1893. Maximo purportedly died in his early seventies in 1913 and Bartola at an unknown date.[697] We still do not know under what conditions they died or where, or even if they were buried. In their wake, however, they left a flourishing entertainment industry. During their lives as freak performers, they were connected to three central pillars of this industry – the freak show, the circus and the ethnic show – and each of them, in their own but interconnected ways, peddled exoticism, wonder and freakishness to a transatlantic population. In fact, although we do not know much about their lives, we do know that Maximo and Bartola gave birth to a new form of sideshow performer: the 'pinheads', 'birds', 'rabbits' and 'Aztec children' who became a staple of the American sideshow.[698] It was this new form of display that rocketed the freak show yet further into public consciousness.

———◦•◦———

CHAPTER NINETEEN

CIRCUS SIDESHOW

T HE GOLDEN AGE of the freak show coincided with the golden age of the circus. Both emerged concurrently by the late nineteenth century from the travelling fairs of England to become conglomerate institutions at the heart of a thriving entertainment industry. The growth of this industry, which confidently emerged in the 1880s and grew at an uncontrollable rate in the following decades, was assisted by the institutionalization of the Saturday half-holiday, restrictions on the hours of industrial work, the value placed on the concept of spare time, and broader economic and social changes which ensured that the working and middle classes had more money in their pockets to spend on leisure. This was also a time when modernity reached new summits: cities were growing, populations expanding, corporations thriving and railroads connecting, and the entertainment industry capitalized on these developments and was flourishing.[699]

Minstrel shows, for example, had evolved from backstreet entertainment for the working classes in the 1830s, and then popular, appealing amusements for the middle classes in the 1840s, to become more organized, lavish, spectacular and racially mocking recreations. Minstrel troupes sometimes featured freak performers, such as the

8ft 2in Chinese Giant and an African dwarf, alongside a strongman and wrestler.[700] As a result of the popularity of minstrelsy, there was even a widespread 'banjo empire', involving the mass production and advertising of an instrument once seen as undignified and associated with slavery.[701] By the late nineteenth century boxing and baseball had also emerged as organized sports, reflecting the industrial mindset: they had centralized and standardized rules, a tight business organization and marketing campaigns that reached the masses.[702]

Wild West shows, a mixture of the circus and ethnic shows, were also on the scene. By 1882 Buffalo Bill (William F. Cody) established the precursor to today's rodeo show and, in 1883, formed 'Buffalo Bill's Wild West', which toured America for three years. The show included cowboys, cowgirls, 'illustrations' of Native American attacks, battle re-enactments, shooting exhibitions, Native American dances, races on horseback, bucking horses, 'genuine buffalo hunts' and real Native Americans from the Plains, including Sitting Bull, who was granted an audience with President Grover Cleveland.[703] In the spring of 1887 the magnificent show sailed across the choppy Atlantic to perform as part of Queen Victoria's Golden Jubilee celebrations. Black Elk, an Oglala Sioux who performed for Her Majesty on 11 May 1887, recalled years later that Victoria 'came to the show in a big shining wagon, and there were soldiers on both sides of her, and many other shining wagons came too. That day other people could not come to the show – just Grandmother England and some people who came with her.'[704]

The circus had also reached its zenith. In 1892, 1898 and 1899, according to Victoria's journals, George Sanger (who had by now dubbed himself Lord Sanger) proudly rode around the grounds of Balmoral and Windsor Castle.[705] In a similar story of circus domination, across the Atlantic Barnum had formed a partnership with James L. Hutchinson and James Bailey, creating Barnum & London (1881–86) and Barnum & Bailey (1887–1919), humongous conglomerate circuses. The latter in particular dominated the circus scene, reflecting larger developments in the US economy as industrialization and modernity intensified.

In America the number of travelling circuses went from fourteen to twenty-two between 1884 and 1889, and the Ringling Brothers and Barnum & Bailey were the ultimate conquerors. As late as 2017, Ringling Brothers and Barnum & Bailey remained significant cultural institutions.[706] Just as Barnum had injected respectability into his American Museum, so he elevated his circus which, even by the late nineteenth century, continued to be associated with moral dubiousness. But Barnum never used the term 'circus' – his was the Greatest Show, even the Great Moral Show – which pitched his enterprise at the middle classes, as well as the working and upper classes.[707] This, in turn, ensured its popularity. And so, back in 1836, after his display of Joice Heth, Barnum had joined a small-scale circus that travelled America under the threat of censure; but by 1889 Barnum's Greatest Show on Earth sailed from America to England, to be seen by British royalty. This was a total transformation within one showman's lifetime.

The circus gave freak performers a stage. Some appeared in the main tent ('midget clowns', as they were called, were a favourite), but the sideshow was the most consistent stage for freak performers. The sideshow was dubbed, by one ex-circus clown, the 'G-string with a G-rating': a space of tamed titillation open to a general audience and featuring the exotic, the wonderful and the extraordinary freaks.[708]

⎯⎯⎯⎯◦◦◦◦⎯⎯

ALSO KNOWN AS the kid show or 'ten in one' (ten exhibits for the price of one), the sideshow was a uniquely American institution that connected the freak show and the circus. These 'out-side shows', as they were initially called, emerged alongside travelling menageries as early as the 1830s, although before the 1860s freak performers were only occasionally present. By the 1880s, however, the sideshow had become an established institution, and by the 1890s it had grown in scope to accommodate around fifteen exhibits, plus a band, often painted in blackface, inside one large tent. This was in addition to the 'pit shows' which, as the name suggests, comprised a pit in the middle of a tent where, down at the bottom, you could see the crawling Wild Man or Wild Woman, sometimes surrounded by snakes.[709] Sideshows were commonly advertised by colourful canvases – also known as sideshow banners, which became an art form in themselves – and the ballyhoo of the talker who'd attract customers with a spiel and perhaps an outside performance to tempt people inside these poorly lit spaces, emitting the smell of old canvas.[710]

The sideshow included so-called born freaks, such as armless wonders, dwarfs and giants, and performers like Maximo and Bartola. William Henry Johnson, who possibly played the What Is It? when the Aztecs were at the American Museum in 1860, reportedly used to guard the best sideshow spot because, in his later years, he saw himself as sideshow royalty (and indeed, he was a popular act). Hiram and Barney Davis were billed as the Astonishing Wild Men from the Island of Borneo; like Maximo and Bartola, they had cognitive disabilities and were short in stature. Born on a farm in Ohio, their father had died when they were young and their mother agreed to release her sons into the care of a showman, initially reluctantly, until he came bearing significant sums of cash, so the story goes. Their exhibition capitalized on an interest in the exotic and foreign: they were frequently displayed against a backdrop that depicted a jungle; they babbled and bounced onstage, and often appeared in chains. They first appeared in exhibition halls, then dime museums and then the sideshow.

Exoticism was a key theme of the sideshow. Indeed, the sideshow also accommodated exotic freaks, such as the Fiji Cannibals and Zulu Warriors, as well as the so-called made (or 'self-made') freaks, a rather nebulous category that included novelty performers whose acts were often steeped in the aroma of the Orient.[711] So, at a late nineteenth- or early twentieth-century sideshow, you might study the great artistic canvas on the tattooed man or, from the 1880s, the tattooed woman; shudder at the thought of the pain being experienced by the Indian Rubber Man, who stretched his skin 18in from his body; feel a slight tingle as your eyes devoured the erotic and exotic Circassian Beauties, who were allegedly, but rarely, from the Caucasus in Eastern Europe; marvel at the jugglers, mind readers, sword swallowers or serpent queens, whose necks and scantily clad bodies were wrapped in living snakes; or even suffer a bout of psychosomatic indigestion when marvelling at the Human Ostrich, who swallowed glass, textiles and paper before your very eyes.

The sideshow was not just a circus phenomenon, but also a space in American carnivals. These travelling enterprises, arranged around a walkway, featured rides, games and sideshows. Carnivals were independent entities, but they could also be connected to circuses and world's fairs. Carnivals got the name 'midway', because they were located between the entrance and the big top or pavilion. The modern carnival emerged from the World's Columbian Exposition held in Chicago in 1893 to celebrate Columbus's discovery of America. The Midway Plaisance, a mile-long strip that featured mechanized rides, including the world's first Ferris wheel, as well as sideshow attractions and food vendors, set the precedent. From that moment, as midway companies emerged across America, the freak had yet another space in which to perform.

———◦◌◦———

BUT WHILE THE sideshow was a particularly American institution, the situation was somewhat different in Britain. The British population could see the sideshow when American circuses came to town, but British circuses did not generally feature freak performers. Instead, they catered to the desire for difference using savages and exotic people. George Sanger, for example, displayed a company of savages in his circus, which he first formed in 1854 as a tributary to the English fairs, after discovering that his competition, the Howes and Cushing American circus, was pawning off 'Red Indians' who were in fact natives of England. Sanger subsequently hired locals from the slums of Liverpool, costumed them in feathers, skins and beads, doused their skins in red pigment and gave them some 'terrible-looking weapons'. They learned to do war dances, 'yell like fiends, and to perform tribal ceremonies', and they appeared in a cage. During circus processions, Sanger would personally feed them fruit and sweetmeats through the iron bars, much to the delight of the crowd.[712]

At roughly the same time, in the latter part of the 1850s, a circus in Glasgow was getting into legal trouble following the successful performance of Ki-hi-chin-fan-foo. He was actually a white Irishman dressed in Chinese garb, his head shaved and his skin dyed yellow. When two genuine Chinese men thought Ki-hi-chin-fan-foo was a fellow countryman being held against his will, they rushed to the police. The circus proprietor was subsequently hauled before the courts and forced to bring his witness: the bald Irishman masquerading as Ki-hi-chin-fan-foo, who could not speak a word of Chinese and had never been to China.

But what was particularly interesting about this episode was the circus proprietor: Pablo Fanque, immortalized in the Beatles' song 'Being for the Benefit of Mr Kite' (1967), was capitalizing on the trend for the exotic. Indeed, even his stage name was meant to give him a foreign tinge; his real name was William Darby, and he was born on 28 February 1796, at St Andrew's workhouse, Norwich, the third son of Mary and John Darby, described as a butler of African descent.[713] At some point between 1820 and 1831 he was apprenticed to the 'strict disciplinarian' William Batty, a skilled equestrian and circus proprietor, noted the chronicler Thomas Frost.[714] By the early 1830s Pablo Fanque – it is not clear when, exactly, he acquired the name – was featuring in Batty's circus, performing tricks on the ropes in Leicester, Brighton and Southampton: on a *corde volante*, a length of rope attached to two points in the ceiling, the American Voltigeur and Flying Mercury impressed audiences with his daring and dangerous stunts; he was also billed as the 'loftiest jumper in England', leaping through narrow hoops fixed with steel daggers.[715] In 1836 Fanque was performing with Batty's circus in Nottingham; he was described by Frost as 'a negro rope-dancer', although at this point Fanque had developed equestrian tricks too.[716] A few years later he was called the the Flying Indian while performing at Astley's Amphitheatre, the ancestral home of the circus.[717]

Around 1841, according to the autobiography of the circus clown W.F. Wallett (who would later meet Queen Victoria), Fanque went solo. 'It was my last night at the circus, and also that of Pablo, who left Batty to start an establishment of his own.'[718] There is little explanation as to why Fanque took this gamble. 'It must be remarked that in those days,' wrote Frost in 1875, 'equestrianism was not so popular as it has since become ... young and struggling beginners had a hard battle to fight.'[719] Going it alone was risky, especially because Fanque had a family to support, and because he was operating during a difficult time for black Britons.

Outside Britain, slavery was still a fact of life at this time. Americans such as Sarah Parker Remond and Henry 'Box' Brown, who was also a magician and mesmerist, were reporting from experience when they exposed the horrors of slavery on speaking tours across Britain which, during the 1840s and 1850s, could pack an audience of over one thousand.[720] While Britain had abolished slavery, racial prejudice and notions of white superiority abounded. Indeed, in 1853 *Punch* bemoaned that the popular abolitionist novel *Uncle Tom's Cabin* (1852) 'roused such a penchant for niggers, that dark skins must now take precedence over white'.[721] At the height of Fanque's fame, Frederick Douglass, the African-American abolitionist and statesman, was noting with dismay the 'pestiferous nuisance' of blackfaced minstrelsy, which brought mocking racial prejudice from America to England.[722]

Yet despite this racist context, within six years Fanque did succeed on his own. He developed one of the finest studs of ponies and horses in the country, having started with only two animals. By the middle of the century he was able to fill a 3,000-capacity, purpose-built amphitheatre in Manchester. There were serious problems along the way – the tragic death of his wife in 1848, familial complications, bankruptcy and the declining fortunes of his circus in the 1860s – but by the time of his death in 1871, he was a respected and renowned circus proprietor who could boast an impressive career.[723] He had offered the country, particularly those in the North, a thrilling circus performance filled with marvels and exoticism. And he wasn't the only one.

Anna Olga Albertina Brown, more commonly known as Lala, was reportedly born on 21 April 1858 to German parents in the now-Polish city of Szczecin. Her mixed-race heritage was used to her advantage in the circus, lending her an air of exoticism when she first stepped inside the ring aged nine. She was variously dubbed Olga the Mulatto, Olga the Negress, the Venus of the Tropics, and the Cannon Woman. In Paris, she was hailed as La Venus Noire and in London stories circulated claiming she was an African princess.[724]

Although small in stature, Lala possessed incredible strength, working as a trapeze artist, hand balancer, wire walker, strength artist and an iron jaw performer, which saw her suspended from on high by her ankles while clamping a great weight in her teeth. She toured in numerous circuses and music halls throughout Europe before partnering with another strength acrobat, Theophila Szterker, their act together being known as Les Deux Papillons ('The Two Butterflies'). Theophila died while performing one of her acrobatic tricks, and afterwards Lala's story becomes harder to trace, though we know she married an American circus performer in 1888 and had three daughters, all of whom became performers.[725]

Lala was a star of the Victorian circus at a time when this form of entertainment had reached its zenith as part of the flourishing entertainment industry. And in the year that Lala was born, Julia Pastrana was mounting the back of a horse at a circus touring Germany. Like Lala, Pastrana performed in circuses across Europe. Also like Lala, Pastrana was exotic because of her heritage. But unlike Lala, Julia Pastrana had a beard and her main stage was the freak show.

CHAPTER TWENTY

PEEPING AT PASTRANA

HERE ARE NO birth, baptism or early records enabling a reconstruction of Julia Pastrana's formative years, but she was probably born in 1834 in the Sierra Madre region of Mexico.[726] She suffered from two rare congenital disorders that meant her face and body were covered in dark hair and her gums were so overgrown it looked as if she had a second set of teeth.[727]

Rumours abound about her early years: she was sold into show business by her parents; she was left to die in a forest but was miraculously rescued; she was protected by her mother, who, hailing from a so-called Root-Digger Indian tribe, fled the community when Pastrana was born. In this version, so the story goes, a group of Mexican herders then found Pastrana in a mountain cave hiding with her mother. Pastrana was subsequently taken to a local orphanage and eventually adopted by Señor Sánchez, the governor for the state of Sinaloa in Mexico, who kept her as his maid. In April 1854 she left Sánchez, having been persuaded by a showman to perform in America, and in December 1854, at the Gothic Hall musical theatre on Broadway, she was billed as the Marvellous Hybrid or Bear Woman.[728]

Pastrana toured under the management of another showman, Theodore Lent, who like Pastrana remains an obscure figure.

Recent research suggests he was an ambitious, optimistic and rather unscrupulous businessman, salesman and auctioneer who occasionally dabbled in prostitution.[729] He probably met Pastrana while she was performing in New York, charming his way into her life and, it would appear, marrying her in Baltimore around 1855.[730]

Why they married we don't know for sure. Pastrana was reportedly generous, sensitive, charitable and intelligent, claiming that Lent 'loves me for my own sake'.[731] Perhaps, though, the marriage was really a way for Lent to exact control: when Barnum met Pastrana in 1857, according to the memoirs of another showman, 'she would not take off the thick veil which covered her face until Mr. Lent came in'.[732] Also, Lent knew Pastrana was a money-maker, so to avoid her changing showmen what better way to keep her than by marrying her?

But it appears that Lent was attracted to bearded ladies. Indeed, in the world of the freak show bearded ladies often found admirers and husbands. Annie Jones, initially billed as the Infant Esau at Barnum's Museum, was allegedly secretly married to a showman when she had just turned sixteen. The marriage lasted fifteen years until 1895, when the pair were divorced, and Jones subsequently married again. Mme Fortune Clofullia, another bearded lady who featured in Barnum's Museum from the 1850s, also had a husband as well as a son who would sometimes appear with his mother onstage.[733] As for Lent, Pastrana would not be his last bearded wife; in the 1860s he married Marie Bartel, a bearded lady from Germany. After promising her father that he would never display Marie, Lent soon had his new wife billed as the sister of Julia Pastrana, under the name Miss Zenora Pastrana. At this time the press described Bartel as 'his property'.[734] But what about Lent and Pastrana? What cemented the marriage? Love, lust or money? Perhaps a bit of all three. Certainly, though, in light of his later actions, it is hard to conclude that it was affection. As we will see, Lent emerges as a monster.

In 1857 Pastrana and Lent – freak and showman, wife and husband – were in London, with Pastrana billed as 'Miss Julia Pastrana, the Nondescript, known throughout the United States and Canada as the BEAR WOMAN' and 'Baboon Lady'.[735] While the mysteries of Pastrana's formative years leave the historians grappling for the truth, these very same mysteries were a deliberate part of her presentation as a freak. To put it bluntly, by suppressing the truth of Pastrana's story, showmen could peddle the claim that she was the product of an unholy union between man and beast: 'Her Remarkable Formation, and Mysterious Parentage,' claimed one piece of publicity, 'and how she was Discovered in a Cave, suckled by her Indian Mother, Dwelling with Baboons, Bears, and Monkeys.'[736] According to the press, 'the delicate inference is obvious', but this didn't stop Lent hammering home the point.[737] Another poster for Pastrana's 1857 exhibition contained a short section on the 'Root-Digger Indians to which Tribe Julia's Mother belonged': 'These remarkable beings inhabit the Mountains, in Mexico, and live in caves with animals of different description, such as Bears, Monkeys, Squirrels, &c., between which and themselves they know no difference; their food consists of grass, roots, insects, barks of tree, &c.'[738]

The Root-Diggers lived with animals and couldn't tell them apart from their own kind, a further insinuation of bestial copulation (accusations commonly aimed at Africans onstage). The bestiality was enhanced by the very association of the term 'Root-Digger', which signalled, to the white Victorian mind, dirty, lazy, bloodthirsty and animalistic sexual savages.[739] In Mexico, where Pastrana's mother was variously claimed to be a native, living in a cave and/or where she gave birth, women were similarly perceived as hypersexual. What's more, hirsute women like Pastrana came to signify hypersexuality, primitivism and bestiality.[740]

So Julia Pastrana – whoever she really was, whatever the true nature of her story – was placed onstage and under the stares of an audience who were informed that she was the horrific product of a bestial union with, as the publicity stated, 'the face of a Baboon – the body and limbs of a Woman – the skin of a Bear ... wherein the nature of woman predominates over the Ourang-Outangs'.[741] She might be part-animal but she was also 'a Lady in every respect'.[742] And all of this was being assiduously promoted by the man she loved.

⚬⚬⚬

JULIA PASTRANA WAS set to perform at the Regent Gallery, at the Quadrant on Regent Street with its lodgings, homes and shops selling imported and exotic delicacies. The colonnades of cast-iron columns, supporting a variety of formal and picturesque facades, offered a covered footway so those with spare time could meander around and possibly head into a freak show.[743] Indeed, the Regent Gallery was a prime location with a proud tradition of freak shows: the Gigantic Youth from Yorkshire was shown at 50 Piccadilly in 1812, having already, allegedly, been introduced to 'Majesties, and Royal Family, at Windsor'.[744] Around 1817 to 1829, a Fat Boy, three years old, was on display for 1 shilling at 183 Piccadilly and, in the mid-1840s, the Human Tripod was exhibited for half a crown at the Quadrant, being declared 'a bipenis, as well as a trisceles' with three legs.[745] Daniel Lambert, Chang and Eng Bunker, and Charles Stratton had all been shown in the vicinity.

At the Regent Gallery Pastrana could be seen three times a day, for the price of 3 shillings from the stalls, 2 shillings from the 'area' and 1 shilling from the gallery. The press, who were given a private view along with men of medicine, praised her 'very pretty whiskers', 'double gums', and strange set of teeth, declaring that 'she dresses with great taste in rich Spanish and other costumes, and after each performance comes among the audience to converse and answer questions'.[746] She was adept at playing up to her billing as the Baboon Lady. She was described as 'sociable and polite, and, besides being undoubtedly the greatest living curiosity, she is a lady in every respect', with 'scientific men', ladies and children being 'highly amused by her strange appearance, her dancing and singing'.[747] She danced the Highland fling, performed English and Spanish songs and conversed easily with the audience.[748] One spectator commended her 'sweet voice' and 'great taste in music and dancing'.[749] Another spectator recalled giving Pastrana a cigarette:

... seating herself in an apish posture astride of a tall chair, she lighted it and smoked it through; looking a perfect fiend, as she sat there before the spectators, her great cavernous eyes flaming and her huge nostrils omitting clouds of smoke. Yet with all this, she was substantially human: she spoke several languages, sang, danced, was lively and intelligent. Of her origin nothing certain was or is known: the story however being that her mother was a Mexican Indian, who was lost for years in a country full of apes & bears. It is held, I believe, that such an union as is this hinted at can never produce conception; the spermatozoa of beasts being unable to germinate in the human female, and vice versa? [750]

The publicity had clearly got this spectator musing. His name was Arthur Munby, seemingly a respectable upper-middle-class gentleman: a graduate of the University of Cambridge, a civil servant in the Ecclesiastical Commission from 1858 and an occasional poet. But he harboured a secret life: a sadomasochistic marriage to his working-class servant Hannah Cullwick from 1873, and an obsessive lust for working-class women. In his alma mater, Trinity College, there are volumes of his diaries, notebooks and photograph albums that document, in minute detail, his fascination with working women, from pit girls to collier girls to acrobats and even women with no noses. He indexed his diaries 'Working Women, studies of'.[751] His obsession was 'all-pervasive', as one contemporary academic suggested, and intimately connected to male pleasure; his relationship to working-class women was infused with pornographic voyeurism.[752] Munby gained a thrill from transgressions, so it was hardly surprising that he would head to Pastrana's freak show in 1857.[753] He didn't write about her, though, until 1862 when he returned to another one of her shows, which was very different to the first.

After her 1857 London exhibition Lent and Pastrana travelled across Europe. Much like Tom Thumb, Pastrana was a gifted performer who starred in her own play, *Der Curierte Meyer*, about a dairyman who falls for Pastrana, whose face is covered in a veil (lifted for the audience's amusement). The show was closed on the grounds of obscenity, but Pastrana continued to perform Spanish dances and popular songs. She then joined the circus, travelling across Germany to Warsaw and, by late 1859, Moscow. Here she gave birth to a boy in March 1860, who was born with the same congenital traits and he died, two days later, from asphyxia.

The delivery had also taken its toll on Pastrana and she died, following complications, in the early hours of 25 March 1860. Her last words were apparently: 'I die happy; I know I have been loved for myself.'[754] But Lent's actions suggest otherwise. After the death of his wife and child, he sold the bodies for £500 and they were sent for embalming at Moscow University with a view to their preservation in the University's Anatomical Museum.[755] After the bodies were embalmed, Lent had a ghastly change of heart: he realized he could make a freak show from the corpses, so he offered the university £800 as a repurchase.[756] Lent returned to London in 1862 determined to continue with the freak show. And so, in 1862, the Embalmed Female Nondescript and Child were displayed at the Burlington Gallery, 191

Piccadilly, a site usually reserved for high art exhibitions. That's where Arthur Munby saw Pastrana for the second time.

AFTER DINNER ONE night Munby headed to the 'show', paid his shilling and stepped inside the darkened room:

> ... there, on a pedestal in the middle of the floor, stood 'The embalmed Nondescript', as they call her now, looking exactly as in life. Wearing a short ballet-dress, which I was told she made for herself; her legs cased in pink stockings, her feet planted wide apart, just as she used to stand – like an animal painfully reared on its hindlegs; her coarse black hair wreathed with flowers; bracelets on the bare and hirsute arms; and a wedding ring upon the hard dead hand![757]

He felt a strange mixture of emotions staring at Pastrana. On the one hand he 'felt scarcely more affected by it than by an ordinary museum specimen', and he had to admit that the embalming was most 'wonderful'. Yet there was also a horror, made worse by the embalmed child who stood erect under a glass case next to his mother: 'the hideous hairy face of this dead Julia Pastrana, staring at you with great glass eyes, & crowned with a ghastly contrast of gay flowers, is enough to fill your fancy with nightmares. It is like seeing a stuffed ape in woman's clothes, & knowing that it is a woman after all'.[758]

She certainly appeared to haunt his dreams for, years later, he wrote a poem entitled *Pastrana* (1909): "'Twas a big black ape from over the sea,' he began, 'And she sat on a branch of a walnut tree,/ And grinn'd and sputter'd and gazed at me ... Such a monstrous birth of the teeming East,/ Such an awkward ugly breed:/... Yet still as I look'd I began to doubt/ If she were an ape indeed ...' And so he continued until he revealed his ultimate response to Pastrana: 'disgust'.[759]

'The Embalmed Female Nondescript and Child'. In 1862, the corpses of Julia Pastrana and her child were on display at the Burlington Gallery, 191 Piccadilly, London.

Disgust would come to dominate responses to freaks, eventually assisting in the decline of the freak show. But disgust has at its core a paradox situated between revulsion and attraction.[760] In Munby's words, disgust engenders a 'hideous fascination'.[761]

Pulled by his own disgust, Munby returned to Pastrana's exhibition, purchasing her photograph, minutely examining her body, stroking her skin and even fondling her breasts: 'The hairy skin of her arms and bosom resembles, to the eye and touch, the hide of a Chinese pig.'[762] His sexual fantasies were filled yet further when he went to see a 'beautiful series' of wax models at the London Anatomical Exhibition, in January the following year, and saw 'one of the most interesting things in the collection ... a full length nude model of Julia Pastrana.'[763]

Munby's interests were of the sexual rather than the scientific variety, yet in his 1862 diary he did ponder whether Pastrana was really human or ape. He mused on the implication of Darwin's theory of evolution: 'She proved her humanity (unless Darwin's views be correct) by producing a child', as he wrote in his diary.[764] Darwin was also interested in Pastrana after Alfred Wallace, his co-theorist on evolution, visited Pastrana's exhibition and told him about her. She became a 'splendid addition' to his *The Variation of Animals and Plants under Domestication* (1868), as Darwin wrote to Wallace.[765]

Darwin used Pastrana in this scientific text to discuss her abnormality as it related to other mammals. He described her as 'a Spanish dancer' who was 'a remarkably fine woman, but she had a thick masculine beard and a hairy forehead' and sported a 'gorilla-like appearance'. Darwin's main interest was her teeth, a cast of which had been taken by a London dentist, which proved, along with examples of hairless dogs, 'that the two orders of mammals – namely, the Edentata and Cetacea – which are the most abnormal in their dermal covering, are likewise the most abnormal either by deficiency or redundancy of teeth.'[766] Pastrana was thus packaged within science, and even featured in a late teratological text, *Anomalies and Curiosities of Medicine* (1896), which claimed she had a 'simian appearance'.[767]

Clearly, then, Pastrana meant different things to different people: Munby was disgusted; Darwin scientific; and another Victorian gentleman was wonderstruck.[768]

FRANCIS BUCKLAND, AN eccentric naturalist whose house on Albany Street in London doubled as a menagerie, first saw the living Pastrana in 1857. He returned to her embalmed exhibition in 1862 with the 'eminent taxidermist' Abraham Dee Bartlett, a zoologist, naturalist and superintendent at London Zoo.[769] On approaching the glass case at the Burlington Gallery, Buckland immediately exclaimed, 'Julia Pastrana!', and the recollections of seeing the living Pastrana flooded back into his mind: 'the huge deformed lips and the squat nose remained exactly as in life: and the beard and luxuriant growth of soft black hair on and about the face were in no respect changed from their former appearance'.[770]

Buckland couldn't quite believe that this was the same Pastrana he saw when she was alive. He struggled to comprehend 'that the mummy was really that of a human being, and not of an artificial model'. Both he and Bartlett were awestruck at this 'most wonderful specimen of the art of preserving' and, as he wrote, 'both he and I are at a loss to know the means which have been employed'.[771] Buckland was also taken aback by Pastrana's beauty. In life, as in death, 'her figure was exceedingly good and graceful, and her tiny foot and well-turned ankle, *bien chaussé*, perfection itself'.[772] Her arms and chest retained 'their former roundness and well-formed appearance', and despite the black hair protruding from her face, as he wrote, 'there was no unpleasantness, or disagreeable concomitant about the figure'.[773]

Moreover, despite her label, the Baboon Lady, and despite Darwin's theories doing the rounds *and* despite all the insinuations that Pastrana was the product of a bestial union, Buckland never referred to her in these terms. The omission is noteworthy, especially because Buckland was greatly fond of simian creatures.[774] Instead, Buckland merely noted that 'an idea was also attempted to be promulgated that she was not altogether human'.[775] But he gives this no credence. Crucially, Buckland consciously avoided raising the spectre of Darwin because, as he stated in 1875: 'I am not a disciple of Darwin or the development theory. I believe in the doctrine – I am sorry to say now old fashioned – that the great Creator made all things in the beginning, and that he made them good.'[776]

This was precisely what Darwin railed against in *On the Origin of Species*: 'It is so easy to hide our ignorance under such expressions as the "plan of creation", "unity of design", etc., and to think that we give an explanation when we only restate a fact.'[777] But Buckland was versed in the tradition of natural theology, or physico-theology, which found expression in the Bridgewater Treatises (1833–40), to which Buckland's father, William Buckland, contributed.[778] These treatises asserted the 'truth' of God's design in nature, and Buckland junior was 'a staunch upholder' of this view.[779] As a result, Buckland was confident that man and monkey were separate: there was no origin in apes, merely God's Creation, and this was the lens through which he viewed Pastrana. It meant, in direct opposition to Munby, that he saw her as 'wonderful'.[780]

B Y THE TIME Buckland's extended discussion of Pastrana was published, in his fourth and final series of *Curiosities of Natural History* (1888), Lent had married the bearded Marie Bartel, who, beside the embalmed Pastrana, performed as her alleged sister. From the mid-1860s and into the 1870s, Bartel and Lent toured with European circuses, while the embalmed corpses continued to be displayed; it's been conjectured that Bartel resented 'her mummified predecessor's ghastly, stiff grin'.[781] In the early 1880s Lent and Bartel retired to Russia, with Lent reportedly going insane around 1884 and ending his days in a Russian mental asylum – perhaps the guilt got too much for him? In 1888, the year Buckland's book was published, Bartel returned to Germany and exhibited herself alongside the embalmed corpses at the Anthropological Society of Munich. Bartel apparently remarried, but to whom it isn't clear, dying around 1900, although the exact date is unknown.[782]

Before she passed away, however, she gave the embalmed Pastrana and child to a German impresario. The bodies moved between different showmen and fairgrounds and were displayed as late as 1973 in Sweden, before disappearing into an underground department at the Institute of Forensic Medicine in Oslo. It was not until 2003 that a Mexican artist, Laura Anderson Barbata, began a campaign to repatriate Pastrana and bury her with dignity. In February of 2013 she was laid to rest in Mexico.[783] No one knows what became of the child.

The story of Pastrana has continued to attract numerous artists, biographers and historians.[784] Both today and then she represented different things to different people and, in light of her life, which at times reads like a Gothic horror story, it seems counterintuitive to suggest that she engendered the emotion of wonder. Indeed, as scientists began explaining away God's Creation, the monster was transformed into a deviant and a defect; what once provoked wonder and fear came to provoke horror and disgust.[785] Munby and Darwin support this reading, yet Buckland serves as a reminder that older notions of wonder could prevail.[786] In fact, in the Victorian era, wonder did not die but thrived as a notion that coalesced around ideas of divinity, imagination and awe, and was described by the psychologist Alexander Bain, in 1859, as a 'rupture' in the expected 'continuity of events' which leads to 'a certain shock ... surprise, wonder, or astonishment'.[787]

In a world of industrialization, standardization, automation and machinery, there was a corresponding need for fantasy and escapism. People retreated into a 'wonderland': a place of Gothic architecture, historical tableaux, fairy tales and make-believe.[788] Dickens's *Hard Times* (1854) juxtaposed Victorian rationalism with the wonder of the circus: a place of escapism and fantasy *and* a space of co-operation and compassion against the hard-nosed self-interest of the outside world. Wonder was inspired through magic shows, spiritual seances, panoramic displays, magic lantern shows and, of course, the freak show.[789] Indeed, in 1871 another marriage was about to take place but, unlike the sinister undertones of Pastrana's, or the publicity stunt of the Aztecs', this was the start of a genuine and happy marriage which, at the time, was perceived as simply wonderful.[790]

CHAPTER TWENTY-ONE

ANNA AND MARTIN

O N 17 JUNE 1871, a dry but overcast day, the thirty-three-year-old groom stood at the altar of St Martin-in-the-Fields, Trafalgar Square, London. Martin Van Buren Bates, a first lieutenant in the American Civil War, stood nearly 8ft tall and weighed over 500lb, appearing almost as large as the Corinthian columns that divided the nave from the aisle. He cut an overpowering but dashing figure with his oval face, jet black hair neatly parted and well-trimmed moustache. He wore a splendid blue dress coat, white waistcoat and fashionable grey trousers. His gold watch, studded in diamonds, was a gift from the Queen of England.

Outside the church was a 'mass of people', Bates recalled in his autobiography, and 'it was with the utmost difficulty that the guardians of the peace kept a passage open for our carriages'.[791] Inside it was equally packed with well-wishers, the curious and journalists. What were they staring at? The giant groom, for sure, but also the bridesmaids, Millie and Christine, African-American conjoined twins, born into slavery in North Carolina and joined at the lower base of the spine. They walked down the aisle and took their seats in the front pew.

They were followed by the bride, Anna Haining Swan, over 7ft tall and twenty-four years old, demonstrating 'something of stateliness and dignity in the skill with which she managed a most imposing train', wrote the *Daily Telegraph*.[792] Her gown was made from approximately 300ft of satin and 150ft of lace; 'elegant jewels adorned her person, among which was a clustered diamond ring, the bridal gift of England's much loved queen', recalled Bates.[793] Anna carried a bouquet of orange blossoms.

EXTRAORDINARY MARRIAGE AT ST. MARTIN'S CHURCH ON SATURDAY LAST.

The marriage of Martin Van Buren Bates and Anna Swan at St Martin-in-the-Fields, 1871. Millie and Christine can be seen to the left.

A couple of weeks before their big day, it's said that Queen Victoria met the engaged couple at Buckingham Palace. According to Bates's autobiography, Victoria remarked, 'I am impressed by the giantess's grace and elegance. Her Southern gentleman is very mannerly.'[794] Allegedly, Victoria presented Anna with the bridal dress she wore down the aisle. It was even possible that the queen helped secure the church, which was in the royal parish.

Anna was 'the most agreeable, good-looking giantess … lady-like in manners and address', according to Francis Buckland, whose wife might have been part of the bridal party (being referred to only as Mrs Buckland). Anna was given away by her manager, Judge Ingalls.[795] The service was conducted by Rev. Rupert Cochran, a family friend from Nova Scotia; he was assisted by Rev. Dr Roberts, the vicar of the church; and the best man was Henry Lee, editor of *Land and Water*, a natural history magazine that took regular contributions from Francis Buckland, who continued to pursue natural history and freak performers long after he saw Julia Pastrana.

After the service, the newlyweds celebrated with a scrumptious wedding breakfast; the couple then headed to the Star and Garter Hotel in Richmond for their wedding night. They arrived back in London four days later, settling into a grand house on Craven Street: 'the entire street bade us "God speed",' Bates recalled.[796] It was the start of a happy marriage.

⁂

ANNA SWAN WAS born on 6 August 1846 in the small rural community of Mill Brook, Nova Scotia. She soon moved to nearby New Annan, where she was raised in a small wooden cabin near dense forests and with coastal views overlooking the Atlantic Ocean. Her parents, Alexander and Ann, were farmers who provided the best they could for Anna and her ten surviving siblings, all of whom were average in height. Alexander was one of the early Presbyterian Scottish settlers to New Annan, and Anna was raised in a religious, loving and close-knit family, although life was far from easy. Money was tight, the winters were merciless and farm work arduous: ploughing the fields, weeding the vegetables and tending livestock.[797]

Anna was healthy, happy and doted on by her parents. According to her great-grand-nephew, Dale Swan, who kindly provided me with family stories and information, Anna's maternal grandmother would tell her to stand tall and be proud of who she was: 'Stand Tall, Lass and be proud. Be proud of who you are, of your ancestry and be the best person you can be.' Anna lived by doing the best she could and entrusting the rest to God. She was known to be kind, generous and had a good sense of humour; she developed a strong sense of personal pride and self-assurance.[798] She needed them in a world that saw her as different.

By the age of four, Anna already stood at 4ft 6in and eventually reached approximately 7ft 11in, probably because of a tumor on the pituitary gland that produces the growth hormone. Her mother knitted her clothes and her father made her shoes, but she kept growing out of them, so providing for her needs was expensive. Aged four and a half she was displayed by her parents as the Infant Giantess in Halifax and other county fairs, apparently so they could afford her new shoes.[799]

Aged six, Anna was attending school near New Annan, but now 5ft 4in tall and already taller than her mother, and eye to eye with her father, she was teased by her classmates. Her father had to raise her desk on wooden blocks so she could write while sitting on her stool. Yet despite the problems she remained good-natured, kind and clever. She thrived academically and decided to become a teacher, enrolling at a teaching college in her teens while living with her Aunt in Truro, Nova Scotia, a small farming community.[800]

But in Truro, as in New Annan, Anna could not escape the stares and comments from the community – she was now around 7ft. Even when she wasn't being exhibited at county fairs, she was always on display whether walking in the streets or studying at school, her body marking her as different. And the practical difficulties increased. She couldn't have her meals at the table and had to eat on the floor with her back to the wall; and walking through doorframes, up flights of stairs, through narrow corridors, entering a room and navigating furniture, everything was an assault course that made her feel ill-fitted to the world. Eventually, she was forced to give up training as a teacher because her size was not conducive to studying or the classroom.[801]

Then one of P.T. Barnum's agents came knocking. He offered Anna a considerable amount of money for her services at the American Museum. Her parents initially refused: they wanted Anna closer to home because she was still in her teens and New York was a remarkably different world to their rural surroundings. But when Barnum offered some $23 a week in gold coins, a large amount for Canadian farmers, plus the provision of a private tutor and a chaperone for the big city, along with accommodation, her parents agreed and Anna was off to the American Museum.[802]

IN THE EARLY 1860s she lived at Barnum's museum. Her furniture and room were built to accommodate her size, and she was provided with custom-made shoes (size 16½) and luxurious clothing. She was given a private carriage, tutored three hours a day and had music and acting lessons. The American Museum was almost a refuge, a place that celebrated her extraordinary body and treated her with respect. She had a good relationship with Barnum.

Her friends included Isaac Sprague, the Living Skeleton, and she performed alongside Commodore Nutt – 'he was the shortest of men and she was the tallest of women', noted Barnum, so the pair were a natural fit.[803] In letters to her family she noted the numerous marriage proposals she received from the likes of Joseph, the museum's French Giant, although she was aware that some proposals emanated from dubious gentlemen with ulterior motives: the Theodore Lents of the world. She could travel back home to see her family and frequently sent them money. In an age when women faced numerous barriers in the public sphere, Anna was earning a healthy living as a celebrated freak performer.

She conversed with audiences, appeared in tableaux and plays (Lady Macbeth was a favourite role) and recited poetry and music. When not performing in Barnum's museum, which burned down in 1865 and again in 1868, she toured across America and Europe, even joining Chang and Eng on an 1868 tour. A few years later, in 1871, she joined the company of Judge H.P. Ingalls, which sailed to Britain in April 1871 as part of a three-year European tour.[804]

Martin Van Buren Bates, known as the Kentucky Giant, was also travelling with Ingalls. The pair had met previously but affection blossomed onboard the *City of Brussels* and, before the ship had even docked in Liverpool on 2 May 1871, they were announcing their engagement. They married in June.

———◦◦◦———

B ATES WAS BORN on 9 November 1837, the youngest of eleven siblings born to John and Sarah from Letcher County, Kentucky. By his fifteenth birthday he was around 6ft tall, eventually (supposedly) hitting 7ft 9in. He worked on the family farm, received a good education and volunteered for the Confederates at the outbreak of the American Civil War, serving as a private with the Fifth Kentucky Infantry.[805]

His courage in battle saw him progress to the rank of first lieutenant and then, as he claimed in his autobiography, to captain. It was noted in his war records: 'He is nearly seven feet and weighs three hundred

and fifty pounds. He is not able to perform military duties on foot
and there is not a horse in the Confederate States Army to carry him
for any length of time.'[806] This was not quite true, according to the
family stories. He gained a chilling reputation as a fearless fighter
on horseback, mercilessly attacking guerrilla outfits plaguing the
mountainous regions of Whitesburg; according to his great-great-
nephew Bruce Bates, who was possibly reporting mythology rather
than reality:

> He used two colossal 71-calibre horse pistols that had been made
> specially for him at the Tredegar Iron Works in Richmond. He
> wore them strapped across his chest in black leather holsters. He
> had a sabre that was 18 inches longer than the standard weapon.
> He rode a huge Percheron horse that he took from a German
> farmer in Pennsylvania.[807]

In 1863 Bates was caught in Pike County, Kentucky, and imprisoned
by the Unionists. It's said the soldiers used to come and stare at his
ginormous proportions, dubbing him the Kentucky Giant. This might
have inspired Bates's next career move: after the Civil War, aged twenty-
eight, he left Kentucky and began working for a small circus, Wiggins
and Benoit, in Cincinnati, Ohio. He claimed in his autobiography that:
'finding my immense proportions was the object of wonder, I decided,
for want of something better to do, to exhibit myself as a curiosity'.[808]
Bates's nephew performed as a trick rider and sharpshooter while he
exhibited as a giant. He also read poetry to demonstrate his education
and superior cast of mind.

Indeed, education and learning were an important part of Bates's
sense of masculinity. On the other hand, he noted in his autobiography
that the war had 'served to bring into active use every muscle of the
body and to enable me to endure hardship' (a comment that revealed

his commitment to late nineteenth-century notions of masculinity: physical stoicism and forbearance).[809] And this was matched by his commitment to strengthening his mind: 'He who would obtain strength, either of mind or body, should be temperate in all things', and as a result he refrained from alcohol.[810] He was versed in the teratological work of Étienne Geoffroy Saint-Hilaire. He studied the lineage of giants back into the mythology of Titans and Cyclopses, and mined the book of Genesis, extracting the numerous cases of heroic giants demonstrating 'remarkable feats and strength'.[811] From these gigantic ancestors, Bates drew pride and convinced himself that humankind would continue to evolve in mind and body, which would be reflected in height: 'There is no reason why physical growth should not keep pace with mental growth. I believe that both will advance so that in centuries to come we shall be looked upon as dwarfs when compared to the physical and mental giants of the future.'[812] Bates, then, took strength from his colossal height, believing it reflected superior development.

'For five years I travelled,' Bates recalled, 'visiting all parts of the United States and Canada', showing off his gigantic proportions and finally accepting an offer from Judge H.P. Ingalls to begin a tour of Europe in 1870. He joined him at Elizabeth, New Jersey. Ingalls had assembled the Ingalls Troupe, which included Millie and Christine (the conjoined twins) and Anna Swan: 'It was then I met my wife,' Bates recalled in his autobiography, and 'our history from that time blends into one.'[813]

———— ◦◯◦ ————

AFTER THEIR INTRODUCTION to Queen Victoria and their marriage at St Martin-in-the-Fields, the couple performed in theatres and concert halls and may have received royalty, although I haven't found any evidence to corroborate the claim that they met Queen Victoria on at least two further occasions. That the rumour exists, however, suggests the extent to which Queen Victoria was seen as part of the freak show milieu. It was also reported that they met Bertie, the Prince of Wales, and his wife, Princess Alexandra.

On 19 March 1872 tragedy struck when Anna gave birth to a daughter who died during the delivery. The child weighed 18lb and was 27in tall, well above the average. Bates wrote in his autobiography that the 'loss affected us both, and by the advice of the doctors I took my wife upon the continent. There we travelled for pleasure, only giving receptions when requested to do so by Royal Command.'[814] The loss profoundly impacted the couple and particularly Anna's health. For the rest of her life she suffered bouts of extreme fatigue and weakness.

They sailed back to America on 2 July 1874 to enter a new phase. In a decision that echoes the choices made by Chang and Eng Bunker, the couple purchased 130 acres of land in the small farming community of Seville, Ohio, a tiny village in rural Medina County, and retired from the freak show: 'I had determined to become a farmer,' wrote Bates, which was no small feat considering the still primitive means of working the land in mid- to late nineteenth-century Ohio.[815] He kept prize livestock, which included shorthorn cattle and Percheron horses, in a specially constructed barn next to a custom-built house known as the House of Giants.[816]

The mansion was built in yellow pine timber and boasted eighteen rooms separated by sliding doors made of rare wood, marble fireplaces and an elegant staircase. The whole house was constructed for the Bateses' convenience: the ceilings were as high as 14ft and the doors over 8ft. In the living room were two large rocking chairs and a grand piano mounted on stilts 3ft high. Their dining room table was raised at one end and lowered at the other, so the married couple and their guests could eat together, and there was also a 10ft walnut wooden bed. There was also a servants' quarter.[817]

Guests from their freak show days included Lavinia and Charles Stratton (who had a mansion of their own) and the Russian Fedor (or Theodor) Jeftichew, billed as Jo-Jo, the Dog-Faced Boy (and later Man), who spoke around five languages. He began by touring with his father, who also had hypertrichosis, leading to excessive hair growth anywhere on the body and face, and was brought to America by Barnum in 1884 when Fedor was sixteen. He had a successful freak show career, earning good money and continuing to perform until he died of pneumonia in the early 1900s, when he was in his mid-thirties. Another friend and visitor was the Living Skeleton (Isaac W. Sprague), who might have fallen for Anna when they lived together at the American Museum.

Born in 1841 in Massachusetts, Sprague laboured with his father at his shoemaking business and grocery store, but his increasingly emaciated body made it hard for him to work. After his parents died, and unable to make a living for himself, he joined Barnum's American Museum. Apparently suffering from an extreme case of muscular atrophy, at the age of forty-four he weighed just 43lb. He did, nonetheless, marry and have three healthy children. At the Bateses' house, Sprague was entertained by their pet monkey and talking parrot but he never made a comfortable living and died in poverty, aged forty-five, in 1887.[818]

The Bateses also embedded themselves in the community. Anna joined the Baptist church on 21 March 1877, the date of her baptism, and Martin formally joined and was baptized there on 25 January 1885. This eight-year gap reflects the family rumours that he was not as religious as Anna. Dale Swan conjectures that Martin might have joined the church to please his wife, who, being a Swan, could be somewhat feisty, as were Anna's sisters and her mother.[819] Today, rumours in Seville claim that the couple chose the Baptist church because the door was rounded at the top, so they didn't have to stoop to enter. The first Sunday they attended they had to stand because the seats were too small, but the church soon constructed a large pew, adding an extra foot, so the Bateses could be one with the community.

———◦◦◦———

ANNA AND MARTIN lived the remainder of their days in this rural, religious community, surrounded by meadows and the Hubbard and Chippewa creeks, briefly returning to the freak show, between 1878 and 1880, to pay for the construction of their house. They joined W.W. Coles Circus for the spectacular (alleged) sum of $20,000 in 1878, billed as the Two Largest People in the World. A year later they were back at their farm where Anna gave birth to a boy on 18 January 1879. Tragically, their second child only lived eleven hours: 'He was 28 inches tall, weighed twenty-two pounds perfect in every respect,' wrote Martin Bates.[820] Anna and Martin, who loved children and desperately wanted one of their own, had to bury their baby. Anna's health deteriorated further, and she once again experienced the cycle of extreme fatigue and weakness that had plagued her since the loss of her first child.

Despite the tragedy, the couple continued to be involved in community life. Anna could be heard occasionally scolding her husband whenever he swore. Martin was always more mischievous and still wore on certain occasions his Confederate uniform in a state that had sided with the Unionists, even training his talking parrot to squawk 'Get off the Property' at a neighbour whom he disliked.[821] According to Dale Swan, the Sunday before Christmas in 1887 Anna attended Seville's Baptist church and, at the end of the service, presented the children with a large shoe filled with gifts. People were shocked by how she looked: despite her beaming smile she had lost weight and looked tired. A ledger at the church, which contains minutes of various meetings, includes the following entry:

> *In Memoriam to Mrs. Annie M. Bates*
> *...*
> *Came to Seville Ohio Feb 20th 1873.*
> *Baptized into the Baptist Church March 21st 1877.*
> *Died August 5th 1888.*
> *Buried in Mound Hill Cemetery Seville Ohio Aug 9th.*
> *Lovely in her character. Earnest in her life.*
> *Liberal in her deeds Simple and sublime in her faith.*
> *She died in the Lord*
> *leaving a multitude of friends to mourn her loss.*
> *The memory of the just is blessed ...*[822]

Anna died on the eve of her forty-second birthday, we think due to heart failure, leaving her two surviving parents $500 each and her five surviving siblings approximately $1,500 each. This was a huge amount of money for a family raised as poor Canadian farmers. The whole community mourned the loss, and family and friends from afar poured into the small town to see her laid to rest. At her memorial service in Seville, Rev. B.F. Ashley paid tribute to Anna's beaming love and compassion as well as her faith, self-sacrifice, grace and sophistication. He read from Mark 14:8: 'She has done what she could.'

Martin was heartbroken but he remarried, on 23 October 1889, to an average-sized woman. He moved out of his marital home and lived with Annette Lavonne Weatherby, daughter of the minister of Seville's Baptist Church, until his death in 1919. He was buried next to Anna and their baby son at Mound Hill Cemetery.

THE LIVES OF Anna Swan and Martin Bates are still celebrated in Seville and Nova Scotia, and they leave us needing to re-evaluate the freak show. This form of entertainment meant they were able to forge a life that was normal and comfortable. This is perhaps an ironic legacy for the freak show, which thrived off the commercialization of bodily difference. Certainly, it provided some performers with a career, a community of friends and a means of turning disabilities into assets.

While ethical issues regarding Barnum's rise to fame have leapt out, with some of the horror stories being shocking and saddening, we should avoid utter condemnation. Barnum treated Anna very well when she joined his museum, which functioned as a refuge for her and others who were marginalized in their communities. When she and Martin semi-retired to Seville, the couple could make easy money if funds were low, by returning to the freak show. And they never expunged their performing lives; friends and acquaintances from Barnum's American Museum remained good friends.

Perhaps two of their closest friends were Millie and Christine, bridesmaids to Anna back in 1871. They sang at the wedding and remained close to the couple, visiting them at their Seville mansion later in life. Like Anna, Millie and Christine also performed at Barnum's American Museum and had risen to great heights in the freak show and circus world, meeting Queen Victoria and earning a fortune from their star appearances across the globe. And like Martin, they wrote an autobiography and were committed to God. They saw themselves as 'fearfully and wonderfully made', a quote from their favourite Bible verse, rising from the ashes of a troubling past to become 'The Eighth Wonder of the World'.

CHAPTER TWENTY-TWO

WONDER OF THE WORLD

ILLIE AND CHRISTINE, variously labelled the Carolina Twins, the Two-Headed Nightingale and the Eighth Wonder of the World, came into the world as slaves. Born in July 1851, they were owned by a North Carolina blacksmith, Jabez Mckay, who had in his possession their mother and father.[823] According to an undated, unattributed and often factually incorrect freak show biography, published somewhere between 1902 and 1912, their mother, Monemia, 'was a handsome woman, finely formed and in excellent health', and their father, Jacob, was 'of Moorish descent, slender and sinewy, with the powerful activity characteristic of his race'.[824]

Millie and Christine, joined at the lower spine and sharing one pelvis, were 'the wonder of the family', growing into lively and agreeable little girls, with 'robust health'. The girls were instantly the talk of the town and, according to their biography, which spoke of them as one person, 'during the first eighteen months of her life nothing of importance occurred to Millie Christine worthy of note'.[825] But this was not true because, before the age of one, Millie and Christine were traded like property and thrust onstage as 'freaks of nature'. It would be the start of a tumultuous early life as the girls were pawned off to another manager, inspected by physicians and displayed at North Carolina's first official state fair in October 1853: 'GREAT ATTRACTION! THE CELEBRATED CAROLINA TWINS will be exhibited at Raleigh during the Agricultural Fair', ran the headlines.[826] The fair was packed with thousands who came to enjoy the carnivalesque atmosphere and trade in farm equipment and livestock, and watch acrobats, jugglers and curiosities including, for 50 cents, the Carolina Twins.

In these early days Millie and Christine were usually accompanied by their mother, but things soon changed when the girls were kidnapped by another showman who displayed them across America, Canada and, from July 1855, Britain. According to the twins, who wrote an account of their lives around 1869, they were taken to Europe because, while being exhibited in Philadelphia, a party of spectators claimed the twins were slaves 'brought into a free State, where we were unjustly deprived of our liberty' – a concern that was notably lacking when Joice Heth was displayed by Barnum. So they were 'spirited ... away before the necessary papers could be served, and in a few hours we were upon the basins of the broad Atlantic *en route* for Europe'.[827] At this point it appears the girls were being exhibited by two showmen, a William Thompson and William Millar, who invited the medical fraternity to inspect the twins in Liverpool. But by August 1855 Millar had abandoned his partner, effectively stealing the twins and taking them on a whirlwind tour across Scotland. A custodial battle ensued.

By this time their legal owner, Joseph Pearson Smith a respected merchant from North Carolina, had tracked down Millie and Christine with the help of a private investigator. Along with their mother, Smith set sail from New York to England in an attempt to reclaim the twins. They arrived in Liverpool on New Year's Day 1857 and, not long after, Monemia was at the Exchange Rooms in Birmingham, staring at her now five-and-a-half-year-old daughters, whom she had not seen since they were two and a half. Eventually, after a protracted custodial battle, Smith gained custody of the twins and brought them back to North Carolina.

⚬⚭⚬

JOSEPH SMITH WAS reportedly compassionate and caring, 'our kind master and guardian' wrote the twins.[828] His wife, Mary, taught Millie and Christine reading and writing, which contravened the slavery laws, and their 'white ma', the twins wrote, 'taught us our first precepts of religion, and assumed the duties of preceptress'.[829] They were trained to play the piano, sing as a duet in soprano and alto voices and to turn their unique sideways walk into a dance. This was in preparation for the freak show under Smith's management. They toured with him until, so the twins wrote, 'the domestic political troubles commenced' (the American Civil War), and they were withdrawn from public life. Shortly afterwards, Smith died:

> *We were old enough then to mourn the loss of our good master, who seemed to us as a father, and we here would render a grateful tribute to his memory, by saying that he was urbane, generous, kind, patient-bearing, and beloved by all. We trust, in fact believe, that he has gone to that heaven we have heard him so often describe to us, when he would impress upon our minds the necessity of leading a good life in the hope of gaining a blessed immortality hereafter.*[830]

It would appear that the twins genuinely loved their master and his wife. Indeed, following the Emancipation Proclamation, Millie and Christine chose to continue living with Mary because, as they wrote, 'We can trust her, and what is more, we feel grateful to her and regard her with true filial affection.'[831] It might seem strange for Millie and Christine to have had such regard for their previous slave owners, but the Smiths had treated them well and, for the girls who had been kidnapped, sold and mistreated, the issue of trust was crucial. After the Civil War, which left 620,000 dead, the girls began touring once more. This time, however, echoing Chang and Eng becoming 'Their Own Men', Millie and Christine stipulated that they would not submit to intimate examinations by medical men.

In 1866 they performed with Chang and Eng as part of the Combination Troupe, as it was known, which was arranged by Judge H.P. Ingalls, the manager and associate of P.T. Barnum. The troupe, which performed in New York, Ohio and further afield into the closing months of 1866, contained two sets of conjoined twins performing in very different circumstances after the Civil War. Millie and Christine had been liberated; Chang and Eng felt financially burdened because their slaves had been emancipated and the debts they were owed had been repaid in worthless Confederacy currency. They had been firmly with the Confederates against the Unionists with two of their sons fighting for the cause, but the conclusion of the war forced them to return to the freak show to recoup their losses.

Chang and Eng were forty-five when they reluctantly had to tour once again. They appeared with two of their children (it's not clear which) wearily answering questions from spectators, while Millie and Christine, aged fifteen, danced and sang. In 1868 Ingalls took Chang and Eng on a tour of Europe while the girls were sent across America, probably writing their autobiography in 1869. They were emphatic: 'One thing is certain, we would not wish to be severed, even if science could effect a separation. We are contented with our lot, and are happy as the day is long. We have but *one heart*, one feeling in common, one desire, one purpose.' They closed their story with the words of the song they sang in the freak show which, as they wrote, 'conveys a good idea of our feelings'. Here are a few sections:

> *Some persons say I must be two,*
> *The doctors say this is not true;*
> *Some cry out humbug, till they see,*
> *When they say, great mystery!*

> *Two heads, four arms, four feet,*
> *All in one perfect body meet;*
> *I am most wonderfully made,*
> *All scientific men have said.*

> *I'm happy, quite, because I'm good;*
> *I love my Savior and my God.*
> *I love all things that God has done,*
> *Whether I'm created two or one.*[832]

Following his European tour with Chang and Eng, Ingalls returned to America and arranged for Millie and Christine's trip to Britain. This was the tour when Anna Swan and Martin Bates fell in love aboard the ship that left New York harbour on 22 April 1871, marrying less than two months later at St Martin-in-the-Fields. Millie and Christine were the bridesmaids. Shortly afterwards Ingalls arranged for the wedding party to appear at the Masonic Hall, where they met the Prince of Wales. A few days later Millie and Christine received their summons to perform before Queen Victoria.

Victoria's world had been shattered in 1861 when her mother, and then her husband, died: 'For me, life came to an end on December 14,' she wrote the day Prince Albert passed away.[833] She was unable to write in her journal for the rest of the year as the royal household was shrouded in mourning. Indeed, just as she and Albert set the trend for freak shows in the 1840s, so Victoria set the trend for mourning in the 1860s: black hats, black-edged stationery and black-embroidered handkerchiefs became the fashion. But when she met Millie and Christine, on 24 June 1871, Victoria was slowly being liberated from her grief and developing into her own woman. She had formed an intimate relationship with her Highland servant John Brown, and she forged a close bond with the flamboyant prime minister, Disraeli, who would soon bestow upon her the title Empress of India. And she remained a fan of the circus and freak show. After breakfast, Victoria saw Millie and Christine at Windsor Castle, writing in her journal: 'There are 2 heads with different brains & will power ... It is one of the most remarkable phenomena possible. They are very dark coloured ... & look very merry & happy ... They sang duets with clear fine voices.'[834]

It would appear, however, that Victoria mistook Millie and Christine for Chang and Eng when she described how they were joined: 'by a sort of bar of flesh not far from the region of the heart'.[835] Although there appears to be no supporting evidence to collaborate the claims that Chang and Eng met Queen Victoria, she was evidently aware of the twins. Her son, the Prince of Wales, had seen them at Barnum's American Museum in 1860.

Like Victoria, the naturalist Francis Buckland was a fan of Millie and Christine (and also of Chang, Eng, the Aztecs and Julia Pastrana), whom he described in 1871 as 'two charming young negress girls, who are united back to back by an indissoluble band'. He found Christine intelligent, joyous, cultured and educated; similarly 'Millie is like her sister in face and in her charming manners. They live in perfect concord, and from long habit walk about and even dance, without any appearance of effort or constraint. They are called the "Two-headed Nightingale," because they both sing very well, and the duets they practice show they have good voices, which have been successfully cultivated. Their age is nineteen.'[836]

In a career reflecting the movements of many freak show celebrities, Millie and Christine proceeded to perform for the dignitaries of Europe which included, besides Queen Victoria, the Prince of Wales, Princess Alexandra, Grand Duke Vladimir of Russia, Prince John of Glücksburg and the royal families of Austria and Russia. During their years in Europe, from 1871 to 1878, they exhibited in England, France, Germany, Belgium, Italy, Hungary, Austria and Holland, and reportedly they mastered French, German, Italian and Spanish. They even performed with General Tom Thumb at Astley's Amphitheatre in London, and they followed Chang, Eng and Julia Pastrana by appearing at the circus in St Petersburg, Russia. Notably, while in Paris in 1874, they continued to refuse intimate examinations, which greatly perturbed the Parisian doctors, who were still eager to inspect and ultimately dissect the bodies of conjoined twins.

The same year that Millie and Christine refused a medical examination in Paris, Chang and Eng were under the knife at the College of Physicians, Philadelphia. It was almost an inevitable conclusion for the Siamese Twins who from the moment they were first displayed were hounded by the medical fraternity. They were desperate to open their bodies to discover the precise nature of the twins' anomalies. By 1874, they had secured their prize.

———— ◦◎◦ ————

CHANG AND ENG's later life on the freak show circuit had not been happy. Chang reportedly developed a strong drinking habit and would frequently appear tipsy onstage, propped up by his brother. Then came their grand tour in 1868. And their last. Since the North had been ambivalent about the slave-owning Confederate twins, they toured

Europe. As was now the common procedure for Chang and Eng, they were accompanied by two of their children, Katherine, aged twenty-four, and Nannie, aged twenty-two, who were physically unexceptional other than being the offspring of the Siamese Twins.

Nannie kept a diary of the tour, describing the 'exceedingly irksome' shows and detesting the crowds of people who 'flocked around us crying here are the "Siamese Twins"' and mistakenly assuming that she and her sister were their 'Wives'.[837] But the turning point was when 'one man – I will not say gentleman – asked me if my grandmother or grandfather was a negro'. 'I was so angry I could scarcely speak.'[838] For the daughter of a slave owner, born and raised in the American South, to be presumed in the lineage of African Americans was a major insult.

Unlike their first appearance in London, the press were now decidedly ambivalent about Chang and Eng. One reporter noted that the Bunkers were simply one of many 'melancholy exhibitions which from time to time disgrace our civilization', a signal that, despite the freak industry thriving, tastes were slowly changing.[839] The *Liverpool Mercury* reported that 'it is impossible to regard them with feelings other than of commiseration and pity'.[840] Another reviewer, who knew the twins well in 1830 and went to their 1869 show at the Egyptian Hall, the scene of their London debut, 'was pained to tears by the contrast ... the features wholly changed, the hair grey, the complexion faded, and an expression of deep melancholy on both faces'.[841] But perhaps the worst experience was their display in the Circus Renz in Germany, 1870. The press described Chang and Eng with 'grey heads' and 'mellow in gait and actions', and the audience laughed at the self-respecting twins as they underwent what was a depressing indignity: 'first they appear on a quickly improvised podium which runs all around the area, then, turning this way and that, sometimes taking a bow, they wander through the aisle which is located between the boxes and the stands'.[842]

When the twins travelled to Russia, performing in Moscow and St Petersburg, their fortunes changed for the better; according to family stories, they met the Russian tsar, the fifty-two-year-old Alexander II, and even enjoyed a theatrical performance at his palace. But their plans to perform in Vienna, Rome, Madrid and Paris were disrupted when France declared war on Prussia, and they were forced to cut short their tour and return home.[843] Shortly afterwards, in the early hours of Saturday 17 January 1874, following a debilitating cold, Chang passed away, aged sixty-two, followed about two hours later by his brother. In the days that followed, the men of science exerted pressure on the Bunker families and finally got their hands on Chang and Eng's corpses. They were dissected; their conjoined livers were preserved and displayed at the Mütter Museum where they can still be seen today; their lungs and entrails mysteriously disappeared; and the twins were sent back to North Carolina for burial.

In 1829 a Parisian journalist had berated the anatomists for dissecting the conjoined Ritta and Christina Parodi, Sardinian twins who were brought to Paris by their parents in the hope of exhibiting them: 'You despoil this beautiful corpse, you bring this monster to the level of ordinary men, and when all is done, you have only the shade of a corpse,' decried the journalist.[844] Dissection, in his eyes, rendered the poetic body a mere cadaver. It substituted the extraordinary for the ordinary body, the abnormal for the normal. It stripped away the wonder. Millie and Christine were determined never to succumb to the same fate as either the Parodis or Chang and Eng. They would continue to refuse medical examinations and keep their status as wonders: 'THE EUROPEAN WONDER, MILLIE CHRISTINE, THE TWO-HEADED NIGHTINGALE, who has no rival', bellowed their publicity in 1881.[845]

Millie and Christine were at the apex of their careers. In 1881 they were performing in Cuba, followed by a star appearance at the renowned Bunnell Museum in New York, a popular museum hosting all manner of entertainments. In 1882 they travelled with the Great Inter-Ocean Railroad Show, earning an astounding $700 a week as one of the main attractions. Billed as the Earth's Greatest Wonder, the Two-Headed Lady, they appeared after the acrobats, athletes, jugglers, magicians, bareback riders and clowns, singing and dancing a polka to the sounds from the circus band. In 1886 they joined the huge travelling circus Barnum & London, joining other human curiosities in the Museum of Living Wonders. They continued in the world of the freak show, moving between popular dime museums and American circuses, and eventually retired from the stage to live out the remainder of their days in North Carolina.[846]

They bowed out from the world in October 1912. Notably, the medical fraternity never got their hands on the corpses of Millie and Christine: they were buried in a 4 x 6ft grave, in a double coffin built of cypress lumber, guarded by a watchman for nine months. The following words marked their grave: 'Millie-Christine … She lived a life of much comfort owing to her love of God and joy following His commands. A real friend to the needy of both races and loved by all who knew her.' And inscribed on raised letters were the words from the psalms: 'A soul with two thoughts. Two hearts that beat as one.'[847]

———⚬⚬⚬———

MILLIE AND CHRISTINE left the world when the freak industry, and the entertainment industry more generally, was at its height in Britain and America. By the late nineteenth century, for example, seaside resorts were flourishing: Blackpool's North Pier, which opened in 1863, was seeing almost half a million visitors a year by 1875.[848] Sports were also thriving, with cricket, boxing, horse racing and football enthusiastically followed, and new popular sports – badminton, cycling, field hockey, lawn tennis and table tennis – emerging.[849] Music halls in England had developed from the penny gaffs to reach a commercial zenith between 1880 and 1919.[850] Shopping, that great recreational activity, had increased as family-run shops were increasingly replaced by larger, multi-employee shops and commercial bazaars by the end of the nineteenth century.[851] And what were once small-scale travelling circuses prone to moral condemnation had, by late in the century, become travelling cities utilizing the railways and attracting all classes (although some still saw circuses as morally reprehensible). Similarly, ethnic shows had developed from small-scale performances into large-scale commercial enterprises tied to mass entertainment, particularly after the 1851 Great Exhibition at the Crystal Palace.[852] The history of the freak show mirrored these broader changes. What began as small-scale exhibitions of human curiosities had developed into large-scale freak shows, part of an international freak industry, which were explicitly connected to commercial dime museums, circuses, world's fairs, carnivals and amusement parks.

Indeed, the growth of American amusement parks provided freak performers with yet another space. Coney Island, for example, had become a busy seaside resort by the 1870s, and at the end of the century featured large-scale amusement parks such as Luna Park, with 4 million paying visitors in 1903 alone, and Dreamland, which opened in 1904. The latter contained 1,000 electric lights, a 25,000sq ft ballroom and a 370ft tower for punters to enjoy the views. There were fairground rides, a menagerie of wild beasts and freak performers such as the woman 'So Fat That It Takes Seven Men to Hug Her', an assemblage of 'aborigines' and, by 1912, William Henry Johnson, who played the What Is It? in Barnum's American Museum. Nonetheless, the popular stall called 'Hit the Nigger – Three Balls for Five [cents]' serves as a necessary reminder that the amusement park was not welcoming to everyone (by 1928, two-thirds of Northern amusement parks practised segregation).[853]

Inside Dreamland was Lilliputia, a so-called 'Midget City', containing three hundred dwarfs. Everything was scaled to size so visitors could wander through the place observing the miniature homes where the dwarfs lived. And this wasn't the only one: in amusement parks and world's fairs across America and Europe, there were more midget cities fitted with miniature halls, fire stations and everything you'd expect to find. There were also 'midget companies', which blossomed in Europe and America in the later nineteenth century. Horwath's Midgets and Singer's Midgets were two of the most renowned, with the Lilliputian Opera Company making its debut in 1890. It featured Lavinia Magri (the widow of Charles Stratton) and her new husband, Count Magri, who were also residents at Lilliputia when it opened.[854]

Freak performers could now be seen in almost every conceivable space associated with entertainment. They were in the sideshow as part of the circus; the sideshow as part of the carnival; in amusement parks and minstrel shows and even Buffalo Bill's Wild West shows. Images of freak performers were everywhere, even in the home. From the 1860s small photographs or *cartes-de-visite* had proliferated with the renowned photographers Matthew Brady and Charles Eisenmann taking hundreds of images, which were sold in the freak shows, and subsequently went directly into people's homes, often side by side with family photographs.[855] By the late nineteenth and early twentieth century, freak performers were even depicted on postcards and comic illustrations.[856]

And Queen Victoria remained part of the action. In the 1880s Victoria was still meeting freak performers, this time 'some wonderful little dwarfs, called midgets', she wrote in her journal in 1881, billed as the 'Royal Midgets', who, the press declared, were 'Under the patronage of her Most Gracious Majesty the Queen, T.R.H. the Prince and Princess of Wales, and the Royal Family'.[857] Allegedly, when the Prince and Princess of Wales went to see the Barnum & Bailey circus in 1898, the princess demanded: 'We want to see the freaks.'[858]

They didn't need to look far. The freak industry had well and truly arrived. But no one would suspect that at the height of such domination in Victorian culture, the seeds of its decline had already begun to sprout.

THE FINAL ACT

O UR HISTORY OPENED with a paradox and so it shall close. The roots of the freak show, right back in the seventeenth century and even before then, were found both in the stigmatized travelling fairs and in the royal courts of Europe, locations low and high in the social and cultural pecking order. As we enter the end of the nineteenth century and move into the twentieth, a new paradox emerges: on the one hand, the freak show was thriving, on the other, its decline was already apparent. In short, the freak show was a victim of its own success. The conglomerate circuses toured nationally and internationally, giving the freak show global dominance, but at the same time this harmed the smaller independent freak shows as performers flocked to the bigger stages.[859]

At the height of the freak show's popularity, demand for performers was strong yet they were not always easy to source, by virtue of their rarity, so 'self-made freaks' supplied the market with tattooed people and Circassian Beauties piling into the circuses and dime museums. At the bottom of the heap were the 'gloaming geeks' who would decapitate live rats, snakes and chickens with their teeth. But these self-made freaks saturated the market, their ubiquity killed their novelty and they became the lowest rung on the freak show ladder.[860]

Furthermore, the showman's long-standing courtship of medical men, while initially imbuing the freak show with respectability, finally resulted in freak performers moving from the stage and into laboratories and institutions. Finally, the broader historical changes that supported a flourishing entertainment industry were also creating a saturated market that would marginalize the freak show. Public tastes were changing and a world war was about to begin. The freak show was nearing an end, although you wouldn't necessarily know it looking at the success of performers like Millie and Christine.

The career of Joseph Merrick, at the end of the century, exemplifies these changing fortunes. He has become the archetypal Victorian freak and has featured in so many documentaries, biographies and texts that he has assumed a celebrity status even today.[861] His deformities included abnormal growths around his feet, legs and left arm; his back and face were covered with lumps of protruding tissue and, due to an injury the young Merrick sustained to his hip, he was left with a permanent limp.

Born on 5 August 1862 into a working-class Leicestershire family, Merrick had extreme deformities which meant that, following the death of his mother in 1873 and the subsequent cruel torments of a step-mother, he struggled to find work, eventually being forced to check himself into the Leicester Union Workhouse in December 1879. According to workhouse registers, the reason for admittance was 'unable to work'.[862] Within twelve weeks, however, he was discharged at his 'own request'.[863] Yet two days later Merrick was forced to return; the reason on the admissions register – 'No Work'.[864] In his autobiography, a six-page pamphlet sold at his freak shows and written around 1880 to 1885, he reveals how he ultimately escaped the degradation of the workhouse: 'so thought I; I'll get my living by being exhibited about the country. Knowing Mr Sam Torr, Gladstone Vaults, Wharf Street, Leicester, went in for Novelties, I wrote to him, he came to see me, and soon arranged matters.'[865]

Sam Torr was a popular entertainer who owned a newly refurbished music hall in Leicester. He established a syndicate of interested businessmen to exhibit Merrick as a 'freak of nature'. The group included Mr J. Ellis, the owner of a music hall in Nottingham, the showmen George Hitchcock and Tom Norman, as well as 'Professor' Sam Roper, who had formed Sam Roper's Fair, which travelled from Nottingham to King's Lynn. Arrangements secured, Merrick was finally discharged from the workhouse, once again, at his 'own request'.[866]

He was probably first displayed at Ellis' music hall in Nottingham as 'The Elephant Man, Half-a-Man and Half-an-Elephant', later travelling with Roper's Fair.[867] He had his own caravan, some privacy and even some friends: 'I am as comfortable now as I was uncomfortable before,' he wrote in his autobiography.[868] Bertram Dooley and Harry Bramley, who worked in the boxing booth at the fair, frequently visited Merrick's caravan to chat. Dooley recalled that he 'would talk on subjects that you never really think a man in that condition would talk about. Very upstage subjects, you know, and he was a bit on the religious side, too …'[869]

Merrick was probably shown in at least two towns before heading to London in 1884, where the twenty-four-year-old showman Tom Norman exhibited him on the Whitechapel Road in London's East End: an area renowned for poverty, immorality and sexual transgression, and where Jack the Ripper stalked. It was home to immigrants and the working classes, and Merrick's show-shop catered to their desire for cheap entertainment. His freak show was more primitive and less commercial than many freak shows in the golden age, revealing how older modes of exhibiting human curiosities still existed: the fairs, the canvases, and the single, transitory shows that were prevalent in the early nineteenth century had not been wholly replaced by the more commercialized age of the freak.

In fact across the field of entertainment, more traditional carnivalesque forms of entertainment remained, despite the shift towards middle-class respectability.[870] In Britain, for example, the prevalence of violence detectable in pre-industrial entertainment merely underwent a process of reinvention and adaption: prizefighting and bare-knuckle boxing were outlawed, but the introduction of the Queensberry Rules in 1867 saw boxing flourish as a popular sport in late-Victorian England.[871]

So, Norman was not completely out of touch when he erected a primitive canvas depicting a human metamorphosing into an elephant. He charged a mere two pence for audiences to see Merrick as he delivered his 'Roll up' outside the show: 'Ladies and gentlemen, I ask you please not to despise or condemn this man on account of his unusual appearance. Remember we do not make ourselves, and were you to cut or prick Joseph he would bleed, and that bleed or blood [sic] would be red, the same as yours or mine.'[872]

Whatever his claims about the universalism of humankind, Norman courted an audience he knew was interested in Merrick's difference. The exhibition was directly opposite the London Hospital, the capital's largest charitable institution for curable patients, and surgeons from the hospital headed to Merrick's show, including the likes of John Bland-Sutton and Frederick Treves.[873] Merrick was displayed as an example of congenital deformity at the Pathological Society of London in 1884.[874] The men of science were encircling the freak once again.

THE NEXT PART of Merrick's story reveals the declining fortunes of the freak show. The police closed his public exhibition on the grounds of decency, forcing Merrick to go on the road with Roper's Fair. The story gets a little murky here but, in the mid-1880s, Merrick was passed on to another showman – some say he was Austrian, others Italian – who took Merrick to the Continent.[875]

According to Francis Carr-Gomm, chairman of the London Hospital, Merrick was forced to exhibit in Belgium 'but the police there too kept him moving on, so that his life was a miserable and hunted one'.[876] He was not perceived as a respectable freak performer but rather as a severely deformed creature who horrified and disgusted both English and European audiences. A burden rather than an asset, in early June 1886 Merrick was abandoned by his showman in Brussels. This showman, whoever he was, stole the £50 Merrick had saved. He was left destitute. His extreme deformities meant he was most probably hounded by people in the streets; he couldn't speak their language and, even if he could, his facial deformities ensured his speech was such that he could often not be understood even in English. But Merrick managed to pawn a few possessions and made his way back to London, possibly on a steamer from Ostend to Dover, finally arriving back in the capital.[877]

According to Carr-Gomm, Merrick headed to 'the only friend he had in the world', Frederick Treves of the London Hospital. As chairman, Carr-Gomm was confronted with an immediate problem expressed in a letter published in *The Times*, December 1886: 'Can any of the readers suggest to me some fitting place where he can be received?'[878]

The hospital was strictly for curable patients and Merrick's condition was by no means curable, yet according to the hospital's minutes one benefactor offered '£50 yearly' if Merrick was kept at the institution; 'the only other suggestions the Chairman had received were to send him to a Hospital for the blind, to lighthouses or to Dartmoor'.[879] The latter may have meant Dartmoor prison or quite simply the vast wilderness of southern Devon; in both cases the suggestion was to ensure Merrick was isolated. As a result of Carr-Gomm's public appeal, a total of £230 was raised in public donations, although he had never explicitly asked for money. In his second letter, published in January 1887, he thanked the public for their kindness and stated that Merrick would reside permanently at the institution.[880] Carr-Gomm relayed that 'Merrick has desired me to convey to them his most grateful thanks', stressing 'that he is deeply sensible of their kindness'.[881] Merrick was now institutionalized.

He spent his days in quiet leisure, attending the hospital's chapel, visiting the theatre and holidaying in a secluded estate, enjoying a retirement reminiscent of Anna and Martin Bates. On the other hand, however, visitors were permitted to see Merrick in a social setting that echoed Daniel Lambert's receptions at the beginning of the century. Moreover, like Tom Thumb, 'it became a cult among the personal friends of the Princess [Alexandra of Wales] to visit the Elephant-Man in the London Hospital', according to the surgeon Bland-Sutton.[882] The Prince of Wales, ever the freak fancier, also met Joseph at the hospital. Merrick's room at the London Hospital was even called the Elephant House by the medical staff who had easy access to his body.[883] He was intimately examined and photographed and, according to Wilfred Thomason Grenfell, a young surgeon who helped care for Merrick, 'he used to talk freely of how he would look in a huge bottle of alcohol – an end to which in his imagination he was fated to come'.[884] He was under no illusions.

On 11 April 1890 he passed away, a funeral was held in the hospital chapel and his body was then 'handed over to Mr Treves the licensed anatomist of the college', claim the hospital minutes.[885] Treves dissected Merrick and arranged his skeleton for the private college museum.[886] Merrick's skeleton was added to the Pathological Museum, joining, among others, a plaster cast of 'an adult microcephalic idiot', a conjoined pair of kittens and a wax model of a 'Chinaman, with a parasitic foetus', according to the catalogue.[887] This museum was never open to the public, so Merrick's skeleton was never officially exhibited but, in the words of the surgeon Bland-Sutton, such a collection was 'little better than a freak-museum'.[888]

⌁⌁

SUBSEQUENT ACCOUNTS OF Merrick's life, written in the early twentieth century, reflected the declining fortunes of the freak show. In *The Elephant Man and Other Reminiscences* (1923), published at the end of a successful career, some thirty-three years after Merrick's death, Frederick Treves was more concerned about his reputation than the truth, writing to his literary editor, Sir Norman Flower, 'I don't want to end up with a failure' and admitting that 'it is a pity that the whole truth cannot always be told'.[889] In the original handwritten manuscript, which contains very few corrections, one is glaring: Treves originally wrote the name 'Joseph Merrick' before crossing-out 'Joseph' and writing 'John'.[890] It can only be conjectured as to why but, for whatever reason, it exemplified a process of distancing that reconstructed Joseph Merrick the man into John Merrick, Treves' literary construct.

According to Treves, 'John' Merrick had a life of appalling suffering: his mother 'basely deserted him when he was very small' (she had in fact died); 'he had had no childhood. He had had no boyhood. He had never experienced pleasure.' [891] His life in the freak show was one of abject horror: 'He was taken about the country to be exhibited as a monstrosity and an object of loathing. He was shunned like a leper, housed like a wild beast, and got his only view of the world from a peephole in a showman's cart.'[892]

Treves claimed a 'Vampire Showman' (that is to say, Tom Norman) treated Merrick like a 'dog'.[893] He lived with the 'fear of people's eyes, the dread of being always stared at, the lash of the cruel mutterings of the crowd'.[894] But Treves offered salvation and the London Hospital a refuge: 'he began to change, little by little, from a hunted thing into

298

a man ... Merrick, I may say, was now one of the most contented creatures I have chanced to meet. More than once he said to me: "I am happy every hour of the day."'[895]

Not so, according to Merrick's London exhibitor, Norman, who responded to Treves' text in 1923. Published in the *World's Fair*, the showman's trade journal, and republished in posthumous memoirs, Norman reversed Treves' claims that the freak show was malevolent and the hospital benevolent. According to Norman, Merrick longed for work and independence, which was ultimately realized when he worked in the freak show, his incarceration at the London Hospital, however, amounted to the deprivation of his liberty. While Treves presented himself as the saviour and Norman as the villain, in the showman's account Treves was the demon and the showman was the redeemer. As Norman said when discussing Mary Ann Bevan, billed as the Ugliest Woman on Earth: 'Here is another instance of the Showman being a freak of nature's salvation.'[896]

We are back at the question of exploitation. According to Merrick's autobiography, the freak show enabled him to leave the degrading workhouse and earn an income as an independent man. His autobiography was written to encapsulate the Victorian values of self-help and hard work, reflecting the popular philosophy of Samuel Smiles, who paid homage to the hardworking individual: 'Labour is the best test of the energies of men.'[897] So, although Merrick was never explicit in his views, other than saying he was well treated in the freak show, perhaps he would have defended the institution that saved him from social marginalization. But then, again, we return to an issue that has underscored this book, and which we saw most clearly in the case of Daniel Lambert's biographies and Józef Boruwłaski's memoirs: many of the sources documenting freak performers were public presentations, moulded by specific agendas, rather than revelations of realities.

Merrick's autobiography (if it was even written by him; the

authorship cannot be clearly verified) was produced for his freak show performance. The veracity is questionable. Moreover, it was written before Merrick was abandoned in Europe and before he was taken into the care of – or confined within – the London Hospital. Perhaps at this point Merrick would have had a different view of his life in the freak show. Ultimately, we are only left with one confident conclusion: there was never one Elephant Man but rather a series of Elephant Men moulded by different texts which had different functions; for Treves and Norman, to fulfil the personal ambitions and vendettas of the surgeon and showman. Despite the antagonism, however, Norman also recognized their similarities, and the injustice of being deemed an exploiter: 'The question is – who really "exploited" poor Joseph? I, the Showman, got the abuse. Dr Treves, the eminent surgeon (who you must admit was also a Showman, but on a rather higher social scale) received the publicity and praise.'[898]

Even the *World's Fair* extolled Treves as the 'brilliant surgeon' who was able to 'remedy some of Fate's mischief' to ensure Merrick spent the remainder of his days 'in something approaching comfort'.[899] Treves' narrative ultimately proved triumphant (it was even the basis for David Lynch's 1980 film *The Elephant Man*) because, by the late nineteenth century, the world of medicine had more authority, and the claims of a surgeon more weight, than the world of freak shows and the assertions of a showman.

TREVES HAD POWER. He was a surgeon entrenched in proliferating institutional structures, the chief centres of confinement being the hospitals, prisons and workhouses: institutional frameworks that isolated 'deviance' and imposed the ideology of work and self-discipline, according to Michel Foucault.[900] In the second half of the nineteenth century the combined number of inmates in lunatic asylums, prisons and workhouses nearly doubled.[901] Medicine was practised in the increasing number of hospitals and, by 1916, hospital wards were swelling as the shellshocked, blind, paralysed and deaf returned from the Great War.[902] The rise of institutions reflected and enhanced medical authority, while giving surgeons more power to appropriate the bodies displayed in the freak show.

But this was a longer trend than such dates suggest. There had been calls for freak performers to be institutionalized as early as General Tom Thumb's display in London. At the height of 'Deformito-Mania', after the suicide of the English painter Benjamin Robert Haydon in 1846, the author Angus Bethune Reach demanded that 'the secrecy of private dwelling or public asylum enwrap' the freak performer.[903] This became an increased reality as medicine was professionalized and backed by the power of the state.

Merrick's confinement at the London Hospital signalled a trend that continued into the twentieth century. Indeed, the novelty performer Daniel P. Mannix, first writing in 1976, recalled a family of 'pinheads' (i.e. with microcephaly) with whom he once worked. With this condition they were presented in the tradition established by Maximo and Bartola, the Aztec Children, in the mid-nineteenth century. 'Sally was the star,' Mannix noted, but 'some conscientious individuals had complained to the police about exploitation' and 'the little group had been broken up and sent to different institutions'. Sally was eventually located: 'She missed her friends and was miserably unhappy. She was sleeping on the floor, the food was terrible, and no one paid any attention to her.' A showman eventually rescued her from the institution.[904]

Schlitzie the 'pinhead' had a similar experience. He was around 4ft tall with the mental capabilities of a toddler. Although very little is known about his early life, it is possible that he was a Simon Metz who was born in 1901. However, he was actually presented as a girl, in part because he was incontinent and required nappies, and a dress was deemed easier to conceal his toilet needs. Schlitzie performed in American sideshows and even featured in films including Tod Browning's cult classic *Freaks* (1932). According to Mannix: 'Schlitzie was in show business for thirty years and then his manager – or to be more explicit about it, his owner – died. The side show wanted to keep Schlitzie, but the state insisted on putting him in an institution.'[905]

He was later found by a showman 'literally dying of loneliness'. The medical attendants 'were far too busy to pay any attention to him and Schlitzie was pining away'.[906] He was eventually released (or rescued) and taken into the care of a showman, continuing to perform in sideshows and circuses until his death, aged seventy, in 1971.

As freak performers increasingly found themselves confined or cared for in medical institutions, the freak body shifted from being a show-stopping wonder to a pathological scientific specimen, non-sensationalized and demystified under the medical gaze. The Photographic Society, founded in 1890 at St Bartholomew's Hospital, produced images depicting physical manifestations of disease. These photographs were used as reference tools for medical students and staff. The patients were mainly taken from the wards of St Bartholomew and many of the subjects, such as those with acromegaly, elephantiasis and achondroplasia, were bodies that could have been found in freak shows.[907]

Perhaps the most vivid portrayal of the dominance of medicine over the freak performer's body is the photograph depicting the surgical separation of the conjoined twins, Radica and Doodica, known as the Orissa Twins or Hindoo Twins, who were first displayed in Britain in 1893. Like Chang and Eng Bunker, they were conjoined by a ligament at the chest and, like the Bunker twins, were constantly subject to medical gossip about the possibility of surgical separation.[908] In the twentieth century medicine would continue to 'correct' and segregate abnormalities in what some have described as a campaign of 'enforced normalization'.[909]

In 1830 Chang and Eng's medical attendant, George Bolton, concluded his paper to the Royal College of Surgeons by thanking the 'owners' for 'the liberal manner in which they have uniformly afforded the means of investigating so curious an object of philosophical inquiry' which, Bolton declared, 'entitle them equally to the thanks of the philanthropist and the lover of science'.[910] By the time of Merrick's display, however, medicine's authority had grown to such an extent that the exceptional body was perceived as the rightful remit of professionals rather than showmen. What's more, while at the beginning of the century medical men stood mystified at the freak performers onstage, by the end of the century and into the twentieth they 'knew' what caused the disability they saw onstage. The ambiguity so central to the appeal of the freak was erased, the fabulous biographies of their lives revealed as fiction. The discovery of the endocrine system, ductless glands that regulate growth, secondary sexual functions and the X-ray further demystified difference and exposed the showmen's freak show stories as falsities.[911]

In a widely circulated article for the *Scientific America Supplement* (1908), the scientific community claimed that the Dog-Faced Man had 'hypertrichosis', Chang the Chinese Giant had 'acromegaly' and the Wild Men of Borneo and Barnum's What Is It? 'we now recognize in the maturer years of professional experience, as cases of microcephalous [*sic*] idiocy'. They continued: 'Most of these humble and unfortunate individuals, whose sole means of livelihood is the exhibition of their physical infirmities to a gaping and unsympathetic crowd, are pathological rarities ... A more refined and a more humane popular taste now frown upon such exhibitions.'[912]

Public tastes and attitudes were changing. Merrick's display was closed by the authorities in the interests of public decency, although these seeds of censure had been planted earlier. There was cultural snobbery directed towards Chang and Eng, the scoffing of genteel classes who criticized the display of Joice Heth in 1835, the anger directed towards Tom Thumb after the suicide of Haydon. Pastrana's exhibitions were closed on the Continent for obscenity, before she was even embalmed, and when Munby expressed his disgust, albeit tinged with eroticism, he signalled a new emotion that increasingly came to define responses to freak performers. Indeed, Treves claimed Merrick was 'the most disgusting specimen of humanity that I have ever seen', and that people react to 'the creature' with 'horror and disgust'.[913]

An introduction to George Sanger's autobiography noted in 1926: 'perhaps the greatest change that has taken place in show-life in our generation is the disappearance of freaks and monstrosities; and this, it will surely be agreed by all, is a change entirely for the good'.[914] Sanger's grandson, George Sanger Coleman, agreed. In the late nineteenth century he joined Barnum and Bailey's Circus and noted with discomfort the 'innumerable freaks that were exhibited in the permanent side-show'.[915] He felt disgust when taking his meals 'opposite the Dog-Faced Man, whose revolting appearance completely put me off my food for several days' and, when he joined Buffalo Bill, he was dismayed to find 'dozens of the freaks that were so beloved of both Barnum and Bailey' noting: 'I did not enjoy meeting them again.'[916]

In Britain, however, he need not worry. The growth of medical power was matched by the creeping power of the state. In 1889 the London County Council (LCC) was formed and began to license venues; one showman predicted to Tom Norman that 'your and mine occupation is gone'.[917] Norman directly blamed the LCC for the freak show's decline, while across the board the state was intervening in all manner of entertainment; indeed, the Metropolitan Board of Works demanded extensive alterations to Astley's Amphitheatre in 1888. With pressure from the LCC and the Ecclesiastical Commission, Sanger sold the land and property, and the ancestral home of the circus was demolished in 1893.[918]

—◦◦◦—

CHANGING PUBLIC TASTES were informed by new ideas. While the masculinity of Daniel Lambert was articulated through his direct speech and love of hunting, and while General Tom Thumb's masculinity was reflected through his sexual vitality, his kisses and fake child, by the late nineteenth and early twentieth century masculinity was located at the level of the body. So-called 'manly independence' was inculcated in public schools through games, athletics, rowing and the establishment of Spartan surroundings.[919] Manliness was expressed through physical strength, which helps explain why Frederick Treves infantilized and feminized Joseph Merrick writing that, at the London Hospital, 'he showed himself to be a gentle, affectionate and lovable creature, as amiable as a happy woman' and he 'still remained in many ways a mere child'.[920] No wonder that, two years after Merrick's death, Treves lamented 'the weakling, the delicate, the misshapen' products of society.[921] Freak performers like the Elephant Man, or women with beards or dwarfs appearing like children, did not fit into this new masculine scheme.

Also, the rediscovery of Mendel's laws of genetics, the rise of eugenics and the advent of Social Darwinism turned freak performers into a national menace. How could you celebrate a freak show marriage, which could lead to 'freak' children, if you believed that physical anomalies were inherited and would cascade down the generations and ultimately enfeeble the nation? In 1895 the first English translation of Max Nordau's *Degeneration* (1892) appeared. Nordau was a German doctor and writer influenced by the work of Cesare Lombroso, the father of modern criminology, who claimed that criminal behaviour was inherited. Nordau's text reflected broader fears about the decline of civilized man, decrying the *fin de siècle*, and anxiously fearing man's descent 'to the lowest degrees of degeneracy, to idiocy, to dwarfishness, etc.'.[922] Increasingly, the likes of the Aztecs, Maximo and Bartola – discussed as dwarfish, degenerate and idiotic – were not to be celebrated but feared. Increasingly, the other side of evolution – devolution – panicked the late Victorians.

Degenerates, it was increasingly thought, would block the evolutionary advance. The rise of eugenics (developed by Darwin's cousin Francis Galton), signalled a corresponding fear that the unfit would hold back the nation. In 1903 Galton asked: 'Our National Physique – Prospects of the British Race – Are We Degenerating?' Luckily, Galton argued, 'a material improvement in our British breed is not so utopian an object as it may seem'.[923] But freak performers were not part of this Utopian breed or indeed the Aryan breed, with eugenics reaching its logical conclusion at the gates of Auschwitz where, behind the sign that read *Arbeit Macht Frei*, dwarfs could be seen.[924]

The treatment of so-called 'imbeciles' tells a similar story. During the Victorian period they were to be pitied, reformed, cured and improved, or displayed in the freak show. Moreover, as the Victorians had large families, it was common for families to have relatives with some form of neurological or physical difference. By the end of the century, however, attempts to 'cure' individuals inside Victorian institutions had largely failed. What's more, as they had done with physical disability, hereditarian beliefs turned the 'imbecile' into a national threat because 'idiocy', it was believed, could be transmitted down the generations. As such, the 'idiot' became a source of family shame, questioning the mental and bodily soundness of the parents. Furthermore, while families became smaller and the nuclear family became the norm, children born different were increasingly abnormal. Unsurprisingly, therefore, they were hidden from public view in proliferating institutions, which reached an apogee in the 1960s.[925]

That very same decade, as Civil Rights activists marched on Washington, the Disability Rights movement was already underway. In 1957 the advocacy group Midgets of America was established, albeit in a publicity stunt, and by 1960 the group had become the Little People of America, which offered support and advocacy to dwarfs. Today it boasts a membership in the thousands, with sister organizations around the world. And as the Disability Rights movement gathered steam, people with disabilities began challenging exploitative practices that ultimately led to a critique of the freak show as dehumanizing displays and the 'pornography of disability'.[926]

However, even before the Disability Rights movement began to demand social and political change, freak performers were also arguing for their right to be accommodated rather than excluded from society, although in a very different form and context. Joseph Merrick finished his own autobiography with a quote from Isaac Watts, an Independent minister who influenced the evangelical revival of the eighteenth century and shaped the evangelicalism of the nineteenth, asking his readers to judge him on his mind rather than his body:

> Was I so tall, could reach the pole,
> Or grasp the ocean with a span;
> I would be measured by the soul,
> The mind's the standard of the man.[927]

Merrick was suggesting to his readers that, in his mind at least, he was one of them, and should be judged accordingly. Only three years after Merrick's autobiography, across the Atlantic the freak performer R.A. Steere made a similar case, presenting a picture of independent manhood in the field of work and stating, on behalf of dwarfs, 'we are quite capable of taking care of ourselves'.[928] By the latter part of the nineteenth century, members and advocates of the blind community were also demanding schemes to enable the blind to work.[929] There were calls from the charitable sector asking for more education and industrial training for 'epileptic and crippled children and adults'.[930] Ben Purse, who led the National League of the Blind and Disabled when it was established in 1899, specifically drew on Samuel Smiles's self-help philosophy to promote employment within the blind community.[931] And then, in April 1903, representatives of the Barnum and Bailey Sideshow complained about the word 'freak'. Barnum had died in 1891 so his partner, James A. Bailey, bore the brunt. It was an expression, the press claimed, of 'Bitter Grief' against a word that was both ugly and stigmatizing and in need of urgent 'remedy'. Ostensibly, this 'revolt' was a moment of protest, akin to workers striking with their trade unions, in a struggle to overcome a linguistic burden that underpinned years of exploitation and social marginalization. The struggle, however, was a 'humbug' masterminded by Bailey's PR expert, Tody Hamilton, but the revolt reflected an increased sense that the term 'freak' was objectionable, and that, as a community, freak performers could demand change.[932]

AS FREAK PERFORMERS entered the twentieth century, a chapter was closed on the history of freakery. They had seen monumental change: the court dwarfs from the seventeenth century had transformed into international Victorian freak show celebrities. The human oddities of the stigmatized travelling fairs had become a community of freak performers in respectable, commercial and permanent venues. A broader entertainment industry had emerged, bolstered by wholescale economic and social changes, with the freak industry a central component. There was, of course, continuity too. While the dwarfs and giants left the royals courts in the eighteenth century to pursue careers onstage, it was Queen Victoria who sparked 'Deformito-Mania' in the 1840s, and who kept the doors of Buckingham Palace open for all manner of freak performers. Similarly, in Europe and America, royals and republicans met the freak performers whose celebrity and ubiquity were enabled by the emergence of a popular culture and a flourishing mass entertainment industry. Moreover, while the rise of teratology, science and evolutionary theories may have demystified difference, the emotion of wonder – that sense of awe at the unexpected – remained a source of continuity well into the nineteenth century.

But in the twentieth century the fortunes of the freak show declined. Increasingly, the wonders, marvels and prodigies of the seventeenth century, who had turned into the 'freaks of nature' in the nineteenth century, had become cases of pathology. The First World War created disabilities on an industrial scale and rendered unpalatable gawping at deformities in the freak show. The Entertainment Tax of 1916, which was designed to raise money for the British war effort, further harmed business. The 1920 Aliens Order meant non-British citizens needed a work permit, which in turn restricted the access of foreign performers and 'exotic freaks' to England.[933]

Between the 1890s and the First World War, a new reforming zeal under the banner of progressivism began to challenge elements of American popular culture that were seen as morally dubious; the amusement parks, for example, were attacked as carnivalesque venues where the working and lower middle classes congregated to enjoy 'vulgar experiences'.[934] By the 1920s, as the entertainment industry continued to grow in leaps and bounds, with movie houses, radios, vaudeville and national sports, the circus suffered amid the competition and so did the sideshow, although the circus as an institution continued into the twenty-first century. By 1929 the fate of fat women appeared sealed: 'the fat lady, for instance, is ceasing to interest the public', claimed circus folk.[935] The American dime museums – the first institution that really rocketed the freak show into popular culture – were also being overshadowed and, by the 1930s, they were shells of their former selves.

The Great Depression of the 1930s further depressed freak show attendance, and in the years after the First World War, the cinema finally replaced the freak show as *the* archetypal expression of popular culture. The movie industry made the once modern Victorian freak show appear old and dated, just as phonograph records were outselling sheet music that had once reflected the Victorian music industry. By the 1940s the display of exceptional bodies was almost a throwback to a bygone age. In 1939–40, at the New York World's Fair, the sideshow of freaks was relegated to the basement, along with the menagerie. By the 1950s the sideshow had divorced itself from the circus, and it would appear that the end was in sight. The lights were finally fading on the freak show.

ENCORE

—◦•◦—

THE FREAK SHOW, however, lived on, lives on and lingers on in more ways than one. In fact, while the freak show was declining as an institution from the late nineteenth century, the freak performer remained salient in twentieth-century cinema, photography, fiction and performance theatre.[936]

The cinema may have marginalized the freak show as an institution, but its performers moved onto the screen. Tod Browning's horror film *Freaks* (1932) featured a group of freak performers, sourced from the stages of the freak show. In the movie, which was set in the circus, freak performers exact their revenge on the beautiful trapeze artist Cleopatra after she seduces, marries and then tries to kill a dwarf in order to steal his inheritance.[937] And while *Freaks* was initially banned in the UK, by the 1960s the film had secured a cult following at a time when 'freaking out' or being a 'freak' was part of a countercultural movement embraced by hippies, the New Left and youth subculture.[938] The freak had become an identity of rebelliousness as the meaning of the word evolved in other ways too: to be a 'jazz freak', for example, meant to be an avid fan.[939] Moreover, while the 1960s saw carnival sideshows abandoned by patrons, who flocked to the bigger and more exciting fairground rides, the sideshow did continue to offer up freak performers into the

1980s.[940] It was only in 2008 that Richard Butchins's documentary could confidently title itself *The Last American Freak Show*.

Yet the freak show was remarkably adaptive. I first saw Mat Fraser in the play *Sealboy: Freak*, a performance inspired by a twentieth-century sideshow act featuring Stanislaus Berent, who, like Fraser, was born with phocomelia (a rare congenital condition affecting the limbs). After a performance of the play, Fraser and I discussed the history and legacy of the freak show. Fraser is a disability activist, writer and actor (who went on to star in the hit series *American Horror Story: Freak Show*, which premiered in 2014), and I was keen to get his perspective on disability and performance. He stressed that, as a person with a disability, he was always stared at on the streets, but onstage he had agency and control.[941]

The disability theorist Terri Thrower described the 'everyday freak show' as when people continue to stare and react unfavourably to a person with a disability in the street.[942] Butchins's documentary *The Last American Freak Show* was even excluded from the London International Disability Film Festival in 2008 because BAFTA's Head of Events was 'uncomfortable' about the film. Mat Fraser lamented at the time: 'Heaven forbid that anyone should be made to feel uncomfortable by a film about disability made by a disabled person.'[943] Moreover, these interactions between people with and without disabilities reveal ongoing freak show dynamics. As one contemporary disability scholar wrote:

> *To be granted fully human status by normates, disabled people must learn to manage relationships from the beginning. In other words, disabled people must use charm, intimidation, ardor, deference, humor, or entertainment to relieve nondisabled people of their discomfort. Those of us with disabilities are supplicants and minstrels, striving to create valued representations of ourselves in our relations with the nondisabled majority.*[944]

Even the interactions between people with and without disabilities require a performance. For Jennifer Miller, the founder of New York's queer performance group Circus Amok and an occasional performer of the Bearded Lady at Coney Island, the freak show is still a lens through which such physical difference is perceived.[945]

Contemporary popular culture is replete with the legacy and dynamics of the freak show. You see it in the American franchise Ripley's Believe It or Not! which started as a newspaper series in the first half of the twentieth century before morphing into various media, including museums like the one in New York, or in Gunther von Hagens's Body Worlds, a display of plastinated corpses that opened in London in 2002.[946] In all manner of popular culture, the legacy of the freak show persists: in talk shows, science fiction, medical documentaries, non-medical documentaries and films, reality TV, the phenomenon of bodybuilding and even in the life of the late 'celebrity freak' Michael Jackson.[947] What has occurred is a relocation and dispersal of the Victorian freaks and their shows, and a continued fascination with the different, the weird and the wonderful.

We are, in short, still interested. It's somewhat of a cliché to say we are all freaks and it is not really true, for the individuals discussed in this book had experiences very different to our own, in a world very different to ours. But there are certainly points of comparison. We live in a world of fake news and alternative facts that emerged from the age of the freaks. The impact of social media, and the blurring of life and performance, has rarely been so relevant. We all have a 'front' we put out there for others to see. We all have or will have bodily imperfections and disabilities we probably want unseen. But this is not our show. So, let us now exit the stage, thank the stars and let them take the final bow.

Notes and References

Curtain Up

1 Phineas T. Barnum, *The Life of P.T. Barnum, Written by Himself*, intro. by Terence Whalen (Urbana: University of Illinois Press, 2000 [1854]), p. 257.

2 Ibid.

3 Ibid., p. 259. Barnum also retold the story of the meeting between Victoria and Tom Thumb in: Phineas T. Barnum, *Struggles and Triumphs; or, Forty Years' Recollections of P.T. Barnum, Written by Himself. Author's Edition* (Buffalo, NY: Warren, Johnson, 1873 [1869]), pp. 176–9. Admittedly, I have taken some artistic licence. It is not really clear whether the Lord-in-Waiting was annoyed at the antics.

4 Queen Victoria's Journals (QVJ), 23 March 1844, <www.queenvictoriasjournals. org> Queen Victoria's Journals can be accessed online through a partnership between ProQuest, the Royal Archives and the Bodleian Libraries [accessed 9 February 2019].

5 *Punch; or The London Charivari*, vol. 10 (London: *Punch*, 1846), p. 262; *Punch; or The London Charivari*, vol. 13 (London: *Punch*, 1847), p. 90.

Introduction

6 Tim Blanning, *The Romantic Revolution* (London: Weidenfeld & Nicolson, 2010), pp. 1–9.

7 *New York Times*, 19 April 1891.

8 A.H. Saxon, *P.T. Barnum: The Legend and the Man* (New York: Columbia University Press, 1989), p. 331.

9 Anon., *Sketch of the Life, Personal Appearance, Character, and Manners, of Charles S. Stratton the Man in Miniature, known as General Tom Thumb, and his Wife, Lavinia Warren Stratton, including the History of their Courtship and Marriage, with some Account of Remarkable Dwarfs, Giants, and other Human Phenomena, of Ancient and Modern Times, also Songs Given at their Public Levees* (New York: Press of Wynkoop & Hallenbeck, 1867), p. 26.

10 The Barnum Museum, Bridgeport, CT (TBMB), Folder, Letters from Lavinia, 9 September 1915.

11 Rosemarie Garland-Thomson, 'Introduction: From Wonder to Error – A Genealogy of Freak Discourse in Modernity', in *Freakery: Cultural Spectacles of the Extraordinary Body*, ed. by Rosemarie Garland-Thomson (New York: New York University Press, 1996), pp. 1–22.

12 Jack Hunter, *Freak Babylon: An Illustrated History of Teratology & Freakshows* (London: Creation Books, 2010), pp. 10–30.

13 A.W. Bates, *Emblematic Monsters: Unnatural Conceptions and Deformed Births in Early Modern Europe* (New York: Rodopi, 2005), pp. 158–9.

14 Edward J. Ingebretsen, *At Stake: Monsters and the Rhetoric of Fear in Public Culture* (Chicago: University of Chicago, 2001), pp. xiii–xvi; Timothy K. Beal, *Religion and Its Monsters* (London: Routledge, 2002), pp. 75–6.

15 Laura Lunger Knoppers and Joan B. Landes, 'Introduction', in *Monstrous Bodies/ Political Monstrosities in Early Modern Europe*, ed. by Laura Lunger Knoppers and Joan B. Landes (Ithaca, NY: Cornell University Press, 2004), pp. 1–22; Julie Crawford, *Marvelous Protestantism: Monstrous Births in Post-Reformation England* (Baltimore, MD: Johns Hopkins University Press, 2005), pp. 2–9.

16 Henry Morley, *Memoirs of Bartholomew Fair* (London: Frederick Warne, 1874), p. 246.

17 Paul Semonin, 'Monsters in the Marketplace: The Exhibition of Human Oddities in Early Modern England', in *Freakery*, ed. by Garland-Thomson, pp. 69–81; London Metropolitan Archives (LMA), Bartholomew Fair Folder, SC/GL/BFS/001-022.

18 Nadja Durbach, *Spectacle of Deformity: Freak Shows and Modern British Culture* (Berkeley: University of California Press, 2010), pp. 2–3.

19 Rosemarie Garland-Thomson, 'Freakery Unfurled', in *Victorian Freaks: The Social Context of Freakery in Britain*, ed. by Marlene Tromp (Columbus: Ohio State University, 2008), pp. ix–xi (p. x).

20 Michael M. Chemers, 'Le Freak, C'est Chic: The Twenty-First Century Freak Show as Theatre of Transgression', *Modern Drama*, 46:2 (2003), pp. 285–304. On the freak show as exploitative see: David T. Mitchell and Sharon L. Snyder, 'Exploitations of Embodiment: Born Freak and the Academic Bally Plank', *Disability Studies Quarterly*, 25:3 (2005) <http://dsq-sds.org/article/view/575/752> [accessed 9 January 2019]; David A. Gerber, 'The "Careers" of People Exhibited in Freak Shows: The Problem of Volition and Valorization', in *Freakery*, ed. by Garland-Thomson, pp. 38–54. For the freak show as a form of empowerment see: Matthew Sweet, *Inventing the Victorians* (London: Faber & Faber, 2001), pp. 136–54; Cheryl Marie Wade, 'Disability Culture Rap', in *The Ragged Edge: The Disability Experience from the Pages of the First Fifteen Years of The Disability Rag*, ed. by Barrett Shaw (Louisville, KY: Avocado Press, 1994), pp. 15–18.

21 Eli Claire, *Exile and Pride: Disability, Queerness and Liberation* (Cambridge, MA: South End, 1999), pp. 70, 93.

22 Frederick Drimmer, *Very Special People: The Struggles, Loves and Triumphs of Human Oddities* (New York: Citadel, 1991), pp. xii–xiii; Leslie Fiedler, *Freaks: Myths and Images of the Secret Self* (Harmondsworth: Penguin, 1981), p. 13.

23 Katherine Dunn, *Geek Love* (New York: Knopf, 1989), p. 20.

24 There is always the possibility of a political analysis, however. See: David T. Mitchell and Sharon L. Snyder, 'Exploitations of Embodiment: Born Freak and the Academic Bally Plank', *Disability Studies Quarterly*, 25:3 (2005) <http://dsq-sds.org/article/view/575/752> [accessed 9 January 2019]. Richard Howells and Michael M. Chemers, 'Midget Cities: Utopia, Utopianism, and the *Vor-Schein* of the "Freak" Show', *Disability Quarterly Studies*, 25:3 (2005) <http://dsq-sds.org/article/view/579/756> [accessed 9 January 2019].

25 'freak, n.1.' *OED Online*, Oxford University Press, December 2018 [accessed 5 March 2019].

26 Robert Bogdan, *Freak Show: Presenting Human Oddities for Amusement and Profit* (Chicago: University of Chicago Press, 1988), p. 6.

27 There were numerous terms for a diverse array of freak performers, including: 'born freaks', 'made freaks', 'novelty acts', 'gaffed freaks' (i.e. fake freaks). Bogdan, *Freak Show*, pp. 6–10.

28 Ibid., p. xi.

29 Cited in Garland-Thomson, 'Introduction', in *Freakery*, ed. by Garland-Thomson, pp. 1–22 (p. 10) and Susan Stewart, *On Longing: Narratives of the Miniature, the Gigantic, the Souvenir, the Collection* (Baltimore, MD: Johns Hopkins University Press, 1984), p. 109.

30 Freak Studies is a body of work that focuses on the freak as a social category. For a helpful overview see: Michael M. Chemers, 'Introduction Staging Stigma: A Freak Studies Manifesto', *Disability Quarterly Studies*, 25:3 (2005) <http://dsq-sds.org/article/view/574/751> [accessed 9 January 2019].

31 Bogdan, *Freak Show*, p. 10.

32 Durbach, *Spectacle of Deformity*, pp. 4–14; Julia V. Douthwaite, *The Wild Girl, Natural Man, and the Monster: Dangerous Experiments in the Age of Enlightenment* (Chicago: University of Chicago Press, 2002), p. 48.

33 Cited in Bogdan, *Freak Show*, p. 3.

34 Durbach, *Spectacle of Deformity*, pp. 14–21.

35 C.H. Unthan, *The Armless Fiddler* (London: George Allen and Unwin, 1935), pp. 261–2.

36 Ibid.

37 Ibid., p. 264.

ACT ONE: Dress Rehearsals

38 The exact details of the banquet are not clear, but I have followed the reasoned conjectures outlined by Nick Page, *Lord Minimus: The Extraordinary Life of Britain's Smallest Man* (New York: St. Martin's Press, 2001), pp. 34–5.

39 Thomas Fuller, *The History of the Worthies of England who for Parts and Learning have been Eminent in the Several Counties: Together with an Historical Narrative of the Native Commodities and Rarities in each County* (London: Printed by J.G.W.L. and W.G. for Thomas Williams, 1662), p. 349.

40 Betty M. Adelson, *The Lives of Dwarfs: Their Journey from Public Curiosity Toward Social Liberation* (Piscataway, NJ: Rutgers University Press, 2005), pp. 97–111.

41 Cited in Ibid., p. 15.

42 Ibid., pp. 7–11.

43 The two contemporary accounts of Hudson's life were Fuller, *History of the Worthies*, and James Wright, *The History and Antiquities of the County of Rutland: Collected from Records, Ancient Manuscripts, Monuments on the Place, and Other Authorities* (London: Bennett Griffin, 1684). For more on the sources and reconstructing Hudson's life see: Page, *Lord Minimus*, pp. 5–7, 243–44.

44 Cited in John Southworth, *Fools and Jesters at the English Court* (Stroud: Sutton Publishing, 1998), p. 156.

45 Fuller, *History of the Worthies of England*, p. 54.

46 In 1568 another dwarf donning a miniature suit of armour and waving a flag emerged from a pie during a festival honouring William, Duke of Bavaria, and Princess Renata of Lorraine.

47 Jane Ravenscroft, 'Invisible Friends: Questioning the representation of the court dwarf in Hapsburg Spain', in *Histories of the Normal and the Abnormal: Social and Cultural Histories of Norms and Normativity*, ed. by Waltraud Ernst (London: Routledge, 2006), pp. 26–52.

48 Lorraine Daston and Katharine Park, *Wonders and the Order of Nature, 1150–1750* (New York: Zone Books, 2001), pp. 21–66.

49 Edward J. Wood, *Giants and Dwarfs* (London: Richard Bentley, 1868), p. 278.

50 Page, *Lord Minimus*, p. 24.

51 Cited in Semonin, 'Monsters in the Marketplace', in *Freakery*, ed. by Garland-Thomson, pp. 69–81 (p. 70).

52 Thomas Frost, *The Old Showmen, and The Old London Fairs* (London: Tinsley Brothers, 1874), p. 18–19.

53 Ibid., p. 19.

54 Ibid., p. 26.

55 Adelson, *Lives of Dwarfs*, pp. 44–9.

56 QVJ, 21 February 1849.

57 Page, *Lord Minimus*, pp. 152–5.

58 Cited in Ibid., p. 160.

59 Walter Scott, *Peveril of the Peak* (London: George Routledge, 1879 [1823]), p. 323.

60 Ibid., pp. 326–7.

61 *Queenslander*, 26 June 1897.

62 Page, *Lord Minimus*, p. 157.

63 Ibid., pp. 166–79.

64 Wright, *History and Antiquities of the County of Rutland*, p. 105.

65 Ibid.

66 For Hudson's later years see: Page, *Lord Minimus*, pp. 206–34.

67 Durham County Record Office (DCRO), Memoirs of the Celebrated Dwarf, Count Joseph Boruwłaski (1801), DU 1/60/11, pp. vii–viii.

68 Joseph Boruwłaski, *Second Edition of the Memoirs of the Celebrated Dwarf, Joseph Boruwłaski, A Polish Gentleman* (Birmingham: J. Thompson, 1792), pp. 2–3.

69 For a helpful biography of Boruwłaski see: Anna Grześkowiak-Krwawicz, *Gulliver in the Land of Giants: A Critical Biography and the Memoirs of the Celebrated Dwarf*, trans. by Daniel Sax (Surrey: Ashgate, 2012).

70 Boruwłaski, *Second Edition of the Memoirs*, pp. 5–6.

71 Grześkowiak-Krwawicz, *Gulliver in the Land of Giants*, pp. 7–10.

72 Boruwłaski, *Second Edition of the Memoirs*, p. 7.

73 Ibid., p. 8.

74 Grześkowiak-Krwawicz, *Gulliver in the Land of Giants*, p. 12.

75 Ambroise Paré, *On Monsters and Marvels*, trans. with intro. by Janis L. Pallister (Chicago: University of Chicago Press, 1982 [1573]), p. 3.

76 Cited in Mark S. Blumberg, *Freaks of Nature and What They Tell Us About Development and Evolution* (Oxford: Oxford University Press, 2009), p. 26.

77 Ibid., pp. 22–30.

78 Boruwłaski, *Second Edition of the Memoirs*, pp. 16–17.

79 Ibid., p. 40.

80 Benedetta Craveri, *The Age of Conversation*, trans. by Teresa Waugh (New York: New York Review of Books, 2005).

81 Boruwłaski, *Second Edition of the Memoirs*, p. 20.

82 Cited in Adelson, *Lives of Dwarfs*, p. 11.

83 Boruwłaski, *Second Edition of the Memoirs*, pp. 21–2.

84 Ibid., pp. 26, 29.

85 Cited in Grześkowiak-Krwawicz, *Gulliver in the Land of Giants*, p. 9.

86 Boruwłaski, *Second Edition of the Memoirs*, pp. 42–3.

87 Ibid., p. 43.

88 Ibid., p. 60.

89 Ibid., pp. 61–2.

90 Boruwłaski, *Memoirs of the Celebrated Dwarf* (London, 1788 [first edition]), cited in Grześkowiak-Krwawicz, *Gulliver in the Land of Giants*, p. 110.

91 Ibid., pp. 115, 117.

92 Boruwłaski, *Second Edition of the Memoirs*, p. 71.

93 Boruwłaski, *Memoirs of the Celebrated Dwarf* [first edition], cited in Grześkowiak-Krwawicz, *Gulliver in the Land of Giants*, p. 120.

94 Boruwłaski, *Second Edition of the Memoirs*, p. 85.

95 Ibid.

96 Ibid., p. 89; Boruwłaski, *Memoirs of the Celebrated Dwarf* [first edition], cited in Grześkowiak-Krwawicz, *Gulliver in the Land of Giants*, p. 127.

97 His sexual vivaciousness earned him an entry in Francis Grose, *A Classical Dictionary of the Vulgare Tongue* (London. S. Hooper, 1785), note 'Buckinger's Boot' was a euphemism for 'cunt'.

98 For Boruwłaski's performances and others see: Grześkowiak-Krwawicz, *Gulliver in the Land of Giants*, pp. 30–2.

99 Ibid., pp. 26–7.

100 Boruwłaski, *Second Edition of the Memoirs*, p. 108.

101 Catherine Hutton, 'A Memoir of the Celebrated Dwarf, Joseph Boruwłaski', *Bentley's Miscellany*, vol. 17 (London: Richard Bentley, 1845), 240–9 (p. 247).

102 Ibid.

103 Boruwłaski, *Second Edition of the Memoirs*, p. 131.

104 DCRO, Library Pamphlets, Tom M. Heron, 'The Little Count', *Joseph Boruwłaski* (City of Durham, 1986), Vol A 14/17, p. 17.

105 Boruwłaski, *Second Edition of the Memoirs*, p. 141; Grześkowiak-Krwawicz, *Gulliver in the Land of Giants*, p. 66.

106 Grześkowiak-Krwawicz, *Gulliver in the Land of Giants*, pp. 43–4.

107 Durham University Library (DUL), Hanna Swiderska, *The Celebrated Polish Dwarf* (21 July 1968), Add. MS 1395/2, p. 15.

108 *Durham University Journal* 20:2 (1910), p. 30.

109 DUL, Letter from Joseph Boruwłaski, 20 May 1818, Add. MS. 180.

110 DUL, Catalogue of Furniture, Books, and other effects, of the late celebrated Polish dwarf, SDG/16/1.

111 Mrs Mathews [Anne Jackson], *Memoirs of Charles Mathews, Comedian*, vol. 3 (London: Richard Bentley, 1839), p. 213.

112 DUL, Commonplace Book of William Van Mildert, Add. MS. 1907, F.31.

113 DUL, Letter from Joseph Boruwłaski, Add. MS. 1079, 27 May 1818.

114 Grześkowiak-Krwawicz, *Gulliver in the Land of Giants*, pp. 59–69.

115 Kerry Duff, 'Biographies of Scale', *Disability Studies Quarterly*, 25:4 (2005) <http:// dsq-sds.org/article/view/617/794> [accessed 28 December 2018].

116 Lavinia M. Magri, *The Autobiography of Mrs. Tom Thumb*, ed. by A.H. Saxon (Hamden, CT: Archon Books, 1979), p. 172.

117 DUL, Correspondence, Accounts, etc., SDG/1/1.

118 *Durham University Journal*, 15:11 (1903), p. 133.

119 DCRO, Correspondence, DU 1/31/251–253.

120 *Durham University Journal*, 10:2 (1910), p. 30.

121 Anon., *The Life of that Wonderful and Extraordinary Heavy Man, the Late Daniel Lambert. From his Birth to the Moment of his Dissolution, with an Account of Men Noted for their Corpulency, and other Interesting Matter* (Stamford: J. Drakard, 1809), p. 4.

122 Jan Bondeson, *Freaks: The Pig-Faced Lady of Manchester Square & other Medical Marvels* (Stroud: Tempus, 2006), pp. 112–36.

123 James Neild, *State of the prisons in England, Scotland, and Wales, extending to various places therein assigned* (London: Nicholas and Son, 1812), p. 338.

124 Anon., *Life of that Wonderful and Extraordinary Heavy Man*, p. 9.

125 Stamford Town Library, Lincolnshire (STL), Daniel Lambert Newspaper Cutting Folder, 'Mr Daniel Lambert'.

126 Sander L. Gilman, *Obesity: The Biography* (Oxford: Oxford University Press, 2010), p. 59.

127 Stamford Town Hall (STH), Daniel Lambert Folder, F52LAM.

128 Anon., *Life of that Wonderful and Extraordinary Heavy Man*, p. 10.

129 Ibid., pp. 9–11.

130 Cited in David Haslam and Fiona Haslam, *Fat, Gluttony and Sloth: Obesity in Literature, Art and Medicine* (Liverpool: Liverpool University Press, 2009), p. 42.

131 Cited in Ibid., p. 53.

132 William Granger, *The New Wonderful Museum and Extraordinary Magazine: Being a Complete Repository of all the Wonders, Curiosities, and Rarities of Nature and Art*, 6 vols. (London: A. Hogg, 1802–8), vol. 5 (1808), p. 2679.

133 Anon., *Life of that Wonderful and Extraordinary Heavy Man*, p. 11.

134 *The Times*, 2 April 1806.

135 Anon., *Life of that Wonderful and Extraordinary Heavy Man*, p. 13.

136 John Tosh, *Manliness and Masculinities in Nineteenth-Century Britain: Essays on Gender, Family, and Empire* (Harlow: Pearson Longman, 2005), pp. 86–98.

137 R.S. Kirby, *Kirby's Wonderful and Eccentric Museum; or, Magazine of Remarkable Characters* 6 vols. (London: R.S. Kirby, 1803–20), vol. 2 (1804), p. 409; Henry Wilson, *The Eccentric Mirror: Reflecting a Faithful and Interesting Delineation of Male and Female Characters* (London: James Cundee, 1806–7, 1813), 1:1 (1806), p. 1.

138 Anon., *The Eccentric Magazine; or, Lives and Portraits of Remarkable Characters*, 2 vols. (London: G. Smeeton, 1812–14), vol. 2 (1814), p. 241.

139 Ibid., p. 248.

140 *York Herald*, 4 June 1808.

141 Tosh, *Manliness and Masculinities*, pp. 86–98.

142 Anon., *Life of that Wonderful and Extraordinary Heavy Man*, p. 14.

143 Ibid., pp. 14–15.

144 Wilson, *Eccentric Mirror*, 1:1 (1806), p. 20.

145 *York Herald*, 17 September 1808.

146 Mrs Mathews [Anne Jackson], *The Life and Correspondence of Charles Mathews the Elder, Comedian* (London: Warne and Routledge, 1860), p. 384.

147 STL, Daniel Lambert Primary References Folder, 'A Contemporary Account of the Death of Daniel Lambert at Stamford – June 1809'.

148 Anon., *Life of that Wonderful and Extraordinary Heavy Man*, pp. 15–16.

149 Ibid., p. 28.

150 Record Office of Leicestershire, Leicester and Rutland (ROLLR), Scrapbook 38'31; The British Library, London (BLL), Sarah Sophia Banks Collection, vol. III: Balloons, Sights, Exhibitions, Remarkable Characters. Katterfelto the Monster, L.R.301.h.5, 22AA.

151 *Caledonian Mercury*, 13 March 1806.

152 ROLLR, 'Life of that Wonderful and Extraordinary Heavy Man', M40.

153 *Morning Post*, 19 June 1806; *Morning Post*, 30 June 1806.

154 The John Johnson Collection: An Archive of Printed Ephemera (TJJC), Human Freaks 1 (25) [accessed 9 February 2019].

155 TJJC, Human Freaks 2 (7d).

156 DCRO, Opinion concerning the fairs in Elvet, 1804, DU 1/60/12, 1804.

157 STL, Daniel Lambert Primary References Folder, *Stamford Mercury*, 23 June 1809.

158 James Gregory, 'Eccentric Lives: Character, Characters and Curiosities in Britain, *c.* 1760–1900', in *Histories of the Normal and the Abnormal*, ed. by Ernst, pp. 73–100.

159 Kirby, *Kirby's*, vol. 2 (1804), p. 422; James Caulfield, *Portraits, Memoires, and Characters of Remarkable Persons, from the Revolution in 1688 to the End of the Reign of George II*, 4 vols. (London: H.R. Young and T.H. Whitely, 1819), vol. 1 (1819), p. vi.

160 Fiona Yvette Pettit, 'Freaks in Late Nineteenth-Century British Media and Medicine' (unpublished doctoral thesis, University of Exeter, 2012), pp. 38–9.

161 Jason McElligott and Eve Patten, 'The Perils of Print Culture: An Introduction', in *The Perils of Print Culture: Book, Print and Publishing History in Theory and Practice*, ed. by Jason McElligott and Eve Patten (Basingstoke: Palgrave Macmillan, 2014), pp. 1–16.

162 Anon., *Life of that Wonderful and Extraordinary Heavy Man*, p. 28.

163 Cited in Victoria Carroll, *Science and Eccentricity: Collecting, Writing and Performing Science for Early Nineteenth-Century Audiences* (London: Pickering & Chatto, 2008), p. 20.

164 Wilson, *Eccentric Mirror*, 1:12 (1806), pp. 1–2.

165 Sander L. Gilman, *Fat: A Cultural History of Obesity* (Cambridge: Polity Press, 2008), pp. 80–5.

166 Durbach, *Spectacle of Deformity*, pp. 26–7.

167 Anon., *Life of that Wonderful and Extraordinary Heavy Man*, p. 16.

168 Thomas Seccombe, 'Lambert, Daniel (1770–1809)', rev. E. L. O'Brien, *Oxford Dictionary of National Biography* <http://www.oxforddnb.com/view/article/15932> [accessed 28 December 2018].

169 Wilson, *Eccentric Mirror*, 1:4 (1806), p. 22.

170 Linda Colley, *Britons: Forging the Nation, 1707–1837* (London: Pimlico, 2003), pp. 147–94; Paul Langford, *Englishness Identified: Manners and Characters, 1650–1850* (Oxford: Oxford University Press, 2000), pp. 267–75.

171 Anon., *Life of that Wonderful and Extraordinary Heavy Man*, p. 12; Thomas Prest, *The Magazine of Curiosity and Wonder* (London: G. Drake, 1835), p. 17.

172 Reva Wolf, 'John Bull, Liberty, and Wit: How England Became Caricature', in *The Efflorescence of Caricature, 1759–1838*, ed. by Todd Porterfield (Surrey: Ashgate, 2011), pp. 49–60.

173 Chris Evans, *Debating the Revolution: Britain in the 1790s* (London: I.B. Tauris, 2006), p. 62.

174 Tamara L. Hunt, *Defining John Bull: Political Caricature and National Identity in Late Georgian England* (Surrey: Ashgate, 2003), pp. 121–69.

175 For the complexities of Lambert's 'Otherness' see: Joyce L. Huff, 'Freaklore: The Dissemination, Fragmentation, and Reinvention of the Legend Daniel Lambert, King of Fat Men', in *Victorian Freaks*, ed. by Tromp, pp. 37–59; Paul Youngquist, *Monstrosities: Bodies and British Romanticism* (Minneapolis: University of Minnesota Press, 2003), pp. 38–41.

176 Herbert Spencer spoke of a 'Daniel Lambert of Learning' in his *Study of Sociology* (1873), and George Meredith's *One of our Conquerors* (1890) referred to London as the 'Daniel Lambert of cities'.

177 BLL, Lysons Collectanea, vol. I, C20452, 31; STH, The Philips Collection, Entertainment Folders 232.

178 National Fairground Archives (NFA), Cyril Critchlow Collection, Newspaper Cuttings, 178G25.4.

179 Ibid.

180 Cited in Pamela Horn, *Amusing the Victorians: Leisure, Pleasure and Play in Victorian Britain* (Stroud: Amberley Publishing, 2014), p. 109.

181 'Lord' George Sanger, *Seventy Years a Showman*, with an intro. by Kenneth Grahame (New York: Dutton and Company, 1926 [1910]), p. 10.

182 Ibid., p. 12.

183 Tom Norman and George Barnum Norman, *The Penny Showman: Memoirs of Tom Norman 'Silver King'* (London: Privately Published, 1985), p. 9.

184 NFA, Shufflebottom Family Collection: Family History Notes Written by Florence Shufflebottom, 178B28.2.

185 Ibid.

186 Norman and Norman, *Penny Showman*, p. 44.

187 Sanger, *Seventy Years a Showman*, p. 13.

188 BLL, Fillinham Collection of Cuttings, vol. IV: Fairs, 1889.b.10/4, p. 7.

189 Vivienne Richmond, *Clothing the Poor in Nineteenth-Century England* (Cambridge: Cambridge University Press, 2013), pp. 121–34.

190 Cited in Hugh Cunningham, *Leisure in the Industrial Revolution, c.1780–c.1880* (London: Croom Helm, 1980), p. 90.

191 See, for example, LeRoy Ashby, *With Amusement for All: A History of American Popular Culture since 1830* (Lexington: University Press of Kentucky, 2006), pp. 41–72; Rosalind Crone, *Violent Victorians: Popular Entertainment in Nineteenth-Century London* (Manchester: Manchester University Press, 2010), pp. 1–11, 257–68.

192 BLL, Fillinham Collection of Cuttings, vol. IV: Fairs, 1889.b.10/4, p. 9.

193 Frost, *The Old Showmen*, pp. 155, 205–6.

194 Charles Dickens, *Sketches by Boz*, ed. and intro. by Dennis Walder (London: Penguin, 1995 [1833–39]), pp. 143–4.

195 Sanger, *Seventy Years a Showman*, p. 23.

196 Ibid., p. 26.

197 Dickens, *Sketches by Boz*, p. 140.

198 Sanger, *Seventy Years a Showman*, p. 83.
199 Ibid., pp. 82–3.
200 Ibid., p. 79.
201 Ibid., p. 18.
202 Ibid., pp. 18–19.
203 Ibid., p. 54.
204 Ibid., p. 51.
205 Ibid., p. 58.
206 Ibid., p. 35.
207 Ibid., p. 36.
208 Dominique Jando, *Philip Astley & The Horsemen who invented the Circus (1768–1814)* (San Francisco: Circopedia, 2018), p. 73.
209 Thomas Frost, *Circus Life and Circus Celebrities* (London: Tinsley Brothers, 1873), p. 17.
210 Cited in Steve Ward, *Father of the Modern Circus 'BILLY BUTTONS': The Life & Times of Philip Astley* (Barnsley: Pen & Sword History, 2018), p. 36.
211 Cited in Ibid., p. 37.
212 Jando, *Philip Astley & The Horsemen who invented the Circus*, pp. 73–108.
213 Ibid., p. 33.
214 Cited in Horn, *Amusing the Victorians*, p. 111.
215 See Vanessa Toulmin, *Pleasurelands* (Sheffield: National Fairground Archive, 2003).

ACT TWO: Show Time

216 Ben Weinreb et al, *The London Encyclopaedia* (London: Macmillan, 2008), pp. 266–7.
217 Cited in Irving Wallace and Amy Wallace, *The Two: A Biography* (London: Cassell, 1978), p. 90.
218 [James W. Hale], *An Historical and Descriptive Account of the Siamese Twin Brothers, from Actual Observations, Together with Full Length Portraits, the Only Correct Ones, Permitted to be Taken by Their Protectors* (London: W. Turner, 1830), p. 7.
219 Cited in David R. Collins, *Chang and Eng: The Original Siamese Twins* (Oxford: Maxwell Macmillan, 1994), pp. 46–7.
220 [Hale], *Historical and Descriptive Account of the Siamese Twin Brothers*, p. 8.
221 *Bristol Mercury*, 1 December 1829.
222 Yunte Huang, *Inseparable: The Original Siamese Twins and Their Rendezvous with American History* (New York: Liveright Publishing, 2018), p. 83.
223 LMA, Bartholomew Fair Folder, 1820–29, SC/GL/BFS/136, 140, 141, 144, 147.
224 Ibid., SC/GL/BFS/126.
225 TJJC, Human Freaks 1 (38a); Human Freaks 2 (11), and 2 (34). For Chabert, the 'Incombustable Man', see Richard D. Altick, *The Shows of London: A Panoramic History of Exhibitions, 1800–1862* (Cambridge, MA: Belknap Press, 1978), pp. 263–5.
226 Pascal Blanchard, Gilles Boëtsch and Nanette Jacomijn Snoep, 'Human Zoos: The Invention of the Savage', in *Human Zoos: The Invention of the Savage*, ed. by Pascal Blanchard, Gilles Boëtsch and Nanette Jacomijn Snoep (Paris: Musée de Quai, 2011), pp. 20–54.

227 Sadiah Qureshi, *Peoples on Parade: Exhibitions, Empire, and Anthropology in Nineteenth-Century Britain* (Chicago: University of Chicago Press, 2011), p. 6.

228 Cited in Huang, *Inseparable*, p. 11.

229 Ibid., p. 13.

230 [Hale], *Historical and Descriptive Account of the Siamese Twin Brothers*, p. 6.

231 George Buckley Bolton, 'Statement of the Principle Circumstances Respecting the United Siamese Twins Now Exhibiting in London', *Philosophical Transactions of the Royal Society of London*, 120 (1830), pp. 177–86 (p. 177).

232 North Carolina State Archives (NCSA), Siamese Twins Collection P.C.916.1, Copy of Contract, 1829.

233 Bolton, 'Statement of the Principle Circumstances', p. 178.

234 Cited in Altick, *The Shows of London*, p. 37.

235 Huang, *Inseparable*, pp. 80–8; John Kuo Wei Tchen, *New York Before Chinatown: Orientalism and the Shaping of American Culture, 1776–1882* (Baltimore, MD: Johns Hopkins University Press, 1999), p. 106.

236 *Morning Post*, 19 November 1829.

237 Cited in Ulrike Hillemann, *Asian Empire and British Knowledge: China and the Networks of British Imperial Expansion* (Basingstoke: Palgrave Macmillan, 2009), pp. 30–1.

238 Ibid., pp. 16–33, 120–141, 152–168.

239 Deborah Cohen, *Family Secrets: Living with Shames from the Victorians to the Present Day* (London: Penguin, 2013), pp. 3–37.

240 Cited in Bill Brown, *The Material Unconscious: American Amusement, Stephen Crane, & the Economies of Play* (London: Harvard University Press, 1996), p. 209.

241 Bogdan, *Freak Show*, pp. 27–9.

242 Qureshi, *Peoples on Parade*, p. 200.

243 Bogdan, *Freak Show*, p. 28.

244 [Hale], *Historical and Descriptive Account of the Siamese Twin Brothers*, p. 3.

245 *The Times*, 2 December 1829.

246 Anon., *The Siamese Twins: Chang and Eng. A Biographical Sketch* (London: J.W. Last, 1869), p. 1.

247 Elizabeth Grosz, 'Intolerable Ambiguity: Freaks as/at the Limit', in *Freakery*, ed. by Garland-Thomson, pp. 55–66 (p. 56).

248 Cited in Erin O'Connor, *Raw Material: Producing Pathology in Victorian Culture* (Durham, NC: Duke University Press, 2000), p. 157.

249 [Hale], *Historical and Descriptive Account of the Siamese Twin Brothers*, p. 3.

250 Ibid.

251 Roy Porter, *Bodies Politic: Disease, Death and Doctors in Britain, 1650–1900* (London: Reaktion Books, 2001), p. 55.

252 [Hale], *Historical and Descriptive Account of the Siamese Twin Brothers*, p. 14.

253 Cited in Sarah Mitchell, 'From "Monstrous" to "Abnormal": The Case of Conjoined Twins in the Nineteenth Century', in *Histories of the Normal and the Abnormal*, ed. by Ernst, pp. 53–72 (p. 61) and M. Sauvage, 'The Period of the First Union of the Siamese Twins', *Lancet*, 29:735 (1837), pp. 29–30.

254 Anon., 'The Siamese Twins at the College of Physicians', *Richmond and Louisville Medical Journal*, 17:4 (1874), pp. 459–73 (pp. 460–1).

255 Huang, *Inseparable*, p. 46; Garland-Thomson, 'Introduction', in *Freakery*, ed. by Garland-Thomson, pp. 1–22.

256 Cited in Blumberg, *Freaks of Nature*, p. 27.

257 Cited in Sarah Mitchell, 'From "Monstrous" to "Abnormal"', pp. 53–72 (p. 61).

258 Lennard J. Davis, 'Constructing Normalcy', in *The Disability Studies Reader*, ed. by Lennard J. Davis (Oxon: Routledge, 2010), pp. 3–19; 'abnormality, n.' *OED Online*. Oxford University Press, December 2018 [accessed 5 March 2019].

259 J.B. Morrell, 'Professionalisation', in *Companion to the History of Modern Science*, ed. by R.C. Olby and others (London: Routledge, 1996), pp. 980–9.

260 Bolton, 'Statement of the Principle Circumstances', p. 185.

261 Ibid., p. 181.

262 Ibid., p. 180–2.

263 Fiedler, *Freaks*, p. 199.

264 Bolton, 'Statement of the Principle Circumstances', pp. 183–4.

265 Ibid., pp. 184–5.

266 Ibid., p. 185.

267 Edward B. Lytton, *The Siamese Twins: A Satirical Tale of the Times. With Other Poems* (New York: J. & J. Harper, 1831), p. 76.

268 Cited in Youngquist, *Monstrosities*, p. xi.

269 Gilles Boëtsch and Pascal Blanchard, 'The Hottentot Venus: Birth of a 'Freak' (1815), in *Human Zoos*, ed. by Blanchard, Boëtsch and Snoep, pp. 62–72 (p. 68).

270 Ibid., p. 62.

271 Clifton Crais and Pamela Scully, *Sara Baartman and the Hottentot Venus: A Ghost Story and a Biography* (Princeton, NJ: Princeton University Press, 2009), p. 140.

272 For recent scholarship see: Pamela Scully and Clifton Crais, 'Race and Erasure: Sara Baartman and Hendrik Cesars in Cape Town and London', in *Journal of British Studies*, 47:2 (2008), pp. 301–323; Crais and Scully, *Sara Baartman and the Hottentot Venus*.

273 *London Times*, 26 November 1810.

274 Scully and Crais, 'Race and Erasure', p. 316.

275 *London Times*, 26 November 1810.

276 [Jackson], *Life and Correspondence of Charles Mathews the Elder*, p. 385.

277 Cited in Scully and Crais, 'Race and Erasure', p. 320.

278 Crais and Scully, *Sara Baartman and the Hottentot Venus*, pp. 138–9.

279 Ibid., p. 140.

280 Royal College of Surgeons, London (RCSL), Museum Letters 1821 RCS-MUS/S/5/6/4; RCSL, Research: Memoranda of Natural History, vol 1 MS0007/1/6/1/8; Research: The Mermaid MS0007/1/6/1/16.

281 Glyn Williams, *Naturalists at Sea: Scientific Travellers from Dampier to Darwin* (New Haven, CT: Yale University Press, 2013), pp. 239–59.

282 BLL, Sarah Sophia Banks Collection, vol. V: Cuttings from Newspapers L.R.301.h.7, *Hottentots in England*, 9 November 1803.

283 Qureshi, *Peoples on Parade*, p. 106.

284 NCSA, Siamese Twins Collection P.C.916.1, Correspondence, Capt. Abel Coffin, 1829–1830, 28 June 1829.

285 Edward W. Said, *Orientalism* (London: Routledge & Kegan Paul, 1978), pp. 1–28, 201–11.

286 Bolton, 'Statement of the Principle Circumstances', p. 178.

287 Mitchell, 'From "Monstrous" to "Abnormal"', pp. 53–72.

288 Douglas C. Baynton, 'Disability and the Justification of Inequality in American History', in *The New Disability History: American Perspectives*, ed. by Paul K. Longmore and Lauri Umansky (New York: New York University Press, 2001), pp. 33–57.

289 Cynthia Wu, *Chang and Eng Reconnected: The Original Siamese Twins in American Culture* (Philadelphia: Temple University Press, 2012), p. 25.

290 Wilson Library, University of North Carolina at Chapel Hill, Ephemera Collection CbB S56f, CbB S56sl, CbB S56p, CbB S56w.

291 [Hale], *Historical and Descriptive Account of the Siamese Twin Brothers*, pp. 4–5.

292 Zachary Lockman, *Contending Visions of the Middle East: The History and Politics of Orientalism* (Cambridge: Cambridge University Press, 2010), pp. 67–70, 83–6.

293 [Hale], *Historical and Descriptive Account of the Siamese Twin Brothers*, p. 6.

294 Bolton, 'Statement of the Principle Circumstances', pp. 178–9.

295 [Hale], *Historical and Descriptive Account of the Siamese Twin Brothers*, p. 8.

296 Ibid.

297 NCSA, Siamese Twins Collection P.C.916.1, Correspondence, Capt. Abel Coffin, 1831–3, 8 January 1831.

298 NCSA, Siamese Twins Collection P.C.916.1, Correspondence, Capt. Abel Coffin, 1829–30, 6 March 1830.

299 Bill Ashcroft, 'Primitive and Wingless: The Colonial Subject as Child', in *Dickens and the Children of Empire*, ed. by Wendy S. Jacobson (Basingstoke: Palgrave Macmillan, 2000), pp. 184–202.

300 NCSA, Siamese Twins Collection P.C.916.1, Correspondence, Capt. Abel Coffin, 1831–3, 8 January 1831.

301 Benjamin Reiss, *The Showman and the Slave: Race, Death and Memory in Barnum's America* (Cambridge, MA: Harvard University Press, 2001), p. 28.

302 Peter Benes, *For a Short Time Only: Itinerants and the Resurgence of Popular Culture in Early America* (Amherst: University of Massachusetts Press, 2016), p. 20.

303 Robert M. Lewis (ed.), *From Travelling Show to Vaudeville: Theatrical Spectacle in America, 1830–1910* (Baltimore, MD: Johns Hopkins University Press, 2003), p. 13.

304 Cited in Richard R. Beeman, 'Trade and Travel in Post-Revolutionary Virginia: A Diary of an Itinerant Peddler, 1807–1808', in *The Virginia Magazine of History and Biography*, 84:2 (1976), pp. 174–188 (pp. 177–8).

305 NCSA, Siamese Twins Collection P.C.916.1, Correspondence, Charles Harris to the Coffins, 1832, 27 January 1832; NCSA, Siamese Twins Collection P.C.916.1, Correspondence, Charles Harris to the Coffins, 1832, 30 March 1832.

306 Cited in Joseph Andrew Orser, *Lives of Chang and Eng: Siam's Twins in Nineteenth-Century America* (Chapel Hill: University of North Carolina Press, 2014), p. 38.

307 Cited in Lewis (ed.), *From Travelling Show to Vaudeville*, p. 5.

308 Cited in Orser, *Lives of Chang and Eng*, p. 40.

309 Cited in Ibid., p. 42.

310 NCSA, Siamese Twins Collection P.C.916.1, Correspondence, James W. Hale and Charles Harris to the Coffins, 1829–31, 22 December 1831.

311 NCSA, Siamese Twins Collection P.C.916.1, Correspondence, Charles Harris to the Coffins, 1832, 9 January 1832. NCSA, Siamese Twins Collection P.C.916.1, Correspondence, Charles Harris to the Coffins, 1832, 8 January 1832.

312 NCSA, Siamese Twins Collection P.C.916.1, Correspondence, Charles Harris to the Coffins, 1832, 16 January 1832.

313 Huang, *Inseparable*, p. 114.

314 *Baltimore Patriot*, 20 August 1831.

315 NCSA, Siamese Twins Collection P.C.916.1, Correspondence, Charles Harris to the Coffins, 1832, 29 May 1832.

316 NCSA, Siamese Twins Collection P.C.916.1, Correspondence, Capt. Abel Coffin, 1831–3, 5 October 1832.

317 Southern Historical Collection, University of North Carolina at Chapel Hill (SHC, UNC), Chang and Eng Bunker 3761/226, Ledger 1832–41, June 1839.

318 SHC, UNC, Chang and Eng Bunker 3761/213-17, Ledger 1832–41, March 1839.

319 SHC, UNC, Chang and Eng Bunker 3761/068, Ledger 1832–41, May 1834; SHC, UNC, Chang and Eng Bunker 3761/037-041, Ledger 1832–41, June–July 1833. For a fuller picture of their lives offstage see: Chang and Eng Bunker Papers, M-3761; Bunker, Chang and Eng, Op3761; Bunker, Chang and Eng, P. 3761.

320 [James W. Hale], A Few Particulars Concerning Chang-Eng, The United Siamese Brothers, Published Under Their Own Direction (New York: John M. Elliott, 1836), p. 1.

321 [Hale], Historical and Descriptive Account of the Siamese Twin Brothers, p. 6; [Hale], Few Particulars Concerning Chang-Eng, p. 5.

322 [Hale], Few Particulars Concerning Chang-Eng, p. 3.

323 NCSA, Siamese Twins Collection P.C.916.1, Correspondence, Charles Harris to the Coffins, 1832, 11 April 1832.

324 [Hale], Few Particulars Concerning Chang-Eng, p. 5; NCSA, Siamese Twins Collection P.C.916.1, Correspondence, Charles Harris to the Coffins, 1832, 2 March 1832.

325 For academics drawing a distinction between onstage performances and offstage realities see, for example, Rikke Andreassen, Human Exhibitions: Race, Gender and Sexuality in Ethnic Displays (Surrey: Ashgate, 2015), pp. 83–114; Rachel Adams, Sideshow U.S.A.: Freaks and the American Cultural Imagination (Chicago: University of Chicago Press, 2001), p. 6; Bodgan, Freak Show, p. 3; Michael M. Chemers, Staging Stigma: A Critical Examination of the American Freak Show (Basingstoke: Palgrave Macmillan, 2008), p. 17.

326 Huang, Inseparable, pp. 163–4.

327 Ibid., p. 191.

328 Orser, Lives of Chang and Eng, pp. 94–101.

329 Cited in Ibid., p. 137.

330 Ibid., pp. 83–4, 110.

331 For more on Chang and Eng's slaves see Huang, Inseparable, pp. 238–45; Orser, Lives of Chang and Eng, pp. 125–6.

332 Greensboro Patriot, 16 October 1852.

333 Ibid., 30 October 1852.

334 Barnum, Life of P.T. Barnum, p. 143.

335 Ibid., p. 148.

336 Ibid.

337 Ibid., pp. 148–9.

338 Ibid., p. 156.

339 Reiss, Showman and the Slave, pp. 211–24.

340 Ibid., p. 218.

341 Ibid.

342 Barnum, Life of P.T. Barnum, p. 153.

343 Reiss, Showman and the Slave, pp. 30–2.

344 William Knight Northall, Before and Behind the Curtain, or Fifteen Years' Observations Among the Theatres of New York (New York: W.F. Burgess, 1851), p. 114.

345 Ibid., pp. 113–14.

346 Neil Harris, *Humbug: The Art of P.T. Barnum* (Chicago: University of Chicago Press, 1973), p. 19.

347 Ashby, *With Amusement for All*, p. 17.

348 Barnum, *Life of P.T. Barnum*, p. 153.

349 Ibid.

350 Ibid., p. 152.

351 Anon., *The Life of Joice Heth, the Nurse of Gen. George Washington, (the Father of Our Country,) Now Living at the Astonishing Age of 161 Years, and Weighs Only 46 Pounds* (New York: Printed for the Publisher, 1835), p. 3.

352 *New York Sun*, 21 August 1835.

353 Barnum, *Life of P.T. Barnum*, p. 155.

354 Cited in Reiss, *Showman and the Slave*, p. 63.

355 Barnum, *Life of P.T. Barnum*, p. 154.

356 Benjamin Reiss, 'Barnum and Joice Heth: The Birth of Ethnic Shows in the United States (1836)', in *Human Zoos*, ed. by Blanchard, Boëtsch and Snoep, pp. 62–72.

357 Huang, *Inseparable*, pp. 268–79.

358 Barnum, *Life of P.T. Barnum*, p. 154.

359 *New York Sun*, 20 August 1835.

360 *New York Herald*, 8 September 1836.

361 Barnum, *Adventures of An Adventurer: Being Some Passages in The Life of Barnaby Diddleum* (1841), cited in James W. Cook (ed.), *Colossal P.T. Barnum Reader: Nothing Else Like It in the Universe* (Urbana: University of Illinois Press, 2005), p. 36.

362 Cited in Reiss, *Showman and the Slave*, p. 74.

363 Barnum, *Life of P.T. Barnum*, p. 156.

364 Cited in Reiss, *Showman and the Slave*, p. 92.

365 Benjamin Reiss, 'P.T. Barnum, Joice Heth and Antebellum Spectacles of Race', in *American Quarterly* 51:1 (1999), pp. 78–107.

366 Cited in Michael P. Costeloe, *William Bullock Connoisseur and Virtuoso of the Egyptian Hall: Piccadilly to Mexico (1773–1849)* (Bristol: Bristol HiPLAM, 2008), pp. 195–6.

367 Barnum, *Life of P.T. Barnum*, p. 157.

368 James W. Cook, *The Arts of Deception: Playing with Fraud in the Age of Barnum* (Cambridge, MA: Harvard University Press, 2001), pp. 8–10, 14–16, 103–4, 117–19. Another conceptualization, 'operational aesthetics', has been used to describe Barnum's exhibitions. See: Harris, *Humbug*, pp. 61–89.

369 *New York Sun*, 26 February 1836.

370 Barnum, *Adventures of An Adventurer*, cited in Cook (ed.), *Colossal P.T. Barnum Reader*, p. 49.

371 Ibid.

372 Reiss, *Showman and the Slave*, p. 136.

373 Harriet A. Washington, *Medical Apartheid: The Dark History of Medical Experimentation on Black Americans from Colonial Times to the Present* (New York: Anchor Books, 2006), p. 88.

374 *New York Sun*, 26 February 1836.

375 Ibid.

376 *New York Evening Star*, 27 February 1836.

377 *New York Sun*, 27 February 1836.

378 *New York Herald*, 27 February 1836.

379 *New York Sun*, 1 March 1836.

380 Reiss, *Showman and the Slave*, p. 160.

381 *New York Herald*, 8 September 1836.

382 Ibid.

383 Barnum, *Life of P.T. Barnum*, p. 175.

384 Ashby, *With Amusement for All*, pp. 21–7.

385 Reiss, *Showman and the Slave*, pp. 35–6.

386 Cook (ed.), *The Colossal P.T. Barnum Reader*, pp. 1–8. Cook notes that 'mass culture' is slightly anachronistic prior to 1950, but that a 'massification' of culture certainly occurred.

387 Ibid., pp. 9–13.

388 Barnum, *Adventures of An Adventurer*, cited in Cook (ed.), *Colossal P.T. Barnum Reader*, pp. 14–56.

389 Reiss, *Showman and the Slave*, p. 177.

390 Saxon, *P.T. Barnum*, p. 84.

391 Barnum, *Life of P.T. Barnum*, p. 180.

392 Ibid., p. 160.

393 Ibid., p. 187.

394 Ibid., p. 207.

395 Ibid.

396 Philip B. Jr. Kunhardt, Philip Kunhardt III and Peter Kunhardt, *P.T. Barnum: America's Greatest Showman* (New York: Knopf, 1995), pp. 34–5.

397 James Dawson Burn, *Three Years Among the Working-classes in the United States during the War* (London: Smith, Elder, 1865), pp. 17–18.

398 Lewis (ed.), *From Travelling Show to Vaudeville*, p. 29.

399 Barnum, *Struggles and Triumphs*, p. 121.

400 Ibid., p. 125.

401 Barnum, *Life of P.T. Barnum*, p. 225; P.T. Barnum, *The Humbugs of the World* (New York: Carleton, 1866), p. 18.

402 Barnum, *Humbugs of the World*, pp. 20–1.

403 Barnum, *Life of P.T. Barnum*, p. 225.

404 Ibid., pp. 226–42.

405 Ibid., p. 232.

406 Ibid., pp. 238–9.

407 Barnum, *Struggles and Triumphs*, p. 110.

408 Cited in Andrea Stulman Dennett, *Weird and Wonderful: The Dime Museum in America* (New York: New York University Press, 1997), p. 23.

409 Ibid., p. 6.

410 Ashby, *With Amusement for All*, p. 52.

411 See Crone, *Violent Victorians*, pp. 1–11, 257–68.

412 Ashby, *With Amusement for All*, pp. 41–72.

413 Dennett, *Weird and Wonderful*, p. xi.

414 Bogdan, *Freak Show*, pp. 35–9.

415 William Livingston Alden, *Among the Freaks* (London: Longmans, 1896), p. 2.

416 Ibid., pp. 2–9.

417 Dennett, *Weird and Wonderful*, pp. 27, 37–40.

418 For primary material relating to Barnum's time with the circus see: BHC, Barnum's American Museum, Draw #6; Circus/Barnum, 1871–1880, Draw #8; Circus/Barnum, 1881–1891, Draw #9.

419 Anon., *The True Lamplighter, and Aunt Mary's Cabin* (Boston: Perkins & Fay, 1854), p. 29.

ACT THREE: Double Act

420 Dennis Todd, *Imagining Monsters: Miscreations of the Self in Eighteenth-Century England* (Chicago: University of Chicago Press, 1995), pp. 45–52.

421 Eric D. Lehman, *Becoming Tom Thumb: Charles Stratton, P.T. Barnum, and the Dawn of American Celebrity* (Middletown, CT: Wesleyan University Press, 2013), pp. 10–13.

422 Ibid., pp. 10–18.

423 Barnum, *Life of P.T. Barnum*, p. 243.

424 Lehman, *Becoming Tom Thumb*, pp. 14–15.

425 Barnum, *Life of P.T. Barnum*, p. 243.

426 Adelson, *Lives of Dwarfs*, pp. 35–7, 62–5.

427 Barnum, *Life of P.T. Barnum*, p. 244.

428 Ibid., pp. 243–4.

429 Ibid., p. 244.

430 Bogdan, *Freak Show*, pp. 147–75.

431 Barnum, *Life of P.T. Barnum*, pp. 244–5.

432 Magri, *Autobiography of Mrs. Tom Thumb*, p. 178.

433 Cited in Raymond Fitzsimons, *Barnum in London* (London: Geoffrey Bles, 1969), p. 60.

434 Philip Hone, *Diary of Philip Hone, 1828–1850*, vol. 2, ed. by Allan Nevins (New York: Dodd, Mead, 1927), p. 664.

435 *Omaha Daily Bee*, 6 February 1883.

436 Barnum, *Life of P.T. Barnum*, p. 223.

437 Cited in Fitzsimons, *Barnum in London*, p. 61.

438 Ibid.

439 *New York Herald*, 1 December 1843.

440 Cited in Lehman, *Becoming Tom Thumb*, p. 24.

441 Ibid.

442 *New-York Daily Tribune*, 9 December 1842.

443 Michael M. Chemers, 'Jumpin' Tom Thumb: Charles Stratton on Stage at the American Museum', *Nineteenth Century Theatre and Film*, 31:2 (2004), pp. 16–27 (p. 16).

444 Cited in George Sullivan, *Tom Thumb: The Remarkable True Story of a Man in Miniature* (New York: Clarion Books, 2011), pp. 66–7.

445 Ibid.

446 Ibid., p. 67.

447 Anon., *An Account of the Life, Personal Appearance, Character, and Manners, of Charles S. Stratton, the American Man in Miniature, known as General Tom Thumb, Twelve Years Old, Twenty-Five Inches High, and Weighing Only Fifteen Pounds* (London: T. Brettell, 1845), p. 9.

448 Tosh, *Manliness and Masculinities*, pp. 86–98; Anon., *Account of the Life, Personal Appearance, Character, and Manners, of Charles S. Stratton*, p. 7.

449 Anon., *Account of the Life, Personal Appearance, Character, and Manners, of Charles S. Stratton*, p. 11.

450 Huff, 'Freaklore', in *Victorian Freaks*, ed. by Tromp, pp. 37–59 (p. 38).

451 Lehman, *Becoming Tom Thumb*, pp. 27–8.

452 TJJC, Human Freaks 1 (62).

453 Anon., *Account of the Life, Personal Appearance, Character, and Manners, of Charles S. Stratton*, p. 9; Charles Dickens, *The Old Curiosity Shop: A Tale* (London: Chapman & Hall, 1843), pp. 28, 286.

454 Stewart, *On Longing*, pp. 111–17.

455 Hone, *Diary of Philip Hone*, p. 664.

456 Anon., *Sketch of the Life, Personal Appearance, Character, and Manners, of Charles S. Stratton, the Man in Miniature, known as General Tom Thumb, Fifteen Years Old, Twenty Eight Inches High, and Weighing Only Fifteen Pounds, with some Account of Remarkable Dwarfs, Giants, and other Human Phenomena* (New York: Van Norden & Amerman, 1847), p. 7.

457 Zygmunt Bauman, *Modernity and Ambivalence* (Oxford: Polity Press, 1991), p. 1.

458 Anon., *Sketch of the Life, Personal Appearance, Character, and Manners, of Charles S. Stratton* (New York, 1847), p. 7.

459 Lori Merish, 'Cuteness and Commodity Aesthetics: Tom Thumb and Shirley Temple', in *Freakery*, ed. by Garland-Thomson, pp. 185–203.

460 Lehman, *Becoming Tom Thumb*, p. 25.

461 Barnum, *Life of P.T. Barnum*, p. 245.

462 Lehman, *Becoming Tom Thumb*, p. 25.

463 Barnum to Sol Smith, 3 March 1841, cited in *Selected Letters of P.T. Barnum*, ed. and intro. by A.H. Saxon (New York: Columbia University Press, 1983), pp. 13–14.

464 Lehman, *Becoming Tom Thumb*, p. 29.

465 Barnum to Moses Kimball, 5 February 1843, cited in *Selected Letters of P.T. Barnum*, ed. and intro. by Saxon, pp. 14–15.

466 Barnum to Moses Kimball, 8 March 1843, cited in Ibid., pp. 16–17.

467 Barnum, *Life of P.T. Barnum*, p. 245.

468 Chemers, *Staging Stigma*, p. 33.

469 Ibid., pp. 27–55.

470 Barnum, *Life of P.T. Barnum*, p. 245.

471 Ibid., p. 246.

472 Ibid.

473 Ibid., p. 247.

474 Dickens, *Sketches by Boz*, pp. 143–4.

475 Barnum, *Life of P.T. Barnum*, p. 252.

476 See: Horn, *Amusing the Victorians*, for a useful introduction.

477 *Freeman's Journal*, 23 January 1844.

478 *Berrow's Worcester Journal*, 25 January 1844.

479 Cited in Saxon, *P.T. Barnum*, p. 83.

480 Charles Dickens, *American Notes* (London: Granville Publishing, 1985 [1842]), pp. 209–30.

481 Jerry White, *London in the Nineteenth Century: A Human Awful Wonder of God* (London: Vintage, 2008); Weinreb and others, *The London Encyclopaedia*, p. 657.

482 Citations from Roy Porter, *London: A Social History* (London: Penguin, 2000), p. 226; Qureshi, *Peoples on Parade*, pp. 17–28; Carl Chinn, *Poverty Amidst Prosperity:*

The Urban Poor in England, 1834–1914 (Manchester: Manchester University Press, 1995), p. 90; Peter Ackroyd, *London: The Biography* (London: Chatto & Windus, 2000), p. 582.

483 Friedrich Engels, *The Condition of the Working-Class in England in 1844, with a Preface written in 1892*, trans. by Florence Kelley Wischnewetzky (London: George Allen & Unwin, 1943 [1892]), p. 64.

484 George Augustus Sala, *The Life and Adventures of George Augustus Sala, Written by Himself*, vol. 1 (New York: Charles Scribner's Sons, 1895), p. 124.

485 *The Times*, 21 February 1844.

486 *Morning Post*, 21 February 1844.

487 *The Times*, 21 February 1844.

488 *Illustrated London News*, 24 February 1844.

489 For Tom Thumb's performance at the Princess's Theatre, and its relationship to 'minor theatre', see Fitzsimons, *Barnum in London*, pp. 73–80.

490 Barnum, *Life of P.T. Barnum*, p. 252.

491 Ibid., pp. 254–5.

492 Ibid, p. 254.

493 *Era*, 3 March 1844.

494 Ibid.

495 Barnum, *Life of P.T. Barnum*, pp. 255–6, 263–4.

496 Frost, *Old Showmen*, p. 148.

497 *The Times*, 12 March 1844.

498 Fitzsimons, *Barnum in London*, p. 87.

499 Ibid., pp. 87–9.

500 Barnum, *Life of P.T. Barnum*, p. 263.

501 Cited in Fitzsimons, *Barnum in London*, p. 89.

502 Matthew Dennison, *Queen Victoria: A Life of Contradictions* (London: HarperCollins, 2013), p. 33

503 QVJ, 28 March 1838.

504 QVJ, 23 February 1838.

505 Cited in A.N. Wilson, *Victoria: A Life* (London: Atlantic Books, 2014), p. 44.

506 Cited in Christopher Hibbert, *Queen Victoria: A Personal History* (Cambridge, MA: Da Capo Press, 2000), p. 42.

507 QVJ, 26 December 1833.

508 QVJ, 10 January 1839.

509 George Rowell, *Queen Victoria Goes to the Theatre* (London: Paul Elek, 1978), pp. 24–5.

510 Cited in Ibid., p. 25.

511 Cited in Wilson, *Victoria*, p. 127.

512 Cited in Lehman, *Becoming Tom Thumb*, p. 2.

513 Barnum, *Struggles and Triumphs*, pp. 174–6.

514 Paul Thomas Murphy, *Shooting Victoria: Madness, Mayhem and the Modernisation of the Monarchy* (London: Head of Zeus, 2012), pp. 207–35.

515 Barnum, *Life of P.T. Barnum*, p. 260.

516 Ibid.

517 QVJ, 1 April 1844.

518 QVJ, 19 April 1844.

519 NFA, John Bramwell Taylor, Box Three 178T1.309; *Era*, 21 April 1844; *The Times*, 12 April 1844.

520 Cited in Lehman, *Becoming Tom Thumb*, p. 7.
521 Cited in Ibid., p. 39.
522 Cited in Saxon, *P.T. Barnum*, p. 133.
523 *The Times*, 12 April 1844.
524 Lehman, *Becoming Tom Thumb*, pp. ix–xv, 6–9.
525 *Punch*, vol. 10 (1846), p. 203.
526 Barnum to Moses Kimball, 18 August 1844, cited in *Selected Letters of P.T. Barnum*, ed. and intro. by Saxon, pp. 28–30.
527 *Punch*, vol. 10 (1846), p. 280.
528 Fitzsimons, *Barnum in London*, p. 134.
529 Ibid.
530 QVJ, 16 December 1844.
531 TJJC, Human Freaks 1 (5).
532 QVJ, 15 May 1846.
533 Cited in Hibbert, *Queen Victoria*, p. 223.
534 TJJC, Human Freaks 1 (42a).
535 *Punch*, vol. 10 (1846), p. 262; *Punch*, vol. 13 (1847), p. 90.
536 Barnum to Moses Kimball, 30 January 1845, cited in *Selected Letters of P.T. Barnum*, ed. and intro. by Saxon, pp. 30–2.
537 Cited in Saxon, *P.T. Barnum*, p. 141.
538 *Douglas Jerrold's Shilling Magazine*, vol. 3 (London: *Punch*, 1846), p. 330.
539 *Punch*, vol. 5 (1843), p. 157.
540 TBMB, P.T. Barnum Letter Copybook, 1845–01–01, pp. 18, 62.
541 Albert Smith, 'Manners and Customs: Sketches of Paris', in *The Mirror of Literature, Amusement, and Instruction*, vol. 33 (London: J. Limbird, 1839), pp. 308–9.
542 Anon., *Sinnett's Picture of Paris* (London: Joseph Masters, 1847), p. 38.
543 Barnum, *Struggles and Triumphs*, p. 189.
544 Ibid., p. 192.
545 Ibid.
546 Ibid.
547 Ibid., p. 202.
548 Ibid., p. 193.
549 Durbach, *Spectacle of Deformity*, p. 4.
550 TBMB, 1845-01-01, P.T. Barnum Letter Copybook, p. 52.
551 Chemers, *Staging Stigma*, p. 44.
552 Barnum, *Struggles and Triumphs*, p. 194.
553 Ibid., p. 203.
554 Ibid., p. 204.
555 Ibid., p. 202.
556 Cited in Saxon, *P.T. Barnum*, p. 129.
557 Lehman, *Becoming Tom Thumb*, pp. 49–51.
558 Barnum, *Struggles and Triumphs*, p. 208.
559 Lehman, *Becoming Tom Thumb*, pp. 53–4.
560 TBMB, 1845-01-01, P.T. Barnum Letter Copybook, pp. 69, 19.
561 Lehman, *Becoming Tom Thumb*, p. 54.
562 Fitzsimons, *Barnum in London*, p. 117.
563 Lehman, *Becoming Tom Thumb*, pp. 60–3.

564 Benjamin Robert Haydon, *Autobiography and Journals of Benjamin Robert Haydon (1786–1846)*, ed. and intro. by Malcolm Elwin (London: Macdonald, 1950 [1853]), p. 290.

565 Ibid., p. 638.

566 Cited in Paul O'Keeffe, *Genius for Failure* (London: Bodley Head, 2009), p. 491.

567 Boyd Hilton, *A Mad, Bad, and Dangerous People? England 1783–1846* (Oxford: Clarendon Press, 2006), pp. 167–84.

568 Cited in O'Keeffe, *Genius for Failure*, p. 357.

569 Haydon, *Autobiography and Journals of Benjamin Robert Haydon*, p. 644.

570 Cited in O'Keeffe, *Genius for Failure*, p. 490.

571 Haydon, *Autobiography and Journals of Benjamin Robert Haydon*, p. x.

572 *Punch*, vol. 10 (1846), p. 203.

573 Haydon, *Autobiography and Journals of Benjamin Robert Haydon*, p. 647.

574 Ibid., p. 650.

575 Cited in O'Keeffe, *Genius for Failure*, p. 507.

576 Haydon, *Autobiography and Journals of Benjamin Robert Haydon*, pp. 643–4.

577 Dickens, *American Notes*, pp. 223–4.

578 *Punch*, vol. 10 (1846), p. 203.

579 Ibid.

580 *The Times*, 2 January 1847.

581 Lambert Adolphe Jacques Quételet, *Letters Addressed to the Grand Duke of Saxe-Coburg and Gotha, on the Theory of Probabilities, as applied to the Moral and Political Sciences*, trans. by O.G. Downes (London: Charles & Edwin Taylor, 1849), p. 104.

582 *Punch*, vol. 13 (1847), p. 90.

583 Lehman, *Becoming Tom Thumb*, pp. 73–86; Bogdan, *Freak Show*, p. 152.

584 *New York Times*, 11 February 1863.

585 Lehman, *Becoming Tom Thumb*, pp. 119–20.

586 Barnum, *Struggles and Triumphs*, p. 567.

587 Anon., *History of Commodore Nutt, The Smallest Man in Miniature in the Known World* (New York: Wynkoop, Hallenbeck & Thomas, 1862), pp. 7–13.

588 TBMB, Barnum Investments #1, Commodore Contract, 12 December 1861, EL 1988.951.

589 Barnum, *Struggles and Triumphs*, p. 602.

590 Ibid.

591 Cited in Bogdan, *Freak Show*, p. 155. See also: Museum of the City of New York (MCNY), vol. 41, Midgets (Barnum-Affiliated) 39.500.1866 and 2.11.18.

592 Sylvester Bleeker, *Gen. Tom Thumb's Three Years' Tour Around The World, Accompanied by his Wife – Lavinia Warren Stratton, Commodore Nutt, Miss Minnie Warren, and Party* (New York: S. Booth, 1872).

593 Bridgeport History Center, Bridgeport Public Library, Connecticut (BHC), Draw #5 Tom Thumb; TBMB, Box TT LW Framed Items 3; STL, Tom Thumb Medallion ST 2833; TBMB, Box TT Daguerreotypes; TBMB, Box TT Album. See also MCNY, vol. 37, Freaks I; MCNY, vol. 38, Freaks II; MCNY, vol. 39, Freaks III.

594 TBMB, Box TT Merchandising Artefacts, Trade Cards (1880–1890) T 2014.35.1; BHC, Box #1 Tom Thumb, Trade Card and Paper Dolls; TBMB, Box TT Merchandising Artefacts, Tom Thumb Segs 2012.12.1; TBMB, Box TT Merchandising Artefacts, 'Tom Thumb Jujubes' EL 1988.195.1.

595 Henry Fielding, *Tom Thumb and the Tragedy of Tragedies*, ed. by L.J. Morrissey (Edinburgh: Oliver & Boyd, 1970 [1730]), pp. 1–10.

596 F.M.L. Thompson, *The Rise of Respectable Society: A Social History of Victorian Britain, 1830–1900* (London: Fontana, 1988), pp. 85–113.

597 Cited in Saxon, *P.T. Barnum*, p. 210.

598 Cited in Bogdan, *Freak Show*, p. 157.

599 F63091, Copy of Minnie Warren Stratton's Death Certificate (No. 325, 25 September 1866), kindly sourced and provided by John Gannon, author of *The Killing of Julia Wallace* (2012).

600 *Brooklyn Daily Eagle*, 29 December 1878.

601 Ibid., 8 August 1878.

602 Ibid.

603 Ibid., 29 December 1878.

604 Hone, *Diary of Philip Hone*, pp. 795–6.

605 TBMB, Manuscript: Bound typescript of "A Journal" by Caroline C. Barnum, 1848–07–05–1848–08–11.

606 Saxon, *P.T. Barnum*, p. 130.

607 *Omaha Daily Bee*, 6 February 1883.

608 Cited in Lehman, *Becoming Tom Thumb*, p. 81.

609 Magri, *Autobiography of Mrs. Tom Thumb*, pp. 169–70.

610 Cited in Lehman, *Becoming Tom Thumb*, p. 81.

611 Barnum, *Struggles and Triumphs*, p. 399.

612 David A. Gerber, 'The "Careers" of People Exhibited in Freak Shows', in *Freakery*, ed. by Garland Thomson, pp. 38–54 (p. 40).

613 Ibid., pp. 38–54.

614 *Omaha Daily Bee*, 6 February 1883.

615 Saxon, *P.T. Barnum*, p. 142.

616 Robert Bogdan, 'The Social Construction of Freaks', in *Freakery*, ed. by Garland-Thomson, pp. 23–37 (p. 35).

617 Bogdan, *Freak Show*, p. 152.

618 Magri, *Autobiography of Mrs. Tom Thumb*, p. 169.

ACT FOUR: The Climax

619 Anon., *Illustrated Memoir of an Eventful Expedition into Central America: Resulting in the Discovery of the Idolatrous City of Iximaya, in an Unexplored Region; And the Possession of Two Remarkable Aztec Children Maximo (the Boy), And Batola (the Girl)* (London, [publisher not identified], 1853), p. 25.

620 Bogdan, *Freak Show*, pp. 127–34.

621 Jonathan Mason Warren, 'An Account of Two Remarkable Indian Dwarfs Exhibited in Boston Under the Name of Aztec Children', in *American Journal of the Medical Sciences* 10:42 (1851), pp. 285–293.

622 Cited in Durbach, *Spectacle of Deformity*, pp. 119–20.

623 Warren, 'An Account of Two Remarkable Indian Dwarfs', p. 293.

624 Cited in Bogdan, *Freak Show*, p. 130.

625 *Liverpool Mercury*, 21 June 1853.

626 *Era*, 26 June 1853.

627 *Liverpool Mercury*, 21 June 1853.

628 Durbach, *Spectacle of Deformity*, pp. 130–43.

629 *Morning Post*, 2 July 1853.

630 *Lancet*, 9 July 1853, p. 44.

631 James Cowles Prichard, *The Natural History of Man; Comprising Inquiries into the Modifying Influence of Physical and Moral Agencies of the Different Tribes of the Human Family* (London: H. Bailliere, 1843), p. 26.

632 James Hunt, *Negro's Place in Nature: A paper read before the London Anthropological Society* (New York: Van Evbie, Hobton, 1864), p. 23.

633 Richard Cull and Richard Owen, 'A Brief Notice of the Aztec Race, followed by a Description of the So-Called Aztec Children Exhibited on the Occasion', *Journal of the Ethnological Society of London* (1848–1856), vol. 4 (1856), pp. 120–37 (p. 136).

634 John Conolly, *The Ethnological Exhibitions of London* (London: John Churchill, 1855), p. 12.

635 Robert Knox, 'Some Remarks on the Aztecque and Bosjieman Children', *Lancet*, 7 (April 1855), pp. 357–60.

636 Ibid., p. 357.

637 Robert Knox, *The Races of Men: A Fragment* (London: Henry Renshaw, 1850), p. 2.

638 *Morning Post*, 5 July 1853.

639 QVJ, 14 June 1853.

640 The images of Martinus, Flora and the Zulus can be accessed via the Royal Collection Trust: <https://www.rct.uk/collection> [accessed 21 February 2019], under the references: RCIN 2905939; RCIN 2905921; RCIN 2905923.

641 Prince Albert, *Prince Albert's Golden Precepts: or, The Opinions and Maxims of his Late Royal Highness the Prince Consort* (London: Sampson Low, 1862), pp. 57–9.

642 Cited in Jules Stewart, *Albert: A Life* (London: I.B. Tauris, 2012), p. 139.

643 Cited in Stanley Weintraub, *Albert: Uncrowned King* (London: John Murray, 1997), p. 250.

644 Cited in Qureshi, *Peoples on Parade*, p. 236.

645 Ibid., pp. 235–8.

646 *Standard*, 5 July 1853.

647 Anon., *Illustrated Memoir of an Eventful Expedition into Central America*, n.p.

648 QVJ, 4 July 1853.

649 *Lancet*, 9 July 1853; *Morning Chronicle*, 16 July 1853.

650 *Illustrated London News*, 23 July 1853.

651 *Berkshire Chronicle*, 23 July 1853.

652 *Household Words*, vol. 7 (London: Bradbury & Evans, 1853), p. 576.

653 There were numerous estimates of their age which, by 1853, had Maximo in the region of eleven to twelve years old and Bartola eight to ten years old.

654 *Household Words*, p. 576.

655 *Era*, 31 July 1853.

656 *New-York Daily Tribune*, 14 November 1860.

657 Barnum, *Struggles and Triumphs*, p. 544.

658 Ibid.

659 Wallace and Wallace, *The Two*, pp. 224–5.

660 Gardner Engleheart, *Journal of the Progress of H.R.H. the Prince of Wales through British North America; and his visit to the United States, 10th July to 15th November, 1860* ([London]: privately printed, [1860]), pp. 90–1.

661 *New-York Daily Tribune,* 1 March 1860.

662 Cook, 'Of Men, Missing Links, and Nondescripts: The Strange Career of P.T. Barnum's "What is It?" Exhibition', in *Freakery,* ed. by Garland-Thomson, pp. 139–57.

663 Cited in Bogdan, *Freak Show,* pp. 136–7.

664 Warren, 'An Account of Two Remarkable Indian Dwarfs', p. 286.

665 Katheryn Hughes, *Victorians Undone: Tales of the Flesh in the Age of Decorum* (London: HarperCollins, 2017), pp. 75–7.

666 Peter Bowler, *Evolution: The History of an Idea* (Berkeley: University of California, 2003), pp. 84–95.

667 Charles White, *An account of the regular gradation in man, and in different animals and vegetables; and from the former to the latter* (London: Printed for C. Dilly, 1799), p. 67.

668 Arthur O. Lovejoy, *The Great Chain of Being: A Study of the History of an Idea* (New York: Transactions Publishers, 2009), p. 234.

669 Susie L. Steinbach, *Understanding the Victorians: Politics, Culture and Society in Nineteenth-century Britain* (New York: Routledge, 2017), pp. 285–90.

670 A. Hodgson, 'Defining the Species: Apes, Savages and Humans in Scientific and Literary Writing of the 1860s', *Journal of Victorian Culture,* 4:2 (1999), pp. 228–51.

671 Janet Browne, 'Darwin in Caricature: A Study in the Popularisation and Dissemination of Evolution', *American Philosophical Society,* 145:4 (2001), pp. 496–509; Jane R. Goodall, *Performance and Evolution in the Age of Darwin: Out of the Natural Order* (London: Routledge, 2002), pp. 47–79.

672 *New York Herald,* 16 March 1860.

673 Durbach, *Spectacle of Deformity,* p. 146.

674 Cited in Ibid., p. 89. See also: Nigel Rothfels, 'Aztecs, Aborigines, and Ape-People: Science and Freaks in Germany, 1850–1900', in *Freakery,* ed. by Garland-Thomson, pp. 158–72.

675 C.R. Darwin, *The Descent of Man, and Selection in relation to Sex,* vol. 1, 1ˢᵗ edn (London: John Murray, 1871), p. 14.

676 Herbert Spencer, *The Principles of Biology* (London: William and Norgate, 1864), p. 444; Darwin, *Descent of Man,* pp. 152, 157, 163.

677 John MacKenzie, 'The Imperial Exhibitions of Great Britain', in *Human Zoos,* ed. by Blanchard, Boëtsch and Snoep, pp. 259–68.

678 Nadja Durbach, 'London, Capital of Exotic Exhibitions from 1830 to 1860', in *Human Zoos,* ed. by Blanchard, Boëtsch and Snoep, pp. 81–8.

679 *Illustrated London News,* 6 November 1852.

680 Cited in Bernth Lindfors, 'Charles Dickens and the Zulus', in *Africans On Stage: Studies in Ethnological Show Business,* ed. by Bernth Lindfors (Bloomington, IN: Indiana University Press, 1999), pp. 62–80 (p. 62).

681 Cited in Ibid., p. 72.

682 Caldecott had actually been to court after the Zulus' Chief Manoys publicly assaulted him, although courts ruled in Manoys' favour.

683 *The Times,* 18 May 1853.

684 Cited in Lindfors, 'Charles Dickens and the Zulus', in *Africans On Stage,* ed. by Lindfors, p. 76.

685 Ibid.

686 Hilke Thode-Arora, 'Hagenbeck's European Tours: The Development of the Human Zoo', in *Human Zoos,* ed. by Blanchard, Boëtsch and Snoep, pp. 165–73.

687 Raymond Corbey, 'Ethnographic Showcases: Account and Vision', in *Human Zoos*, ed. by Blanchard, Boëtsch and Snoep, pp. 95–103; MacKenzie, 'The Imperial Exhibitions of Great Britain', in *Human Zoos*, ed. by Blanchard, Boëtsch and Snoep, pp. 259–68.

688 See Charles Darwin, *On the Origin of Species By Means of Natural Selection; or, The Preservation of Favoured Races in the Struggle for Life* (London: John Murray, 1859 [first edition]), p. 44.

689 Palmira Fontes da Costa, 'The Meaning of Monstrosities in Charles Darwin's Understanding of the Origin of Species' <http://dx.doi.org/10.14195/978-989-26-0342-1_8> [accessed 9 January 2019], pp. 81–2.

690 Blumberg, *Freaks of Nature*, pp. 30–7.

691 Wood, *Giants and Dwarfs*, p. 106.

692 General Register Office, Application Number: 8128770-1.

693 Anon., *Illustrated Memoir of an Eventful Expedition into Central America*, p. 25.

694 This argument was mounted by Durbach, *Spectacle of Deformity*, pp. 143–6.

695 Boruwłaski, *Second Edition of the Memoirs*, pp. 21–2.

696 Kunhardt Jr., Kunhardt III and Kunhardt, *P.T. Barnum*, pp. 336–8.

697 Rothfels, 'Aztecs, Aborigines, and Ape-People', in *Freakery*, ed. by Garland-Thomson, p. 160.

698 Irina Podgorny, 'Falsehood on the Move: The Aztec Children and Science in the Second Half of the 19th Century', *Medicina Nei Secoli* 25:1 (2013), pp. 223–44 (p. 226).

699 Ashby, *With Amusement for All*, pp. 73–142.

700 Ibid., p. 85.

701 Ibid., p. 91.

702 Ibid., pp. 92–106.

703 The William F. Cody Archive, Buffalo Bill Center of the West and University of Nebraska-Lincoln <http://codyarchive.org/life/wfc.bio.00002.html> [accessed 9 January 2019].

704 Cited in *Masterpieces of American Indian Literature*, ed. and intro. by Wills G. Regier (Lincoln: University of Nebraska Press, 2005), p. 571.

705 QVJ, 13 July 1892; QVJ, 17 June 1898; QVJ, 17 July 1899.

706 Ashby, *With Amusement for All*, p. 77.

707 Cited in Ibid.

708 Cited in Ibid., p. 78.

709 Bogdan, *Freak Show*, pp. 45–6; Matthew Wittmann, *Circus and the City: New York, 1793–2010* (New York and New Haven: Bard Graduate Center and Yale University Press, 2012), pp. 36, 43, 55, 63.

710 Joe Nickell, *Secrets of the Sideshows* (Lexington: University of Kentucky, 2005), pp. 45–79.

711 'Self-made freaks' were also called 'created oddities' and included the 'gaffed freaks'. For some, the 'made' freaks were different to the novelty performers, who were described as 'working acts'. See Nickell, *Secrets of the Sideshows*, pp. 178–259.

712 Sanger, *Seventy Years a Showman*, p. 196.

713 NFA, Turner Online Database.

714 Frost, *Circus Life and Circus Celebrities*, pp. 142, 192.

715 Cited in Gareth H.H. Davies, *Pablo Fanque and the Victorian Circus: A Romance of Real Life* (Cromer: Poppyland Publishing, 2007), pp. 33–4.

716 Frost, *Circus Life and Circus Celebrities*, p. 97.

717 *Era*, 21 July 1839.

718 W.F. Wallett, *The Public Life of W.F. Wallett, The Queen's Jester: An Autobiography*, ed. by J. Luntley (London: Bemrose and Sons, 1870), p. 74.

719 Frost, *Circus Life and Circus Celebrities*, p. 196.

720 David Olusoga, *Black and British: A Forgotten History* (London: Pan, 2017), pp. 244–6.

721 Cited in Sadiah Qureshi, 'Meeting the Zulus: Displayed Peoples and the Shows of London', in *Popular Exhibitions, Science and Showmanship, 1840–1910*, ed. by Joe Kember, John Plunkett and Jill A. Sullivan (London: Pickering & Chatto, 2012), pp. 185–198 (p. 195).

722 Cited in Olusoga, *Black and British*, pp. 280–2.

723 Thomas Dawson Walker, known as the Whimsical Walker, was particularly wedded to Pablo Fanque. Whimsical Walker, *From Sawdust to Windsor Castle* (London: Stanley Paul, 1922), pp. 8–10.

724 D.L. Chandler, 'Little Known Black History Fact: Olga Kaira', <https://blackamericaweb.com/2016/10/28/little-known-black-history-fact-olga-kaira/> [accessed 9 January 2019].

725 It would appear that Lala applied for an American passport in 1919.

726 Jan Bondeson, *Cabinet of Medical Curiosities* (Ithaca, NY: Cornell University Press, 1997), pp. 216–44.

727 Jan Bondeson and A.E.W. Miles, 'Julia Pastrana, The Nondescript: An Example of Congenital, Generalized Hypertrichosis Terminalis with Ginger Hyperplasia', *American Journal of Medical Genetics*, 47:2 (1993), pp. 198–212.

728 Christopher Gylseth and Lars Toverud, *Julia Pastrana: The Tragic Story of the Victorian Ape Woman*, trans. by Donald Tumasonis (Stroud: Sutton Publishing, 2003), pp. 1–11.

729 Kathleen Godfrey, *Julia Pastrana Online* (2016) <http://juliapastranaonline.com/exhibits/show/who-was-theodore-lent-/nyc> [accessed 9 January 2019].

730 American and Commercial Advertiser, 'Trouble about a Hybrid', *Julia Pastrana Online* <http://juliapastranaonline.com/items/show/13> [accessed 9 January 2019].

731 Cited in Gylseth and Toverud, *Julia Pastrana*, pp. 75–6.

732 G. Van Hare, *Fifty Years of a Showman's Life; or, The Life and Travels of Van Hare* (London: W.H. Allen, 1888), p. 46.

733 Drimmer, *Very Special People*, pp. 106–26.

734 *Morning Post*, 2 March 1865.

735 TJJC, Human Freaks 3 (6); Wellcome Library London (WLL), Freaks Ephemera Box 3 EPH 499B, 'Curious History of the Baboon Lady'.

736 WLL, 'Curious History of the Baboon Lady'.

737 *Era*, 19 July 1857.

738 TJJC, Human Freaks 3 (6).

739 Allan Lonnberg, 'The Digger Indian Stereotype in California', *Journal of California and Great Basin Anthropology*, 3:2 (1981), pp. 215–23.

740 Galia Ofek, *Representations of Hair in Victorian Literature and Culture* (Surrey: Ashgate, 2009), pp. 56–62.

741 Anon., *Account of Miss Pastrana, The Nondescript; and the Double-Bodied Boy* (London: E. Hancock, 1860), p. 4.

742 WLL, Oversize Ephemera EPH+33:3.

743 Weinreb, *The London Encyclopaedia*, p. 686.

744 TJJC, Human Freaks 2 (10).

745 TJJC, Human Freaks 2 (9); TJJC, Human Freaks 2 (82).

746 *Daily News*, 3 July 1857.

747 *Standard*, 3 July 1857.

748 TJJC, Human Freaks 3 (6).

749 Francis T. Buckland, *Curiosities of Natural History: Fourth Series* (London: Richard Bentley, 1888), p. 42.

750 Trinity College Library, Cambridge, Papers of A.J. Munby (TCLC, MUNB), 12, pp. 205–7.

751 TCLC, MUNB, 4, 1 January-18 March, 1860, n. p.

752 Cited in Angela V. John, *By the Sweat of Their Brow: Women Workers at Victorian Coal Mines* (London: Routledge, 1984), p. 104.

753 See: TCLC, MUNB, Arthur Munby's Notebooks MUNB, 97; Albums of Photographs, MUNB, 111–121.

754 Cited in Bondeson, *Cabinet of Medical Curiosities*, p. 230.

755 J. Sokolov, 'Julia Pastrana and her child', *Lancet*, 1 (1862), pp. 467–9.

756 Hare, *Fifty Years of a Showman's Life*, p. 46.

757 TCLC, MUNB, 12, pp. 208–9.

758 TCLC, MUNB, 12, pp. 209–10.

759 A.J. Munby, *Relicta: Verses* (London: Bertram Dobell, 1909), pp. 5–13.

760 Daniel Kelly, *Yuck! The Nature and Moral Significance of Disgust* (Cambridge, MA: MIT Press, 2011), pp. 35–41.

761 TCLC, MUNB, 12, p. 207.

762 TCLC, MUNB, 13, p. 192.

763 TCLC, MUNB, 17, p. 83.

764 TCLC, MUNB, 12, p. 207.

765 Darwin to Wallace, [12–31] Mar [1867], *Darwin Correspondence Database* <http://www.darwinproject.ac.uk/entry-5440> [accessed 9 January 2019].

766 Charles Darwin, *The Variation of Animals and Plants under Domestication*, vol. 2 (London: John Murray, 1868), p. 328.

767 George M. Gould and Walter L. Pyle, *Anomalies and Curiosities of Medicine* (Philadelphia: W.B. Sanders and Company, 1901 [1896]), p. 229.

768 Lillian Craton, *The Victorian Freak Show: The Significance of Disability and Physical Differences in 19th-Century Fiction* (Amherst, NY: Cambria Press, 2009), p. 3.

769 WLL, Oversize Ephemera EPH+33:4.

770 Buckland, *Curiosities of Natural History: Fourth Series*, p. 41.

771 WLL, Oversize Ephemera EPH+33:4; TJJC, Human Freaks 3 (8).

772 Buckland, *Curiosities of Natural History: Fourth Series*, pp. 42.

773 Ibid., p. 41.

774 George C. Bompas, *Life of Frank Buckland by His Brother-In-Law* (London: Smith, Elder, 1885), pp. 129–37.

775 Buckland, *Curiosities of Natural History: Fourth Series*, p. 40.

776 Francis T. Buckland, *Log-Book of a Fisherman and Zoologist* (London: Chapman & Hall, 1875), p. xii.

777 Darwin, *On the Origin of Species By Means of Natural Selection*, pp. 481–2.

778 Peter Harrison, *The Bible, Protestantism and the Rise of Natural Science* (Cambridge: Cambridge University Press, 1998), p. 171.

779 Buckland, *Log-Book of a Fisherman and Zoologist*, p. xi. Buckland's personal scrapbook contains two pages dedicated to his father's work on the Bridgewater Treatises: RCSL, The Papers of Francis Buckland, vol. I MS0035/1.176-177.

780 Robert C. Fuller, *Wonder: From Emotion to Spirituality* (Chapel Hill: University of North Carolina Press, 2006), pp. 1–41.

781 Bondeson, *Cabinet of Medical Curiosities*, p. 235.

782 Drimmer, *Very Special People*, pp. 316–19.

783 Bondeson, *Cabinet of Medical Curiosities*, pp. 233–41; Laura Anderson Barbata, 'Julia Pastrana: Brief Chronology' <http://www.lauraandersonbarbata.com/work/mx-lab/julia-pastrana/3.php> [accessed 21 February 2019].

784 Rebecca Stern, 'Our Bear Women, Ourselves: Affiliating with Julia Pastrana', in *Victorian Freaks*, ed. by Tromp, pp. 200–33.

785 Rosemarie Garland-Thomson, *Extraordinary Bodies: Figuring Physical Disability in American Culture and Literature* (New York: Columbia University Press, 1997), pp. 70–80; Garland-Thomson, 'Introduction', in *Freakery*, ed. by Garland-Thomson, pp. 1–22.

786 Wonder, in short, was accommodated by the new age of scepticism: Sarah Tindal Kareem, *Eighteenth-Century Fiction and the Reinvention of Wonder* (Oxford: Oxford University Press, 2014), pp. 1–30.

787 Cited in O'Connor, *Raw Material*, p. 158.

788 A.N. Wilson, *The Victorians* (London: Arrow Books, 2003), pp. 322–9.

789 Martin Willis, 'On Wonder: Situating the Spectacle in Spiritualism and Performance Magic', in *Popular Exhibitions, Science and Showmanship, 1840–1910*, ed. by Kember, Plunkett and Sullivan, pp. 167–82.

790 Heather McHold, 'Even as You and I: Freak Shows and Lay Discourse on Spectacular Deformity', in *Victorian Freaks*, ed. by Tromp, pp. 21–36.

791 Martin Van Buren Bates, *A Historical Sketch of the Tallest Man and Wife, That Have Ever Existed, Captain Martin Van Buren Bates and Mrs. Bates, Formerly Anna Swan, Together with a Short Description of Mythological, Ancient, Medieval and Modern Giants* ([Place of publication, publisher and date not identified]), p. 9.

792 *Daily Telegraph*, 19 June 1871.

793 Bates, *Historical Sketch of the Tallest Man and Wife*, p. 9.

794 Cited in Shirley Irene Vacon, *Giants of Nova Scotia: The Lives of Anna Swan and Angus McAskill* (East Lawrencetown, NS: Pottersfield Press, 2008), p. 40. However, I have not found any reference to this meeting in Queen Victoria's Journals.

795 Bompas, *Life of Frank Buckland*, p. 253.

796 Bates, *Historical Sketch of the Tallest Man and Wife*, p. 9.

797 For modern biographies of Anna Swan see: Vacon, *Giants of Nova Scotia*, pp. 17–78; Anne Renaud, *Extraordinary Life of Anna Swan* (Sydney, NS: Cape Breton University Press, 2013).

798 My thanks to Dale Swan for sharing these family histories.

799 Dale Swan, private correspondence.

800 For Anna Swan's early years see: Vacon, *Giants of Nova Scotia*, pp. 17–25.

801 Renaud, *Extraordinary Life of Anna Swan*, pp. 7–8.

802 Barnum, *Struggles and Triumphs*, p. 573.

803 Ibid.

804 Vacon, *Giants of Nova Scotia*, pp. 26–38; Renaud, *Extraordinary Life of Anna Swan*, pp. 9–22.

805 Vacon, *Giants of Nova Scotia*, p. 38.

806 Cited in Renaud, *Extraordinary Life of Anna Swan*, p. 26.

807 Louise Carson, 'The Rest of the Story About the Civil War Giant', *FNB Chronicle* 9:3 (1998) <http://www.tngenweb.org/scott/fnb_v9n3_giant.htm> [accessed 9 January 2019].

808 Bates, *Historical Sketch of the Tallest Man and Wife*, p. 7.

809 Ibid., p. 7.

810 Ibid., p. 22.

811 Ibid., p. 16.

812 Ibid.

813 Ibid., p. 8.

814 Ibid., p. 11.

815 Ibid.

816 Cited in Vacon, *Giants of Nova Scotia*, p. 47.

817 Vacon, *Giants of Nova Scotia*, pp. 47–9; Renaud, *Extraordinary Life of Anna Swan*, pp. 33–6.

818 Marc Hartzman, *American Sideshow: An Encyclopedia of History's Most Wondrous and Curiously Strange Performers* (London: Penguin, 2005), pp. 51–2, 88–9.

819 Thanks to Dale Swan and members of the First Baptist Church of Seville, Ohio, I was provided with further information about the Bateses' life in the community.

820 Bates, *Historical Sketch of the Tallest Man and Wife*, p. 12.

821 Cited in Vacon, *Giants of Nova Scotia*, p. 61.

822 Kindly supplied by the First Baptist Church of Seville, Ohio.

823 For a modern biography see: Joanne Martell, *Millie-Christine: Fearfully and Wonderfully Made* (Winston-Salem, NC: John F. Blair, 2000).

824 Anon., *Biographical Sketch of Millie Christine, the Carolina Twin, Surnamed the Two-Headed Nightingale, and the Eighth Wonder of the World* (Cincinnati, OH: Hennegan [between 1902 and 1912]), p. 4.

825 Ibid.

826 Cited in Martell, *Millie-Christine*, p. 8.

827 Millie and Christine McCoy, *The History of the Carolina Twins: "Told in Their Own Peculiar Way" by "One of Them"* (Buffalo: Buffalo Courier Printing House [c. 1869]), pp. 8–9.

828 Ibid., p. 8.

829 Ibid., p. 14.

830 Ibid., pp. 15–16.

831 Ibid., p. 16.

832 Ibid., p. 21.

833 Cited in Dennison, *Queen Victoria*, p. 90.

834 QVJ, 24 June 1871.

835 Ibid.

836 Bompas, *Life of Frank Buckland*, p. 255.

837 NCSA, Siamese Twins Collection P.C.916.1, Nannie Bunker's Diary, 1868–9, pp. 22–26 December 1868; NCSA, Millie-Christine Collection PC.266.4, First European Tour, Edinburgh, Scotland, January 1857.

838 NCSA, Siamese Twins Collection P.C.916.1, Nannie Bunker's Diary, 1868–9, 26 December 1868.

839 Cited in Orser, *Lives of Chang and Eng*, p. 168.

840 Cited in Wallace and Wallace, *The Two*, p. 273.

841 Cited in Ibid., p. 274.

842 Cited in Ibid., p. 279.

843 Ibid., pp. 283–6.

844 Cited in Armand Marie Leroi, *Mutants: On the Form, Varieties and Errors of the Human Body* (London: HarperCollins, 2003), p. 26.

845 Cited in Martell, *Millie-Christine*, p. 198.

846 Ibid., pp. 198–237.

847 Cited in Ibid., p. 270.

848 Horn, *Amusing the Victorians*, p. 200.

849 Ibid., p. 222.

850 Barry J. Faulk, *Music Halls and Modernity: The Late-Victorian Discovery of Popular Culture* (Columbus: Ohio University Press, 2004), pp. 7–22.

851 Tammy C. Whitlock, *Crime, Gender and Consumer Culture in Nineteenth-Century England* (Surrey: Ashgate, 2005), pp. 20–6, 30–6, 43–60.

852 Qureshi, *Peoples on Parade*, pp. 2–4, 271–84.

853 Cited in Ashby, *With Amusement for All*, p. 140.

854 Bogdan, *Freak Show*, pp. 55–8; Ashby, *With Amusement for All*, pp. 132–42.

855 Christopher Smit, 'A Collaborative Aesthetic: Levinas's Idea of Responsibility and the Photographs of Charles Eisenmann and the Late Nineteenth-Century Freak-Performer', in *Victorian Freaks*, ed. by Tromp, pp. 283–311.

856 Anne Featherstone, 'Showing the Freaks: Photographic Images of the Extraordinary Body', in *Visual Delights: Essays on the Popular and Projected Image in the 19th Century*, ed. by Simon Popple and Vanessa Toulmin (Towbridge: Flicks Books, 2000), pp. 135–42.

857 QVJ, 26 February 1881; *Standard*, 1 March 1881.

858 Cited in Linda Simon, *The Greatest Show on Earth: A History of the Circus* (London: Reaktion Books, 2014), p. 227.

The Final Act

859 Durbach, *Spectacle of Deformity*, pp. 173–4.

860 Bogdan, *Freak Show*, pp. 234–56.

861 Helen Davies, *Neo-Victorian Freakery: The Cultural Afterlife of the Victorian Freak Show* (Basingstoke: Palgrave Macmillan, 2015) pp. 159–96.

862 ROLLR, Leicester Workhouse Admissions and Discharges, 1879–1905, G/12/60/1, Entry: 1434, 29 December 1879.

863 Ibid., Entry: 1902, 22 March 1880.

864 Ibid., Entry: 1947, 24 March 1880.

865 Merrick, *The Life and Adventures of Joseph Carey Merrick* (Leicester: H. & A. Cockshaw, 1880 [1885 (?)]), n.p.

866 ROLLR, Leicester Workhouse Admissions and Discharges, 1879–1905, G/12/60/1, Entry: 8506, 3 August 1884.

867 Michael Howell and Peter Ford, *The True History of The Elephant Man* (Harmondsworth: Penguin Books, 1983), pp. 86–92.

868 Merrick, *Life and Adventures of Joseph Carey Merrick*, n.p.

869 Cited in Howell and Ford, *True History of The Elephant Man*, p. 108.

870 Ashby, *With Amusement for All*, p. 64.

871 Crone, *Violent Victorians*, p. 264.

872 Norman and Norman, *Penny Showman*, pp. 103–4.

873 John Bland-Sutton, *The Story of a Surgeon* (London: Methuen, 1930), p. 139.

874 *British Medical Journal*, 6 December 1884, p. 1140; Anon., 'Pathological Society of London', *Lancet*, 6 December 1884, pp. 1000–2.

875 Howell and Ford, *The True History of The Elephant Man*, p. 111.

876 *The Times*, 4 December 1886.

877 Howell and Ford, *The True History of The Elephant Man*, pp. 111–16.

878 *The Times*, 4 December 1886; A.E. Clark-Kennedy, *The London: A Study in the Voluntary Hospital System, Volume II: The Second Hundred Years, 1840–1948* (London: Pitman Medical Publishers, 1963), pp. 40–93.

879 Royal London Hospital Archives and Museum (RLHAM), London Hospital Committee Minutes, 28 September 1886–18 December 1888, LH/A/5/43, p. 82.

880 *The Times*, 5 January 1887.

881 Ibid.

882 Bland-Sutton, *Story of a Surgeon*, p. 140.

883 Wilfred Thomason Grenfell, *A Labrador Doctor: The Autobiography of Sir Wilfred Thomason Grenfell* (London: Hodder & Stoughton, 1954 [1919]), p. 65.

884 Ibid.

885 RLHAM, London Hospital Committee Minutes, 1 January 1889–2 December 1891, LH/A/5/44, p. 236.

886 Howell and Ford, *The True History of The Elephant Man*, pp. 192–202.

887 *Descriptive Catalogue of the Pathological Museum of the London Hospital*, ed. by F. Charlewood Turner, Frederick S. Eve and T.H. Openshaw (London: London Hospital Medical College, 1890), pp. 122–3.

888 Bland-Sutton, *Story of a Surgeon*, p. 8.

889 BLL, The Papers of Frederick Treves R.P.3008/1, 19 October 1922; BLL, The Papers of Frederick Treves R.P.3008/1, 30 October 1922.

890 ROLLR, *The Elephant Man*: Manuscript by Sir Frederick Treves, 1925, DE 2226, p. 3.

891 Frederick Treves, *The Elephant Man and Other Reminiscences* (London: W.H. Allen, 1980 [1923]), p. 15.

892 Ibid., p. 11.

893 Ibid., pp. 17, 8.

894 Ibid., p. 17.

895 Ibid., pp. 19–20.

896 Norman and Norman, *Penny Showman*, p. 45.

897 Samuel Smiles, *Self-Help; with Illustrations of Character and Conduct* (London: John Murray, 1859), p. 24.

898 Norman and Norman, *Penny Showman*, p. 110.

899 Anon., 'The Elephant Man: Story of a Freak that Fiction has Never Equalled', *World's Fair*, 17 February 1923, no. 962.

900 Michel Foucault, *Madness and Civilization: A History of Insanity in the Age of Reason*, trans. by Richard Howard (London: Routledge, 2009), pp. 35–60 (p. 41).

901 Although the proportion of the confined population remained much the same: Richmond, *Clothing the Poor in Nineteenth-Century England*, p. 261.

902 Ben Shephard, *A War of Nerves* (London: Jonathan Cape, 2000), pp. 73–5, 157–9.

903 Cited in Fitzsimons, *Barnum in London*, p. 137.

904 Daniel P. Mannix, *Freaks: We Who Are Not As Others* (New York: RE/Search, 1999 [1976]), pp. 11–12.

905 Ibid., p. 91.

906 Ibid.

907 Wellcome Images, St Bartholomew's Hospital Archives and Museum MU/14/48/68, MU/14/1/3/2, MU/14/1/9/1, MU/14/48/68, MU/14/1/3/2, MU/14/1/9/1.

908 Fiona Pettit, 'The Afterlife of Freak Shows', in *Popular Exhibitions, Science and Showmanship, 1840–1910*, ed. by Kember, Plunkett and Sullivan, pp. 61–78.

909 Cited in Durbach, *Spectacle of Deformity*, p. 182.

910 Bolton, 'Statement of the Principle Circumstances', p. 186.

911 Bogdan, *Freak Show*, pp. 62–7.

912 Cited in Ibid., pp. 64–5.

913 Treves, *Elephant Man*, p. 11.

914 Sanger, *Seventy Years a Showman*, p. xvii.

915 George Sanger Coleman, as told to John Lukens, *The Sanger Story: The Story of His Life with His Grandfather 'Lord' George Sanger* (London: White Lion Publishers, 1974 [1956]), p. 193.

916 Ibid., p. 209.

917 Norman and Norman, *Penny Showman*, p. 13.

918 Other regulations on entertainment included: the Street Music Act (1864), the Fairs Act (1871) and the Children's Dangerous Performances Act (1879).

919 J.A. Mangan and Callum McKenzie, 'The Other Side of the Coin: Victorian Masculinity, Field Sports and English Elite Education', in *Making European Masculinities: Sport, Europe, Gender*, ed. by J.A. Mangan (London: Frank Cass, 2000), pp. 62–85.

920 Treves, *Elephant Man*, pp. 16, 21.

921 Frederick Treves, *Physical Education* (London: J. & A. Churchill, 1892), p. 1.

922 Max Nordau, *Degeneration* (London: William Heinemann, 1898), p. 34.

923 Cited in Michael Boulter, *Bloomsbury Scientists: Science and Art in the Wake of Darwin* (London: UCL Press, 2017), p. 106.

924 At Auschwitz the Ovitz family, who once performed as the Lilliput Troupe, were forced to dance naked to SS soldiers while Mengele experimented on their bodies.

925 Cohen, *Family Secrets*, pp. 77–112.

926 Cited in David A. Gerber, 'Pornography or Entertainment? The Rise and Fall of the Freak Show', *Reviews in American History* 18:1 (1990), pp. 15–21 (p. 16).

927 Merrick, *Life and Adventures of Joseph Carey Merrick*, n.p.

928 Cited in Duff, 'Biographies of Scale' <http://dsq-sds.org/article/view/617/794> [accessed 9 January 2019].

929 Mansfield Turner and William Harris, *A Guide to the Institutions & Charities for the Blind in the United Kingdom* (London: Robert Hardwicke, 1871), pp. vii–xi.

930 Family Welfare Association, *The Epileptic and Crippled Child and Adult: A Report on the Present Condition of These Classes of Afflicted Persons, With Suggestions for their Better Education and Employment* (London: Swan Sonnenschein, 1893), pp. 99–100.

931 Ben Purse, *The Blind in Industry: Fifty Years of Work and Wages* (London: Edson, 1925), pp. 95–101.

932 Bogdan, *Freak Show*, pp. 270–2.

933 Durbach, *Spectacle of Deformity*, pp. 177–8.

934 Cited in Ashby, *With Amusement for All*, p. 145.
935 Cited in Haslam and Haslam, *Fat, Gluttony and Sloth*, p. 47.

Encore

936 Adams, *Sideshow U.S.A.*, pp. 60–209.
937 The film was just one example of freak performers onscreen. Another well-known example being the Munchkins in *The Wizard of Oz* (1939).
938 Fiedler, *Freaks*, pp. 300–19.
939 Mary J. Russo, *The Female Grotesque: Risk, Excess and Modernity* (London: Routledge, 1994), pp. 75–6.
940 Nickell, *Secrets of the Sideshows*, pp. 345–52.
941 Mat Fraser, personal interview, 12 November 2012.
942 Terri Thrower, 'Overcoming the Need to "Overcome": Challenging Disability Narratives in *The Miracle*', in *Different Bodies: Essays on Disability in Film and Television*, ed. by Marja Evelyn Mogk (London: McFarland, 2013), pp. 205–18 (p. 212).
943 Mat Fraser, 'Go Ahead – Take a Look', *Guardian*, 15 February 2008 <http://www.theguardian.com/film/2008/feb/15/disability.baftas2008> [accessed 21 February 2019].
944 Garland-Thomson, *Extraordinary Bodies*, p. 13.
945 Elizabeth Stephens, 'Geeks and Gaffs: The Queer Legacy of the 1950s American Freak Show', in *Queer 1950s: Rethinking Sexuality in the Postwar Years*, ed. by Heike Bauer and Matt Cook (New York: Palgrave Macmillan, 2012), pp. 183–95 (p. 190).
946 Nadja Durbach, '"Skinless Wonders": Body Worlds and the Victorian Freak Show', *Journal of the History of Medicine and Allied Sciences*, 69:1 (2014), pp. 38–67.
947 See chapters under the heading 'Relocation of the Freak Show' in *Freakery*, ed. by Garland-Thomson, pp. 315–84.

Sources

ARCHIVAL DOCUMENTS

BRIDGEPORT HISTORY CENTER, BRIDGEPORT PUBLIC LIBRARY, CONNECTICUT (BHC)
Box #1 Tom Thumb
Box #2 Tom Thumb
Draw #5 Tom Thumb
Draw #6 Barnum's American Museum
Draw #8 Circus/Barnum, 1871–1880
Draw #9 Circus/Barnum, 1881–1891

BRITISH LIBRARY, LONDON (BLL)
1889.b.10/1, Fillinham Collection of Cuttings, vol. IV: Fairs
C20452, Lysons Collectanea, vol. I
L.R.301.h.5, Sarah Sophia Banks Collection, vol. III: Balloons, Sights, Exhibitions, Remarkable Characters.
L.R.301.h.7, Sarah Sophia Banks Collection, vol. V: Cuttings from Newspapers
R.P.3008/1, The Papers of Frederick Treves

DURHAM COUNTY RECORD OFFICE (DCRO)
DU 1/31/251–253, Correspondence regarding Boruwłaski's wedding ring
DU 1/60/11, Memoirs of the Celebrated Dwarf, Count Joseph Boruwłaski (1801)
DU 1/60/12, Opinion concerning the holding of fairs in Elvet, 1804
Vol A 14/17, Library Pamphlets

DURHAM UNIVERSITY LIBRARY (DUL)
Add. MS. 180, Letter from Joseph Boruwłaski
Add. MS. 1079, Letter from Joseph Boruwłaski
Add. MS. 1395/1–3, Copy of Hanna Swiderska's article
Add. MS. 1907, Commonplace book of William Van Mildert
SDG/1/1, Correspondence, Accounts, etc.
SDG/16/1, Catalogue of Furniture, Books, and Other Effects

LONDON METROPOLITAN ARCHIVES (LMA)
SC/GL/BFS/001, Bartholomew Fair Folder

MUSEUM OF THE CITY OF NEW YORK, MANHATTAN (MCNY)

Vol. 37, Freaks I
Vol. 38, Freaks II
Vol. 39, Freaks III
Vol. 41, Midgets (Barnum-Affiliated)

NATIONAL FAIRGROUND ARCHIVES, SHEFFIELD (NFA)

178B28, Shufflebottom Family Collection
178G25, Cyril Critchlow Collection
178T1.296–178T.342, John Bramwell Taylor, Box Three
Turner Database (Online resource accessed onsite)

NORTH CAROLINA STATE ARCHIVES, RALEIGH (NCSA)

OS mss Pc266, Millie-Christine Collection
PC.266.1, Millie-Christine Collection, 1855–1974
PC.916.1, Siamese Twins Collection, 1829–1969

RECORD OFFICE OF LEICESTERSHIRE, LEICESTER & RUTLAND (ROLLR)

38'31, Scrapbook
DE 2226, *The Elephant Man*: Manuscript by Sir Frederick Treves, 1925
G/12/60/1, Leicester Workhouse Admissions and Discharges, 1879–1905
M40, 'Life of that Wonderful and Extraordinary Heavy Man'

ROYAL COLLEGE OF SURGEONS, LONDON (RCSL)

MS0007/1/6/1/5, Research: Book of scraps relative to the specimens in the museum
    and to natural history
MS0007/1/6/1/8, Research: Memoranda of Natural History vol. I
MS0007/1/6/1/16, Research: The Mermaid
MS0035/1, The Papers of Francis Buckland, vol. I
RCS-MUS/S/5/6/4, Museum Letters 1821

ROYAL LONDON HOSPITAL ARCHIVES AND MUSEUM, BARTS HEALTH NHS TRUST (RLHAM)

LH/A/5/43, London Hospital Committee Minutes, 28 September 1886–18 December 1888
LH/A/5/44, London Hospital Committee Minutes, 1 January 1889–2 December 1891

SOUTHERN HISTORICAL COLLECTION, THE UNIVERSITY OF NORTH CAROLINA AT CHAPEL HILL (SHC, UNC)

3761, Bunker, Chang and Eng
4822-Z, Christopher Wren Bunker Papers
M-3761, Chang and Eng Bunker Papers
Op3761, Bunker, Chang and Eng
P.3761, Bunker, Chang and Eng

SOURCES

STAMFORD TOWN HALL, LINCOLNSHIRE (STH)

230–234, The Philips Collection, Entertainment Folders
F52LAM, Daniel Lambert

STAMFORD TOWN LIBRARY, LINCOLNSHIRE (STL)

Folder, Daniel Lambert Newspaper Cutting
Folder, Daniel Lambert Primary References
ST 2833, Tom Thumb Medallion

THE BARNUM MUSEUM, BRIDGEPORT CONNECTICUT (TBMB)

1845-01-01, P.T. Barnum Letter Copybook, 1845–1846
1848-07-05-1848-08-11, Manuscript: Bound typescript of 'A Journal' by
    Caroline C. Barnum
Barnum Investments #1
Box TT Album
Box TT Daguerreotypes
Box TT LW Framed Items 3
Box TT Merchandising Artefacts
Folder, Letters from Lavinia

TRINITY COLLEGE LIBRARY, CAMBRIDGE, PAPERS OF A.J. MUNBY (TCLC, MUNB)

MUNB, 1–65, Diaries of A.J. Munby
MUNB, 97, Arthur Munby's Notebooks
MUNB, 111–121, Albums of Photographs

WELLCOME LIBRARY, LONDON (WLL)

EPH+33, Oversize Ephemera
EPH 499B, Freaks Ephemera Box 3
SBHB MU/14, St Bartholomew's Hospital Archives & Museum, Wellcome Images

WILSON LIBRARY, THE UNIVERSITY OF NORTH CAROLINA AT CHAPEL HILL

CbB S56f, Ephemera Collection
CbB S56p, Ephemera Collection
CbB S56sl, Ephemera Collection

ELECTRONIC ARCHIVES

Darwin Project, <http://www.darwinproject.ac.uk>
Disability Museum, <http://www.disabilitymuseum.org>
Evanion Catalogue, <http://www.bl.uk/catalogues/evanion>
Godfrey, Kathleen, Julia Pastrana Online, <www.juliapastranaonline>
John Johnson Collection (TJJC), <http://johnjohnson.chadwyck.com> (Accessed via
    the Senate House Library Catalogue)

Lost Museum, <https://lostmuseum.cuny.edu/archive/>
Queen Victoria's Journals (QVJ), <http://www.queenvictoriasjournals.org>
Royal Collection Trust, <https://www.rct.uk/collection>
Victorian Popular Culture, <http://www.victorianpopularculture.amdigital.co.uk/>
William F. Cody Archive, Buffalo Bill Center of the West and University of Nebraska-
    Lincoln, <http://codyarchive.org>

PRIMARY SOURCES (INCLUDING MODERN REPRINTS)

Albert, Prince, *Prince Albert's Golden Precepts: or, The Opinions and Maxims of his
    Late Royal Highness the Prince Consort* (London: Sampson Low, 1862)
Alden, William Livingston, *Among the Freaks* (London: Longmans, 1896)
Anon., *Account of Miss Pastrana, The Nondescript; and the Double-Bodied Boy*
    (London: E. Hancock, 1860)
Anon., *An Account of Chang and Eng, The World Renowned Siamese Twins, Elegantly
    Illustrated* (New York: T.W. Strong, 1853)
Anon., *An Account of the Life, Personal Appearance, Character, and Manners, of
    Charles S. Stratton, The American Man in Miniature, known as General Tom
    Thumb, Twelve Years Old, Twenty-Five Inches High, and Weighing Only Fifteen
    Pounds* (London: T. Brettell, 1845)
Anon., *Biographical Sketch of Millie Christine, the Carolina Twin, Surnamed the Two-
    Headed Nightingale, and the Eighth Wonder of the World* (Cincinnati: Hennegan
    [between 1902 and 1912])
Anon., *History of Commodore Nutt, The Smallest Man in Miniature in the Known
    World, is Eighteen Years Old, Twenty-Nine Inches High, and Weighs 24 pounds.
    Now Exhibiting at Barnum's Museum, New York* (New York: Wynkoop,
    Hallenbeck & Thomas, 1862)
Anon., *Illustrated Memoir of an Eventful Expedition into Central America: Resulting
    in the Discovery of the Idolatrous City of Iximaya, in an Unexplored Region; And
    the Possession of Two Remarkable Aztec Children Maximo (the Boy), And Batola
    (the Girl)* (London, [publisher not identified], 1853)
Anon., *The Eccentric Magazine; or, Lives and Portraits of Remarkable Characters*,
    2 vols. (London: G. Smeeton, 1812–1814)
Anon., *The Life of Joice Heth, the Nurse of Gen. George Washington, (the Father of Our
    Country,) Now Living at the Astonishing Age of 161 Years, and Weighs Only 46
    Pounds* (New York: printed for the publisher, 1835)
Anon., *The Life of that Wonderful and Extraordinary Heavy Man, the Late Daniel
    Lambert. From his Birth to the Moment of his Dissolution, with an Account
    of Men Noted for their Corpulency, and other Interesting Matter* (Stamford: J.
    Drakard, 1809)
Anon., *The Siamese Twins: Chang and Eng. A Biographical Sketch* (London: J.W.
    Last, 1869)
Anon., *Sinnett's Picture of Paris* (London: Joseph Masters, 1847)

Anon., *Sketch of the Life, Personal Appearance, Character, and Manners, of Charles S. Stratton, the Man in Miniature, known as General Tom Thumb, and his Wife, Lavinia Warren Stratton, including the History of their Courtship and Marriage, with some Account of Remarkable Dwarfs, Giants, and other Human Phenomena, of Ancient and Modern Times, also Songs Given at their Public Levees* (New York: Press of Wynkoop & Hallenbeck, 1867)

Anon., *Sketch of the Life, Personal Appearance, Character, and Manners, of Charles S. Stratton, the Man in Miniature, known as General Tom Thumb, Fifteen Years Old, Twenty-Eight Inches High, and Weighing Only Fifteen Pounds, with some Account of Remarkable Dwarfs, Giants, and other Human Phenomena* (New York: Van Norden & Amerman, 1847)

Anon., *The True Lamplighter, and Aunt Mary's Cabin* (Boston: Perkins & Fay, 1854)

Barnum, Phineas T., *Selected Letters of P.T. Barnum*, ed. and intro. by A.H. Saxon (New York: Columbia University Press, 1983)

——*Struggles and Triumphs; or, Forty Years' Recollections of P.T. Barnum, Written by Himself. Author's Edition* (Buffalo, NY: Warren, Johnson, 1873 [1869])

——*The Humbugs of the World* (New York: Carleton, 1866)

——*The Life of P.T. Barnum, Written by himself*, intro. by Terence Whalen (Urbana: University of Illinois Press, 2000 [1854])

Bates, Martin Van Buren, *A Historical Sketch of the Tallest Man and Wife, That Have Ever Existed, Captain Martin Van Buren Bates and Mrs. Bates, Formerly Anna Swan, Together with a Short Description of Mythological, Ancient, Medieval and Modern Giants* ([place of publication, publisher and date not identified])

Bland-Sutton, John, *The Story of a Surgeon* (London: Methuen, 1930)

Bleeker, Sylvester, *Gen. Tom Thumb's Three Years' Tour Around The World, Accompanied by his Wife – Lavinia Warren Stratton, Commodore Nutt, Miss Minnie Warren, and Party* (New York: S. Booth, 1872)

Bompas, George C., *Life of Frank Buckland By His Brother-In-Law* (London: Smith, Elder, 1885)

Boruwłaski, Joseph, *A Second Edition of the Memoirs of the Celebrated Dwarf, Joseph Boruwłaski, A Polish Gentleman. Containing A faithful and curious Account of his birth, education, marriage, travels, and voyage. Written by himself and carefully revised and corrected. And translated from the French by Mr. S. Freeman* (Birmingham: J. Thompson, 1792)

Buckland, Francis T., *Curiosities of Natural History: Fourth Series* (London: Richard Bentley, 1888)

——*Log-Book of a Fisherman and Zoologist* (London: Chapman & Hall, 1875)

Burn, James Dawson, *Three Years Among the Working-classes in the United States during the War* (London: Smith, Elder, 1865)

Caulfield, James, *Portraits, Memoires, and Characters of Remarkable Persons, from the Revolution in 1688 to the End of the Reign of George II. Collected from the Most Authentic Accounts Extant*, 4 vols. (London: H.R. Young and T.H. Whitely, 1819)

Coleman, George Sanger, as told to John Lukens, *The Sanger Story: The Story of His Life with His Grandfather 'Lord' George Sanger* (London: White Lion, 1974 [1956])

Conolly, John, *The Ethnological Exhibitions of London* (London: John Churchill, 1855)

Darwin, Charles, *On the Origin of Species By Means of Natural Selection; or, The Preservation of Favoured Races in the Struggle for Life* (London: John Murray, 1859 [first edition])

——*The Descent of Man, and Selection in Relation to Sex* (London: John Murray, 1871 [first edition])

——*The Variation of Animals and Plants under Domestication*, 2 vols. (London: John Murray, 1868)

Dickens, Charles, *American Notes* (London: Granville Publishing, 1985 [1842])

——*Sketches by Boz*, ed. and intro. by Dennis Walder (London: Penguin, 1995 [1833–1839])

——*The Old Curiosity Shop: A Tale* (London: Chapman & Hall, 1843)

Engels, Friedrich, *The Condition of the Working-Class in England in 1844, with a Preface written in 1892*, trans. by Florence Kelley Wischnewetzky (London: George Allen & Unwin, 1943 [1892])

Engleheart, Gardner, *Journal of the Progress of H.R.H. the Prince of Wales through British North America; and his visit to the United States, 10th July to 15th November, 1860* ([London]: privately printed, [1860])

Fairholt, F.W., *Eccentric and Remarkable Characters. A Series of Biographical Memoirs of Persons Famous for Extraordinary Actions or Singularities. With Illustrations* (London: Richard Bentley, 1849)

Family Welfare Association, *The Epileptic and Crippled Child and Adult: A Report on the Present Condition of These Classes of Afflicted Persons, With Suggestions for their Better Education and Employment* (London: Swan Sonnenschein, 1893)

Fielding, Henry, *Tom Thumb and the Tragedy of Tragedies*, ed. by L.J. Morrissey (Edinburgh: Oliver & Boyd, 1970 [1730])

Frost, Thomas, *Circus Life and Circus Celebrities* (London: Tinsley Brothers, 1873)

——*The Old Showmen, and The Old London Fairs* (London: Tinsley Brothers, 1874)

Fuller, Thomas, *The History of the Worthies of England who for Parts and Learning have been Eminent in the Several Counties: Together with an Historical Narrative of the Native Commodities and Rarities in each County* (London: Printed by J.G.W.L. and W.G. for Thomas Williams, 1662)

Gould, George M., and Walter L. Pyle, *Anomalies and Curiosities of Medicine* (Philadelphia: W.B. Sanders, 1901 [1896])

Granger, William, *The New Wonderful Museum and Extraordinary Magazine: Being a Complete Repository of all the Wonders, Curiosities, and Rarities of Nature and Art*, 6 vols. (London: A. Hogg, 1802–1808)

Grenfell, Wilfred Thomason, *A Labrador Doctor: The Autobiography of Sir Wilfred Thomason Grenfell* (London: Hodder & Stoughton, 1954 [1919])

Grose, Francis, *A Classical Dictionary of the Vulgare Tongue* (London: S. Hooper, 1785)

[Hale, James W.], *A Few Particulars Concerning Chang-Eng, The United Siamese Brothers, Published Under Their Own Direction* (New York: John M. Elliott, 1836)

——*An Historical and Descriptive Account of the Siamese Twin Brothers, from Actual Observations, Together with Full Length Portraits, the Only Correct Ones,*

Permitted to be Taken by Their Protectors (London: W. Turner, 1830)

Hare, G. Van, *Fifty Years of a Showman's Life; or, The Life and Travels of Van Hare* (London: W.H. Allen, 1888)

Haydon, Benjamin Robert, *The Autobiography and Journals of Benjamin Robert Haydon (1786–1846)*, ed. and intro. by Malcolm Elwin (London: Macdonald, 1950 [1853])

Hone, Philip, *Diary of Philip Hone, 1828–1850*, vol. 2, ed. by Allan Nevins, (New York: Dodd, Mead, 1927)

Hone, William, *The Every-Day Book*, vol. 1 (London: Thomas Tegg, 1840 [1828])

Hunt, James, *Negro's Place in Nature: A paper read before the London Anthropological Society* (New York: Van Evbie, Hobton, 1864)

Hutton, Catherine, 'A Memoir of the Celebrated Dwarf, Joseph Boruwłaski', *Bentley's Miscellany*, vol. 17 (London: Richard Bentley, 1845), pp. 240–9

Kirby, R.S., *Kirby's Wonderful and Eccentric Museum; or, Magazine of Remarkable Characters*, 6 vols. (London: R.S. Kirby, 1803–1820)

Knox, Robert, *The Races of Men: A Fragment* (London: Henry Renshaw, 1850)

Lytton, Edward B., *The Siamese Twins: A Satirical Tale of the Times. With Other Poems* (New York: J. & J. Harper, 1831)

McCoy, Millie and Christine, *The History of the Carolina Twins: 'Told in Their Own Peculiar Way' by 'One of Them* (Buffalo: Buffalo Courier Printing House [1869])

Magri, M., Lavinia, *The Autobiography of Mrs. Tom Thumb*, ed. by A.H. Saxon (Hamden, Conn: Archon Books, 1979)

Mathews, Mrs. [Jackson, Anne], *Memoirs of Charles Mathews, Comedian*, vol. 3 (London: Richard Bentley, 1839)

——*The Life and Correspondence of Charles Mathews the Elder, Comedian* (London: Warne and Routledge, 1860)

Merrick, J.C., *The Life and Adventures of Joseph Carey Merrick* (Leicester: H. & A. Cockshaw, 1880 [1885])

Morley, Henry, *Memoirs of Bartholomew Fair* (London: Frederick Warne, 1874)

Munby, Arthur Joseph, *Relicta: Verses* (London: Bertram Dobell, 1909)

Neild, James, *State of the Prisons in England, Scotland, and Wales: Extending to various places therein assigned* (London: Printed by J. Nichols and Son, 1812)

Nordau, Max, *Degeneration* (London: William Heinemann, 1898)

Norman, Tom and George Barnum Norman, *The Penny Showman: Memoirs of Tom Norman 'Silver King'* (London: privately published, 1985)

Northall, William Knight, *Before and Behind the Curtain, or Fifteen Years' Observations Among the Theatres of New York* (New York: W.F. Burgess, 1851)

Paré, Ambroise, *On Monsters and Marvels*, trans. with intro. by Janis L. Pallister (Chicago: University of Chicago Press, 1982 [1573])

Prest, Thomas, *The Magazine of Curiosity and Wonder* (London: G. Drake, 1835)

Prichard, James Cowles, *The Natural History of Man; Comprising Inquiries into the Modifying Influence of Physical and Moral Agencies of the Different Tribes of the Human Family* (London: H. Bailliere, 1843)

Quételet, Lambert Adolphe Jacques, *Letters Addressed to the Grand Duke of Saxe-Coburg and Gotha, on the Theory of Probabilities, as applied to the Moral and Political Sciences*, trans. by O.G. Downes (London: Charles & Edwin Taylor, 1849)

Sala, George Augustus, *The Life and Adventures of George Augustus Sala, Written by Himself*, vol. 1 (New York: Charles Scribner's Sons, 1895)

Sanger, 'Lord' George, *Seventy Years a Showman*, with an intro. by Kenneth Grahame (New York: Dutton, 1926 [1910])

Scott, Walter, *Peveril of the Peak* (London: George Routledge, 1879 [1823])

Smiles, Samuel, *Self-Help; with Illustrations of Character and Conduct* (London: John Murray, 1859)

Smith, Albert, 'Manners and Customs: Sketches of Paris', in *The Mirror of Literature, Amusement, and Instruction*, vol. 33 (London: J. Limbird, 1839), pp. 308–9

Spencer, Herbert, *The Principles of Biology* (London: William and Norgate, 1864)

Treves, Frederick, *Physical Education* (London: J. & A. Churchill, 1892)

——*The Elephant Man and Other Reminiscences* (London: W.H. Allen, 1980 [1923])

Turner, F. Charlewood, Frederick S. Eve and T.H. Openshaw, eds., *Descriptive Catalogue of the Pathological Museum of the London Hospital* (London: London Hospital Medical College, 1890)

Turner, Mansfield and William Harris, *A Guide to the Institutions & Charities for the Blind in the United Kingdom* (London: Robert Hardwicke, 1871)

Unthan, C.H., *The Armless Fiddler* (London: George Allen and Unwin, 1935)

Walker, Whimsical, *From Sawdust to Windsor Castle* (London: Stanley Paul, 1922)

Wallett, W.F., *The Public Life of W.F. Wallett, The Queen's Jester: An Autobiography*, ed. by J. Luntley (London: Bemrose and Sons, 1870)

White, Charles, *An Account of the Regular Gradation in Man, and in different Animals and Vegetables; and from the former to the latter* (London: Printed for C. Dilly, 1799)

Wilson, Henry, *The Eccentric Mirror: Reflecting a Faithful and Interesting Delineation of Male and Female Characters* (London: James Cundee, 1806–7, 1813)

Wood, Edward J., *Giants and Dwarfs* (London: Richard Bentley, 1868)

Wright, James, *The History and Antiquities of the County of Rutland: Collected from Records, Ancient Manuscripts, Monuments on the Place, and Other Authorities* (London: Bennett Griffin, 1684)

SECONDARY SOURCES

Ackroyd, Peter, *London: The Biography* (London: Chatto & Windus, 2000)

Adams, Rachel, *Sideshow U.S.A.: Freaks and the American Cultural Imagination* (Chicago: University of Chicago Press, 2001)

Adelson, Betty, *The Lives of Dwarfs: Their Journey from Public Curiosity Toward Social Liberation* (Piscataway, NJ: Rutgers University Press, 2005)

Altick, Richard D., *The Shows of London: A Panoramic History of Exhibitions, 1800–1862* (Cambridge, MA: Belknap Press, 1978)

Andreassen, Rikke, *Human Exhibitions: Race, Gender and Sexuality in Ethnic Displays* (Surrey: Ashgate, 2015)

Ashby, LeRoy, *With Amusement for All: A History of American Popular Culture since 1830* (Lexington: University Press of Kentucky, 2006)

Ashcroft, Bill, 'Primitive and Wingless: The Colonial Subject as Child', in *Dickens and the Children of Empire*, ed. by Wendy S. Jacobson (Basingstoke: Palgrave Macmillan, 2000), pp. 184–202

Bates, A.W., *Emblematic Monsters: Unnatural Conceptions and Deformed Births in Early Modern Europe* (New York: Rodopi, 2005)

Bauman, Zygmunt, *Modernity and Ambivalence* (Oxford: Polity Press, 1991)

Baynton, Douglas C., 'Disability and the Justification of Inequality in American History', *The New Disability History: American Perspectives*, ed. by Paul K. Longmore and Lauri Umansky (New York: New York University Press, 2001), pp. 33–57

Beal, Timothy K., *Religion and Its Monsters* (London: Routledge, 2002)

Bedini, Silvio A., *Ridgefield in Review* (Ridgefield, CT: Ridgefield 250th Anniversary Committee, 1958)

Beeman, Richard R., 'Trade and Travel in Post-Revolutionary Virginia: A Diary of an Itinerant Peddler, 1807–1808', in *The Virginia Magazine of History and Biography*, 84:2 (1976), pp. 174–88

Benes, Peter, *For a Short Time Only: Itinerants and the Resurgence of Popular Culture in Early America* (Amherst: University of Massachusetts Press, 2016)

Blanchard, Pascal, Gilles Boëtsch and Nanette Jacomijn Snoep, 'Human Zoos: The Invention of the Savage', in *Human Zoos: The Invention of the Savage*, ed. by Pascal Blanchard, Gilles Boëtsch and Nanette Jacomijn Snoep (Paris: Musée du quai Branly, 2011), pp. 20–54

Blanning, Tim, *The Romantic Revolution* (London: Weidenfeld & Nicolson, 2010)

Blumberg, Mark S., *Freaks of Nature and What They Tell Us About Development and Evolution* (Oxford: Oxford University Press, 2009)

Boëtsch, Gilles, and Pascal Blanchard, 'The Hottentot Venus: Birth of a "Freak"' (1815), in *Human Zoos: The Invention of the Savage*, ed. by Pascal Blanchard, Gilles Boëtsch and Nanette Jacomijn Snoep (Paris: Musée du quai Branly, 2011), pp. 62–72

Bogdan, Robert, *Freak Show: Presenting Human Oddities for Amusement and Profit* (Chicago: University of Chicago Press, 1988)

——'The Social Construction of Freaks', in *Freakery: Cultural Spectacles of the Extraordinary Body*, ed. by Rosemarie Garland-Thomson (New York: New York University Press, 1996), pp. 23–37

Bondeson, Jan, *A Cabinet of Medical Curiosities* (Ithaca, NY: Cornell University Press, 1997)

——*Freaks: The Pig-Faced Lady of Manchester Square & other Medical Marvels* (Stroud: Tempus, 2006)

Bondeson, Jan, and A.E.W. Miles, 'Julia Pastrana, The Nondescript: An Example of

Congenital, Generalized Hypertrichosis Terminalis With Ginger Hyperplasia',
American Journal of Medical Genetics, 47:2 (1993), pp. 198–212

Boulter, Michael, *Bloomsbury Scientists: Science and Art in the Wake of Darwin*
(London: UCL Press, 2017)

Bowler, Peter, *Evolution: The History of an Idea* (Berkeley: University of California, 2003)

Brown, Bill, *The Material Unconscious: American Amusement, Stephen Crane, & the
Economies of Play* (London: Harvard University Press, 1996)

Browne, Janet, 'Darwin in Caricature: A Study in the Popularisation and Dissemination
of Evolution', *American Philosophical Society*, 145:4 (2001), pp. 496–509

Carroll, Victoria, *Science and Eccentricity: Collecting, Writing and Performing Science
for Early Nineteenth-Century Audiences* (London: Pickering & Chatto, 2008)

Carson, Louise, 'The Rest of the Story About the Civil War Giant', *FNB Chronicle* 9:3
(1998) <http://www.tngenweb.org/scott/fnb_v9n3_giant.htm> [accessed
9 January 2019]

Chemers, Michael M., 'Introduction Staging Stigma: A Freak Studies Manifesto',
Disability Quarterly Studies, 25:3 (2005), <http://dsq-sds.org/article/
view/574/751> [accessed 3 February 2016]

——'Jumpin' Tom Thumb: Charles Stratton on Stage at the American Museum',
Nineteenth Century Theatre and Film, 31:2 (2004), pp. 16–27

——'Le Freak, C'est Chic: The Twenty-First Century Freak Show as Theatre of
Transgression', *Modern Drama*, 46:2 (2003), pp. 285–304

——*Staging Stigma: A Critical Examination of the American Freak Show* (Basingstoke:
Palgrave Macmillan, 2008)

Chinn, Carl, *Poverty Amidst Prosperity: The Urban Poor in England, 1834–1914*
(Manchester: Manchester University Press, 1995)

Claire, Eli, *Exile and Pride: Disability, Queerness and Liberation* (Cambridge, MA:
South End, 1999)

Clayton, Tim, *Caricatures of the Peoples of the British Isles* (London: British Museum
Press, 2007)

Cohen, Deborah, *Family Secrets: Living with Shames from the Victorians to the Present
Day* (London: Penguin, 2013)

Colley, Linda, *Britons: Forging the Nation, 1707–1837* (London: Pimlico, 2003)

Collini, Stefan, *Public Moralists: Political Thought and Intellectual Life in Britain,
1850–1930* (Oxford: Clarendon Press, 1991)

Collins, David, *Chang and Eng: The Original Siamese Twins* (Oxford: Maxwell
Macmillan, 1994)

Connell, Philip, *Romanticism, Economics and the Question of 'Culture'* (Oxford:
Oxford University Press, 2001)

Cook, James W., 'Of Men, Missing Links, and Nondescripts: The Strange Career of
P.T. Barnum's "What Is It?" Exhibition', in *Freakery: Cultural Spectacles of the
Extraordinary Body*, ed. by Rosemarie Garland-Thomson (New York: New York
University Press, 1996), pp. 139–57

——*The Arts of Deception: Playing with Fraud in the Age of Barnum* (Cambridge, MA:
Harvard University Press, 2001)

——ed., *The Colossal P.T. Barnum Reader: Nothing Else Like It in the Universe* (Urbana: University of Illinois Press, 2005)

Corbey, Raymond, 'Ethnographic Showcases: Account and Vision', in *Human Zoos: The Invention of the Savage*, ed. by Pascal Blanchard, Gilles Boëtsch and Nanette Jacomijn Snoep (Paris: Musée du quai Branly, 2011), pp. 95–103

Costa, Palmira Fontes da, 'The Meaning of Monstrosities in Charles Darwin's Understanding of the Origin of Species' in Darwin, *Evolution, Evolutionisms: Ciências e Culturas*, Vol. 18, ed. by Ana Leonor Pereira, João Rui Pita and Pedro Ricardo Fonseca (Coimbra: Imprensa da Universidade de Coimbra, 2011), <http://dx.doi.org/10.14195/978-989-26-0342-1_8> [accessed 9 January 2019]

Costeloe, Michael P., *William Bullock Connoisseur and Virtuoso of the Egyptian Hall: Piccadilly to Mexico (1773–1849)* (Bristol: University of Bristol HiPLAM, 2008)

Crais, Clifton and Pamela Scully, *Sara Baartman and the Hottentot Venus: A Ghost Story and a Biography* (Princeton, NJ: Princeton University Press, 2009)

Craton, Lillian, *The Victorian Freak Show: The Significance of Disability and Physical Differences in 19th-Century Fiction* (Amherst, NY: Cambria Press, 2009)

Craveri, Benedetta, *The Age of Conversation*, trans. by Teresa Waugh (New York: New York Review of Books, 2005)

Crawford, Julie, *Marvelous Protestantism: Monstrous Births in Post-Reformation England* (Baltimore, MD: Johns Hopkins University, 2005)

Crone, Rosalind, *Violent Victorians: Popular Entertainment in Nineteenth-Century London* (Manchester: Manchester University Press, 2010)

Daston, Lorraine, and Katharine Park, *Wonders and the Order of Nature, 1150–1750* (New York: Zone Books, 2001)

Davies, Gareth H.H., *Pablo Fanque and the Victorian Circus: A Romance of Real Life* (Cromer: Poppyland Publishing, 2007)

Davies, Helen, *Neo-Victorian Freakery: The Cultural Afterlife of the Victorian Freak Show* (Basingstoke: Palgrave Macmillan, 2015)

Davis, Lennard J., 'Constructing Normalcy', in *The Disability Studies Reader*, ed. by Lennard J. Davis (Oxon: Routledge, 2010), pp. 3–19

Dennett, Andrea Stulman, *Weird and Wonderful: The Dime Museum in America* (New York: New York University Press, 1997)

Dennison, Matthew, *Queen Victoria: A Life of Contradictions* (London: HarperCollins, 2013)

Douthwaite, Julia V., *The Wild Girl, Natural Man, and the Monster: Dangerous Experiments in the Age of Enlightenment* (Chicago: University of Chicago Press, 2002)

Drimmer, Frederick, *Very Special People: The Struggles, Loves and Triumphs of Human Oddities* (New York: Citadel, 1991)

Duff, Kerry, 'Biographies of Scale', *Disability Studies Quarterly*, 25:4 (2005) <http://dsq-sds.org/article/view/617/794> [accessed 28 December 2018]

Dunn, Katherine, *Geek Love* (New York: Knopf, 1989)

Durbach, Nadja, 'London, Capital of Exotic Exhibitions from 1830 to 1860', in *Human Zoos: The Invention of the Savage*, ed. by Pascal Blanchard, Gilles Boëtsch and Nanette Jacomijn Snoep (Paris: Musée du quai Branly, 2011), pp. 81–8

—— '"Skinless Wonders": Body Worlds and the Victorian Freak Show', *Journal of the History of Medicine and Allied Sciences*, 69:1 (2014), pp. 38–67

—— *Spectacle of Deformity: Freak Shows and Modern British Culture* (Berkeley: University of California Press, 2010)

Evans, Chris, *Debating the Revolution: Britain in the 1790s* (London: I.B. Tauris, 2006)

Faulk, Barry J., *Music Halls and Modernity: The Late-Victorian Discovery of Popular Culture* (Columbus: Ohio University Press, 2004)

Featherstone, Anne, 'Showing the Freaks: Photographic Images of the Extraordinary Body', in *Visual Delights: Essays on the Popular and Projected Image in the 19th Century*, ed. by Simon Popple and Vanessa Toulmin (Towbridge: Flicks Books, 2000), pp. 135–42

Fiedler, Leslie, *Freaks: Myths and Images of the Secret Self* (Harmondsworth: Penguin, 1981)

Fitzsimons, Raymund, *Barnum in London* (London: Geoffrey Bles, 1969)

Foucault, Michel, *Madness and Civilization: A History of Insanity in the Age of Reason*, trans. by Richard Howard (London: Routledge, 2009)

Fuller, Robert C., *Wonder: From Emotion to Spirituality* (Chapel Hill: University of North Carolina Press, 2006)

Garland-Thomson, Rosemarie, *Extraordinary Bodies: Figuring Physical Disability in American Culture and Literature* (New York: Columbia University Press, 1997)

—— 'Freakery Unfurled', in *Victorian Freaks: The Social Context of Freakery in Britain*, ed. by Marlene Tromp (Columbus: Ohio State University, 2008), pp. ix–xi

—— 'Introduction: From Wonder to Error – A Genealogy of Freak Discourse in Modernity', in *Freakery: Cultural Spectacles of the Extraordinary Body*, ed. by Rosemarie Garland-Thomson (New York: New York University Press, 1996), pp. 1–22

Gerber, David A., 'Pornography or Entertainment? The Rise and Fall of the Freak Show', *Reviews in American History* 18:1 (1990), pp. 15–21

—— 'The "Careers" of People Exhibited in Freak Shows: The Problem of Volition and Valorization', in *Freakery: Cultural Spectacles of the Extraordinary Body*, ed. by Rosemarie Garland-Thomson (New York: New York University Press, 1996), pp. 38–54

Gilman, Sander L., *Fat: A Cultural History of Obesity* (Cambridge: Polity Press, 2008)

—— *Obesity: The Biography* (Oxford: Oxford University Press, 2010)

Goodall, Jane R., *Performance and Evolution in the Age of Darwin: Out of the Natural Order* (London: Routledge, 2002)

Gregory, James, 'Eccentric Lives: Character, Characters and Curiosities in Britain, c. 1760–1900', in *Histories of the Normal and the Abnormal: Social and Cultural Histories of Norms and Normativity*, ed. by Waltraud Ernst (London: Routledge, 2006), pp. 73–100

Grosz, Elizabeth, 'Intolerable Ambiguity: Freaks as/at the Limit', in *Freakery: Cultural Spectacles of the Extraordinary Body*, ed. by Rosemarie Garland-Thomson (New York: New York University Press, 1996), pp. 55–66

Grześkowiak-Krwawicz, Anna, *Gulliver in the Land of Giants: A Critical Biography* and the Memoirs of the Celebrated Dwarf, trans. by Daniel Sax (London: Routledge, 2012)

Gylseth, Christopher, and Lars Toverud, Julia Pastrana: The Tragic Story of the Victorian Ape Woman, trans. by Donald Tumasonis (Stroud: Sutton Publishing, 2003)

Harris, Neil, Humbug: The Art of P.T. Barnum (Chicago: University of Chicago Press, 1973)

Harrison, Peter, The Bible, Protestantism and the Rise of Natural Science (Cambridge: Cambridge University Press, 1998)

Hartzman, Marc, American Sideshow: An Encyclopedia of History's Most Wondrous and Curiously Strange Performers (London: Penguin, 2005)

Haslam, David, and Fiona Haslam, Fat, Gluttony and Sloth: Obesity in Literature, Art and Medicine (Liverpool: Liverpool University Press, 2009)

Hibbert, Christopher, Queen Victoria: A Personal History (Cambridge, MA: Da Capo Press, 2000)

Hillemann, Ulrike, Asian Empire and British Knowledge: China and the Networks of British Imperial Expansion (Basingstoke: Palgrave Macmillan, 2009)

Hilton, Boyd, A Mad, Bad, & and Dangerous People? England 1783–1846 (Oxford: Clarendon Press, 2006)

Hodgson, A., 'Defining the Species: Apes, Savages and Humans in Scientific and Literary Writing of the 1860s', Journal of Victorian Culture, 4:2 (1999), pp. 228–51

Horn, Pamela, Amusing the Victorians: Leisure, Pleasure and Play in Victorian Britain (Stroud: Amberley Publishing, 2014)

Howell, Michael, and Peter Ford, The True History of The Elephant Man (Harmondsworth: Penguin, 1983)

Howells, Richard, and Michael M. Chemers, 'Midget Cities: Utopia, Utopianism, and the Vor-Schein of the 'Freak' Show, Disability Quarterly Studies, 25:3 (2005) <http://dsq-sds.org/article/view/579/756> [accessed 3 February 2016]

Huang, Yunte, Inseparable: The Original Siamese Twins and Their Rendezvous with American History (New York: Liveright Publishing, 2018)

Huff, Joyce L., 'Freaklore: The Dissemination, Fragmentation, and Reinvention of the Legend Daniel Lambert, King of Fat Men', in Victorian Freaks: The Social Context of Freakery in Britain, ed. by Marlene Tromp (Columbus: Ohio State University, 2008), pp. 37–59

Hughes, Kathryn, Victorians Undone: Tales of the Flesh in the Age of Decorum (London: HarperCollins, 2017)

Hunt, Tamara L., Defining John Bull: Political Caricature and National Identity in Late Georgian England (Surrey: Ashgate, 2003)

Hunter, Jack, Freak Babylon: An Illustrated History of Teratology & Freakshows (London: Creation Books, 2010)

Hunter, Kay, Duet for a Lifetime: The Story of the Original Siamese Twins (London: Michael Joseph, 1964)

Ingebretsen, Edward J., At Stake: Monsters and the Rhetoric of Fear in Public Culture (Chicago: University of Chicago, 2001)

Jando, Dominique, *Philip Astley & The Horsemen who invented the Circus (1768–1814)* (San Francisco, CA: Circopedia, 2018)

John, Angela V., *By the Sweat of Their Brow: Women Workers at Victorian Coal Mines* (London: Routledge, 1984)

Kareem, Sarah Tindal, *Eighteenth-Century Fiction and the Reinvention of Wonder* (Oxford: Oxford University Press, 2014)

Kelly, Daniel, *Yuck! The Nature and Moral Significance of Disgust* (Cambridge, MA: MIT Press, 2011)

Knoppers, Laura Lunger, and Joan B. Landes, 'Introduction', in *Monstrous Bodies/ Political Monstrosities in Early Modern Europe*, ed. by Laura Lunger Knoppers and Joan B. Landes (Ithaca, NY: Cornell University Press, 2004), pp. 1–22

Kunhardt, Philip B. Jr., Philip Kunhardt III and Peter Kunhardt, *P.T. Barnum: America's Greatest Showman* (New York: Knopf, 1995)

Langford, Paul, *Englishness Identified: Manners and Characters, 1650–1850* (Oxford: Oxford University Press, 2000)

Lehman, Eric D., *Becoming Tom Thumb: Charles Stratton, P.T. Barnum, and the Dawn of American Celebrity* (Middletown, CT: Wesleyan University Press, 2013)

Leroi, Armand Marie, *Mutants: On the Form, Varieties and Errors of the Human Body* (London: HarperCollins, 2003)

Lewis, Robert M., ed., *From Travelling Show to Vaudeville: Theatrical Spectacle in America, 1830–1910* (Baltimore, MD: Johns Hopkins University Press, 2003)

Lindfors, Bernth, 'Charles Dickens and the Zulus', in *Africans On Stage: Studies in Ethnological Show Business*, ed. by Bernth Lindfors (Indiana: Indiana University Press, 1999), pp. 62–80

Lockman, Zachary, *Contending Visions of the Middle East: The History and Politics of Orientalism* (Cambridge: Cambridge University Press, 2010)

Lonnberg, Allan, 'The Digger Indian Stereotype in California', *Journal of California and Great Basin Anthropology*, 3:2 (1981), pp. 215–23

Lovejoy, Arthur O., *The Great Chain of Being: A Study of the History of an Idea* (New York: Transactions Publishers, 2009)

MacKenzie, John, 'The Imperial Exhibitions of Great Britain', in *Human Zoos: The Invention of the Savage*, ed. by Pascal Blanchard, Gilles Boëtsch and Nanette Jacomijn Snoep (Paris: Musée du quai Branly, 2008), pp. 259–68

Mangan, J.A., and Callum McKenzie, 'The Other Side of the Coin: Victorian Masculinity, Field Sports and English Elite Education', in *Making European Masculinities: Sport, Europe, Gender*, ed. by J.A. Mangan (London: Frank Cass, 2000), pp. 62–85

Mannix, Daniel P., *Freaks: We Who Are Not As Others* (New York: RE/Search, 1999)

Martell, Joanne, *Millie-Christine: Fearfully and Wonderfully Made* (North Carolina: John F. Blair, 2000)

McElligott, Jason, and Eve Patten, 'The Perils of Print Culture: An Introduction', in *The Perils of Print Culture: Book, Print and Publishing History in Theory and Practice*, ed. by Jason McElligott and Eve Patten (Basingstoke: Palgrave Macmillan, 2014), pp. 1–16

McHold, Heather, 'Even as You and I: Freak Shows and Lay Discourse on Spectacular Deformity', in *Victorian Freaks: The Social Context of Freakery in Britain*, ed. by Marlene Tromp (Columbus: Ohio State University, 2008), pp. 21–36

Merish, Lori, 'Cuteness and Commodity Aesthetics: Tom Thumb and Shirley Temple', in *Freakery: Cultural Spectacles of the Extraordinary Body*, ed. by Rosemarie Garland-Thomson (New York: New York University Press, 1996), pp. 185–203

Mitchell, David T., and Sharon L. Snyder, 'Exploitations of Embodiment: Born Freak and the Academic Bally Plank', *Disability Studies Quarterly*, 25:3 (2005) <http://dsq-sds.org/article/view/575/752> [accessed 9 January 2019]

Mitchell, Sarah, 'From "Monstrous" to "Abnormal": The Case of Conjoined Twins in the Nineteenth Century', in *Histories of the Normal and the Abnormal: Social and Cultural Histories of Norms and Normativity*, ed. by Waltraud Ernst (London: Routledge, 2006), pp. 53–72

Morrell, J. B., 'Professionalisation', in *Companion to the History of Modern Science*, ed. by R.C. Olby and others (London: Routledge, 1996), pp. 980–9

Murphy, Paul Thomas, *Shooting Victoria: Madness, Mayhem and the Modernisation of the Monarchy* (London: Head of Zeus, 2012)

Nickell, Joe, *Secrets of the Sideshows* (Lexington: University of Kentucky, 2005)

O'Connor, Erin, *Raw Material: Producing Pathology in Victorian Culture* (Durham, NC: Duke University Press, 2000)

Ofek, Galia, *Representations of Hair in Victorian Literature and Culture* (Surrey: Ashgate, 2009)

O'Keeffe, Paul, *A Genius for Failure: The Life of Benjamin Robert Haydon* (London: Bodley Head, 2009)

Olusoga, David, *Black and British: A Forgotten History* (London: Pan, 2017)

Orser, Joseph Andrew, *The Lives of Chang and Eng: Siam's Twins in Nineteenth-Century America* (Chapel Hill: University of North Carolina Press, 2014)

Page, Nick, *Lord Minimus: The Extraordinary Life of Britain's Smallest Man* (New York: St. Martin's Press, 2001)

Pettit, Fiona, 'The Afterlife of Freak Shows', in *Popular Exhibitions, Science and Showmanship, 1840–1910*, ed. by Joe Kember, John Plunkett and Jill A. Sullivan (London: Pickering & Chatto, 2012), pp. 61–78

——'Freaks in Late Nineteenth-Century British Media and Medicine' (unpublished doctoral thesis, University of Exeter, 2012)

Podgorny, Irina, 'Falsehood on the Move: The Aztec Children and Science in the Second Half of the 19th Century', *Medicina Nei Secoli* 25:1 (2013), pp. 223–44

Porter, Roy, *Bodies Politic: Disease, Death and Doctors in Britain, 1650–1900* (London: Reaktion Books, 2001)

——*London: A Social History* (London: Penguin, 2000)

Purse, Ben, *The Blind in Industry: Fifty Years of Work and Wages* (London: Edson, 1925)

Qureshi, Sadiah, 'Displaying Sara Baartman, The "Hottentot Venus"', *History of Science* 42:2 (2004), pp. 233–57

——'Meeting the Zulus: Displayed Peoples and the Shows of London', in *Popular Exhibitions, Science and Showmanship, 1840-1910*, ed. by Joe Kember, John Plunkett and Jill A. Sullivan (London: Pickering & Chatto, 2012), pp. 185–98

——*Peoples on Parade: Exhibitions, Empire, and Anthropology in Nineteenth-Century Britain* (Chicago: University of Chicago Press, 2011)

Ravenscroft, Jane, 'Invisible Friends: Questioning the representation of the court dwarf in Hapsburg Spain', in *Histories of the Normal and the Abnormal: Social and Cultural Histories of Norms and Normativity*, ed. by Waltraud Ernst (London: Routledge, 2006), pp. 26–52

Reay, Barry, *Watching Hannah: Sexuality, Horror and Bodily De-formation in Victorian England* (London: Reaktion.Books, 2002)

Regier, Willis Goth, ed., *Masterpieces of American Indian Literature* (Lincoln: University of Nebraska Press, 2005)

Reiss, Benjamin, 'Barnum and Joice Heth: The Birth of Ethnic Shows in the United States (1836)', in *Human Zoos: The Invention of the Savage*, ed. by Pascal Blanchard, Gilles Boëtsch and Nanette Jacomijn Snoep (Paris: Musée de quai Branly, 2011), pp. 73–80

——'P.T. Barnum, Joice Heth and Antebellum Spectacles of Race', in *American Quarterly* 51:1 (1999), pp. 78–107

——*The Showman and the Slave: Race, Death and Memory in Barnum's America* (Cambridge, MA: Harvard University Press, 2010)

Renaud, Anne, *The Extraordinary Life of Anna Swan* (Sydney, NS: Cape Breton University Press, 2013)

Richmond, Vivienne, *Clothing the Poor in Nineteenth-Century England* (Cambridge: Cambridge University Press, 2013)

Rothfels, Nigel, 'Aztecs, Aborigines, and Ape-People: Science and Freaks in Germany, 1850–1900', in *Freakery: Cultural Spectacles of the Extraordinary Body*, ed. by Rosemarie Garland-Thomson (New York: New York University Press, 1996), pp. 158–72

Rowell, George, *Queen Victoria Goes to the Theatre* (London: Paul Elek, 1978)

Russo, Mary J., *The Female Grotesque: Risk, Excess and Modernity* (London: Routledge, 1994)

Said, Edward W., *Orientalism* (London: Routledge & Kegan Paul, 1978)

Saville, J. F., 'Eccentricity as Englishness in *David Copperfield*', *Studies in English Literature*, 42:4 (2002), pp. 781–97

Saxon, A.H., *P.T. Barnum: The Legend and the Man* (New York: Columbia University Press, 1989)

——*The Life and Art of Andrew Ducrow & The Romantic Age of the English Circus* (Hamden: Archon Books, 1978)

Scully, Pamela and Clifton Crais, 'Race and Erasure: Sara Baartman and Hendrik Cesars in Cape Town and London', in *Journal of British Studies*, 47:2 (2008), pp. 301–23

Semonin, Paul, 'Monsters in the Marketplace: The Exhibition of Human Oddities in Early Modern England', in *Freakery: Cultural Spectacles of the Extraordinary*

Body, ed. by Rosemarie Garland-Thomson (New York: New York University Press, 1996), pp. 69–81

Shephard, Ben, A War of Nerves (London: Jonathan Cape, 2000)

Simon, Linda, The Greatest Show on Earth: A History of the Circus (London: Reaktion Books, 2014)

Smit, Christopher, 'A Collaborative Aesthetic: Levinas's Idea of Responsibility and the Photographs of Charles Eisenmann and the Late Nineteenth-Century Freak-Performer', in Victorian Freaks: The Social Context of Freakery in Britain, ed. by Marlene Tromp (Columbus: Ohio State University, 2008), pp. 283–311

Southworth, John, Fools and Jesters at the English Court (Stroud: Sutton Publishing, 1998)

Steinbach, Susie L., Understanding the Victorians: Politics, Culture and Society in Nineteenth-century Britain (New York: Routledge, 2017)

Stencell, A.W., Seeing Is Believing: America's Sideshow (Toronto: ECW Press, 2002)

Stephens, Elizabeth, 'Geeks and Gaffs: The Queer Legacy of the 1950s American Freak Show', in Queer 1950s: Rethinking Sexuality in the Postwar Years, ed. by Heike Bauer and Matt Cook (New York: Palgrave Macmillan, 2012), pp. 183–95

Stern, Rebecca, 'Our Bear Women, Ourselves: Affiliating with Julia Pastrana', in Victorian Freaks: The Social Context of Freakery in Britain, ed. by Marlene Tromp (Columbus: Ohio State University, 2008), pp. 200–33

Stewart, Jules, Albert: A Life (London: I.B. Tauris, 2012)

Stewart, Susan, On Longing: Narratives of the Miniature, the Gigantic, the Souvenir, the Collection (Baltimore, MD: Johns Hopkins University Press, 1984)

Sullivan, George, Tom Thumb: The Remarkable True Story of a Man in Miniature (New York: Clarion Books, 2011)

Sweet, Matthew, Inventing the Victorians (London: Faber & Faber, 2001)

Tchen, John Kuo Wei, New York Before Chinatown: Orientalism and the Shaping of American Culture, 1776–1882 (Baltimore, MD: Johns Hopkins University Press, 1999)

Thode-Arora, Hilke, 'Hagenbeck's European Tours: The Development of the Human Zoo', in Human Zoos: The Invention of the Savage, ed. by Pascal Blanchard, Gilles Boëtsch and Nanette Jacomijn Snoep (Paris: Musée du quai Branly, 2011), pp. 165–73

Thompson, C.J.S., The History and Lore of Freaks (London: Random House, 1996)

Thrower, Terri, 'Overcoming the Need to "Overcome": Challenging Disability Narratives in The Miracle', in Different Bodies: Essays on Disability in Film and Television, ed. by Marja Evelyn Mogk (London: McFarland, 2013), pp. 205–18

Tosh, John, Manliness and Masculinities in Nineteenth-Century Britain: Essays on Gender, Family, and Empire (Harlow: Pearson Longman, 2005)

Toulmin, Vanessa, Pleasurelands (Sheffield: National Fairground Archive, 2003)

Vacon, Shirley Irene, Giants of Nova Scotia: The Lives of Anna Swan and Angus McAskill (East Lawrencetown, NS: Pottersfield Press, 2008)

Wade, Cheryl Marie, 'Disability Culture Rap', in The Ragged Edge: The Disability Experience from the Pages of the First Fifteen Years of The Disability Rag, ed. by Barrett Shaw (Louisville, KY: Avocado Press, 1994), pp. 15–18

Wallace, Irving, and Amy Wallace, *The Two: A Biography* (London: Cassell, 1978)

Ward, Steve, *Father of the Modern Circus 'BILLY BUTTONS': The Life & Times of Philip Astley* (Barnsley: Pen & Sword History, 2018)

Washington, Harriet A., *Medical Apartheid: The Dark History of Medical Experimentation on Black Americans from Colonial Times to the Present* (New York: Anchor Books, 2006)

Weinreb, Ben, et al, *The London Encyclopaedia* (London: Macmillan, 2008)

Weintraub, Stanley, *Albert: Uncrowned King* (London: John Murray, 1997)

White, Jerry, *London in the Nineteenth Century: A Human Awful Wonder of God* (London: Vintage, 2008)

Whitlock, Tammy C., *Crime, Gender and Consumer Culture in Nineteenth-Century England* (Surrey: Ashgate, 2005)

Williams, Glyn, *Naturalists at Sea: Scientific Travellers from Dampier to Darwin* (New Haven, CT: Yale University Press, 2013)

Willis, Martin, 'On Wonder: Situating the Spectacle in Spiritualism and Performance Magic', in *Popular Exhibitions, Science and Showmanship, 1840–1910*, ed. by Joe Kember, John Plunkett and Jill A. Sullivan (London: Pickering & Chatto, 2012), pp. 167–82

Wilson, A.N., *The Victorians* (London: Arrow Books, 2003)

——*Victoria: A Life* (London: Atlantic Books, 2014)

Wittmann, Matthew, *Circus and the City: New York, 1793–2010* (New York and New Haven: Bard Graduate Center and Yale University Press, 2012)

Wolf, Reva, 'John Bull, Liberty, and Wit: How England Became Caricature', in *The Efflorescence of Caricature, 1759–1838*, ed. by Todd Porterfield (Surrey: Ashgate, 2011), pp. 49–60

Wu, Cynthia, *Chang and Eng Reconnected: The Original Siamese Twins in American Culture* (Philadelphia: Temple University Press, 2012)

Youngquist, Paul, *Monstrosities: Bodies and British Romanticism* (Minneapolis: University of Minnesota Press, 2003)

Acknowledgements

⸻

I WANT TO BLAME (and thank) my parents, for they have instilled in me an obsession which has lasted the best part of twenty years. That I am only thirty is saying something about my freakish fanaticism.

One of the highlights of writing this book has been travelling around the UK and America, immersing myself in archives, and I am indebted for the help I have received along the way. My thanks to all the archivists, librarians and staff who have assisted me from London to Durham, Sheffield to Cambridge, New York to Connecticut. I would also like to thank John Gannon, Dale Swan and the staff at the First Baptist Church, Seville, Ohio, for providing me with research, family histories and insightful primary materials, and to Mat Fraser for discussing his insights into the history and legacy of the freak show.

This project began as a doctoral dissertation at Goldsmiths, University of London, following my time at the University of Cambridge, and I am grateful for the funding I have received along the way, and to all the historians who have taught me, directed me and inflamed my passion for the past; notably, but by no means exclusively, Dr Colin Shindler, Dr David Pratt, Dr Paul Millett, Dr Vivienne Richmond, Professor Jan Plamper, Professor Nadja Durbach and Professor Matt Cook. Dr Shindler was a source of great support when the world didn't seem so wonderful, and his late wife, Lynn, helped me battle dyslexia and dyspraxia, so they deserve a special thanks. Thanks, also, to the numerous historians and biographers who have studied the subjects of this book, while blazing the trail for a better understanding of the history of disability and the study of freaks.

As a rookie writer, I am extremely grateful to my agent, Andrew Lownie, who took me on, and to my editor, Fiona Slater, for taking this project up. She has had to endure working with a neurotic writer finding his way in the world of non-fiction writing; this book would not exist without her. Alongside this project, I had the privilege of writing with Nick Baker and Stephen Fry; a big thank you to them for their guidance and encouragement. Acknowledgements are also due to Dr Lillian Craton for her helpful comments, and Rachel Woolf, Dr Michael Woolf, Guy Woolf, Professor Vernon Trafford, Fran Smith, Richard Rosenfeld, Jo Whitford and Robin Dennis for their careful eyes. Any mistakes and oversights are all my own.

A special shoutout to my brother, who remains my inspiration, and to the love of my life, my wife, for all her support. Finally, a heartfelt thanks to my whole family for indulging my obsessions and reminding me that while the past is filled with wonder the present is just as enriching.

Illustration Credits

Handbill for an appearance of Joice Heth, printed by J. Booth and Son, 1835. Reproduced courtesy of the Bridgeport History Center, Bridgeport Public Library

Barnum's American Museum, New York. Artist John Reuben Chapin, wood engraving by Samuel Putman Avery, 1853. From the Art and Picture Collection, The New York Public Library. 'Barnum's American Museum, New York'. The New York Public Library Digital Collections. 1853-01-29

P.T. Barnum and the young Charles Stratton, daguerreotype attributed to Marcus Aurelius Root and Samuel Root, c. 1850. Reproduced courtesy of the Bridgeport History Center, Bridgeport Public Library

Charles Stratton with his father, photograph copy of original daguerreotype, photographer unknown, original daguerreotype c. 1843. Reproduced courtesy of the Bridgeport History Center, Bridgeport Public Library

P.T. Barnum with the 'Fairy Wedding Party'. Illustration by A.M. Curtis, 1863. Reproduced courtesy of the Bridgeport History Center, Bridgeport Public Library

'General Tom Thumb, Wife and Child'. *Cartes de visite*, anonymous photographer, c. 1860s. From the Billy Rose Theatre Division, The New York Public Library. 'Tom Thumb' The New York Public Library Digital Collections. 1838-1883

Advert for an exhibition of Maximo and Bartola, the Aztecs, c. 1867–1899. Reproduced courtesy of the Wellcome Collection. CC BY 4.0

Handbill for P.T. Barnum's Greatest Show on Earth, the Courier Company, 1881. Reproduced courtesy of the Bridgeport History Center, Bridgeport Public Library

Barnum & Bailey circus poster, Strobridge Lithography Company, c. 1899. Reproduced courtesy of the Library of Congress, Prints & Photographs Division, [LC-DIG-ppmsca-54832]

Julia Pastrana poster, the 'Nondescript'. Colour woodcut by W. Brickhill's Steam Printing Works, c. 1857. Reproduced courtesy of the Wellcome Collection. CC BY 4.0

Julia Pastrana photograph. Process print after George Wick, early 1860s. Reproduced courtesy of the Wellcome Collection. CC BY 4.0

Francis Trevelyan Buckland, photograph by S.A. Walker, 1879. Reproduced courtesy of the Wellcome Collection. CC BY 4.0

Anna and Martin Bates photograph. Thanks to Dale Swan, Nova Scotia, for the photograph

Millie and Christine McKoy, photograph by Gihon and Thompson, 1871. Reproduced courtesy of the Wellcome Collection. CC BY 4.0

Barnum and Bailey Show, photograph by James E. Hunt, c. 1898. Reproduced courtesy of the Bridgeport History Center, Bridgeport Public Library

'Royal American Midgets', anonymous poster, c. 1880. Reproduced courtesy of the British Library, Evan. 201

Joseph Merrick, anonymous photographer, 1889. Reproduced courtesy of the Wellcome Collection. CC BY 4.0

Radica and Doodica, anonymous photograph, 1902. Reproduced courtesy of the Library of Congress, Prints & Photographs Division, [LC-DIG-ggbain-11619]

Index
